SALVATOR

Bes

LAWYERING

JAMES C. FREUND

LAWYERING

A Realistic Approach to Legal Practice

JAMES C. FREUND

Library of Congress Cataloging in Publication Data

Freund, James C   1934–
    Lawyering, a realistic approach to legal practice.

    Includes bibliographical references.
    1. Practice of law—United States.   I. Title.
KF 300.F73   347'.73'5   79-16274

DEDICATION

*To my mother, who nurtured achievement;
To my wife, who has borne the brunt of
my labors with supportive equanimity; and
To my sons, in the hope that they don't grow up
to be orthodontists.*

ACKNOWLEDGEMENTS

Many lawyers, both inside and outside my firm, have offered helpful suggestions which have been incorporated into this book—ranging from shrewd substantive insights to chiding over my repeated misuse of the word "alternatives". My particular gratitude, for their acute views on the entire project, is directed to Barry Garfinkel, Fred Gerard, Larry Goodman, Sherwin Kamin, Morris Kramer, and Carl Schneider. Others who deserve sincere thanks are Harris Amhowitz, Hank Baer, Mike Diamond, Stu Freedman, John French, John Fricano, Mitch Gitin, Dan Goldwasser, Lew Lowenfels, Neal McCoy, Jim O'Rorke, Jerry Raikes, Tom Schwarz, Joan Secofsky, and Stu Shapiro. Finally, I can't say enough for the dedicated services provided—with intelligence and enthusiasm—by Sue Tholl and Susan Mackin.

Need I say that these good people are exonerated from responsibility for all opinions, errors, excesses or omissions in the pages which follow.

James C. Freund

New York, N.Y.
May 1, 1979

Dedication

Acknowledgements

CHAPTER 1   AN INTRODUCTION TO THE LAWYER'S CRAFT

CHAPTER 2   LEGAL ANALYSIS—THE INTELLECTUAL ELEMENT

CHAPTER 3   WRITTEN AND ORAL EXPRESSION—THE COMMUNICATIONS ELEMENT

CHAPTER 4   THE INTANGIBLE SKILLS

CHAPTER 5   DEALING WITH PARTNERS AND OTHER COLLEAGUES

CHAPTER 6   HANDLING CLIENTS

CHAPTER 7   DEALING WITH OTHER LAWYERS

CHAPTER 8   THE EXERCISE OF GOOD JUDGMENT

CHAPTER 9   PUTTING IT ALL TOGETHER: AN ILLUSTRATIVE SEPTET

CHAPTER 10   A WORD TO THE PARTNERS

CHAPTER 1

AN INTRODUCTION
TO THE LAWYER'S CRAFT

Let's face it: this is the most presumptuous of books. One lawyer, having the temerity to say to other lawyers, here's how you do it. As the writing progressed, I felt (in Harold MacMillan's elegant phrase) "forever poised between a cliché and an indiscretion."[1] Work hard; be diligent and analytical; my God, is this me—or Polonius, boring the daylights out of Laertes? How does one avoid the cardinal sin of pomposity? Am I telling tales out of school?

And yet, I have not been able to escape the conclusion that there exists a large and significant gap in the education of a lawyer—a gap this book attempts to partially fill. Law school teaches us how to think, gives us the tools of the trade. But other than being the proud possessor of an analytical attitude and a batch of disparate legal principles, the law school graduate is not a lawyer in the true sense of the word. As for continuing legal education programs, these are principally designed to provide a great quantum of substantive information about relatively circumscribed areas of practice—an important function, to be sure, but really only helpful in terms of subject matter. And perhaps surprisingly, few lawyers have carved out the time from their busy careers to write books or articles on what it takes to be an effective practitioner.

Ah, you say, but what about on-the-job training? Lawyers tend to practice in law firms, and surely young lawyers will learn their trade in real-life situations under the painstaking tutelage of more seasoned attorneys. And, of course, there's much truth in this—at least up to a point. But that point, unfortunately, isn't too far along the pedagogical trail.

---

[1]   MacMillan's statement in April 1956 concerning the post of Foreign Secretary was quoted in Safire, *Essayettes*, N.Y. Times, May 30, 1977, at 15, col. 4.

1

For the young associate in a law firm, all too often the entire emphasis is on *doing*—on accomplishing a particular project. Investigate those facts. Research that point and write a memo. Do a first draft of the contract. Convene a meeting. There is very little stress on *how* to go about performing those tasks—just do them, and with a little luck they'll be critiqued, and the associate can learn from his mistakes. There is even less said, at least in an instructional sense, about such larger topics as how to handle a client, how to impress superiors, and what is encompassed in the concept of "good judgment." Lawyers, who tend toward specificity, aren't prone to utter broadly-based dicta on intangible issues.

But how about the feedback? Isn't one word of constructive criticism, spoken in the context of a specific problem, worth a bushel of *a priori* maxims? Perhaps so; but will that one word emerge? The partner in charge has a hundred matters on his mind. Unfortunately, constructive criticism of the associate's performance on a regular basis doesn't always rate a high priority. And the associate is in an awkward position to ask for help. His draft of a letter comes back from the partner all marked up, but the reasons for the changes are rarely articulated and not always self-evident. When time permits, and the criticism is verbalized, it is often so specific that the associate has difficulty abstracting a general principle which can prove helpful to him in other situations.

And then, at the end of the year when the partners collectively evaluate the associate's performance, the report on his progress all too frequently produces unenlightening information. "You've done a good job, Jarvis." Or: "Generally satisfactory work, Smitty, but your writing could use a little tightening up." Or: "Your work habits seem somewhat disorganized, Pete; why don't you try to get yourself better organized?" Does it sound familiar? Is it helpful?

Perhaps some of this might be mitigated if the young lawyer asked his seniors for a more detailed critique or otherwise sought out generalized advice on how to practice law. But associates rarely solicit this sort of tutorial. It reminds me of J.P. Morgan's dictum to the effect that if you have to ask the boat dealer the price, you've got no business buying a yacht. Perhaps unwittingly, senior attorneys have nurtured an atmosphere in which young lawyers clambering up the professional ladder are made to feel that, if they have to *question* what qualities comprise the successful lawyer, then they should probably be out peddling real estate.

So this is the territory I choose to stake out in these pages. It's partly what I find myself saying to associates who work with me; more often, these are the points I never seem to get around to expressing. It represents an attempt to dig below the surface, to analyze in depth the principal qualities that make up the compleat attorney. I'm thinking of such vital attributes as a keen analytical sense, the capacity to communicate (orally and on paper), the ability to turn out work on time and under pressure, and that most crucial of all lawyerly intangibles, the exercise of good judgment. I'm interested in a lawyer's skills in handling people—clients, adversaries, regulators, the partners and associates of the firm. And along the way, I won't be able to resist passing on a few tricks of one man's trade—not to elevate these minor gambits to the status of holy writ, but simply to get the reader thinking along possibly productive lines.

Well, that's a mouthful, I'll admit. And I realize such an ambitious agenda can only have meaning if some useful points and usable techniques emerge. The point or technique can neither be too general ("write with clarity") nor too specific ("behold the pronoun's antecedent"). So I've aimed at such pertinent topics as how to disclose (without calling undue attention to) a salient adverse fact in a letter requesting agency permission to take some action; how to end a seemingly interminable meeting; how to handle a disagreement with the partner in charge; how to react to a client who says: "Let me pose a hypothetical question to you. . . .";[2] how to devise an off-beat compromise to a seeming impasse; and how to defer making a decision without antagonizing anyone. And to make all this more meaningful, I've tried to provide a specific example—hypothetical but drawn from actual practice—to illustrate each important principle involved.

To pause for a moment of self-analysis (which I promise will not be a recurring motif), I suppose there does emerge in these pages a point of view about the nature of legal practice, not necessarily shared by the entire legal community. For want of a better term, I consider myself an activist lawyer—I believe that what a lawyer does or doesn't do, the initiative he takes or forsakes, can have a significant impact on the outcome of most matters and transactions; and that accordingly, the practitioner must at all times be alert, reach out and *accomplish.* There are also a great number of highly professional attorneys who take a less expansive, more reflective view of lawyering—and who nonetheless manage to accomplish much of value. The breed of lawyers, however, for whom I have little regard treat their practice as nothing more than reacting to external stimuli; ask me a specific question and I'll give you an even more specific answer—but not if it's part legal, part business; here are the problems I see, but don't look to me for a solution—the *practical* (dirty word!) aspects, the suggested course of action, that's up to the client; *que*

---

[2] One notable omission in the book: how you should react when the same client tells you "The check is in the mail."

sera, sera, and nothing I do will have much effect anyway (lawyers just tend to cancel one another out); and so on. These fellows hang out the same shingle, arrive home in the bosom of their families by 5:30 P.M., and probably sleep a whole lot better at night; but they won't find too much to chew on in the chapters of this book.

LAWYERING is, of course, primarily intended for lawyers, prospective lawyers, and others interested in what lawyers do (or should be doing). Because I felt the need to be addressing a tangible being directly, much of the first nine chapters is aimed rather pointedly at a person I know rather well and often converse with in similar—but hopefully less pedantic—terms: the quintessential law firm associate. I guess this is the view from the bridge—the partner exhorting the associate.[3] It's *not* one associate passing along the inside scoop to his brethren, and the intimacy of a peer group skull session is undoubtedly lacking. But after all, only a partner is really in a position to advise an associate exactly what it is that the partners look for in his work and attitudes. And by the way, I have found a degree of apparent misconceptions among associates in terms of what goes on in a partner's mind[4] which is reminiscent of some of the more bizarre street notions about sex I possessed at age nine. Hopefully, modification of some of these associate distortions may prove a collateral benefit of the book.

This is probably as good a place as any to digress for a few moments on the subject of the partner and associate makeup of a law firm.[5] It's not telling any tales out of school to note the flourishing in American law firms of a very cozy style of organization, bearing no resemblance to the more hierarchical structures that exist in business, education and elsewhere.[6] The basic fact of law firm life is that there is one group of individuals called "partners" and another called "associates". Put aside the subtleties; forget that although all partners may have been created equal, some are obviously more equal than others; disregard the slender differences between a senior and

---

[3] In this regard, I don't think there is too much of a large firm-small firm distinction (except perhaps in a few places—such as Sections 5.2 and 9.4—where layers of associates are the topic). The firm in which I practice was a small one, fifteen or so attorneys, when I first joined it—that was one of its most attractive aspects—and is now on the verge of passing the 200-lawyer mark; but although the changes have been plentiful, I haven't noticed much difference in the scorecard as to what constitutes a good lawyer.

[4] See, e.g., the examples cited in Section 10.5.1.

[5] Many aspects of this topic are explored throughout the book, but particularly in Chapters 5 (from the associate's point of view) and 10 (from the partner's standpoint).

[6] For an interesting sociological study of one type of firm, see E. Smigel, *The Wall Street Lawyer* (1964).

junior associate. The bottom line is that the partners enjoy the bulk of the gratifications and make most of the money; the associates are overworked, under-appreciated, and often appear to be in a state of perpetual disorientation.[7]

I recall, when making the decision whether to attend law school, receiving this morsel of venerable advice: go ahead, you can't lose; even if you decide not to be a lawyer, the legal background will be terrific. It took only a few weeks of the law school grind to realize how misguided my advisor was. Sure, the background is nice to have, but no one in his right mind would knowingly endure that headache unless he wanted very much to be a lawyer. In a similar vein, I've always felt that an associate should aspire to become a partner. He should view his associate status as an apprenticeship, with full admission to the craft occurring only when he's joined the partnership ranks. I am aware of the attitude of some associates at large firms—sensing the lack of partnership opportunity, they nevertheless remain in order to put a few more years of valuable experience under their belts before taking on the outside world. It's entirely logical—but I just can't see it. When no laurel wreath exists to crown your achievements, my personal view is that the effort isn't commensurate with the rewards.

So that's part of this book's message: what you should be doing to impress the partners of the firm, so that one day you'll be added to their number. But most of the material in these pages is equally applicable to lawyers outside firms—those in corporate law departments, or in government, or on their own. The knack of reaching good judgments, skill at negotiating, the ability to write—these really know no boundaries. So, to all you other lawyers, I ask your indulgence if I seem to be addressing my remarks to associates; it's just that they happen to be the handiest target around. And I would hope that there might be some useful reading for partners here, too—not only in the chapter directed to them, but in terms of helping them (as the act of writing has helped me) to articulate a more meaningful message to associates.

Now, as you peruse these pages, it will quickly become obvious that many of the matters covered involve intensely subjective judgments—and subjective judgments within subjective judgments. Per-

---

[7] Much of this disorientation stems from insecurity. In this regard, see Rosenberg, "Are Your Associates Insecure?", 51 *New York State Bar Journal* 103-105 & 129 (1979), in which the author traces the roots of this insecurity through the "intellectually humbling experience" of legal practice and concludes: "It is only when we are at last finally able to recognize that the wisdom and competence of our colleagues is also finite that our own deficiencies cease to wreak havoc on our sense of security."

haps no one can quarrel that the ability to communicate effectively or handle clients well is important—but there are any number of different approaches to achieving those goals. Although I would hope that experienced lawyers would concur in many of my judgments, not all will; and never forget, you're working for *him*, not me! (But then again, adjusting to your particular mentor is a subject to which appropriate attention is devoted[8]. . . .)

But let's understand one another from the outset. I sense that skeptical readers will characterize some of my suggestions as merely "cosmetic" or a matter of optics, and as a result undeserving of a serious lawyer's attention. Well, I won't deny the cosmetics label—but I do reject the notion of resultant insubstantiality. If there's one thing you learn in lawyering—as with the rest of life—it's that appearances rank only a shade behind reality in significance. If you know what you mean but can't communicate it to partners, clients and adversaries—then your effectiveness is questionable. If you operate on a well-ordered basis but give off disorganized vibes, it defeats your purpose. So when I talk about matters of optics, it's not to suggest hypocritical role-playing for which we're all ill-suited; rather, it's for the purpose of bringing appearances into line with realities.[9]

My professional background is in corporate and securities law, and I suppose this shows through in some of the substantive emphasis and particular examples used in the book.[10] It seems to me, though, that the principles are equally applicable to young lawyers who are cutting their teeth on litigation or tax work or almost any of the other disciplines; and, where possible, I have tried to construct hypotheticals from other fields. You won't learn how to prepare a brief or argue a

---

[8]   See Section 5.1.1.

[9]   This is really unpardonable, but I don't seem to have the willpower (or good sense) to refrain from quoting some words I previously wrote on this subject (in the context of affiliate merger transactions):

"The cardinal rule in these affiliate merger transactions is that both the reality and the appearance of the transaction must exhibit as high a degree of fairness as possible to the minority stockholders of the controlled company. If the deal is neither fair in substance nor appearance, then you possess the virtue of candor but little else. If the transaction appears fair but in reality is not, you will eventually get into a lot of trouble. If the deal is actually fair but its appearance is otherwise, you are just plain stupid and deserve any lumps you may be forced to take." J. Freund, *Anatomy of a Merger* (1975) [hereinafter cited as *"Anatomy"* without further cross-reference] at 475-6.

[10]   I have made a particular effort, however, to avoid examples which require any detailed prior knowledge of the subject matter; and if any statement of the legal context doesn't make sense, just ignore it and concentrate on the practice principle involved.

case—but then again, it's not my intention to advise a securities law-yer on drafting a prospectus. Everyone, however, has to deal with clients; we all have to communicate within and without the firm; most lawyers negotiate with other lawyers.—and these are the kinds of mat-ters that are the backbone of the book.

Finally, may I apologize in advance to female attorneys if a dis-proportionate number of "he's" and "his's" slip between the cracks. We are all creatures of habit ("When they spotted the *Bismarck*, they realized what a massive warship she was . . ."), and no distinctions are intended or implied.

At this point, I think it may be helpful to outline the subject matter format of the book. Chapters 2, 3 and 4 represent an attempt to cover what I consider the essential skills a lawyer must possess. Chapter 2 is about legal analysis, which is basic to all else; if you don't under-stand the dimensions of the problem at hand, the ultimate product will inevitably reflect your disorientation. I realize that anyone who makes it through law school and into a firm must possess some quantum of analytical skills. But it is in the application of these skills that the men (or women) are separated from the boys (or girls). The superficiality with which some young lawyers—who really ought to know bet-ter—approach problem-solving is striking. And so the book begins with this critical threshold matter, probing into such subjects as the process of analysis, the way to go about analyzing a problem, and the realization that your basic assumptions need not remain frozen. The chapter concludes with discussions of how the analytical approach can be applied to related non-legal issues, and the obviously signifi-cant role of legal knowledge.

Chapter 3 deals with the broad subject of expres-sion—communication, if you will—of both the written and oral varieties. The focus is less on the preparation of formal instruments (such as a brief or a contract) and formal utterances (such as court-room oral argument) and more on the everyday modes of expression by which a lawyer communicates effectively with those around him—the writing of memoranda or letters, presenting an oral report of a conversation or the results of an inquiry, conducting a meeting. My interest is in a lawyer's ability to communicate findings and ob-servations in a way that will impress others with his grasp and judg-ment. You can possess all the grasp and judgment in the world, but if these qualities are not well communicated, your effectiveness as a lawyer is diminished and you're penalized in the partnership chase. On the writing level, we zero in on such topics as ascertaining pur-pose, organization, the necessity for rewriting, and four key attributes of good writing: clarity, conciseness, interest to the reader and per-suasiveness.

Chapter 4 deals with getting the job done. Here we have the essentially unglamorous skills of diligence, organization, thoroughness,
meeting timetables, productivity, self-starting, working under
pressure, and the like—all of which assume a much greater importance in terms of your progress at the firm than might be expected
in some abstract, Blackstonian view of legal practice. The fact is that
until the job is done—and done with care and dispatch—no one gets
any credit; and conversely, when the job lags or is performed improperly, the associate is likely to shoulder the blame. The subjects in
this chapter are obvious ones, but I've tried to shed some new light
on how you should go about honing these particular skills.

The next part of the book—Chapters 5, 6 and 7—is devoted to the
lawyer's dealings with the principal categories of people he comes
across in his work. Chapter 5 examines an associate's relations with
the partners of the firm, as well as with other associates. These people
are on your side, part of your team; they are also scrutinizing and
evaluating you constantly, and their combined reactions will ultimately determine your future. The stress is on adapting to a
particular partner's idiosyncracies, on getting your message across to
him. I've also touched on such thorny issues as disagreements with
the partner, and the sticky situation that can exist when the two of
you just don't seem to get along. Interacting with other associates—seniors, juniors and peers—is also explored.[11] Finally, there
are separate sections dealing with the practice of law outside the law
firm context—in a corporate counsel's office, in a government
agency, or on your own as a solo practitioner.

Chapter 6 is aimed at handling clients, a subject of obvious
significance. We lawyers don't operate in a vacuum; no one is sub-
sidizing our pursuit of truth and justice. We are essentially advocates
who are hired and paid to advance a client's interest—consistent, of
course, with ethical proprieties and our own dictates of good
taste—and unless we earn the client's confidence and trust, we could
quickly find ourselves reduced to formulating hypotheticals in an
otherwise inactive library. Again, the focus is on discerning quirks in
the client's makeup and adjusting the lawyer's style accordingly. The
key issue is how far to go in giving advice—how to be constructive
while still ensuring that the ultimate decisions are made by the client.
And there's an attempt to detail a few tricks of the trade that may not
have occurred to the reader. The chapter concludes with an examination
of the lawyer's relation to the client's other professionals—primarily accountants.

---

[11]   One topic that's not explored—I have to save something for another
book!—is the relationship among the partners of a firm.

Chapter 7 concerns dealings with other lawyers outside the firm. These relationships can be of very different types. For purposes of our analysis, we have divided the inter-lawyer universe into matters of joint representation, parallel representation, friendly adversaries and hostile adversaries. The principal issue of joint representation is the delicate relationship between inside and outside counsel; we also look at the interaction of generalist and specialist. In parallel representation, where the lawyers represent such clients as co-defendants or parent and majority-owned subsidiary, the main concern is conflict of interest. For friendly adversaries (e.g., two lawyers representing buyer and seller in an acquisition), both of whom are committed to working out a deal although representing differing interests, the key is negotiating—a combination of attempting to get a leg up and devising workable compromises. Hostile adversaries, locking horns in court or over an unfriendly tender offer—where ultimately a winner and a loser will emerge—have their own type of problems with professional relationships. At this point, various aspects of the litigation process are also examined. The final portion of the chapter is concerned with activities involving governmental regulatory officials, including some thoughts on the right question to ask, the right person to see, and obtaining the desired answer.

The next part of the book is an attempt to put it all together. Chapter 8 is devoted to the mystical issue of good judgment, which cuts across all other areas and is the true hallmark of the successful lawyer. Decision-making is definitely the focus here. The topics include anticipating and deferring decisions, some differences between go/no-go determinations and those involving the choice of a particular course of action, and processing and packaging judgments. Then, in Chapter 9, I've conjured up seven extended hypothetical situations which lawyers can (and do) find themselves in; the reader rides along on a step-by-step analysis of legal problem-solving. These situations have been designed not only with a view to the judgmental matters involved, but also to the other concerns covered in earlier parts of the book.

Finally, in Chapter 10, there's a message to partners on the treatment of associates. I suppose this is doubly presumptuous on my part, but so many thoughts came to me in the preparation of this book that I want to pass them along. The principal topics here are the partner's role in educating associates and providing specific and general feedback on the associate's performance.

So now, without further ado, let's explore what lawyering is all about.

CHAPTER 2

LEGAL ANALYSIS—THE INTELLECTUAL ELEMENT

2.1. SUPERFICIAL ANALYSIS AND OTHER CRIMES AGAINST NATURE

Much as you look for a good pair of hands on a surgeon or short-stop, in evaluating a lawyer you always have to start with his analytical skills. I won't attempt a formal definition of this quality—some term it, with classic circularity, the ability to think like a lawyer![1]—but I know this much: it's the absolute *sine qua non* of the successful attorney. True, a lawyer may be a veritable fount of rational thought and still not make it to the top, since (as we shall see) there's a lot more to lawyering than intellect; but if you find yourself incapable of thinking analytically, you might as well chop your shingle into firewood because your future at the bar is bleak.

Harsh words; indeed they are. But it's a tough profession. And the legal problems that come across our desks seem to grow increasingly difficult. I find myself dealing with few matters of substance that can be characterized as simple or relatively routine or that are capable of rote solutions. Charting the contours and byways of a problem may not yield a solution, but at least it puts you on the right track; then, having spotted the issues, the use of your brainpower to devise a well-reasoned solution is really what lawyering is all about.

The ability to think analytically is the single quality most dramatically forged in the law school experience, where the emphasis is on teaching students—through Socratic method or otherwise—to reason in this special kind of way. It seems unlikely that someone devoid of basic analytical skills would have survived the rigors of law

---

[1] Thomas Reed Powell of Harvard put it this way: "If you . . . can think about a thing inextricably attached to something else without thinking of the thing which it is attached to, then you have a legal mind." As quoted in M. Mayer, *The Lawyers* (1966), at 86.

school and been subsequently hired by a law firm. Therefore, I begin
with the assumption that the reader possesses the necessary mental
equipment and training to approach legal problems analytically. The
real question, however, is whether you are using these skills to full
advantage in your practice.

My thesis is that far too many young lawyers fail to apply their
maximum analytical abilities to the problems with which they must
deal. As a result, they produce shoddy work that doesn't stand up to
critical examination by a partner, or worse, by the lawyer on the
other side, or—worst of all—by the client or the court. And I think I
know the principal cause of this malaise. Let me illustrate through a
painful reminiscence.

Although more years have now passed than seem possible, I can
still remember vividly those agonizing days in law school when final
exams rolled around. I always utilized the special examination room,
where students were permitted to bring their typewriters—figuring I
would make up in neatness and sheer quantity of response for
whatever lack of clarity or acumen my answers might otherwise
possess. The exam booklets would be handed out on the hour, following which about fifteen minutes would pass with the room in total
silence.[2] At that point, a typewriter or two would strike a few tentative keys, and then within minutes the room was a cacophony of
sound. During those first fifteen minutes, everyone was *thinking*
rather than composing—reading the first question thoroughly (with a
less detailed look at the others), sorting out its various elements, planning an approach, outlining the answer. We were in an exam environment, where we knew what was expected of us—no one doubted for a
moment that this kind of advance planning was essential before striking out in pursuit of answers. In effect, we forced ourselves to be
analytical.[3]

In your legal practice, however, no one hands you a booklet with
the admonition: ''Be analytical.'' And problems are rarely presented
to the associate in the neatly packaged fashion of a law school exam.
For one thing, in practice it's not always clear what issue is being
posed. At the conclusion of each law school exam question, the
professor would inquire: ''How should the judge decide this case?'',
or ''What torts?''. But when a client embarks on a particular course

---

[2]   I will never forget the day when, about 30 seconds after the exam was distributed, a single typewriter began to function furiously—to a great chorus of
boos from the uptight multitude.
[3]   I should note for the record the corollary phenomenon: namely, that once the
typewriters started in earnest, it was almost impossible to continue the process
of pure thought. There was a great fear of being left at the analytical post! I
readily admit to breaking off my analysis prematurely on a number of occasions,
in order to catch up with more facile classmates.

of action, you often have to devise your own questions. (Is there a statute that this action might violate? Hmm. . . . what about the Robinson-Patman Act. . . ? Let's have a look at the wording. . . .) I'll have more to say on this subject in the next section.[4]

Moreover, on an exam the facts were almost never in dispute, and you were (supposedly) familiar with the applicable law. In real life, the relevant facts of a situation are almost never clear-cut: there are disputed facts, or facts about which your information is incomplete, and some purported facts consist of little more than assumptions. In addition, the law on the subject may well be unfamiliar to you, requiring a round of initial research to ascertain which facts are indeed relevant.

And so, each new problem presented requires a period of analytical thought—of examining the potentialities, of deciding what facts and law you need to know, of structuring the form and substance of your response. But unfortunately, the good habits developed in law school are too often neglected by eager associates. They go off half-cocked on a problem, not quite sure of the question being asked, lacking the necessary facts, and without having set into motion their reasoning faculties. 'Tis a grievous fault; and correct it we must, before the rest of that lawyerly superstructure—communications, dealing with people, making judgments—can be stacked upon the analytical base.[5]

2.2. HOW PROBLEMS APPROACH THE PRACTITIONER (AND VICE-VERSA)

I know what some of you are thinking: "Look, Jim, it's one thing to be comfortably ensconced in the pristine intellectuality of a law school examination room, and quite another to find yourself in a conference room with real lawyers and bona fide clients. You no longer enjoy the luxury of pure thought; you have to be up on your toes, ready to move with alacrity and confidence into relatively uncharted waters."

And (if those thoughts were on your mind), in many respects you are absolutely right. One hallmark of the mature lawyer is his ability to size up the dimensions of a problem right there in the meeting and proffer some tentative legal or practical conclusions on the spot. This is particularly true when the question involved is of the kind that (at

---

[4]   The subject of properly defining the applicable question in a written document is discussed in Section 3.2.1.

[5]   This is particularly highlighted in written communications, where the associate often puts pen to paper without any idea of the structure the document is to take—a failing almost always painfully apparent in the finished product. See Section 3.2.2.

least in the client's perception) a lawyer should be able to handle.[6]

But there will be a number of occasions—in a meeting with the client, or perhaps alone with a partner[7]—when the question presented just cannot be handled on the spot. The reasoning is too complex, the dimensions are too broad; further investigation and thought are required. When this is the case, don't be embarrassed to say so. "I can't give you an answer on that one right off the bat." (If you feel the need, you can usually attribute partial responsibility to other disciplines: "I want to check how that might affect the accounting for the transaction.") It's not the worst thing in the world for the client to understand just how difficult these problems he's creating really are.

So, my opening piece of advice is: never shoot from the hip when your chances of being wrong are other than insignificant. And remember, even the right *legal* response may be the wrong overall answer—as where the client's proposed action is legally permissible but potentially disastrous on a practical level. As you gain in confidence and knowledge—as your sense of judgment[8] matures—you will work out neat ways of avoiding the Scylla of seeming uninformed and the Charybdis of putting your foot in your mouth. Your responses will be couched in such careful terms as: "My initial reaction is that we can work this out, but I would like the comfort of a few precedents"; or "Something tells me you won't be able to get away with that, but before we nix such an imaginative plan let me see if there's a loophole in the regulation"; or (assuming it's so) "I believe one of my colleagues had a similar problem several months ago; I'd like to check with him as to what position the Branch Chief took"—to say nothing of the comfortable standby: "It's essentially a factual determination, and I wouldn't want to answer prematurely without having all the facts."

But now I want to say a few words about the broader issue of just how questions come up in your practice—a consideration which so often influences the amount of analytical energy that is ultimately brought to bear. Obviously, problems are presented to a law firm in many different guises. For example, in large firms with major corporate clients possessing their own legal staffs, some questions might

[6] For example, if I were the client being represented in a purchase of property by a competent real estate lawyer, and for some reason the deed could not be recorded immediately, I would expect the lawyer to be able to tell me—without consulting treatises or colleagues—whether in *this* state the act of recording is requisite to the passage of title between seller and buyer or merely perfects it against third parties. See also Section 6.3.
[7] For a more general discussion of the proper handling of client and partner questions, see Chapter 6 and Section 5.1, respectively.
[8] A subject discussed at length in Chapter 8 and the hypothetical examples of Chapter 9.

be forwarded to the firm in a rather structured form. XYZ Company, which has an outstanding trust indenture, wants to repurchase shares of its preferred stock—an action that might or might not be in violation of Section 13(e)(2)(iii) of the indenture. The memo from company counsel outlines the dimensions of the problem, the factual background, the relevant sections of the indenture, the alternative conclusions—and your firm is asked to render a judgment. When a problem is presented to you in this highly sculpted fashion—and in my experience, such a phenomenon is definitely the exception, not the rule—it's relatively easy to get yourself into a reflective, analytical frame of mind.

Generally, however, problems come to your desk in much more of a state of disarray. A client indicates that he wishes to take a certain action and asks if there are any problems. *You* have to identify the potential source of trouble ("What about the trust indenture?") and ferret out the sections that might possibly be violated. *You* have to decide whether there are tax implications which present a serious enough issue to be brought to a tax expert. It's a rare client who can frame precisely the correct inquiry; your role is to define the issue in legal terms and then answer the question he should have posed (but didn't). But at least here you've been *asked* to look for problems, and that usually eases you into the proper attitude.

At other times, though, you may not even have been asked to identify the problems. A client is pursuing a business course of action, in which you are assisting. No one at the client's office anticipates any obstacles; they just want to get the job done—and fast. You have to supply the self-discipline to stop, look and listen—even to halt the proceedings temporarily so that you can check out certain areas of inquiry before going forward. This is not always easy to do—you're cast in the role of obstructionist, slowing the momentum, interfering with the client's plans.[9] But you just have to muster the necessary will-power and courage; because if you don't, and something goes wrong, your client's prior impatience will furnish absolutely no excuse.

And finally, you might find yourself in a situation where not only haven't you been asked to spot problems for client X, but at the moment you're engaged on matters involving other clients of the office. Then, something comes across your desk in another context, which (if you're not asleep at the analytical switch) touches off a reaction. Perhaps some form of affirmative action is required on the part of client X, in order that his inaction (or continuation of a past course of action) not be deemed violative of a new law or interpretation, or con-

---

[9]   The importance of a lawyer being perceived as one who makes (not breaks) deals is discussed in Section 6.6.

travene a recently executed instrument. This requires a little thought.
When a new regulation or ruling or case is circulated around the office for informational purposes, never assume that someone will ask
you: "Does this have any applicability to X Corporation's situation?"
When you read it, stop—*think*—and decide for yourself if some inquiry or action may be appropriate. There's no question but that the
word of good unsolicited advice—the demonstration to the client of
your eternal vigilance in support of his interests—can win you
plaudits far beyond the measured response to a question expressly
posed for your consideration.

2.3. REVVING UP THE ANALYTICAL MOTOR

Let me illustrate the essential formlessness in which problems arrive though a hypothetical—but definitely not unusual—situation.[10]
What I want you to keep in mind as we proceed is the frequent need
for the lawyer to create his own analytical framework; nothing is
handed to him on a silver platter.

Phil, a sometime acquaintance, enters your office seeking legal advice. He is a very low-key, unaggressive type. You are aware that he
serves as an executive with a good small company, privately owned
by others (and not represented by your firm). After a few pleasantries,
Phil reports that the outfit he works for is about to be acquired by a
public company. Phil has been asked to sign an employment contract,
and he wonders what his response ought to be. And that's it from
Phil. Leaning back in his chair, he awaits your counsel.

All right, where do you start? You know, it's very much as if Phil
were visiting a physician and complaining of a curious pain in his
side. The doctor's going to have to make his diagnosis; Phil is unlikely to do the doctor's job for him—and the chances are, not yours
either. There's no one around to point you in the right direction. Like
the doctor probing the tender flesh in the vicinity of the ribcage, you
just have to fend for yourself.

Well (to switch metaphors), this is the time to rev up your
analytical motor. Just as your car engine requires gas for propulsion,
your analytical motor needs facts. And intentions. And motivations.
And a sense of the time structure within which you're operating. And,
of course, more than a dose of legal knowhow.

So, I would suggest beginning by asking Phil a series of questions,
ranging over the full dimensions of the problem. I'd start with the
selling company (let's call it "Cellar Corp.") Who holds its stock?

---

[10]   For a detailed example of the analytical mind at work, see the problem
"Stud or High Stakes" contained in Section 9.1.

Does Phil own any? Does he have any options to buy stock—or were any promises of equity participation ever made to him? How about pensions or termination rights? I would also probe the present state of Phil's relations with Cellar's principles. Which individual asked you to sign the contract, Phil—the principal of Cellar or an executive from the purchaser corporation (which we'll call "Byre Inc.")? And, by the way, Phil, what kind of shape is Cellar Corp. in?

Then I'd turn to the proposed contract. Which company—Cellar or Byre—is the named contracting party? How long does the contract run? How do the financial provisions seem to you, Phil? What else is in there?

My next series of questions would be aimed at finding out something about Phil and his inner feelings. What are his employment options? Does he want to continue working in the business? And, almost as important as *his* feelings, what do the key individuals at Cellar and Byre *think* Phil wants to do?

Then I would inquire about the acquisition itself. What stage is it presently at—has an agreement been signed or have the parties simply agreed in principle? When is the deal due to close? Are there any substantial conditions to closing? Is the consideration cash, or stock of Byre, or something else? Is the price substantially above the value of the Cellar's assets? And so on.

As the answers flow, the issues—as well as the opportunities—begin to come into perspective. The facts, the state of knowledge, the motives, the timing—all these tend to shape one's thinking and anchor the analysis firmly in the real-world context where situations like this develop. And gradually, there emerges a tale of unrequited love, rivaling a late afternoon soap opera.

It seems that Phil has virtually been running Cellar's business these last few years, as the company's aging and somewhat enfeebled patriarch has gradually slowed down, while his glib but essentially brainless son-in-law has more than confirmed initial impressions of his ineptitude. There have been promises of partnership over the years—"Don't worry, Phil, I'll treat you like the son I never had. . . ."—but no follow-through; at present Phil has a zero equity stake in the business and little in the way of pension or termination benefits. As a result of such broken pledges, Phil's personal relations with the patriarch have become strained, and Phil lacks any residue of loyalty toward him. While the business is essentially sound, it is badly in need of a substantial cash transfusion.

Significantly although in form the contract is with Cellar, it was Byre's president who asked Phil to sign it. After more than a little probing to overcome Phil's natural modesty, he finally admits his belief that the executives of Byre may actually be unwilling to go through with the transaction if Phil doesn't sign the employment contract—since they realize they can't cope with the intricacies of Cellar's business on their own at this point, they're wary of the patriarch's failing health, and the son-in-law's inadequacies are clear to all.

As for the contract Byre is offering to Phil, it would run for three years at a salary level $5,000 above what he has been earning—satisfactory perhaps, but certainly not exciting. The contract also contains a sweeping two-year non-competition provision that disturbs Phil greatly. Aside from that, he has no objections to signing an employment contract. Phil likes the business, feels he's good at it, has considerable respect for Byre, and would like to stay just where he is.

Finally, you learn that the deal has been publicly announced, but although Phil isn't sure, it's doubtful that a definitive agreement has been signed. (You infer this from the fact that Phil hasn't quite completed the compilation of some contractual schedules the lawyers have asked him to prepare.) The closing will probably take place in about five weeks, when Cellar's year-end financial results have been certified by its auditors. The purchase price, which is being paid solely in the form of Byre's common stock, exceeds the value of Cellar's assets by quite a bit.

The process is not unlike feeding a carload of data into a computer and waiting for it to spit out an answer. The main differences are that you—the computer—have to derive the raw data yourself, that the evidence is often highly subjective, and that the judgments can be exceedingly subtle. Still, as you sort out the various strands, it becomes clear that Phil (who doesn't realize it) is sitting on top of a magnificently leveraged position.

Your analytical motor starts to hum. Byre wants Phil, in fact won't go ahead without him; therefore the patriarch, anxious to sell his cash-poor business, needs Phil's cooperation also. Patriarch's equitable position is poor because he's violated past promises; no feelings of loyalty need inhibit Phil's conduct. *Hrrummm. Hrrummm.* Phil wants to stay on, wouldn't mind signing a contract. The acquisition agreement hasn't been signed. With stock as consideration, the deal is probably structured as a tax-free reorganization; and in view of the disparity between price and Cellar's asset value, Byre will undoubtedly want to account for the acquisition on a pooling of interests basis, to avoid the costly amortization of goodwill created in a purchase transaction.[11] *Hrrummm. Hrrummm.*

Now, you're breaking out of traffic and hitting the open road, as you examine Phil's alternatives. He could openly confront the patriarch, demanding his promised share of the business (to take effect be-

---

[11]   For a discussion of these accounting principles and their importance in understanding and negotiating acquisitions, see Section 4.4 of *Anatomy.*

fore the transaction is consummated); then Phil would end up with stock of Byre in the exchange. But that might create tax problems, both for Phil personally and also in terms of the reorganization. Even worse, from Byre's point of view, it might well destroy the pooling. *Honk. Honk.* Alternatively, Phil could insist on better terms in his contract—more dough, less non-compete, and an insistence that the contract be with (or guaranteed by) Byre so he doesn't have to rely on Cellar's shaky credit.

And now you shift into high gear, as your analysis turns to strategic considerations. We'll try the make-me-a-partner routine first—and let Byre know what we're up to. . . . No, wait, I've got it! Let Phil do it alone, without a lawyer, and totally ignorant of reorganizations and poolings; he just wants what's coming to him. When he'd been told that everyone would love to oblige him but it just won't work tax- and accounting-wise, *then* enter the lawyer. At which point, you'll nod sagely, agree with the analysis, but say: "All right, then Phil should receive the equity that you admit he deserves in a different way. Perhaps a bonus, keyed to the annual earnings of Cellar during the employment contract years—it's in your best interests, Mr. Executive of Byre, to provide Phil with the incentives he's being deprived of by *not* having that stock interest." *Flash the brights. Pass. Resume lane.* "And by the way" (if you feel things are going your way), "Byre ought to commit to keep Cellar adequately capitalized at all times during the bonus period. . . ."

Well, there's no need to spin this out further; I'm sure you understand the point. It's an example of legal (and factual, and practical, and strategic) analysis at work, in the law office context—taking a shapeless, formless request for advice, getting the information, sorting out the possibilities, and coming up with a plan for action—diagnosing the curious pain and prescribing a treatment. To me, that's what practicing law is all about.

2.4. THE MODES AND MOODS OF THE REFLECTIVE PROCESS

By the way, how do *you* think? Have you ever considered the reflective process? When my son asks, "Where are my blue socks?" and my wife replies "In the top drawer"; and, after a short pause, he calls back "I don't see them"; and she goes in there and pulls out the socks, and he says "Oh"—he may have been *looking*, but he hasn't been *seeing*. Is it possible that you *imagine* you've been thinking about a problem, but you haven't really given it the kind of thought that generates bright ideas, new approaches, practical solutions, materiality judgments, and so forth?

Let's assume you've been presented with a problem; you have done some preliminary digging into the factual context; you possess some grasp of the legal principals involved. It's now time to do some hard thinking. How do you go about it? Obviously, everyone has his own preferred method, and there are no easy generalizations on this subject. But the point I want to make is that different types of problems may well require differing approaches to the thinking process. A method that works well with a certain kind of question may not be the best means of wrestling with another issue having dissimilar characteristics. Let me illustrate this thesis by examining three rather typical species of problems that arise in the securities law area[12]—each of which, to my mind, calls for a different mode of thought.

Ishyouer Corporation, a medium-sized public company, is about to have an underwritten public offering of its common shares. Although Ishyouer has been a client of the firm for several years, this is your first assignment on its behalf. As often happens in this type of situation, there exists a great sense of time pressure; you've had to find out the facts about the company on the run. It would have been preferable to do your investigation, reflect, and then draft a prospectus; but you were forced to turn out a quick first draft based mainly on Ishyouer's previous filings, with confirmation of the information coming after the fact. Company personnel, while not uncooperative, have limited themselves to answering your direct queries. They appear extremely loath to analyze the business and, in particular, shy away from areas of its prospective vulnerability.

The date for filing Ishyouer's registration statement is rapidly approaching. You are concerned that, although the description of the company's business which you've prepared contains an abundance of factual material, it doesn't really get to the heart of what makes Ishyouer tick—and significantly, it doesn't focus in on whether any foreseeable future developments could adversely affect the company in the near term. You feel it's important to isolate any such factors, since a warning of the potential risk in the prospectus would clearly help your client avoid criticism and possibly litigation down the road were the adverse event to come about.

For me, analytical thought of the kind needed in this situation is best done alone—without people, papers, pencils or other artificial aids. I find, for instance, that some of my best thinking is performed when I'm alone in the car, driving on a highway with no distracting turns or red lights, and I can cut my mind loose to dwell on a

---

[12]   Don't worry about your possible lack of familiarity with the various legal principles mentioned; they are incidental to the thought process focus of this section.

particular problem. You will discover that as more and more divergent, complex and seemingly urgent matters compete for your attention, the luxury of uninterrupted reflective thought about a problem is to be greatly treasured. This is probably akin to the benefits others find in meditation; for me, continuing to reflect on a problem beyond the point at which its potentialities seem to have been exhausted can prove extremely beneficial. Merely concentrating on the problem—even if nothing productive seems to be happening at the moment—often leads to startling insights. This is especially beneficial for (i) separating what is material from what is not;[13] (ii) grasping the real significance of an already known but previously unobtrusive fact; (iii) recognizing how the modification of a basic assumption can drastically alter your perception of the dynamics of a situation;[14] and (iv) formulating a new and different course of action.

And this is just what can happen when you put away that draft prospectus and all those other documents, take leave of the multitude of lawyers and businessmen and accountants and investment bankers, and think hard about Ishyouer. Clear shafts of sunlight filter through the haze. The future of the company, you realize, is dependent on its consumer line of business, which has accounted for the bulk of bottom line growth in recent years; the balance of the company's activities pretty much constitute a holding action. So your search for significance should be in consumer goods. But where? What's unique to Ishyouer's business? What about the competition? You recall that one principal common component exists in each of the company's successful products. It does seem an item capable of duplication by a competitor—but then you've been told that Ishyouer has a solid wall of patent protection around its products. . . . Wait, though, wasn't there *one* patent with an expiration date next year, much earlier than the others? Could it possibly be the one which guards this particular technology? And so on and on, until you've arrived at your point of special significance. But it might not have happened if you hadn't gotten away from the mass of detail and people, to do some hard solitary thinking.

Let's look at a quite different type of securities problem. Remember your buddy, Phil?[15] Well, three years have now passed and he's returned for some more advice. Everything has worked out beautifully—Phil has proved a great success in running the Cellar division of Byre—and now, in order to induce Phil to renew his employment contract, Byre is offering to sell Phil 25,000 shares of

[13] Discerning materiality is a recurring theme of this book; see, e.g., Section 3.2.5.
[14] In this regard, see Section 2.5.
[15] See Section 2.3.

Byre stock on very sweet terms, payable over a period of years. However, in addition to the restrictions imposed by the securities laws on Phil's resale of these shares, there would also be contractual restrictions requiring Phil to sell an annually decreasing percentage of the shares back to the Company at his cost upon termination of his employment; and only shares which were freed up from these restrictions (i.e., which had become vested) could be sold by him in the open market.

Without delving too deeply into the applicable substantive law, let me just say that as a matter of securities law, Phil's right to sell shares publicly is regulated by Rule 144 under the Securities Act of 1933. His ability to commence such sales is a function of both when the shares fully vest and when they are fully paid; and once sales are permitted, he is limited at present during any three-month period to an amount equal to the greater of 1% of the Company's capitalization or the stock's average weekly volume over the four weeks preceding his sale. Tax considerations also come into play here; since Phil will realize income as the various restrictions come off, he'll have to be in a position to sell enough shares to raise the funds necessary to pay the tax. You will undoubtedly ask the Company for registration rights;[16] but in view of the relatively small number of shares involved, you will probably be offered only so-called "piggy-back" rights; and you wonder how hard to negotiate on this point, at the risk of antagonizing the Company.

Well, with a complex, mathematical-type problem of this sort, there's simply no substitute for outlining the various permutations and combinations on paper.[17] You have to classify these factors into their various elements, a task that most people can't do in their heads. It might work out that Phil really doesn't need any registration rights for the first few years (because of the contractual restrictions) and also in the later years (when Rule 144 can help him), but he could use some help in those middle years when he's hung up in between—free to sell some shares contractually but not under the securities laws—and subject to tax. And perhaps, if you approach Byre with a narrowly-based logical demand of this kind, with the equities working in your favor (tax hardships always create sympathy), you may receive favorable consideration—at least, your position will be understandable and won't alienate anyone. But to do

---

16   For a discussion of registration rights, see Chapter 9 of *Anatomy*.
17   The problem in Section 9.1 is another good example of the use of an analytical matrix.

the analysis, you have to get down on paper those calculations as to what his sales and tax status will be for each year.[18]

Take a still different kind of securities problem. Multifaceted Corp., a client of the firm, has an effective "shelf" registration which certain stockholders are using to sell their otherwise restricted shares on the American Stock Exchange from time to time. The Company has outstanding publicly-held warrants to purchase shares, which are presently exercisable (although the market price of the stock exceeds the warrant exercise price by quite a few points). You are aware that Multifaceted is contemplating a public offering of long-term debt, and that it has had preliminary conversations on the subject with a prospective underwriter, although no final decision has yet been reached. The Company president now calls to inform you that he will be appearing tomorrow before a group of financial analysts, at which time he would like to announce a new product discovery destined to revolutionize the oven-cleaning business. How about it, fella?

With this type of inquiry, I find there is no substitute for commandeering another lawyer in the firm and bouncing the problem off him. I don't mean this as an abdication of responsibility; it's just that the interplay of two minds on something of this sort geometrically improves your chances of arriving at an intelligent solution. This is especially true if the other lawyer is knowledgeable in the particular area at issue, or has exceptionally good judgment, or (with luck) both. But even if he's untutored and a trifle immature, I find that the very act of articulating the problem to another lawyer helps *me* to analyze what is significant and what is not, to discover how much I know about the problem and what I need to find out, to ascertain which assumptions I am making, to see how differing alternatives can lead to different results, and so on. Even a lawyer who serves only as a laconic sounding board can be of substantial utility in this regard.

I can think of a number of legal issues in this hypothetical problem on which another lawyer might have a good fix, or where exploration of the problem can help you focus on what's involved and reason accordingly. How early in the proposed debt offering process should your client stop being bullish in order to avoid "gun-jumping" problems? Can he wait longer when the offering is of debt securities, as contrasted with stock? What's the significance of the shelf registra-

---

[18] Incidentally, I find that the ability to do relatively simple, approximate math calculations in one's head ("Let's see, he's got 350,000 shares, and together with her 75,000, that's over 20% of the nearly 2,000,000 shares outstanding . . .") impresses business clients, who are suspicious that real world numbers never intrude into the attorney's ivory tower. Try it sometime.

tion, where the Company itself is not a seller? How about the warrants? Is it relevant that they are "out of the money"? And then there
are the factual issues to be sorted out. How significant really is the
new product discovery? Will the news be released simultaneously in
a press release? Does the president intend to make any sales or
earnings projections to the assemblage? These are the kinds of issues
that a pair of knowledgeable lawyers can thoroughly dissect, with the
end product much improved by the cross-pollination of resulting
ideas.

Well, that's a sampling of analytical modes. I haven't meant to be
comprehensive here; I simply wanted to illustrate that different
problems may call for distinctive approaches. By all means, use the
methods which *you* find the most congenial. But—and this is the real
concept here—give a little thought to the *way* you should be thinking.
And make sure you're seeing those socks in the drawer.

2.5. CRACKING THE ASSUMPTION MOLD

Most tasks you are assigned will contain prescribed parameters
within which you're asked to operate. For example, take that estate
plan you were requested to prepare for the new client. He's made it
very clear that he does not want to yield control of any significant
portion of his property during his lifetime. If, in your zeal to minimize
taxes, you concoct grandiose schemes involving massive *inter vivos*
gifts to kith and kin, you're not carrying out your charge. Or assume
your finance company client is taking additional security on a
short-term loan to an extremely shaky enterprise. You will undoubtedly move heaven and earth to have the transaction completed
by a date more than four months prior to the due date on the borrower's long-term unsecured debt—since you properly anticipate the
possibility of a default, followed by the filing of a petition for bankruptcy, and you want the transaction to escape attack as a preference.
These kinds of parameters, which are actually basic assumptions
about the solution to a problem, will be fed to you by the client or the
partner in charge, and obviously should not be ignored; you can't just go
off and operate in a vacuum where such restraints don't exist.

Most lawyers understand this pretty well, but they are less atten-
tive to an important corollary point, which is: if you encounter great
difficulty working within a given framework, step back for a moment
and re-examine the premises upon which you've been operating. You
might just discover that they're not quite as iron-clad as they seemed
at first blush—that you're not irretrievably bound to adherence. I have
found that clients are remarkably flexible in their approach to

problem-solving—often in inverse relationship to the rigidity with which they set forth their initial position!

Take the following example. A client corporation is proposing to make an acquisition. In the course of your initial briefing, the president mentions (among other things) that the transaction must be accomplished in a manner so as to avoid providing dissenting shareholders of the acquired corporation with appraisal rights under applicable state law. Back at the analytical drawing board, you labor mightily to come up with a form of acquisition transaction that not only fulfills all the other important requirements set forth by the client (e.g., that you end up with 100% of the seller, that only a majority stockholder vote is needed, etc.), but also deprives the seller's stockholders of their appraisal rights. You twist and you turn, but every gimmick to accomplish this either creates severe tax problems or accounting headaches, or involves bizarre corporate maneuvers.

I suggest you stop at this point, go back to the client, and have a little talk with him on the subject of appraisal rights.[19] Explain how the courts of the seller's jurisdiction of incorporation have a definite pro-management bias and are extremely chary of granting minority stockholders meaningful dissenters' rights. Point out that the value being offered in the acquisition exceeds both the market price and book value computations on which the appraisal would primarily be based, so that the exposure is minuscule. Educate him on the reluctance of stockholders to pursue this elusive remedy, in recognition of the time, expense and uncertainty involved. You may observe your client's apparent resolve on the point suddenly crumbling, as he finds he can live quite nicely with a not-so-significant practical problem. Instead of shoehorning the deal into an ill-fitting mold in order to achieve an unimportant objective, you will then be able to restructure it along more traditional corporate lines, with resulting tax and accounting benefits. But it might not have happened, if you had felt unalterably bound by every assumption you were handed.

In my experience, the most brilliant ideas are simple rather than complex—a fresh way of looking at a problem rather than a convoluted scheme—and many involve not much more than the rejection of an implicit assumption. So, merge the elephant into the mouse. You sue *him* first, so you can pick the court. Cracking the assumption mold is the true mark of a first-class analytical lawyer.

---

[19]   On the general subject of discoursing with the client, see Chapter 6.

2.6. THE APPLICATION OF ANALYTICAL REASONING TO NON-LEGAL PROBLEMS

I have become acutely aware, with each passing year, that less and less of what I actually do as a lawyer involves purely legal matters, while an ever-increasing amount of time is spent motivating, persuading and just dealing with people, devising practical courses of action, and so on. As you find this happening in your own practice, you will also discover the ready applicability of analytical modes of thinking to matters which go well beyond the merely legal aspects of a problem.

The difficulty here, though, is that while we've been taught to think analytically about legal issues, we haven't been as well trained in analyzing other kinds of problems. There is a definite tendency to treat these as comprising an inferior species, scarcely entitled to the full measure of brainpower brought to bear on more traditional subjects. It takes more self-discipline and forethought to approach these other matters in the same fashion as a problem having principally legal dimensions.

Your client is attempting to sublease some surplus office space on which he is paying rent as the tenant. You've prepared and submitted to your client a first draft of a sublease with a proposed subtenant. Your client's comments, which took a long time in coming, were rather extensive, and you have now prepared a second draft incorporating their substance. The subtenant's attorney has informed you that he will be out of town all next week, so you are anxious for the sublease to get to him as soon as possible. Should you send him the second draft now, or should you run it by your client first and risk further delay? If you consider it unwise to ignore your client, how about calling him up and suggesting that the sublease be sent immediately to the other lawyer—with a notation that your client hasn't seen the draft and may want to modify it. Would this proposal offend your client? Should you try to convince the client that this is the better course, or should you just lay out the situation and let him decide what's to be done? If you do call the client, which individual should you contact? The president might be more inclined to understand the exigencies of the situation and clear the immediate delivery of the sublease, but would the vice president with whom you've worked then feel miffed that you went over his head? And there you are—dealing with a number of alternatives just as ripe for analysis as the question of whether to include a liquidated damages clause in the sublease.

Or, you have a client who has retired from a life-long business partnership, leaving his younger partner to run the financially troubled show. Your client has left certain funds in the business, with respect to which he occupies limited partner status. At lunch with him one day, in the course of his usual diatribe over his partner's short-comings, your client illustrates his point by remarking on the increasingly frequent visits which the firm's top salesman has been paying to his home—visits (obviously flattering to the client) in which the salesman not only complains about the new regime, but also bounces ideas off your client, seeking advice on sales methods and opportunities. That's curious, you think (as the client drones on), why should that clever young salesman be making those visits? It's unusual; your client mentioned that the two of them were never that close when he was active. What possible motivation could the salesman have? And then it dawns on you: perhaps the salesman, concerned that the firm might go under owing him back commissions, is setting up your client for an allegation that he's only masquerading as a limited partner and is, in fact, a *general* partner—still active in the business and giving advice—and thus fair game for any claims the salesman might have against the firm. But you have to think analytically—some might say, cynically—about motivation in order to stumble upon that hypothesis, and be in a position to advise your client to disengage himself from the situation.

2.7. THE ROLE OF LEGAL KNOWLEDGE

In re-reading this chapter, I realize that in stressing the analytical element, I may have understated the obvious point that, in order to reason analytically about a legal problem, a lawyer needs to know the state of the law. Otherwise, all he can really do is think hypothetically about the problem—if the law were thus-and-so, then certain conclusions might logically follow—but that's *not* what we're really interested in or paid to accomplish. Issue-spotters and alternative-identifiers may make Law Review but they often flunk the larger professional tests. Coming to some sort of reasoned *conclusion* is basic to the practice of law. So permit me to digress from legal reasoning for a few words on the related subject of legal knowledge.

After soaking up wads of legal knowledge in law school and preparation for the bar exam, you'll probably never use 90% of it again. Yet your practice may require you to have at your fingertips a roughly equal quantity of law—the difference being that it consists of more detailed knowledge about much narrower areas. You can't for the life of you remember whether they held for or against the negligent defendant in *Palsgraf*, but you're fully knowledgeable about an obscure SEC staff position equating officers to the corporation for

purposes of Rule 10b-6. And the mass of information you accumulate
is rarely learned in a classical academic manner; rather, you absorb it
as you go, in conjunction with each new legal task undertaken.

Nevertheless, I am often struck by the differences that exist
among various associates in terms of legal knowledge—differences that
can't be explained in terms of intellect, length of practice, or exposure to particular matters. At one extreme, some lawyers give off the
impression they're still in law school—learning for the sake of learning—fascinated by minutiae, relatively uninterested in the practical
utilization of their knowledge. At the other end of the spectrum are
lawyers who seem to possess a peculiar mental block in terms of absorbing new legal knowledge. When you ask them a question about a
matter on which they're working ("What percentage vote does Virginia require for a charter amendment?"), the invariable answer is "I
don't know but I'll check it out." It's as if they were saying, why
should I store up a lot of excess knowledge in my head—I'll hit the
books and find the answer if and when I have to.

I'm aware that a law firm should be more than a collection of
clones—that room exists for all types. Still, as a matter of personal
predilection, the know-nothing exponent is as bothersome as the hypothetical windmill-tilter. Partners—to say nothing of clients—tend to
be unimpressed by lawyers who are perpetually without an answer.[20]
Moreover, the associate who lacks legal knowledge and must
research the underlying law for each new problem, is frequently unable to put his best analytical foot forward. In practice, things don't
come up in an orderly way. The man who has the facts on a particular
matter, seated there in your office today, may be leaving the country
tomorrow, completely out of reach for a week. If you have a basic
knowledge of the applicable law, you will realize the relevant facts
you need and can obtain them on the spot; if you need to hit the
books first, your only chance to gain that information may be lost.[21]

So read some articles. Go to seminars. Keep up with developments
in your area of specialization. Analyze the significant recurring legal
problems with which you commonly deal, and become knowledgeable

---

[20] In this regard, one should distinguish between (i) knowledge that a lawyer
ought to have at his fingertips (if he practices corporate law, for example, he
should be alert to the fact that repurchases of stock can affect a company's
ability to account for a subsequent merger as a pooling of interests; and if he
practices corporate law in Pennsylvania, he should know whether Pennsylvania
law permits a corporation to repurchase its stock out of capital surplus); and (ii)
knowledge that it's reasonable to expect he will have to look up (that pooling
issue for a real estate lawyer; that Pennsylvania repurchase question for an Ohio
attorney). See also Section 6.3.
[21] In this connection, see Section 8.2 on anticipating the need to make
decisions.

about the major details. Hone your memory, which is one of the lawyer's most valuable tools. I would also recommend, prior to a meeting where you expect certain issues to surface, that you run a quick check on them in the library. If you've guessed right and are able to make an intelligent comment on the state of the law—to all appearances, just one of the tidbits retained in your vast repository of knowledge—it can be very impressive.

Being on top of any subject, with lots of useful information at your fingertips, does wonders for your self-esteem. And if you get to the point where other lawyers in the firm are coming to you for advice on legal questions—if you're the man or woman to see when someone has a problem under the Uniform Commercial Code or ERISA—this can stand you in good stead at the time those decisions on partnership are ultimately made.

When one talks about legal knowledge in conjunction with the analytical approach, the ability to do skillful legal research looms very large. This is a somewhat technical subject on which I just want to mention a few brief thoughts. First, don't feel that because you did legal research in law school you're an expert in the field. There's plenty to learn on a practical basis, and you shouldn't feel embarrassed to seek out the assistance of older and wiser heads. Second, there's no excuse for not being thorough in your research;[22] the missed case in point or the overlooked applicable regulation can be absolutely devastating—destroying client relationships, subjecting the firm to claims of malpractice, and irreparably damaging a budding career.[23] Finally, be imaginative in your research. Don't limit yourself to the precise issue in point if the answers aren't satisfactory; look for analogies, figure out possibilities for alternative avenues of approach. In short—as the man from the computer company so well put it—*THINK*.

---

[22] If the deficiencies in your work are explainable due to lack of time or unavailability of sources, this must be noted for the partner evaluating your work; see Section 3.2.8.

[23] For an example of such an omission, see "A Tale of Two Associates" in Section 9.4.

·

CHAPTER 3

WRITTEN AND ORAL EXPRESSION— THE COMMUNICATIONS ELEMENT

3.1. THE SIGNIFICANCE OF COMMUNICATION IN A LAWYER'S WORLD

In macabre moments, I occasionally fantasize over how I would fare professionally without particular limbs or faculties. If, for example, I were suddenly to lose the use of my legs, could I overcome the defect and continue to practice law? What if my eyes went? And the verdict is usually somewhat encouraging—legs often seem a fossil appendage in our sedentary lives; think of the blind lawyers who have made it through law school and into practice; and so on. The one possibility I can never face up to, however, since it would clearly signal the end of my legal career, is loss of the ability to communicate—to speak, to listen, to write.

If you think about it, all the most fundamental aspects of practicing law involve communication. By contrast, a physician can examine a wound, clean it, and apply the sutures without any verbal expression whatsoever—the patient might well be unconscious the entire time. But legal practice requires a constant flow of intelligent communication. The client has to tell you his problem. You must interrogate him to ascertain the relevant factual details. In working with your supervisory partner, there's a need for communication back and forth—to ensure you're on the same wavelength, to know what's expected of you, to test your tentative conclusions for positive feedback. Your firm's position must then be transmitted to the client, in order for him to make the necessary business decision. Along the way, you will communicate with other lawyers, with administrative agencies, perhaps in the courts, and so on. Inadequate communica-

31

tion can result in misunderstandings which undermine any course of dealings and lead to no end of mischief.[1]

As lawyers, we tend to pride ourselves on an ability to communicate; and generally speaking, because it's so much a part of our daily lives, we're probably better at the task than most executives, academics, and other professionals who don't go at it with such intensity. And yet, I never fail to wonder at the inability of some lawyers to effectively communicate the important points inherent in particular situations. While this failing can be anticipated from non-lawyers, and allowances made—I always go out of my way, for example, to avoid having Smith quote me to Jones, much preferring to deliver the message to Jones myself—a negative communication experience involving another lawyer is generally unexpected and leaves a feeling of acute disappointment in its wake.

Perhaps we're asking too much. Communicating effectively, without ambiguity and with all the nuances correctly in place, can be a prodigious task indeed. It often calls for a hand-tailored approach, both to the individual or group to whom one happens to be speaking or writing, and to the particular circumstances in which the communication is taking place. Merely accurate reportage of unemphasized views, for instance, may be insufficient. Identical substantive reports on a single issue may vary widely, based on whether the report is being made to the partner, the client, or the adversary. The context may require thorough exploration of various options, or it may cry out for decisive action; the able lawyer must quickly size up the situation and communicate accordingly.

In my view, however, the solution to this problem is rather simple. Much along the same lines as my criticism of lawyers who don't stop and think analytically before they speak or act,[2] I believe that many lawyers fail to spend enough time thinking about communications *per se*. They wrap themselves in the substantive problem, satisfied that the communication will take care of itself—but that isn't always the case. An effective attorney really must focus separately on the *expression* of his analysis, quite apart from its substance.

Make no mistake: you are as likely to be judged on the basis of your ability to communicate the results of your legal analysis as on the results themselves. To be sure, if you've failed to analyze a problem properly, then no amount of transmission skills will enable you to render an effective report to a discerning observer. (Oh, you

---

[1] As Brandeis said: "Nine-tenths of the serious controversies which arise in life result from misunderstanding, result from one man not knowing the facts which to the other man seem important, or otherwise failing to appreciate his point of view." As quoted in G. Nierenberg, *The Art of Negotiating* (1968), at 41.
[2] See Section 2.1.

might be able to sneak by a client who doesn't really understand what's involved, or a fuzzy adversary lawyer, or even a partner harassed by other demands on his time; but sooner or later, shabby analysis and superficial treatment will catch up with you.) What is truly heartbreaking, though, is to witness the inability of an associate who has performed a superb analytical job to communicate that fact to the listener—with the result, more often than not, that the listener fails to realize the soundness of the actual analysis and transmutes the communications failure into a substantive shortcoming.

As lawyers, we communicate both orally and in writing. There may be some exceptions (the attorney trying a larger number of small personal injury actions on a daily basis comes to mind), but the great bulk of lawyers spend much of their time writing. Not just the legal draftsmanship found in formal documents such as contracts, prospectuses and briefs; what interests me (and will occupy the greater part of this chapter) is a lawyer's ability to compose a memorandum or letter which sets forth the writer's views on the subject in crisp, clear, interesting prose. At a minimum, these views should be readily understandable by the reader; if the reader can also be impressed by the lucidity and sprightliness the writer brings to his task, so much the better; and when, in appropriate circumstances, the reader is persuaded by the writer's thesis, then the writing has accomplished its purpose. By the way, if you can also allude to disquieting facts without alarming the reader, introduce caveats and other qualifications without irritating the reader's desire for certainty, and make your suggested course of action appear so implicit that the reader feels he's arriving at his own decision, then you're really writing well.

But as often as we lawyers write, our prose is dwarfed by the sheer volume of oral communication in which we daily engage. You will undoubtedly notice that the amount of time you spend conversing with clients and other lawyers increases geometrically with the number of years you've been practicing law. Your early days at the firm are likely to be spent in research, preparing memos and briefs, drafting documents, and performing other tasks that entail little personal communication, except with those for whom you're working. But then, as time goes by, the telephone becomes a hideous extension of your left ear, and you begin to wonder whether you're an attorney or a go-between. Countless hours are spent rehashing matters with your client, fencing with your adversary, repeating to Peter what Paul said earlier in the day—situations in which your ability with words, your sense of the proper interpretive shading, can be critical.

So, a large portion of this chapter will be concerned with the informal kinds of situations where you are called upon to communicate

orally. I'm interested in the effect your words have on the other
people with whom you deal—with your ability to listen to and lead
others, to conduct a meeting, to compose differences—and perhaps
most of all, with your ability both to recognize and deal with ambiguity and subtlety in the speech of others, while keeping your own
verbal communications unambiguous and to the point. As a keynote,
let me refer you to the small plaque in my office that sums up the point
rather aptly:

> "I know you believe you understand what you think I said,
> but I am not sure you realize that what you heard is not what
> I meant."

3.2. THE WRITTEN WORD

At the risk of oversimplifying such an obviously complex matter as
a lawyer's writings, let me postulate my two rules of three thumbs
each. First, there are three key techniques involved in the craft of
writing a memorandum, letter or similar document, namely: perceiving
the purpose the document is to serve, organizing thoughts into a logical
pattern, and rewriting prior drafts. Then, there are three stylistic goals
toward which a lawyer's writing should strive: clarity, conciseness, and
interest to the reader. These subjects, together with some thoughts on
writing persuasively and other odds and ends, make up this section of
the book.

3.2.1. Discerning the Purpose of the Document.

A central—and seemingly difficult—consideration for a young lawyer to keep in mind is that each document he writes is intended to
serve a quite distinct purpose. I'm not referring to the obvious differences between a letter and a legal brief, or a memorandum and a
contract; my point is that not all memoranda are the same—not all letters fall into the same category—and you won't communicate effectively until you're conditioned to ascertaining the document's purpose
in terms of the potential reader and the intended goal.

This search for purpose involves at least two separate aspects:
what's the question to be addressed, and what's the proposed use of
the document? The first of these is more obvious and perhaps less
troublesome. Before putting pen to paper, make sure you understand
the legal or practical question you're being called upon to answer. If
you don't articulate the question properly, then your answer, how-

ever well reasoned, may be irrelevant.[3] When the matter is solely
legal, then devising the proper question from a formless presentation
is essentially an analytical matter. But if, as is so often the case, not
only legal but also factual, practical and strategic considerations are
involved, knowing exactly what's expected of you can sometimes be
a problem. Does the partner expect you to advise him as to the best
course of action? Or would he consider that presumptuous—desiring
instead a simple dissertation on the state of the law and a synopsis of
the available facts, in order to reach his own judgment on the matter?
Should a document intended for the client elaborate on the business
realities of the subject as they appear to you—which might have a
decisive impact on the outcome—or is it wiser to confine yourself to
the legal aspects where you possess a measure of expertise?

The simple solution here is to find out what's desired *before* submitting the document. No associate should be bashful about asking a
partner to clarify what he had in mind.[4] If the partner is unavailable,
then indicate the assumption you have made (either in the document
or a note accompanying it), and try to keep the various strands
separate—so that if he had less (or more) in mind, at least your
sub-conclusions are readily apparent.

For example, assume your views on a certain matter to be that the
proposed conduct could be deemed actionable at law, but no obvious
plaintiff exists and the damages would be highly conjectural; moreover, the business realities point strongly in favor of taking the action.[5]
Be sure to make clear the three separate elements of your analysis.
The partner might want to make his own practical judgment about
the likelihood of litigation. And he might wish to let the client
make the ultimate business decision. Still, your views on each of
these matters can be helpful. If, however, you fuse all the elements
together, the partner will be unable to determine whether your conclusion favorable to the action was primarily based on legal rationale,
practical considerations or business judgment.

One little piece of advice (explored more deeply in later chapters[6]),
to which I can't conceive of any exceptions: come to a conclusion—however hedged, however tentative. The on-the-one-
hand-it-can-be-argued approach, which served you so well in law school
at exam time, will *not* endear you to the partner who must make a decision (without having read all the cases and authorities), or to the client

---

[3] "It is a very common thing for attorneys to spend a great deal of time finding
out the answers to questions which are not involved." Arthur A. Ballantine, as
quoted in M. Mayer, *The Lawyers* (1966), at 307.
[4] See Section 5.1.2.
[5] See Section 8.6 on the subject of developing a risk-reward ratio analysis.
[6] See Sections 5.1.2. and 6.3.

who isn't paying big fees for abstract jurisprudential exercises.

The second aspect of the search for purpose takes place on a different, more subtle level. With every letter, memo or other piece of paper you write, you simply must focus on its likely use. Is it an internal document, designed for a partner's eyes only? Will it go to the client? Could it be subject to discovery in a lawsuit? Is it intended for transmission to the other side? If so, will it go only to the lawyer, or will it reach his client? Should you just lay out the various options for others to decide or recommend a desirable course of action? Does it make sense as a think piece, or a research effort, or something else entirely?

For some reason, even relatively senior attorneys often fail to pause and consider these matters. And yet, the answers to questions such as those just posed will obviously affect both the style and the substance of the document. In stylistic terms, perhaps the most important distinction is whether the writing is intended for lawyers or for clients. You can communicate with other lawyers in legalistic modes, but clients have to be able to understand what you're trying to convey. A letter shot through with lawyer's jargon, far from impressing the client with your erudition, may merely infuriate him. I have a small fit each time I review an associate's draft letter to the client containing such cutesy legalisms as *inter alia*, or client memos with string cites and *but contra* indications. What kind of effective communication is this? The client will presumably be just as bewildered by Latin phrases and invocations of long-departed jurists as you are when he talks about inventory turns and abstruse budgetary components.

But you miss my point if you conclude that excision of a few legalistic phrases converts a lawyer-to-lawyer memo into one fit for businessmen. What is called for, rather, is an altered tone to the entire piece, an appreciation of the framework within which the business reader operates and the conflicting pressures upon him, a recognition that the intermediate steps so requisite to you and your supervising partner—the stately path of logic and authority along which you proceed to your ultimate conclusion—may be unimportant to the client. (Would you want your shoemaker to belabor you with details as to how he positioned each nail and applied the adhesive—or is it enough that the heel and sole have been replaced?)

Even with an intra-office document, intended solely for your supervising partner, some thought should be given to its style. Considerations involving the subject matter of the piece, the circumstances involved, and your sense of the predilections of the particular partner[7] are all relevant here. For example, if you've been charged

---

[7] On adapting to a partner's idiosyncracies, see Section 5.1.1.

with developing the legal theories for a potentially major litigation matter, you ought to be comprehensive and precise, following up all leads, providing extensive citations, going into some detail on each court's holding, and so on. On the other hand, if your purpose is to brief an imperturbable partner on some general legal principles which may be useful for a meeting with the client tomorrow, you should get up more of an outline/check-list sort of document, with the main points readily accessible, and not too much in the way of detail or back-up. Most situations will fall somewhere between these extremes, but good judgment should always enter into the selection of a stylistic approach.

More important than style though, the discernment of a document's purpose may well affect its substance. You can make statements in an internal firm memo that would clearly be inappropriate in a document earmarked for the client. For example, in a memorandum discussing litigation threatened against your corporate client over a contract prepared by its inside counsel, the level of candor as to certain unfortunate drafting ambiguities has to be affected by the identity of the recipient. Or, you may feel it necessary to include certain caveats in a memorandum of advice to the client on which he intends to act—caveats that would be superfluous in an internal document; you wouldn't want the failure to point out a possible pitfall (which later, unfortunately, occurs) coming back to haunt you.[8]

One principal consideration should be whether there is any likelihood that the document will become discoverable in a lawsuit or investigation.[9] (This applies not only to final documents but drafts.) I don't intend to go into the whole question of privileged communications, but simply want to sound a warning: no document that you prepare, which is likely to surface in litigation or an investigation, should contain unnecessary material which is potentially embarrassing. There is no canon of ethics requiring you to manufacture useful evidence for your adversary.

Documents ultimately intended for the other side introduce a whole new set of considerations.[10] The balanced approach you adopted with the partner—even the low-key recommendation to your client (with due regard to alternatives and caveats)—is no longer sufficient. When dealing with an adversary (even a friendly one), you should undoubtedly strive for a more persuasive presentation.[11] The task of bringing someone around to your position, without making the memo sound like a brief, is a difficult one, but significant to the partner and

---

[8] See Sections 3.2.8 and 6.5.
[9] See also Section 3.2.9.
[10] Communications with other lawyers are discussed throughout Chapter 7.
[11] See Section 3.2.7 on persuasive writing.

astute clients; and a draft memo intended for the other side which doesn't accomplish this—a document too even-handed, or which isn't sufficiently oblique where some craft is required—will garner you few plaudits.

Taken all together, my point is that you should never do work which is neither fish nor fowl. If you're not sure of the question being asked, or of who will see the document, or of its purpose, then make sure to query the partner involved. If you can't reach him, then select what you consider to be the most desirable mode and include with the draft document a note as to the assumptions you've employed. For example, you might state: "I assumed you were looking for a recommendation from me here, so I haven't gone deeply into other possibilities. If you want more detail on the seemingly less desirable courses of action, please let me know." Or "I am writing this on the assumption that it's for your eyes only. If the memo is to go to the client, I would propose to modify some of the legalistic language and remove the somewhat introspective discussion on page 18." Or, "This is written in lay language, without extensive detail, since I assume it's intended for the client. I have the citations to back up the various points made, if you care to see them." Or "I have assumed that the purpose of this memo is to develop, in conjunction with our client, a proper bargaining posture. If you should want to send this memo to the other side, I would propose to eliminate the discussion of alternatives in Section 3 and make a more persuasive case for the proposed solution." In each case, the partner knows what was in your mind, and what modifications you would propose for other purposes—a giant step in the right direction of effective communication.

3.2.2. The Importance of Organization.

Singing a paean to the role of organization in a document is a little like boosting mom and apple pie. Clearly, a well-organized document creates a much more positive impact on the reader than a disorganized one. When the concepts are approached in an orderly manner and flow naturally from one to the other, when the various possibilities are sorted out for separate discussion, when the conclusion seems to follow inevitably from the chain of reasoning, the reader is swept along in the direction of the writer's viewpoint. The same concepts might be there in a disorganized document, but the sense of disarray causes the reader—unsure of where he's heading, dubious of the writer's subject matter mastery—to take issue with the conclusion. Good organization represents the writer's imprimatur on his material; and since the reader is presumably less knowledgeable on the subject than the writer, this seal of approval can be influential in assuring the reader that the writer knows his stuff.

And yet, too many documents cross our desks lacking in this basic structure. It's almost as if the associate—who can't be blind to the value of organization—has made an unconscious decision that the material will organize itself. But things don't always work out that way. Legal problems are too complex, have too many facets, don't fit into neat categories. A lawyer simply must outline his material before starting to write. This would seem so basic; my fifth grader had to outline his book report on *The Prince and the Pauper*! And it's not just cosmetic; outlining actually helps you to decide what to include, what to excise, what to stress—which ties in neatly with the analytical approach.[12] But it can't be done after the fact; the organization must be inherent in the document.

Let me give you an example. A partner calls you in and presents the following problem. Bidder Corp., your client, has begun to contemplate an acquisition of Target Inc., whose stock is traded on the American Stock Exchange. Bidder has not yet approached Target, however; and at this point, it hasn't been decided whether the approach will be: (i) solely on a friendly basis (where, if turned down, Bidder will exit quietly); or (ii) initially on a friendly basis, but where, if turned down, Bidder may institute a hostile tender offer; or (iii) on an initial unfriendly tender or "bearhug" approach. Bidder's president has asked the partner to advise with respect to permissible purchases of both Target shares and Bidder shares, by Bidder and by the president personally, in the weeks to come. The partner asks you to prepare a memorandum on the subject.

Now, this is a very tricky problem because it involves different substantive considerations and a number of variables. There are various regulatory provisions under the Securities Exchange Act of 1934 potentially affecting these purchases, including Section 16(b) for short-swing profits, Rule 10b-5 for misuse of information, Rule 10b-6 for purchases in connection with a distribution of securities (on the basis that Bidder might utilize its stock in the ultimate transaction), and Rule 10b-13 under the Act prohibiting contemporaneous purchases outside of an announced tender offer. There are also tax aspects, accounting considerations (the purchases could impair pooling treatment), and undoubtedly other matters as well. As for variables, well, purchases by an individual affect certain questions (Section 16(b), for example) but not others (e.g., pooling transactions); the stock purchases could take place

---

[12] See Chapter 2.

prior to Bidder's approach to Target, or after an approach but before any formal offer, or after a formal offer—timing distinctions which may create differing results in securities law terms; Bidder's stock may be used or not; the ultimate transaction may be a negotiated merger or an unfriendly offer; the stock purchases could be in the open market or in block transactions (which may or may not be solicited)—all of which could lead to divergent conclusions.

The only way to approach this kind of exercise is through strict organization of your thoughts. At the point you cite a case or make an observation, it should be absolutely clear to the reader which assumptions are applicable. Are you discussing purchases by an individual or a company? Are you talking about open market purchases or solicited block transactions? The reader requires a frame of reference. This type of problem cries out for the lawyer's favorite organizational tool—a division of the memo into sections and subsections, numbered (Roman and Arabic) and lettered (small letters and capitals), each with titles indicating what is presently under discussion.

There's no single "right" way to organize this material. The substantive provisions of law, for example, could constitute the major headings with the various factual variables serving as sub-headings and sub-sub-headings. Or, if the major distinction seemed to be between whether the individual or the corporation was doing the buying, or which company's stock was being bought, then the appropriate two categories could serve as the main headings. But remember: over-organization, while not as undesirable as the absence of organization, can also impede forceful presentation. For example, let me illustrate an eminently logical (but perfectly dreadful) way in which the material from this problem could be organized:

    I.   Purchases by Bidder Corp.
        A. Of Target Inc. Stock
            1.   Open market transactions
                a.   Prior to any approach
                    (1) Friendly deal only
                        (i) Deal will utilize Bidder stock
                            (u) 16(b)
                            (v) 10b-5
                            (w) 10b-6
                            (x) 10b-13
                            (y) tax-free
                            (z) pooling
                      (ii) Deal will utilize cash
                            (u) 16(b), etc.

            (2) Start friendly, turn unfriendly
                (i) Deal will utilize Bidder stock, etc.
                (u) 16(b), etc.
            (3) Start unfriendly
                (i) Deal will utilize Bidder stock, etc.
                (u) 16(b), etc.
        b. After initial approach, but prior to formal offer
            (1) Friendly deal only, etc.
                (i) Deal will utilize Bidder stock, etc.
                (u) 16(b), etc.
        c. After formal offer
            (1) Friendly deal only, etc.
                (i) Deal will utilize Bidder stock, etc.
                (u) 16(b), etc.
     2. Block transactions, solicited
        a. Prior to any approach, etc.
            (1) Friendly deal only, etc.
                (i) Deal will utilize Bidder stock, etc.
                (u) 16(b), etc.
     3. Block transactions, unsolicited
        a. Prior to any approach, etc.
            (1) Friendly deal only, etc.
                (i) Deal will utilize Bidder stock, etc.
                (u) 16(b), etc.
   B. Of Bidder Corp. stock
     1. Open market transactions, etc.
        a. Prior to any approach, etc.
            (1) Friendly deal only, etc.
                (i) Deal will utilize Bidder stock, etc.
                (u) 16(b), etc.
 II. Purchases by Bidder's President
   A. Of Target Inc. stock, etc.
     1. Open market transaction, etc.
        a. Prior to any approach, etc.
            (1) Friendly deal only, etc.
                (i) Deal will utilize Bidder stock, etc.
                (u) 16(b), etc.

And you can see that the outline would have been ten times as long if I hadn't omitted secondary and tertiary repetitions of all the different variables!

What's wrong with this outline? Well, for one thing, each time you reach the bottom line of the variables, you have to run through six different legal considerations. Wouldn't it be better to use the six considerations as your major headings, to avoid the constant repetition? It's also functionally preferable, since the theory of whether 16(b) or 10b-5 applies to a particular transaction should really be developed coherently in the memo—which is hard to do when it's discussed in several dozen separate pieces at the bottom of a chain of subsections.

"Aha," you say, "that may be fine for the *partner*, but didn't I hear that the memo will ultimately go to the *client*? Wouldn't his purposes be better suited by focusing on the *situation* rather than on the rules. Then he'll know that in a particular situation certain rules are applicable—as contrasted with working his way through an abstract essay on securities law." Well, that's not such a bad point—you're learning!—although for the initial draft to the partner I would still organize it under the various rules; you could mention in a cover note, however, that it can be switched around in organizational terms for the client if the partner considers that desirable. A better alternative is to close (or open[13]) with a conclusion that constitutes a summing up, to wit: "Thus, the principal bite of Rule 10b-6 occurs in connection with the following transactions. . . ."

You can also simplify the matter somewhat by eliminating a number of the possibilities. For instance, assuming that individual purchases wouldn't affect a pooling, this whole area can simply be blocked off in the section on accounting treatment. Inherently improbable situations—Bidder purchasing its own stock after a formal offer—can be given short shrift. And simplification can occur through positions you adopt; for example, you might conclude that once it appears a deal is in the offing, the president should personally stay out of the market under *all* of the factual circumstances—whether or not a specific regulation is applicable.

For the record, here's the way I would outline one of the sections of the memo—let's say the section dealing with Rule 10b-13:

I. 10b-13
  A. General Discussion of Rule.
    1. Background of rule; reason for promulgation; SEC comments upon adoption.
    2. Judicial and administrative interpretations.
  B. Possible Applicability to Instant Situation.
    1. Eliminate as inapplicable all purchases by individual, all

---

[13] For an analogy in the area of oral expression, see Section 3.3.1.

purchases of Bidder's stock, all purchases where a
merger (as contrasted with a tender or exchange offer)
is involved, all distinctions between block and open
market transactions.
2. Clearly applies to purchases by Bidder of Target
stock after commencement of tender or exchange
offer.
C. Key Question: Does 10b-13 apply to purchases by Bidder of Target stock, after approach by Bidder to Target
but before any announcement?
1. Analysis of pros and cons.
2. Possible distinctions based on whether a merger or a
tender offer is proposed and state of Bidder's mind.
D. Conclusion as to applicability.

Can you see why this is a preferable—although not immuta-
ble—approach? In addition to avoiding unnecessary repetition, the organization focuses the reader on the *real* considerations, to the
exclusion of peripheral concerns.

Now, a simpler sort of problem may not require this sec-
tion/subsection approach, and it's rarely utilized in a letter. There are
other, less visible means of cementing the organization. For example, it
helps to remind the reader what point he's at in a complex analysis. So
you might begin a new paragraph with something like "Now, on the
other hand, if the situation involved purchases made *prior* to Bidder's
approach. . . ."

Keep in mind that dividing a paper into sections is no substitute for
analytical organization. I've seen plenty of documents over the years
with subsections and sub-subsections galore—the most elaborate num-
bering and lettering systems—and all to no avail; the writer's thoughts
were hopelessly disorganized. Analytical shortcomings cannot be rectified by cosmetic overlays.

There's one other putative organizational device that aggravates
me: dividing a matter into sections which are merely chronological or
consecutive. No real attempt is made to organize the underlying
material—yet you're left with the disquieting suspicion that the writer
really thought he was accomplishing something. It's easier to illustrate this "absence of organization" than to analyze it, but I'm sure
you'll recognize the syndrome. Let's say you were writing an essay
on your typical early morning's activities. You decide to outline the
essay in advance. The pseudo-chronologist would probably go at it
something like this:

1. Alarm rings.
2. Roll over and want to go back to sleep.
3. Have orange juice.
4. Shower.
5. Shave.
6. Check son's homework.
7. Dress.
8. Eat cereal.
9. Drink coffee.
10. Read newspaper.
11. Enter checks in checkbook.
12. Leave for office.

Is that familiar? And yet, it would be so easy to place a stamp of organization on the proceedings, for instance along the following lines:

1.   Awakening.
      A.   Alarm rings.
      B.   Desire to remain asleep.
2.   Preparation for the day.
      A.   Shower.
      B.   Shave.
      C.   Dress.
3.   The Meal.
      A.   Orange juice.
      B.   Cereal.
      C.   Coffee.
4.   Miscellaneous activities before leaving house.
      A.   Read paper.
      B.   Check son's homework.
      C.   Enter checks in checkbook.

The difference may seem inconsequential, but it's reflected in spades in your legal prose.

3.2.3. The Key to Good Writing is Rewriting.

I won't rule out the possibility that somewhere in this fair land a lawyer exists who can dictate or write out his thoughts in final form for transmission—but he would certainly be a rare bird. As far as I'm concerned, the key to good writing by lawyers is rewriting[14], with the

---

[14]   Brandeis put it this way: "There is no such thing as good writing. There is only good rewriting." As quoted in E. Biskind, *Simplify Legal Writing* (1975) [hereinafter cited as "Biskind"], at 31. Mr. Biskind's book, which goes into much detail about legal prose, was of considerable help to me in the following Sections 3.2.4, 3.2.5 and 3.2.6.

degree of subsequent modifications dependent upon the complexity and importance of the particular document. By contrast, the novelist's penchant for spontaneity may best be captured in the first blush of his original prose, which rewriting merely serves to stultify. The lawyer—less artist and more craftsman—can only achieve the necessary specificity, root out redundancy and ambiguity, and concentrate on what's truly significant after several go-arounds.

There is another consideration at issue here, which is not limited to lawyering. Most of us have suffered through the inability to begin composing a difficult document—writer's block, I believe it's sometimes termed. Rather than freezing into futility, you're much better off getting something—anything—down on paper, in order to break out of the starting gate. The necessary corollary, however, is the requirement to edit. But the two-step process may take you across the finish line sooner, and certainly wiser, than continuing to flounder around, waiting for perfection to issue forth.

While everyone should adopt his own approach to writing, it might be helpful if I outline one procedure which I often use, although this too will vary depending upon the assignment. For these purposes, I'm assuming there is enough time to do a workmanlike job—different rules for short-circuiting apply when time is of the essence. As a point of reference, I'm picturing an assignment to write an article for a periodical on a legal/practical subject about which I already possess knowledge—more of a think piece than a law review-type article, although with some discussion of regulations, authorities, citations, etc. I think the general principles are equally valid for a memorandum or similar document lawyers are called upon to produce in the office.

My first step would be to think through the structure of the article in general terms, recognizing that this is tentative and subject to change as content is added, but convinced of the desirability of having scribbled out some sort of outine in advance. Never overorganize a paper at this early stage, because you can never be sure what will be forthcoming until you start to write.

What I like to do next, prior to any detailed review of secondary sources, is to try to get bits and pieces of my thoughts on the subject down on paper. I have the distinct feeling that these morsels become more productive (in the sense of leading to other thoughts) and more malleable into a coherent whole when reduced to writing than stored away in the crevices of my mind. The easiest way to accomplish this is to dictate into a small portable machine that I can clutch while pacing about the room.[15] For me, the key here is *not* to try to refine what is said, *not* to struggle to find the best word—in some cases *not* even to worry about completing sentences. I don't think about paragraph structure; I'm not concerned with the order in which the thoughts tumble out. If along the way I recognize that elaboration will be necessary, or an example would be appropriate, or a cross-reference is apt, then I will simply say "elaborate" or "give example" or "cross-reference to later discussion." All I'm interested in at this point is getting the thoughts down in front of me (through a typed transcript of the dictation), where they can be worked into something meaningful.

To be sure, I could (and sometimes do) write out the initial thoughts, a technique much favored by lawyers, which certainly results in better initial copy. This is a much slower process, however, and involves you in a mechanical function that inhibits your mind from performing at its free-flowing best. I have the feeling that many lawyers write their initial thoughts in longhand because they can't face reviewing their disorganized dictation or are hoping to avoid substantial re-writing—neither of which rationale has any real merit.

As I revise the typed dictation, turning these fragments into sentences and paragraphs, two things usually happen. First, the thoughts on paper prod my mind to reach out for other ideas, which further elaborate or qualify the point made, or introduce analogous matter. Second, the material begins to shape itself into a certain order and overall design. Sure, this requires a little help from me; and as I go through the draft, I will jot down on a single sheet of paper brief phrases describing the various subtopics, in an attempt to visualize their optimum arrangement.

This is also the point at which I would turn to other written material on the subject. I find that if I start with someone else's observations, it impedes my own free thought; I'm stuck in the ruts of those who have travelled this road before. But at this juncture, after my own thoughts have been committed to paper but still early enough to change directions or modify my thinking, the secondary sources can be most helpful.[15a]

---

[15] Some lawyers might prefer dictating to a secretary, although I sense that others might become inhibited by the stenographer's presumed reactions to the dictator's errors in grammar, repetitions, disorganizational tendencies, and the like. The little machine cannot speak back (except at the operator's bidding) and is incapable of even implicit reprimand.

[15a] There's a contrary view here, holding that research done after analysis is rarely as thorough—since you're just looking for cases to support your thesis.

So, the second draft of the document accomplishes a number of purposes. The scraps of thought are turned into English sentences and paragraphs; elaborations, caveats and examples[16] are supplied; secondary sources are included; and the piece is organized into logical sections and subsections. What I make a point of *not* doing on this second draft is to attempt to write well. I don't strive for the precise word, the elegant phrase. Clarity isn't foremost in my mind, and I don't worry at all about conciseness or engaging the reader's interest. It's too early to be concerned with these matters; you can't really do an effective job on the fine points until you have that second draft in front of you.

When the second draft is typed, then I'm ready for the necessary polishing job so requisite to effective legal writing. Is the organization suitable? Are some parts too long? If so, I can make intelligent cuts. I can relegate to footnotes certain material that now appears peripheral.[17] Ambiguities can be eliminated,[18] cross-references inserted, the prose sharpened, perhaps a few sprightly dicta worked in, and so on. And if I want to be persuasive, or subtle, or oblique, I can make the words perform for me. But the process only works at *this* step—attempting it earlier would have been counter-productive.

Remember, we lawyers are often judged by our prose. At times, we have to move very fast, but there is seldom an excuse for putting out an unpolished document. And polish can't be accomplished as the thoughts first tumble out of your mind onto the paper. So write—and then rewrite.

3.2.4. Clarity: Rooting out the Remnants of Ambiguity.

The dominant attribute of effective legal writing is clarity. A novelist or playwright (Pinter springs immediately to mind) may be intentionally obscure; a humorist toys with whimsy and indulges in double entendre; but the legal craftsman, writing hard-nosed analytical prose, must strive for accuracy and precision. He is engaged in an endless struggle to rid the language of ambiguity and exterminate half-truths. Fuzziness has no place in this no-nonsense universe. Con-

---

The lawyer who researches first, without preconception, tends to be more painstaking, reviewing all of the authorities.

[16] For a discussion of the use of examples, see Section 3.2.6.
[17] In this regard, see Section 3.2.5.
[18] The goal of clarity is discussed in Section 3.2.4.

clusions are conclusive unless clearly labeled tentative; the unexplained assumption is dangerous; the unattributed statement,
anathema.

The essence of clarity is for each word, phrase and sentence to be
unmistakeable in meaning and not reasonably susceptible to another
interpretation. Lawyers rarely *intend* a written thought to convey ambiguity; it just comes with the territory—given the complexity of ideas
and the sometime imprecision of language to convey the intended nuance adequately. Rooting out ambiguity requires the writer to go over
his finished product just one more time with a view to clarity, pretending
for the exercise that he is the relatively uninformed reader rather than
the know-it-all draftsman.

Let's try an example. Assume your firm represents a client which
purchases produce under written contract with a grower.[19] For
reasons having to do with size and color—the goods also seem a bit
overripe—your client wishes to reject a certain shipment of peaches
that has just arrived at his doorstep. The contract contains a provision
giving your client the right to reject produce if "more than 10 days
elapse" between the picking of the fruit and delivery to your client;
the grower's accompanying certificate constitutes "prima facie
evidence" of the date the produce was picked. Another contractual
provision obligates the grower to deliver only "fresh" produce; the
industry rule of thumb for freshness in peaches is about one week between picking and delivery. This particular shipment was delivered to
your client on August 20th, with a grower's certificate stating it was
picked on August 10th. However, one of the shipper's representatives
has informally advised your client that the peaches were loaded onto
the carrier on August 8th. The partner asks you for a quick
memorandum on the subject.

Well, you can see the outlines of the analysis involved here. If the
produce was actually picked on or prior to August 8th, the client can
clearly reject it as not meeting the contractual 10-day-old test. This involves a credibility question of the grower's certificate against the
word of the shipper's representative. Query, what does "prima facie
evidence" mean in this context? It's something less than conclusive, but
more than contractual silence on the certificate. Then there's the further
issue of whether, even if the produce were picked on the 10th, more than
10 days have "elapsed" when it's delivered on the 20th—which depends

---

[19]   Please be advised that I know nothing about produce contracts, industry
practice or the like; what follows is strictly for illustrative purposes, and may not
be in accordance with the applicable facts, law or practice.

on whether you count the day of picking as the first day elapsed. (Prior dealings between the parties might be relevant here.) And, if these arguments don't work for your client, there's the additional possibility that he has a general right of rejection based on the grower's breach of his obligation to ship "fresh" produce. This contains a factual component (was the produce actually fresh?), and several legal elements (do you measure freshness by custom in the trade; is the contractual 10-day rejection provision controlling, or at least relevant; and if a breach has occurred, is rejection of the shipment a permissible remedy, or is your client relegated to damages?).

So, you go about your analysis of the problem, draft your memo touching all the bases, and conclude as follows:

"As a result of the foregoing, it seems obvious that our client can avoid the necessity of accepting the produce because of the grower's failure to fulfill the obligations imposed under the contract."

What's wrong here? Well, for one thing, the statement reeks with ambiguity. Although your bottom line conclusion is apparent, there's no way of telling whether you arrived at that result on the basis of the grower's failure to fulfill the 10-day express condition or the implied obligation to supply "fresh" produce. If the former, did you rely on the statement of the shipper's representative or a legal construction of 10 days having elapsed? If the latter, did you base your findings on a factual conclusion as to non-freshness or a legal view as to the usage in the trade? Your imprecise statement—even though couched in perfectly acceptable legal terms, which under other circumstances might have been clear and unambiguous—involved too many unexplained assumptions.

Moreover, could you really feel as certain about your conclusion as the statement implies? Unless there is some binding authority, it does seem to depend on a number of questions of law and fact upon which judges and juries might disagree. Wouldn't it be preferable, not only for purposes of clarity but to identify your position, to state the premises; e.g., "Assuming a court would accept the oral testimony of the shipper's representative . . ." or "Assuming the 7-day trade custom could be proven and wouldn't be adjudged foreclosed by the specific 10-day clause in the contract. . . ."

In the struggle for clarity of meaning, the lowly comma and the inconsequential parenthesis can be significant allies. Compare "The defendants say the plaintiffs breached the contract" with "The defendants, say the plaintiffs, breached the contract"; who's accusing whom very much depends on the punctuation. Sometimes the ambiguity can't be cured by simply inserting punctuation, but a slight shift in the word order is required. For example, assume a certain statute creates crimes of intentional fraud and reckless misrepresentation. In the case of reckless misrepresentation (but not intentional fraud), there is a statutory defense if the party to whom the misrepresentation was made failed to exercise due care. In reporting on this to the partner, your memo states:

> "The statute renders unlawful both intentional fraud and reckless misrepresentation, unless the other party has not exercised due care."

Your phrasing makes it sound very much like lack of due care is also a defense to intentional fraud. Moving the comma from after "misrepresentation" to after "fraud" would help but has an ungrammatical appearance. Another way would be as follows:

> "The statute renders unlawful both intentional fraud and, unless the other party has not exercised due care, reckless misrepresentation."

An even better solution would be:

> "The statute renders unlawful both reckless misrepresentation (unless the other party has not exercised due care) and intentional fraud."

This latter format illustrates the utility of the parenthesis in clarifying matters. For some unknown reason, many writers condemn the use of parentheses, but I find them extremely helpful in sorting out meanings in complex sentences, where the alternative of commas might still leave room for possible confusion. For example, take the following sentence, which has its fair share of commas but still requires several readings to parse:

> "The 1974 amendments to the statute, which, among other things, introduced the concept of scienter, that form the basis of the appellant's defense, had been enacted when the case was argued but were not in effect at the time the acts were committed."

How much better to wrap a brace of parentheses around the "which" clause, so that the sentence reads:

> "The 1974 amendments to the statute (which, among other things, introduced the concept of scienter) that form the basis of the appellant's defense had been enacted when the case was argued but were not in effect at the time the acts were committed."

3.2.5. Conciseness: The Quest for Materiality.

One of the grim realities of our profession is that lawyers tend to be terribly long-winded. I remember well one of my first mentors in the law, an able and articulate attorney who tended to be verbose in his writing style. He was quite aware of this trait, often candidly confessing to me how much easier he found writing a five-page letter than undergoing the discipline of compressing the same material into two.[20] As the years have passed, I've realized time and again the truth of his words. But you simply must exercise the willpower—make that extra effort—to shorten letters and memoranda intended for others.[21] All too often, the purpose of a writing—to inform, to alert, to persuade—is lost in a miasma of words and immateriality.

How many lawyers have you known—perhaps even yourself!—who are fascinated by richly textured but essentially irrelevant factual details in presenting the contours of a problem or investigation. How often have you seen an attorney intrigued by some intricate complexity in the applicable law, by nice distinctions between the decided cases—all of which hover on the periphery of the problem he's supposed to be solving? This thoroughness, this inquisitiveness of mind, can be one of the hallmarks of a good lawyer (or a good scientist, or a number of other professions), but it must be subjected to discipline—particularly in the written word.

The most common enemy of conciseness is the lawyer's reluctance to sort out the material from the insignificant. One hopes this doesn't evidence his *inability* to do so; a lawyer who can't tell the one from the other suffers from the most serious of shortcomings in his chosen profession. If he *can* distinguish significance but chooses not to do so—out of laziness, or a misconception of its importance, or bad judgment in his utilization of time—he is not beyond redemption; but the adverse effect on the reader is precisely the same as if he totally lacked the capacity.

I find conciseness in a written communication to be quite difficult to achieve at the outset. One doesn't start out to write a concise piece. Until all the thoughts are in front of you, deciding what's material and what isn't can be a tricky task. Crispness is usually the product of a late draft in your rewriting process. As you re-read your draft memo, try to decide which of the thoughts are essential to the analysis, which are collateral to it (but still of some significance), and which are essentially irrelevant or immaterial. This last category should be deleted, as tending to interfere with the flow of thought. Matters that

---

[20] Pascal was also aware of this phenomenon. "The present letter is a very long one," he wrote, "simply because I had no leisure to make it shorter." As quoted in Bisking, *supra* note 14, at 41.
[21] With documents that are written solely to form a record, such as a memo to the files, you are hereby granted permission to ramble on at any length you see fit.

are collateral/relevant, however, should be retained without throwing the reader off the main track. The question is, how best to accomplish this.

I very much like the use of footnotes to handle this sort of thing. I've always found it odd that attorneys, who dearly love to employ legions of footnotes in scholarly articles and briefs, use them sparingly in informal memoranda and virtually abjure them in letters. Footnotes are useful; they enable the reader who wants to pursue the subject to do so, without interrupting the main flow of the action. Like the newspaper editor who makes decisions on which news rates a front page story, your relegation of a thought to footnote status represents your judgment that this is not a primary matter—the corollary of which is that placement of a concept in the principal text marks it as deserving of attention on the part of the serious reader.

It's not only a matter of the document's sheer volume. Particularly when writing for a non-lawyer, long sentences with multiple facets pose an impediment to the reader; and paragraphs which wind on page after page do definite harm to your image. I fully realize how impossible it is to write short, Hemingway-like sentences, when dealing with weighty legal matters.[22] Most sentences (except, strangely enough, this one) contain at least two or three thoughts. One concept depends upon the other, or constitutes a necessary qualification without which the original thought is misleading. But where you have a multiplicity of thoughts, break them up into separate sentences, or at least learn to use a semicolon. And try to keep your paragraphs short enough so as not to discourage all but the hardiest readers.

Let me attempt to illustrate trenchant writing with a before-and-after example—a bit of a straw man, but perhaps instructive. A partner has assigned you to write a memo concerning the predicament faced by your client (Whitehat), who is about to be squeezed out of a closely-held corporation by his former friend and colleague (Blacksocks). The memo will probably be sent to the client. You have just finished the section analyzing the buy-out alternative—Blacksocks, who is president of the company, has recently caused it to make a quite inadequate offer to purchase Whitehat's shares—and you now turn to the possibilities of instituting litigation against the president. Your draft of the memo's next paragraph reads as follows:

---

[22] There is such a thing, of course, as being too concise, too highly tuned—at which point the very terseness of the material makes comprehension difficult and tends to put off the reader. "When I struggle to be terse, I end by being obscure." Horace, *Ars Poetica*.

"I now want to discuss the question of whether White-hat has a potential lawsuit against Blacksocks. One possibility would be to base a claim on the obvious conflict of interest inherent in the Arizona deal. You will recall that this was a situation involving a joint investment by the Company and by Blacksocks individually in real estate properties located on a seven-acre tract in Tempe, Arizona, which included two single occupancy residence hotels and a pawnshop, where the Company advanced approximately 87% of the funds in excess of a non-recourse purchase-money mortgage of $3,000,000, and Blacksocks ended up taking a multitude of tax deductions through prepayment of interest and the use of accelerated depreciation. As it happened, this was also the deal on which Blacksocks first met Accessory, who, as you know, is one of the three other directors whose votes Blacksocks has in his pocket. The property is on the books of the Company at an inflated price, and that, of course, figures into the valuation question that was discussed in the prior section of this memo. I suppose Blacksocks could raise the defense of laches, since this did happen several years ago and Whitehat has never done anything about it. There is an interesting question of corporate opportunity involved here. In *Smith v. Jones*, the 19th Circuit was called upon to deal with the issue of whether it makes a difference if the corporate opportunity initially comes to the individual in his individual capacity. The court said it did not. In this instance, however, I believe the opportunity came to the Company first, so that question may not really be at issue. There is also an interesting disclosure issue, which I want to look into further, as to whether the Board of Directors was given full information on the joint transaction back at the time the funds were first authorized. Finally, there is the possible misuse of corporate funds, but it seems to me, without knowing more about the facts, that we will have to hire an accountant to probe into the details. I would say, however, that all of this represents a fruitful direction for us to pursue."

All right. It's wordy but not illiterate. The paragraph does deal with a single subject. The sentences do follow a logical progression. How could it be improved? Let's try.

"Turning now to the question of potential lawsuits against Blacksocks, one possible conflict of interest claim could be based on the Tempe, Arizona real estate deal.

Evidently the Company put up most of the funds to purchase the properties, and Blacksocks got most of the tax deductions.* If Whitehat can overcome the affirmative defense of laches (several years having transpired since the purchase), this might be a real chink in Blacksocks' armor.

As I see it, there are three avenues of possible attack on the deal: one, corporate opportunity;** two, the adequacy of the original disclosure to the Board when it authorized the purchase; and three, possible misuse of corporate <u>funds</u>. We need more facts to evaluate our position.''

* These properties are on the Company's books at an inflated price—see the discussion on valuation in Section 2.

** In the 19th Circuit, the question of whether the opportunity came to the Company or the individual is irrelevant; *Smith v. Jones.*

Well, it does read a little better, doesn't it? What did we do? We became concise. First, we split up the one long paragraph into two, at a logical breaking point. Second, we eliminated a host of irrelevant or immaterial details: the description of the Tempe tract; the details of the mortgage; the mechanics of Blacksocks' tax deduction; the meeting with Accessory; and so on. Third, we dropped into footnotes two collateral points—the overstatement of the properties on the company's books and the 19th Circuit decision. Fourth, we shortened the sentences and introduced some semicolons. Fifth, we grasped the fact that there were three distinct legal theories and identified them as such in a single sentence, so as to make the maximum impact on the reader.

The greatest enemies of succinctness are the fear of leaving something out and the desire to display the breadth of your subject matter grasp. Forget it. Most of what you delete is far from crucial; if you're worried, salt it away in a footnote or appendix. For the client (and even for the partner), less is more. Bravura displays only serve to irritate and raise doubts about your bottom-line competence; brevity is what pays the rent.[23]

3.2.6. Whetting the Reader's Interest.

It's not telling any tales out of school to observe that most writing on legal subjects by lawyers—the style, as contrasted with the sub-

[23]   For an analogous discussion in another context—namely, how to slim down a legal document to please your client without foregoing any essential protections—see Section 5.1.4 of *Anatomy*, which analyzes several methods of making an acquisition agreement appear less imposing than usual.

stance—tends to be extremely dull. There is a pre-packaged, monochromatic quality to the prose that dulls the edges of even the most fascinating issues. It's almost as if the author were seeking the Somber Seal of Approval, fearful that any injection of sprightliness or creativity into the writing will stamp him as a lightweight thinker or lacking in total dedication to a ponderous profession. And then too, most lawyers are so concerned with the substance of what they're saying—organizing the piece, developing their thesis, etc.—that once having achieved precision, they give little or no thought to style.

I have minimal sympathy for this point of view. Whatever merit total sobriety may have in formal legal documents (another subject for another day), it strikes me as altogether unnecessary in less formal (and formidable) writings such as letters or memos, where you are attempting to educate or persuade—particularly when your reader is not a lawyer. You may have succeeded in rendering your document clear and concise, but if it's dry and monotonous the reader may experience difficulty keeping his mind on the subject at hand. I'm sure we've all experienced the sensation (I hope you're not feeling it right now . . .) of reading through a boring piece on a superficial level of consciousness, realizing at the finish how little has been absorbed. How can the lawyer-writer capture the reader's interest? Well, I have a few thoughts on the subject, which fall into the general categories of vocabulary, grammar, punctuation, sentence and paragraph structure, and the use of examples.

Let's start with vocabulary. My wife is from Sweden; and in order to be able to converse with her parents, I studied Swedish briefly after our marriage. I was struck by the fact—which she readily confirmed—that there was a noticeable shortage of adjectives in the language. Each of the relatively few adjectives had to do rather heavy duty over a broad conceptual range, making it extremely difficult to achieve certain subtleties in meaning through the use of single words. It's different with English, a tongue so richly endowed that the choice of words to express most thoughts is virtually unlimited. And yet, time and again, lawyers fall back on the same tired words in their writing.

I say, why not reach out and give some of those other words a try. If they don't spring to mind, use a thesaurus (which is a much handier tool for an attorney than Black's Law Dictionary). It's more than just the proper use of words to achieve precision of meaning; I'm also talking about word selection to avoid repetition of the same adequate word. If you've employed the word "used" for six sentences in a row, then switch to "utilized"; "short" can become "brief"; "complex", "complicated." And you don't always have to employ the stuffiest words. Let a "transaction" loosen its tie on occasion and become a "deal." Oh, there may be instances where this might come across as too slangy; but in typical informal writing, terms like "transaction" create a deadening effect while "deal" imparts a touch of liveliness to jostle the reader.

Try to avoid legalisms in your informal writings. One can defend the use of such words as "hereof" and "herein" in an agreement, to eliminate ambiguity over whether the reference is to the particular document; but I think they have little place in the kind of writing we're talking about, especially when the reader isn't a lawyer. This can impose a slight burden at times. For example, one of the most useful phrases to make a logical point is *a fortiori*. It gets the thought across in fewer words and with more punch than any equivalent I can think of. And yet, there's no reason in the world for a non-lawyer to understand that expression; so you must use a circumlocution, such as "And the case becomes even more compelling when you look at. . . ."

By the way, avoiding word repetition and using sprightly terms aren't matters to bother about in the early drafts of a writing. Rather, they're a proper subject for your final document review. After everything else has fallen into place, you can scan the pages to see if you've used "somewhat" in three consecutive lines (a stylistic monotony easily remedied—if not the diffidence implied—by changing the middle one to "rather").

Turning now to grammar, I want to touch on just two matters. First, in order to comply with so-called rules of grammar, we often torture our prose unnecessarily. Two rules that come to mind are those warning against split infinitives and sentences with the temerity to end on a prepositional note. Modern writers on the subject deny these the status of absolute rules, counseling (with befitting audacity) that to fully achieve a livelier style, they should be dispensed with. One authority cites the statement by a union leader with regard to management: "They are difficult to negotiate with." Recast to avoid the final preposition, this would read: "They are people with whom it is difficult to negotiate." The first formulation is clear and direct; the second is merely pompous. As for the split infinitive, he points to the newspaper slogan: "If you want to be fully informed, read *The New York Times*." Recast as "To be informed fully", the rhythm of the sentence is destroyed.[24] And rhythm, in addition to clarity, is the criterion here. If fear of splitting produces a stilted or ambiguous sentence, or has an awk-

---

[24]   Biskind, *supra* note 14, at 59-63.

ward, pedantic ring, then—if you're willing to invoke the wrath of highly vocal traditionalists—go right ahead and split.[25]

Second and more important grammatical point: a major cause of stilted writing is lawyers' overuse of the passive tense. (I group in the same category the use of such phrases as: "It is a fact that" or "It is clear that.") Nothing can deaden your prose more quickly than excessive dependency on the passive tense. Am I overreacting to suggest it implies a laziness of mind, an unwillingness to stand up and be counted? "The resolution was passed by the Board by a 5 to 1 vote." Bah! "The Board approved the resolution by a 5 to 1 vote" is stronger. "It was alleged by the plaintiff that. . . ." Humbug! Use "The plaintiff alleged. . . ." Occasionally the passive tense may be preferable, as where you lack the facts to state the matter in the affirmative. "The acquisition was approved by all necessary corporate action" is all right, if you're not sure whether this required board or stockholder approval, or both. But on that last trip through the document, check for your overuse of passives, and try to turn some thoughts around to the more punchy active tense.

Next, punctuation—which can sometimes be employed to increase the reader's interest. An exclamation point certainly demands attention, and is appropriate for a thought that's startling or amusing. You can see in these pages that I like to use the dash, which is not only useful in setting off a thought from the rest of the sentence, but gives the reader a slight jolt in a way that long successions of commas, semicolons and periods cannot. And question marks—turning statements into questions—can prove a useful device. "The question is: should the words of the agreement be read to override the statute?" is more provocative than: "The issue is whether the words of the agreement should be read to override the statute".

Underlining and italicization are helpful in emphasizing a point, particularly where there might otherwise be some question as to your thrust. Italics are ideal for comparing two concepts: "Although they had no conversations on this point *prior* to the Board meeting, there is proof that on July 27 (seven days *after* the meeting) they were seen together in a small cafe. . . ." Italics can lose effectiveness, however, with indiscriminate usage. Similarly, the use of capital letters (where not required) should be kept to a minimum, limited to distinguishing a

---

[25] In the following ambiguous sentence, a split infinitive would have eliminated any doubt: "The Thanksgiving Day setback was sure to defer further American hopes of keeping pace with the Soviet Union in lunar exploration." Does the word "further" modify "defer" or "hopes"? If the infinitive is split to read "further defer", the ambiguity is eliminated. Biskind, *supra* note 14, at 60.

defined term such as the "Company" from references to companies generally.

We have talked previously about sentences and paragraphs.[26] I would only add that a balance must be struck between overly long sentences and short, staccato ones that could better be meshed into a whole. Take the following example:[27] "He stole his mother's money. He forged her signature. He left her destitute. He has no conscience." This would probably be extremely effective in an oral summation to the jury, delivered with appropriate outrage; on paper, however, its force is dissipated. A much better phrasing would be: "Without the slightest twinge of conscience, he closed out his mother's savings account by forging her signature, leaving her destitute."

Always keep in mind that the reader doesn't know your subject as well as you do. A busy lawyer or executive who reads your prose on the run can't be trusted to give it his undivided attention. Do the concepts penetrate into his subconscious, so that he realizes the full significance of what's been said; or is he merely skimming the surface, not really focusing on the complex thoughts you've tried so hard to convey? Simply to state your hypothesis may not be sufficient; rather it must be reinforced in a second, different manner to bring it home more vividly.

One of the best means to accomplish this reiteration is the use of an example to illustrate the point. More than any other technique, this takes the reader off the superficial level and brings him down there with you in the trenches.

For example, let's say that in the course of your tax discussion of a "C"-type reorganization under Section 368 of the Internal Revenue Code, you state the current ruling position of the IRS; namely, that the "substantially all" element is satisfied if the assets transferred represent at least 90% of the fair market value of the acquired corporation's *net* assets and at least 70% of the fair market value of the acquired company's *gross* assets.[28] Now, if you move right on to the next point, you haven't really pinned this down for the reader. It's much better to stop and give an illustration of how this would work on hypothetical facts.[29] "For example, let us assume that the acquired corporation has gross assets of $1,000,000 and net assets of $800,000. Now, if you apply the 90% test. . . ."

---

26   See Section 3.2.5.

27   Biskind, *supra* note 14, at 32.

28   This sentence contains good examples of appropriate italicization.

29   If the issue is only peripheral to the main discussion, you might consider putting the example in a footnote.

It's not always necessary to provide an example. Another effective technique is to state something "in other words." For instance, in the same memo, you may have discussed the specific tax treatment of a subsidiary merger under Section 368(a)(2)(D) for several sentences. At this point, it might be appropriate to say: "In other words, this sort of merger is treated pretty much like an 'A'-type direct merger, with a few exceptions and certain unanswered interpretive questions." This eases the reader into a pre-existing frame of reference (i.e., what an "A"-type reorganization is all about).

3.2.7. The Technique of Persuasiveness.

As will become increasingly evident in these pages,[30] I think it's very important for a lawyer—be he associate or partner—to present a point of view in his written or oral communications. Pointing out problems, identifying issues, suggesting alternative solutions, and then leaving the reader to make his own choice, in my view constitutes an incomplete work product. Most memoranda should contain the writer's choice of the best solution to the question raised. A letter to the client addressing several courses of action should generally indicate which path the writer recommends.

Don't get me wrong. Not every letter or memorandum should approximate a brief. Particularly when writing for a partner, to present only one side of the story is insufficient; he will want to hear the counter-arguments, so that he can evaluate them too. Clients should be advised that other options exist, but that for the reasons stated, the course you recommend is preferred. Judgment must be rendered, and the ability to put choices into a pecking order marks the mature lawyer. Never avoid a legal conclusion on the grounds that you may appear too opinionated or are pre-empting the partner's or client's right to decide. Reach balanced judgments on the basis of disclosed possibilities.

Then, once you have decided what form your opinion will take or which alternative you'll recommend, sculpt your writing so as to make your conclusion persuasive. Without ever overstating the case or omitting rebuttal or options[31], you should lead the reader by the hand in the direction of your judgment. A memorandum which rambles on for pages stating various possibilities, and then suddenly—without forewarning—announces the writer's position, has an almost arbitrary tone. How

---

[30]   See, e.g., Sections 3.3.1, 5.1.2 and 6.3, as well as most of Chapter 8.
[31]   If you feel the necessity to state a contrary view undeserving of much credence, put it in a footnote—which is a good way to emphasize your reaction to its lack of substance. See also Section 3.2.5.

much better to have prepared the reader for the conclusion by taking him step-by-step through your reasoning process.

I don't intend to explore the skill of writing persuasively in any detail. It involves such matters as the choice of words, the manner in which thoughts are expressed, logical development, the placement of alternatives so as not to interrupt the flow, and so on. The use of the "although" sentence can be helpful—the first clause containing the counter-argument, with the second clause stating the more forceful rebuttal ("Although a respectable body of opinion would confer holder in due course status on a finance company assignee of installment paper, the better view seems to be that . . .").

Rather than lecturing in the abstract, however, let me illustrate the point by an example. Compare these two extracts on the issue of whether Mr. Clout should be deemed (for SEC purposes) to be in control of Model Corporation. Here's the first:

"The authorities suggest that control in fact is the key determinant, and this can either be actual control or the power to control. Mr. Clout, who is one of the directors, holds 27% of Model Corporation's stock. This is not as large as the combined total of the other directors, but it is larger than any single holder. The other directors also include one individual who is on the outs with the others and wouldn't necessarily vote with them; if his holdings are subtracted, the rest hold less shares than Mr. Clout. In terms of whether Mr. Clout is part of a control group, it appears that Mr. Clout and the others on the Board are not close; they are not at war either.

"Mr. Clout does not call the day-to-day shots. We know he is consulted on certain decisions, such as the one as to whether to expand into a new territory. On other decisions, he is not consulted; for example, no one asked him about hiring the new assistant sales manager.

"The SEC does not have any fixed rule in this area. I note that in the 1940 Act a holding of 25% or more results in a presumption of control. Model Corporation does not, however, come under the 1940 Act.

"On balance, I have to come out that Mr. Clout is a controlling person."

Now here's the second extract:

"The authorities suggest that control in fact is the key determinant, and this can either be actual control or the power to control. Although Mr. Clout doesn't call the day-to-day shots, his 27% holding and board seat strongly suggest that he possesses the power to control and therefore must be deemed a controlling person. The stock ownership, which parenthetically exceeds the SEC's presumption of control under the 1940 Act (not directly applicable here), is larger than the holdings of any other single stockholder.* Mr. Clout is consulted on such key decisions as expanding into a new territory; the fact that he was not consulted on the seemingly minor decision to hire a new assistant sales manager does not detract substantially from this point. Finally, given the circumstances, it would be difficult to argue that he was *not* part of the control group of Model Corporation, since his relations with the other directors, while not close, have never been strained.''

* Although the directors collectively hold more shares than Mr. Clout, one of their members who holds the plurality shares would presumably not vote with the group.

You can see, can't you, the increased strength of the second statement. (It might even be *too* strong—a bit overstated to emphasize my point; be careful in real life not to carry persuasiveness to the extreme of not making a fair statement.) Although no thought was omitted, everything was contained in a perspective which led the reader toward the same conclusion as the writer. By contrast, in the first excerpt *I* wasn't even sure how it would come out until the final sentence!

Somewhere between an adversarial litigation brief and writings intended for a partner or client (where author and reader are on the same side of the fence) lies the request to an administrative agency[32] on behalf of your client. This consists generally of a factual presentation and the marshalling of arguments in favor of the position you espouse. But unlike a court—which will have the benefit of your adversary's version of the facts and applicable law—the agency has no means of knowing the facts other than through your letter. As a result, the agency's determination is only as definitive as your statement of facts; if you omit facts of significance, you can't rely on the ruling.[33] Moreover, from an ethical standpoint, full disclosure is the only proper course. You must present the complete story while attempting to be persuasive.[34]

It's a rare case where every factor points in a single direction; some negatives will undoubtedly exist. Don't try to sweep these under the

---

[32] On the general subject of dealing with an administrative agency, see Section 7.5.
[33] See Section 7.5.4.
[34] The same is true with a request for a tax ruling directed to the Internal Revenue Service.

rug. Face up to them, but use some intelligence in your manner of presentation. You're not required to bludgeon the reader over the head with the potentially damaging significance of such a factor. If the regulator wants to make the adverse link, that's his business; but there's no need for you to suggest that he should. Thus the matter of placement can assume importance. It may be possible to introduce the hot potato into the narrative at a point where its negative significance is less readily ascertainable—making certain, however, that it doesn't stand out like a sore thumb but relates naturally to its surroundings.

As an example, let's assume you're asking an agency to treat as confidential a certain license agreement, on the grounds that disclosure of its terms might have an adverse competitive effect on your client. When the license agreement was first signed, an article which appeared in a trade publication referred in passing to a few of the details for which you now seek confidentiality. This isn't exactly a favorable fact for your cause; yet you would feel concern on both ethical and practical grounds if you failed to mention the article's existence in your request letter. This is *not* to say, however, that you need state in the section where you're arguing for confidential treatment: "Oh, by the way, the guts of the license agreement were spread out in a trade publication for the world to see." Your responsibility is to reveal the fact that an article about the license agreement in fact appeared: if the agency is interested in how its contents might bear on their determination, they can ask you for a copy.

So, the idea is to scrutinize the forepart of your letter for a logical spot to insert this information with a minimum of fuss. For example, right at the start, where you're discussing the importance of this license agreement to the company, you could add a sentence (or a footnote) stating: "Its significance to the Company is illustrated by the fact that, shortly after its signing, the agreement became the subject of an article in Copper Week, a trade journal." If the agency considers the state of public knowledge about the agreement as relevant to its determination, then they know where to look; but at least you haven't called undue attention to the linkage.

3.2.8. Caveats, Other Qualifications and the Use of Forms.

There will undoubtedly be times when you're forced, usually by the exigencies of time, to produce less than first-class work on a written project. The letter or memo had to be completed by a certain date, and there simply weren't enough hours to perform as thorough a factual investigation or legal research effort as you would have liked. Perhaps certain facts were simply unavailable. Or the relevant legislative history, which might have tipped the scales in one direction or the other, could not be located. The possibilities for second-class work are nearly limitless.

When this happens, don't fret over such inadequacies or freeze into indecision.[35] Do the job as best you can under the circumstances. But—and this is the crucial point for our purposes here—make sure that the product going to the partner, the client or the other lawyer is qualified by appropriate caveats. As a partner, I can live with this kind of incompleteness,[36] as long as I know what the underlying limitations are; then I'm in a position to exercise my judgment accordingly. If the omission constitutes a basic deficiency, I might well discount the conclusion and await further elucidation. If the omission is relatively minor, or of a type that has previously caused no ill effects, then I can see myself ignoring it. But if I don't *know* that you faced impediments in reaching your conclusions, I have no basis for judgment. Unqualified work is presumed to be your best work, and you'll be evaluated on it accordingly.[37] So if, for reasons beyond your control, it doesn't measure up, by all means let the reader know.

Of course, you can also carry this caveat business too far. Unless the qualification is so crucial as to call for particular stress, I find it's best not to be terribly defensive. Beginning a memorandum with six pages of negative caveats leaves an impression of indecisiveness, of uncertainty. In most cases, a footnote or parenthetical reference will be sufficient to get across the point. It's also a good idea to provide your own assessment of the qualification. If you think it's minor and unlikely to cause a problem or interfere with the overall conclusion, let the reader share your unconcern.

In this regard, let me mention an important principle of partner review that I have only rarely heard discussed: the relative demerits of sins of omission and commission. Most partners are too busy to review your draft document *de novo*. The partner's cursory review might reveal errors you have made in the material he reads; he can tell if your description of the terms comport with what the parties agreed upon in his presence; he can comment on the failure of certain paragraphs to hang together, or their apparent overlapping; he might even pick up an ambiguity created by imprecise use of language. But

---

[35]   In this regard, see also Section 4.4.

[36]   I'm assuming here that the limitations on your work are valid ones within the time allotted for the project.

[37]   On a related point, if you have not had an opportunity to proofread a document, you should so indicate to the partner who is the recipient. Otherwise, he will (and ought to) assume that you have done so. From a partner's point of view, an error-strewn document that clearly hasn't (but should have) been proofread by the associate creates an extremely negative reaction.

it is much, much harder for a partner, in the course of a relatively hasty review, to discover what you may have *omitted*. And the distinction can be very significant.

This principle is analogous to the greater difficulty of proving a negative fact than an affirmative one. The reviewing reader has a real problem in calling to mind the full range of material that should (or might) have gone into the document. If it's a form of instrument he's reviewed many times (such as a formal opinion letter) and the omission is glaring (such as the usual caveat regarding the genuineness of signatures), then he might unearth it. But in most cases, to the extent you seek a measure of comfort from a partner's review, you should recognize that you can only rely on his reaction to what was placed in front of him. And while a partner is unlikely to become angry with you if something in what he *reviewed* proves offensive to the client or provides ammunition to the adversary, he will feel no such inhibition with regard to a damaging omission.

The obvious response to this situation—throwing in everything but the kitchen sink—is unsatisfactory, since the partner may feel you lack judgment. So how should you deal with the problem? Well, in close questions over whether to include or omit a certain item, the better practice is to bring the matter to the partner's attention, but in a way (such as by inclusion in a bracketed clause) which signals the partner that you aren't certain the item should be included. If you favor omission but want the partner to focus, then consider a footnote in which you "talk" to the partner; e.g., "I have omitted reference to the Smith transaction, which didn't seem relevant to the purpose of the letter."

Speaking of inclusion/exclusion, if you're drafting a document for which you have precedents—a Rule 10b-6 exemption letter request, a memorandum providing officers and directors with guidelines for insider trading—there's no substitute for taking a look at what others have done before you start. And this is true even if you know the subject cold. Not only is it easier to begin writing with something other than a blank page staring up at you,[38] but another lawyer's reflections on the same problem are bound to have produced some ideas that might not otherwise occur to you. You don't have to—and certainly shouldn't—accept your colleague's views blindly, but at least you ought to be aware of their existence.

Let me say a word about the use of forms generally. I am sure some laymen have the notion that we lawyers keep a well-stocked cabinet full of forms suitable for every occasion—somewhat like those tiny bureau drawers in a dentist's office with a different drill or

---

[38] In this regard, see Section 3.2.3.

utensil for each troublesome molar—and when faced with a fresh legal problem requiring some drafting, we merely reach in, find the proper form, fill in the names, and charge a whopping fee. In the great bulk of situations (I exclude the tenth supplemental indenture), nothing could be further from the truth. Still—and it's nothing to be ashamed of—we all do use forms in our practice, to greater or lesser extents. Were it otherwise, and if each new transaction required us to reinvent the wheel, the legal costs to clients would be even higher than they already are.

A good example of a document for which a proper form is helpful—but only as a starting point—is an acquisition agreement.[39] Having a basic form saves time for associates in drafting, for partners in reviewing, and for clients in being able to pass up the boilerplate; and it insures that the particular needs of clients, reflected in past agreements, won't be overlooked. But it is totally non-professional to use a prior draft without giving considerable thought to the particular exigencies of the transaction at hand. Always question the applicability of prior provisions to your present deal, and consider the advisability of inserting additional provisions to meet current needs.[40]

3.2.9. Should You Put It in Writing?

Before leaving the subject of writing, I have a few thoughts on whether or not a particular matter should be reduced to writing, and a related question of timing. We begin with a rebuttable presumption that once you've gone to the trouble of examining a particular matter in any detail—investigating facts, looking up law, analyzing an instrument or situation—the results should be recorded on paper. In the

---

[39] See Section 5.1 of *Anatomy*.

[40] There is one cardinal sin of form abuse that I find committed so often by young lawyers. The ABC deal comes into the office. The partner evaluates it, calls in an associate, gives him the facts, and tells him to prepare a draft "modeled on the XYZ acquisition that we did in January." The associate goes to the shelf, pulls down the thick black binder on the XYZ deal, makes a photocopy of the agreement and proceeds to mark it up for the ABC deal. Fatal, fatal error. Do you know why? The reason is that the XYZ agreement which found its way into that binder was the final, executed, negotiated agreement. Using it as the model for a first draft bequeaths to the ABC lawyer, gratis, the work product of the XYZ lawyer. All the provisions that you struggled so hard to resist and finally compromised—the additional purchaser's representations, the "materiality" limitations, the "knowledge" caveats—are fixed firmly in place. What the associate should have done, of course, was to go back to the *first draft* of the XYZ deal in the files, and mark that up. But believe me, this happens over and over, and you don't always catch it before the draft agreement is delivered to the other side.

press of other business, it's simply too easy to forget your conclusions or line of reasoning; a written record prepared while the issues are fresh insures ultimate retention. Writing permits an orderly exposition of your views (not always possible in an oral presentation) and enables the recipient to peruse the matter at his convenience when he's not under other pressure.

There are three principal exceptions I can think of to this general rule. By far the most important arises in situations which have the potential for becoming litigious—either between your client and his direct adversary, or as instituted by a third party (such as the government or a minority shareholder). This changes the entire framework of your thinking. You operate on the premise that all documents will be subject to subpoena, and that although certain privileges exist with regard to attorneys' writings, these can easily be waived (as by delivery of a privileged document to a third party, such as an accountant or investment banker). This calls for extreme caution in committing your thoughts to paper. In a hostile discovery situation, the exploratory, undigested musings of a quizzical attorney are transmuted into conspiratorial plottings, actionably omitted from contemporaneous public filings.

The second exception is created by the pace of modern-day legal transactions. What was critical yesterday is irrelevant tomorrow. Always make certain before embarking on a memorandum that it's not an exercise in futility, but represents information that someone in authority is still interested in pursuing.

The third situation is where the practical value of the writing is marginal at best, the client is not well-heeled, and the partner in charge makes a judgment that under the circumstances there's no need to run up the time in preparing a memorandum. This is a decision for the partner to make, not the associate; but if you suspect that this might be the case, be sure to inquire of the partner before getting started.

As for timing, you may just want to check the partner's (or client's) thinking on a particular matter before committing yourself in writing. As discussed in more detail elsewhere,[41] there may be some variations in the tenor (if not the substance) of a memo on a close question on the basis of the expectations of others. If you leap into print without looking, you may lose some desirable flexibility.

Conversely, there will be times when you can score handily by producing the unexpected document.[42] A partner hands you an assignment on Friday afternoon without specifying when he needs

---

41   See Section 6.5.
42   On the general subject of handling partners, see Section 5.1.1.

your input; the subject of whether there will eventually be a writing is not even discussed. You work on the matter all weekend and, when the partner arrives in his office Monday morning, there is a completely unexpected memo on his desk. Believe me, the impact is very powerful—much more impressive than an oral report. You have just gone off the top of the diligence scale.[43]

3.3 ON A VERBAL LEVEL[44]

3.3.1. The Oral Report.

The most basic of all lawyers' communications is the oral report: a description of what you've found through research, investigation or analysis; repeating to X the recent remarks of Y; telling Z what he should say to A; and so on. As with the analytical issues[45] and those involving written communications[46], the starting point here is to think before you speak—not preparation in the sense of rehearsing a set speech, but thought given to interpreting and distilling the essence of what you've learned and organizing your remarks in some coherent fashion.

The enemy here is the disorganized, rambling report, which lays equal stress on the trivial and the significant, wears everyone out, and lowers your stock several notches. Moreover, a half-baked report won't help you—as a well-prepared narrative often will—to decide on the advice being rendered.

Distilling the essence in an oral report—simplifying complex substantive rules, forcing yourself to generalize from the facts, etc.—presents much the same problem as whittling a five-page letter down to two pages.[47] You cannot function simply as a play-back recorder. Typically, you're reporting to busy people who want refined conclusions—not rough facts. If, for example, you're relating the results of a factual investigation, try to classify and organize the facts into helpful patterns, rather than serving them up to the listener in an unvarnished state. Strive to keep your report unencumbered by minor

---

[43] The quality of diligence is discussed in Section 4.3. Similarly, a partner may have given you a problem, the answer to which is more complex than either of you had imagined. Although he didn't ask for a memo, you realize it will be difficult for him to grasp the subject in an oral report interspersed between phone calls. So you furnish him with a clear, concise and interesting memo for perusal on the train home. This can also garner innumerable points.

[44] Most of the material in this section deals with oral communications between you and a partner or client. Communicating with adversaries and other lawyers is covered in Chapter 7.

[45] See Chapter 2.

[46] See Section 3.2.

[47] See Section 3.2.5.

details; such phrases as "with certain immaterial exceptions" and "There are certain nuances here that I'll go into later if you desire, but the main thrust is as follows . . ." are invaluable for keeping on the track—while still indicating that it's not quite as simple as it sounds.

With legal issues, the question is how deeply you should delve into the reasoning by which you arrived at your conclusion. The answer depends in large measure on the person to whom you're making the report and the surrounding circumstances. A rendition which would be entirely proper to a partner might be quite inappropriate for a client, and vice versa. Reporting to a partner on a complex matter of vital interest to him—with the entire morning reserved for the discussion—obviously differs from a report on a simple subject to an overextended partner whom you've managed to corner for a moment near the elevator.

When you're dealing with a partner who has the time and interest, he may very well want you to go through your reasoning, in order to judge whether he agrees with the conclusions you've reached. Still, the safer course is to begin your report with something along these lines: "The bottom line is that I think this proposed deal violates the loan agreement. Would you like me to go through the steps by which I arrived at that conclusion?" That puts it squarely up to the partner. If he replies affirmatively, then you supply the rationale.[48] If he declines, that's his way of saying that he trusts you to have reached the right conclusion. This will probably make you a little nervous at first—can *he* actually be relying on *my* judgment completely?—and if the question is a squeaker you should probably add: "It's a close call, though, and I'd like very much to go through my reasoning to see if you agree."

As for the client, each one is different. Some are completely uninterested in your reasoning—they just want the results. In their minds, having you plod through an analysis would be somewhat akin to a dentist, about to embark on a root canal excursion, saying: "Now first, I'm going to cover your mouth with this rubber sheet; then I'm going to stick these little pins into you; and then I'll . . ." Just do it, Doc; and many clients react this way toward lawyers. If you feel the need to reveal how you reached your conclusion—perhaps you want him to know the basis of your reliance, so that when things backfire later he can't say he wasn't warned[49]—then try a statement like this: "In arriving at this conclusion, my major assumption was that the

---

[48] If he says "yes" enough times in similar circumstances, then you probably should furnish the reasoning as a matter of course.

[49] In this regard, see Section 8.4.

deal would be characterized as an acquisition of securities under the indenture. I am sending you a short memo on the subject, so that you can see how I arrived at that premise.''

Occasionally, you run into a client who *is* interested in the workings of your mind—usually an executive who's a lawyer himself, or whose involvement with the matter under consideration has risen to the level of an obsession.[50] Even here, let him draw you out—and the first time through, avoid technicalities, delete references to section numbers, simplify the mechanics, and limit yourself to the principal steps of your reasoning process.

Let's try to underscore this important point with a particularly tortuous example. Your client, Outraged Corp., has asked you to make a factual and legal investigation into whether the current activities of David Disloyal, a former employee of Outraged, sufficiently violate the non-competition covenant of his prior employment contract to warrant injunctive relief. You complete your investigation and now find yourself in the office of Hector Harried, the president of Outraged Corp. Although the question is not insignificant, you can surmise that it's not the most important item in Harried's multi-pressured day.

All right. Here's a textbook presentation—and absolutely the *wrong* way to go about making your report. To set the stage, begin with a brief general dissertation on the terms of the non-competition provisions in Disloyal's contract. Next, describe the facts you have been able to unearth regarding Disloyal's conduct. Inasmuch as you interviewed several people, hired a detective to follow him around, and picked up a number of specifics regarding his business, customers and localities, make sure to load this with excruciating detail. To round out the overall picture, summarize succinctly the state of the law in this jurisdiction regarding non-competition covenants— basically that the courts are loathe to enforce them in situations *not* involving acquisitions of a business—including some discussion of a few recent cases.

The stage being set, you're now ready to home in on the specific questions involved in the case. There are two major legal issues: first, whether the contract prohibits competition with the business of *affiliates* of the particular subsidiary for which David Disloyal worked (since that is the nature of his present activity); and second, since the non-compete area is limited to the single county in which Outraged Corp. actually conducts business, do the limited acts which Disloyal

[50] When the client consists of the company's inside general counsel, then you have to treat the situation more as if he were a supervising partner than a businessman. Relations with the inside general counsel are covered in Section 7.2.3.

has performed in that county constitute the prohibited competition (or are they merely peripheral, the real competitive effort having taken place in a permitted zone)? But as in any complex matter like this, there are a number of other possible questions; and your sharp eye has picked up at least four of these. So now you turn to Hector Harried and proceed to list all half-dozen issues, one at a time, without identifying which are the crucial ones and without attempting to reach any conclusions—merely to be comprehensive. Then, you go back through them one by one (restating each issue, of course, for total clarity), giving your evaluation of their relative importance and presenting the conclusions you have reached with respect to each.

On the two main issues, although the questions are close, you conclude that Disloyal is, in fact, engaging in proscribed competition. However, now you must get into the question of whether the local court would enforce the covenant—i.e., the application of the law you discussed earlier in general terms to the particular fact pattern emerging here. And reluctantly, you arrive at the conclusion that although there has been a breach, it is of such marginal magnitude, both in terms of the area and the degree of competition, that the court would be unlikely to provide Outraged Corp. with any kind of meaningful relief. So, having plowed through this beautifully organized exercise for the better part of an hour, you now advise Harried that it's probably not worth attempting to sue Disloyal.

All very precise, all very logical, all very legalistic. (Some people might even term it "lawyerlike", although I would reject the appellation.) And what you have probably succeeded in doing is to drive Hector Harried right up the wall and out the air-conditioning vent! Given the relative significance of the situation and in view of the ultimate conclusion, you have taken up far too much of Harried's valuable time. The whole affair could have been handled with considerable brevity, while accomplishing the same purpose. For example, your presentation might have gone along the following lines:

"Disloyal's activities probably do constitute a violation of the non-competition covenant. The two principal issues here are, first, whether the contract covers competition with the business of an *affiliate* of Disloyal's former subsidiary (which is what he's engaged in)—and on that score, although it's far from clear, I come out that businesses of affiliates *are* covered; the second involves the place in which the competitive activies are carried out—on which we have concluded (although again, there are arguments the other way) that his acts in this county constitute sufficient competition to invoke the contract.

"However, the violations are so marginal that, given the negative predilection of the local courts, I don't think we could expect any meaningful judicial assistance if we attempted enforcement. So I have to recommend against bringing litigation.

"I would be happy to go into detail on any of these points or our investigative findings if you would like me to do so, although I realize you have a busy schedule."

Now, *that's* the kind of report most businessmen I know really appreciate. I'll grant that you have to possess some self-confidence to pull it off. In talking at such length, the first lawyer was probably unconsciously trying to convince *himself* that his conclusions were right—thus the subliminal need to have the client follow and appreciate the workings of the lawyer's mind. But which lawyer has done his client more of a service?

If you do have a lengthy report to make—where you have considered the matter in advance and decided that it's important for the listener to grasp some richness of detail and nuance—at the very least you ought to provide a short summary of your principal conclusions or observations right at the outset (much as you would do at the beginning of a long memorandum). Knowing where the speaker is heading makes it so much easier for the listener to fit everything he hears into place—to appreciate the significance of various details, to decide if he's in agreement at checkpoints along the journey, to assess what additional facts may be needed. I often find myself listening to an associate's report with increasing feelings of annoyance—tantalized by facts and inferences but with no idea of the direction in which things are heading.[51] Suspense might be *de rigeur* for authors of mysteries, but it's out of place in the workaday, pressurized worlds of law and business. Top executives must bring their mental processes to bear on a problem *while* they're hearing about it. Anything you can do to help them in this regard will be appreciated.

Oh yes, there's another side to this particular coin. Assume you're wading through a necessarily detailed report for a partner or client. The listener, however, isn't just listening; rather, he's continually interrupting you with questions—some directed to the issue under discussion, others related to matters you intend to cover later in the report. How do you handle this? On the one hand, you can't simply ignore your interrogator; after all, the client is paying your fees and

---

[51] This sometimes calls for a dramatic gesture on the part of the partner, as discussed in Section 10.4.1.

the partner your salary! On the other hand, you dearly want to stay on the point and follow your prescribed course, so that the full logic of your analysis will come through loud and strong.[51a]

Here's my rule of thumb for this difficult problem. If the interruption relates to what you've just been discussing—calling for elaboration or questioning something you've said—then as much as you'd prefer to defer it, you have to respond right then and there. But if the interrupter is anticipating a point you have in mind for later, I find nothing at all wrong with politely declining to break your train of thought; "That's an important point," you can say, "which I intend to cover in just a few minutes."

In my view, the most important aspect of reporting is the necessity to function not only as a reporter but also as an interpreter. The lawyer must put his own imprimatur on the events he reports. What is the *significance* of the facts he's passing along? What did that fellow really *mean* when he said those things? The client deserves your reasoned interpretation of what might otherwise seem to be objective facts.

Let's review that ubiquitous situation where you're repeating to Larry Listener certain remarks made by Ted Talker in a recent phone conversation with you. You don't have a verbatim transcript of what Talker said; at most, you may have taken rough notes.[52] As you find yourself dealing with increasingly more sophisticated legal problems, the subtleties of Talker's remarks—the veiled threats, the deliberate obfuscations, the obvious sensibilities, the tone of voice—and the significance of things left *unsaid,* can be more important than the actual words spoken. You must be sensitive to this, and supply the interpretive quotient along with accurate reportage. Try to arrive at the *sense* of Talker's remarks, for the benefit of Listener who wasn't in a position to derive his own conclusions.

In this regard, never feel bound to report the details of a conversation in the precise order in which they occurred. Oral communications don't necessarily progress in a logical pattern; for purposes of transmission to a third party, the sequence can be rearranged for maximum comprehension. Occasionally, however, the order in which things came up can be important—for example, where it's critical to know whether, at the time the speaker made a certain statement, he was aware of a particular fact that you conveyed during the course of the phone call—and in such cases, you should not ignore the chronology.

Here's another comparative example—this time, of inadequate and

---

[51a] For the analogous problem in the context of courtroom argument, see Section 7.4.4.

[52] This can be important to do, especially if there's a time lag between the two conversations or Talker's remarks have continuing significance.

imaginative reporting. You represent a corporate client which is the subject of a potentially damaging inquiry by the staff of the SEC. Although no formal investigative order has yet issued, the staff has been requesting documents and taking testimony. You're aware that just yesterday, the young staff member ("Gumshoe") who is carrying the laboring oar took the testimony of the one witness ("Tattler," a disgruntled ex-employee) you fear could prove harmful to your client. Naturally, you're curious about Tattler's testimony, but Gumshoe has been notably uncommunicative about such matters in the past and you've decided to refrain from any direct inquiries.

At this point, the phone rings; it's Gumshoe calling. You converse with him for about 15 minutes. When the call is completed, you dial your client to report on the conversation. A technically accurate, but totally inadequate, report might go something like this:

"Gumshoe called a few minutes ago. Although we talked for a while, the only significant developments were, one, he asked how we were coming on that other submission he had requested last week; and two, he asked me for a letter setting forth the amount of business the company currently does in the particular product line that's the subject of the investigation. He didn't say anything about Tattler's testimony, and I didn't ask. So, I guess I really don't have very much to report; but I just wanted to keep you up to date."

Contrast a report along the following lines:

"I received a call today from Gumshoe. It seems to me that the specific matters we discussed were less significant than the overall tone of the conversation. As you recall, Gumshoe has always been very brusque with me in the past, very businesslike, seemingly never interested in engaging in small talk. All of a sudden today, things were quite different, and I had the distinct feeling that he had plenty of time and some desire to discourse at length. Viewed in the light of that possibly adverse testimony yesterday, I feel that the positive tone to our conversation is a favorable indication.

"Several other facets of the call also pointed in the same direction. For instance, Gumshoe asked me for a letter on the amount of business the company now does of the type that's under investigation. A month ago, I told him orally that it was minuscule. So this could also be positive— the kind of written statement a staff member would want in his records if he were going to wrap up an investigation without taking adverse action.

"He also questioned how we were progressing on that other submission he mentioned last week. At first blush, the import of this question is ambiguous: it could mean that the investigation is still going on hot and heavy, or it could mean that it's virtually over and he just wants to close his files. I lean to the latter theory, based on the timing of when he raised this in the conversation—nestled in among some pleasantries that portended no trouble at all.

"I also have to mention that at one point, in referring to Tattler, Gumshoe made a slip of the tongue and used the name of Wardheeler [a prior witness, favorable to the client]. It's hard to imagine Gumshoe making that slip if Tattler had testified harmfully against us yesterday. Also, in mentioning that affidavit he requested last week, Gumshoe specifically stated that his superior would be most interested in seeing it. He said this in such a way that I felt he might be trying to indicate it wasn't *his* idea; that he—Gumshoe—didn't think it was necessary but was merely humoring his superior.

"So I would have to say—although obviously, all this is inference and we have no hard facts or assurances—that the tone and certain other matters in this conversation were sufficiently positive to give us some reason to believe Tattler didn't do the hatchet job we feared he would."

Now, you can be wrong and perhaps end up with egg all over your face. But you haven't misled anyone. You've labeled inferences as such and haven't tried to pass off interpretation as fact. You've provided the client with the underlying observations so that he can draw his own conclusions (he might, for example, see nothing at all positive in that slip of the tongue). And at least you attempted to give him a *sense* of what was going on in the conversation—what he might have surmised himself if he were on the line with you—which makes your account far more useful than the first cursory report. I hasten to add that, if the sense of the phone call with Gumshoe had been negative (as these matters often are!), you would be similarly obliged to alert your client. He's entitled to be chilled by those same cold winds that buffeted you.

There's a real paradox here for the lawyer-communicator. How often have you set forth your own views on something to A, only to hear those views repeated back to you by B with completely different emphasis. Either A didn't report your remarks accurately to B, or B didn't listen very well, or B is now taking some liberties with what he heard. We all want our own remarks repeated verbatim, without the reporter's personal interpretation. And yet, when you're trying to convey what someone else has said, to be really effective you may have to take great liberties with the actual words. It's just one of the small burdens you bear as a professional.

3.3.2. The Client Interview.

I want to focus this section on the client interview—not the formal preparation for litigation, but the everyday situation where a client comes to your office to relate his problem.[52a] Although most of the principles discussed are equally applicable to interviews with existing clients, they can more easily be visualized at the outset of a new client relationship.

I suppose it's somewhat of a cliché by now, but still true: that in an interview of this type, there's simply no substitute for being a good listener—an intelligent, alert audience, who is able to discern more than the words being said, and who acts on what he hears. Remember the Senator in the Watergate hearings who never followed up his own question? The answer might be explosive or devious—fairly crying out for some additional inquiries—but he would just cross the item off his list and move on to the next prepared question. Listening is emphatically *not* a passive exercise. What you hear should be instrumental in determining the direction to proceed, the key to guiding the speaker into productive areas and away from trivia and repetition. If you're not concentrating—if your mind is elsewhere or you're just taking notes without really focusing—then you won't be effective.

When a new client enters the office, some attorneys pull out a yellow pad and begin to take comprehensive notes on every word the client utters. Personally, I can't see it. Not only is this disconcerting to the client (who might as well be talking to a dictating machine), but a lawyer who's busy writing is not busy thinking. He's not sorting out what the client says, attempting to see some pattern in the disorganized facts, establishing significance, figuring out areas worth pursuing, and so on.

My advice is, just listen for a while before you start writing. Try to get an overview of what the problem is all about. Once you're aware of the significant aspects, you'll know what to take notes on; and don't worry, clients *love* to repeat their story. It may also be that many of the items you would have struggled to get down on paper are incorporated in documents that the client has in his briefcase—but just didn't get around to pulling out at this early point in the proceedings. So resist that urge to scribble; don't hunch over your foolscap. Rather, establish eye contact with your new client, nod in

---

[52a] For a lengthy example of an initial client interview, see Section 2.3.

appreciation of his insightful observations, appear a bit quizzical when he's not making sense. Begin to size up the man or woman across your desk. And start thinking about the significance of what is being said.

First cousin to the incessant scrivener is the lawyer who, before a dozen words are out of the client's mouth, starts peppering him with questions, turning the initial interview into a full-scale interrogation. I don't recommend starting out this way. It destroys the client's concentration, which may result in his omitting material facts. He wants to tell *his* story; for all you know, he may have been rehearsing it all week. Let him at least get under way.

On the other hand, interspersing an occasional question makes good sense in several respects. At the very least, it shows the client you're awake and interested in his situation. An intelligent question or comment can indicate to an astute client how readily you grasp his complex problem. The answer may also help you focus on the significance of other facts you'll be hearing. For example, if the client keeps mentioning a certain corporation as the focal point of the problem, you might interject a question as to that company's state of incorporation; your knowledge of the laws of that jurisdiction may then assist you in evaluating the situation.

So, generally speaking, it's good practice to let a client proceed through the main points of his story, in his own fashion, with a minimum of prodding and note-taking from the lawyer. Sure, this can result in a waste of some time—especially with a client who isn't skilled at sorting significance from trivia—but it can also pay important dividends. There will, however, be days when your new client is irredeemably long-winded. After a few minutes, you realize that this fellow just wants to talk, to have somebody listen to him. You can try to get him to "skip the minor details for this first run-through"; but if that doesn't work, then you simply have to cut him off and start directing the interview.

After the client's initial presentation, you begin the guided portion of the interview. What happens in this part depends to a considerable degree on what is involved, which makes generalization somewhat difficult. Basically, if you've been listening you will have a pretty good idea of the legal issues involved, and your questions should be designed to fill in the factual gaps relevant to these issues. In this portion, you ought to take notes—although I suggest that before you start writing, ask the client which information is available in documents. In no case would I recommend taking such voluminous notes that the interview slows down to a tedious pace. You can always find out the facts in more detail later on; right now, consideration of what you want to learn is more important than recording what you've heard.

In the quest for information, your evaluation as to the reliability of the client's comments has real consequence. Verbal descriptions and recollections by a layman—particularly one who is emotionally or financially involved in a situation—can be notoriously unreliable; and while you should make an effort to conceal your skepticism over his version of the facts, your questions ought to probe into these issues. You simply can't accept his version at face value.

In this regard, be sure to make the client distinguish among fact, opinion, hearsay, and speculation. These distinctions may not seem important to the client, who will gloss over them in his dissertation; to you, however, they can be crucial. If he makes a statement of apparent significance, you should query: "How do you know that?" If he describes a scene, ask: "Did you witness this personally or hear about it from someone else?" If he mentions the report of another person, pry a little: "Do you trust that person to be accurate and telling the truth?"

As you proceed, you should be forming your own judgment as to how precise this new client is in reporting details; the more precise, the more comfortable you can feel. If, on the other hand, he tends to vague or grandiose statements, you can begin to decide just how to go about investigating these matters yourself. A more difficult judgment to make on the occasion of the first meeting, but one you might as well start in on, is whether the client is being completely truthful with you. You can operate without precision, but fabrication signals a quick end to the attorney-client relationship.[53]

Ending the interview is your business. You have to decide when you've heard enough; the client can't be expected to make that judgment. Always close with an affirmative statement as to what you propose to do next, such as: "I have enough facts now to do a little research and see if we have a good case. Then we'll meet again—I would say in about a week—and take it from there." Or, "I want to read these documents over and talk to those two people you mentioned before deciding what further steps to take. Have them call me to set up appointments. And remember to send me those other three memoranda we discussed." Don't let the client leave the office without a sense that you are taking this matter under your wing and proceeding expeditiously.

3.3.3. Running an Informal Meeting.

A much neglected skill in the lawyer's repertoire is the ability to conduct a meeting. Not a meeting in the formal sense (such as an an-

---

[53]   More on this subject in Chapter 6.

nual meeting of stockholders), where the concerns are with *Robert's Rules* and other quasi-parliamentary affairs; and not what might be termed an adversarial meeting, where clients and lawyers on opposite sides of contested or negotiated matters come together.[54] What I have in mind is the typical meeting involving lawyers from the same side of the table (including an inside counsel from the client corporation), several company executives, perhaps an outside auditor or investment banker, and a few others with various interests in the issue under discussion. And in using the word "conduct", I'm not referring to situations where you have been formally designated as the chairperson of the assemblage (by dint of some office you hold or otherwise) or where you're clearly *not* expected to be the leader—perhaps a partner is present, or another lawyer (who's more involved in the matter) or your client is calling the shots. Rather, I'm interested in meetings, often called at your instance, to discuss a problem, or provide a status report, or decide on a course of action—meetings where the directions taken, the tempo of the proceedings, and the ultimate duration are pretty much up for grabs (and thus within your prospective control).

I have the distinct feeling that few lawyers attempt to plan in advance what they hope to accomplish in a meeting (other than when the goal is obvious, as with a meeting to mark up a prospectus proof and get it back down to the printer). The problem may well stem from the calling of the meeting in the first instance; it's obviously difficult to outline intelligent aims for meetings which aren't necessary to hold. I proceed on the theory that, except for those occasions when some client hand-holding is in order, no meeting should be convened without a definite purpose in mind. In retrospect, the worst meetings I have ever attended—seemingly interminable and notably non-productive—were sessions that should probably never have taken place.

Once you've discerned the purpose of the meeting, try to decide where you would like to come out on various hypotheses. I recognize that you might not be able to predict results, since this depends on what develops at the meeting—how much information can be provided by those who are present, whether questions are raised that require answers by outside sources, and so on. But without goals and direction, what transpires will seem haphazard at best. By all means, remain flexible, prepared to direct the meeting into different channels; but at least have a game plan.

Here's an example. Your friend Charlie has asked you to assist in forming a new stock brokerage firm. There will be four partner-share-

---

[54]   See Sections 7.3 and 7.4.

holders: Charlie, two of his friends who are brokers at other firms, and a fourth individual, Sawbuck, who will not be active in the running of the business but is putting up a good deal of the initial capital. You sense a potential conflict of interest; you can "handle the situation" and represent the three brokers, but you've suggested to Sawbuck that he retain his own counsel (which he intends to do). At an early point in the proceedings, before either the details of the agreement among the parties or the mechanics of running the company have been settled, a meeting is scheduled for you, the three brokers, and their accountant.

On the basis of your experience in such matters, you realize that the key factor in this assignment will be to work out the business deal between the three active partners and the passive financial partner. The critical issues to be resolved and embodied in the corporate documents and shareholders' agreement include additional contributions to capital, the disposition of shares upon withdrawal from the firm or death, and managerial control. You are also aware of a myriad of other details (unrelated to the basic issues) involved in starting up a business—matters such as registering as a broker-dealer with the SEC, becoming a member of the NASD, leasing office space, and so on.

It's clear in your mind what the purpose of this meeting ought to be: to develop, among the three individuals with relatively similar interests, a negotiating position vis-à-vis the fourth partner, Sawbuck, with respect to decision-making and the potential termination of a partner's interest. Until the shareholders' agreement incorporating these provisions has been signed, no money will be put up and the project won't get off the ground. And you can expect some negotiations on this subject. When the parties get right down to discussing imponderables such as death and the future, it often develops that each person has very different things in mind. That's why a meeting is useful at this point. It's not something you can accomplish dealing with each man individually; this is one of the few times you'll be able to get them all together in the same room. You're hopeful that the interplay of their minds in reaction to your specific questions will provide the impetus to arrive at a satisfactory consensus position.

However, you may be surprised to discover that your clients don't realize the importance of all this. They may well be more interested in the operational questions—broker-dealer qualification and the like. They'll want to get on with filling out questionnaires (which can be handled on an individual basis) and inquiring about matters such as FICA (which are more in the realm of what their accountant will do for them). And unless you make them hew the line on the main purpose of this meeting—to develop this negotiating position—they will tend to get off the subject. Therefore, when one of them starts to bring up these other matters, it's incumbent upon you to say: "No, let's finish *my* agenda first as regards the shareholders' agreement. If we have time left, we can handle these other matters; if not, they can be done individually. Now, who will comprise the board of directors?"—and you proceed directly into your checklist of important items.

Once you have set the direction of a meeting, you may still have a problem maintaining momentum. After all, you're not a czar or chairman with dictatorial powers; you can't just cut people off in mid-sentence—particularly paying clients. Everyone has to feel he's been given full opportunity to record his sentiments. But unfortunately, the other participants may not always appreciate the need to stay on track, to be concise, to discuss what's significant. So what do you do?

Well, as with so much else in the practice of law, this calls for a mixture of adroit diplomacy and a firm hand. For openers, you have to convey the impression that *you* are in the best position to know what should be accomplished at the meeting—as well as the optimal means of arriving at that goal. If you're able to establish that climate, then you can break into another's lengthy dissertation with a line such as: "That's a good point you're making, but I think it might be a good idea at this time for us to move ahead to the other issue we need to cover; we'll have a chance to come back to your point later." (Incidentally, saying that you'll come back to something later—even if you have little intention of so doing—makes it much easier for the speaker to yield; he hasn't really lost face since he believes he'll get another chance.) A related device for cutting off discussion, which is most effective early in the meeting, runs as follows: "Let's pause now on this particular issue and go on to the others, so that we get an overall grasp of everything we want to cover; then we'll come back and explore each issue in detail."

Another technique I find very helpful in conducting a meeting is to sum up or characterize the unstructured statements of others. The ability to take ten minutes of meandering remarks and encapsulate them in a sentence or two—making sure, of course, that the speaker agrees with your characterization—can be a giant step in the direction of the ultimate consensus you're trying to develop. A phrase such as "Well, the main thrust of your remarks appears to be that you would like to go after the scoundrel" represents a polite attempt to force the speaker into making the concise summary he's been resisting all along.

It's important at a meeting to attempt to develop a consensus. People on the same side of a legal-type problem want to feel they're in basic agreement with respect to both the situational analysis and proposed courses of action. As the points come up and are decided, I like to get each participant to indicate his acquiescence—using such obvious techniques as: "What do you think, Frank?" or "Are you in agreement with us on that, Sam?". I must confess that one rationale of this—I would hope, not too ostensible—is to avoid future second-guessing by an otherwise silent attendee.

With some clients, it may be desirable that the ultimate conclusion emanate from them rather than from you. No problem; and by the way, this leads to less second-guessing than when you appear to be shoving a judgment down your client's throat. There are times when you just have to conquer the lawyer's natural ego—that transcendent sensation of being the font from which all knowledge flows. Bite your tongue and let the client take the credit.

I have this theory about meetings, that attendance at them is the *least* demanding task anyone will be called upon to perform on that particular day; and as a result, unless someone takes affirmative action, the meeting will probably continue well beyond the point where it has ceased to be fruitful—since no one wants to leave the comfort of the conference room to go back to some real work. And so, the final aspect of meetings to explore is how to end one. Many inexperienced lawyers appear timorous about calling a halt to the proceedings; they prefer to let the client or some other participant call that shot. As you gain more confidence, however, you will definitely want to take the initiative in this regard, since it's possible that no one else will and you have better things to do with your time than to sit there non-productively.

The best way to end a meeting is to decide upon a particular course of action, or do something else of a resolute nature. Once a determination has been made, it's obvious to everyone that there's no further point in remaining on the premises. The subtle aspect is that sometimes the decision is lurking there, unarticulated, waiting for you to unearth it for the edification of all. For example, take a meeting to put the pricing amendment for the debenture prospectus in shape for filing. All of a sudden, the accountant concedes that the capsule numbers for the most recent fiscal quarter aren't really firm; the underwriter announces that interest rates are temporarily quite soft; and the inside counsel expresses concern that the Justice Department is about to indict the president of a subsidiary for price fixing. Bingo! You get up, put on your coat, and reveal what should be obvious to everyone: that since you're obviously not going to become effective this week, why stay up all night at the printer? But sometimes you just have to put it in words, or everyone will sit around commiserating without knowing what to do.

At other times, however, concluding a meeting is not so simple because, for one reason or another, no decision has been reached, no consensus has developed. Still, when it's clear to you that the meeting has gone about as far as it can go, you have to make an attempt to close things out in as orderly a manner as possible. This becomes primarily a matter of summing up, looking ahead and handing out assignments. The key is to set a date for a follow-up meeting, and then try to develop a program so that whatever remains unresolved will be taken care of by then. If there are unknown or disputed factual questions, assign these to various people, telling them whom to interview and what to investigate in order to be ready for the next go-around. If additional legal questions have surfaced during the meeting which require research, assume the burden of that yourself and fix a self-imposed time limit for the answers.

Take that disappointing prospectus meeting, for instance. Don't just leave. Tell the inside lawyer to make some calls to ascertain how imminent the indictment is, and you start drafting the necessary disclosures. Get an estimate from the underwriter on when he thinks interest rates will firm up sufficiently to proceed. Ask the accountants how much time they need to feel comfortable with the capsule numbers. And fix a date for a new meeting, with each participant aware of what he has to do to make that next conference more successful than the one being adjourned.

3.3.4. Keeping the Oral Laxity Vigil.

The more I practice law, the more convinced I am that a prime function of the effective lawyer is to recognize ambiguity, lack of clarity and other forms of oral laxity in discourse occurring among individuals (one of whom may be the lawyer himself!), point out the problem, and resolve it then and there—rather than allowing it to fester and crop up later with resulting misunderstandings and crossed signals. This is the verbal analogue to the concern with clarity and rooting out ambiguity in writings;[55] and it requires a special appreciation of the fact that when people speak in an informal setting, they don't always use words and phrases with as much precision as when their utterings are reduced to writing. So vigilance on your part is the byword.

Here's what I mean. Nibs, the president of Client Corp., and Boss, your supervising partner, are engaged in a discussion, with you in more or less silent attendance. Client Corp. has recently entered into an agreement to be acquired, which contains several negative

---

[55] See Section 3.2.4.

covenants restricting its freedom of action pending the closing. Client also has a loan agreement with its lender bank, which prohibits Client from a number of activities without the bank's consent. References to both agreements have been made in the course of the discussion.

Time passes. Your gaze shifts to the window. You're getting drowsy. You catch yourself, shaking off your stupor in time to hear Nibs say: "But if we do that, wouldn't it violate the agreement?" "No," replies Boss, "it's no problem." "That's *very* interesting," says Nibs.

Curious, you think. Boss has always seemed acutely concerned—Nibs much less so—about possible violations of the acquisition agreement, something that would serve to give the purchaser an out at the closing. Hmmm. . . . Nibs, on the other hand, keeps bringing up the loan agreement, which Boss has been treating as, in effect, a practical nullity since the loan will be refinanced at the closing. Still, a formal waiver would have to be sought for any transaction prior to closing which violated the express terms of the loan agreement, especially since the acquisition might never be consummated. Hmmm. . . . The particular action I think they were discussing is clearly not a violation of the relatively loose regime of the acquisition agreement, but it's probably caught up somewhere in the snares of that complex loan agreement. . . .

Wait a minute! Could it be that when Nibs referred to "the agreement" he meant the *loan* agreement; while Boss, thinking Nibs meant the *acquisition* agreement, replied in those terms. And maybe that's why Nibs, whom we've lectured *ad nauseam* about the broad scope of the loan agreement, seemed so surprised by Boss's answer. These thoughts rush through your head in a moment, and you blurt out: "Hey, wait a minute. I think you fellows may not have been talking about the same document." And more often than not, right you are. Fortunate too, because otherwise Nibs might have taken the action without bothering to obtain the necessary bank waiver, on the premise that his lawyer had advised him it wasn't necessary.

Just as this sort of thing can happen between two people to whom you're listening (and where, as an inactive participant, you tend to be more objective and alert to such problems), ambiguity and lack of mutual understanding can creep into your own communications with others. Make sure at all times that what you're saying is being clearly understood. Avoid legalistic gibberish that clients don't understand. If a proposition is complex, try to state it in several different ways, so no doubt can exist that the client understands. If you suspect he's still lost, then question him on the point.[56] Avoid the situa-

---

[56] As a last resort, you may have to write out your proposition, not only to aid the client's understanding but to avoid being misquoted. See generally Chapter 6.

tion where the client *thinks* he knows what you're saying and agrees with you, but in fact doesn't realize what this entails—and if he did, might well disagree. Get on the same wavelength.

Suppose you're advising a relatively unsophisticated client (who desperately doesn't want to appear as such) on the tax consequences of a certain transaction. You run through the relatively favorable aspects and then drop in a line like "Of course, there will be recapture of depreciation" or "We can't, however, avoid the imputed interest." The client is reluctant to let on that he hasn't the foggiest notion what you mean by these formidable-sounding terms, so he nods his head knowingly—which you take to mean that he realizes the transaction contains these disadvantages but he's prepared to live with them. I say the fault is yours, not his. With concepts like these, you have to dig in and explain what's going on. It just might be that, once the client appreciates the hefty dose of ordinary income to be realized, he may want you to consider restructuring the deal.

The other aspect here is to appreciate that businessmen and others with whom you deal don't always mean what they say—not through any venal motives or intention to mislead, but simply because they're less likely to be precise with words. This is particularly noticeable when clients toss around legal terms. For instance, the client comes into your office and starts talking about a block of stock, which he refers to as "registered"—with a certain trace of pride in his voice at knowing enough law to realize this can be significant. Don't let him bluff you. "Registered" is a legal concept which shouldn't be entrusted to a layman; and besides, it can mean different things (with widely differing results) under different circumstances.[57] Decline his characterization politely, and inquire into the facts.

This can also happen with non-legalese. I've noticed, for instance, that businessmen commonly tend to overstate the firmness of a deal in its early stages. You must become inured to a certain measure of hyperbole. A call comes in from your client, who says: "I just bought XYZ Company". Your first impulse is to cry out: "How could you have done that? Did you sign any papers? We haven't investigated; we haven't made adequate disclosure", etc. Take it easy—because as you will soon learn, the client has merely ascertained that XYZ might be a willing seller if the parties can agree on a price and several other

---

[57] For example, it might refer to the company's registration under the Securities Exchange Act of 1934, or to the fact that the shares were issued in a public offering under the Securities Act of 1933. It might refer to the fact that the shares are freely saleable without an investment letter, but then again it may not—since this turns on how they were issued, the nature of the proposed transaction and the character of the seller.

important elements. Countless examples of comparable phenomena abound.

3.3.5. When Should You Speak Face-to-Face?

The oral correlative to the question of whether to put something into writing[58] is the identification of situations where face-to-face handling is preferred over use of the telephone.

For many of us, the telephone has become a hateful instrument of eternal bondage—the prime cause of so much of the pressure we feel. It rings constantly, interrupting whatever you're doing, wreaking havoc on any pattern of coherent thought. Your stomach knots up when you arrive back from lunch to find a dozen phone messages on your desk, silently but relentlessly demanding responses before you can attempt anything meaningful. And there is little in life more frustrating than trading "He's out" or "Busy on the other line" responses back and forth with someone you want to reach.

In weaker moments, though, we have to concede the convenience the telephone affords—the avoidance of unappetizing trips, the ability to communicate instantaneously with clients at long distances, and so forth. And because of this, in order to address the question posed by this section, I think we should begin with a rebuttable presumption that most matters *can* be handled by telephone. So, what are the exceptions to the rule, where a face-to-face meeting is especially appropriate? Here, in no special order, are several situations that I think require the personal touch.

The most important of the face-to-face meetings involves a number of participants from different locations, each of whom is likely to have something to say. When it's impossible to get together, conference calls have a certain utility; but for any sustained give-and-take, they just don't fill the bill. You have to strain to hear what's said; the sense of when it's appropriate to butt in with your own two cents' worth is never clear; and you just don't get the facial and postural signals from the other participants that you do when seated around a table. Important meetings of a board of directors or committee should always be held in person if possible, even where the applicable corporate law permits them to be conducted by telephone. Decisions should emerge from the active interplay of ideas, a desideratum easily undermined by a balky conference telephone.

Face-to-face is also best whenever the subject matter to be discussed is very serious or important. Heavy negotiations over an

---

[58] See Section 3.2.9.

agreement should always be conducted in person and not on the phone. The discussion of delicate issues with the client—something, for instance, along the lines of so-called "sensitive payments"—should be handled across the table.

I don't know how you feel about it, but long-winded telephone calls are a real thorn in my side. If I know the conversation is going to take several hours—which for me is just too long a time to be on the telephone—I make every effort to handle such a matter face-to-face.

The fourth exception is very important. This occurs when you want to size someone up for yourself. You want to meet him, see how he looks, examine his gestures—you want to feel physically the force he brings to his utterances, or perhaps his indifference. In short, you want to measure the man; and for this, there's no substitute for being there in person.

Finally, when the client lets it be known that he wants to see his lawyer—especially when he suggests that the meeting take place at his office—my inclination would be to accede to his wishes. Need I elaborate?

I'm sure each of you can think of other examples when the phone just won't do. What's important is that you give this point some thought *beforehand,* and make a conscious decision whether the action you're about to take should be the subject of a phone call or a face-to-face meeting.

CHAPTER 4

THE INTANGIBLE SKILLS

4.1. WHAT'S LEFT TO LAWYERING?

I'll be candid; this is the chapter of the book I approach with the most trepidation. I have the uneasy feeling that every thought is a near cliché, a parody of some Victorian gentleman lecturing his Horatio Alger-like clerk on getting ahead—work hard, be cheerful, show initiative. But no book on lawyering would be complete without at least a cursory examination of those highly intangible qualities extending beyond the frontiers of analytical prowess and communications skills—qualities essential to the favorable evaluation of a young lawyer.

Let's take a quick overview of these overlapping attributes in the context of a typical situation. The president of a major corporate client, Vehicle Inc., advises me (the partner on the account) that the company has decided to finance its new plant by means of a public offering of common stock. He has held preliminary talks with the company's investment bankers, who have suggested a tentative time schedule that looks pretty tight. I envision a lot of work over a relatively short period of time. This will be the first offering we've ever handled for Vehicle, which hasn't been to the public trough in over five years. The associate who had been handling Vehicle matters has recently left the firm to teach. I check with the partner in charge of associates' assignments, who informs me that you (an associate with five years of general corporate experience, including several public offerings) are nearing completion of some other matters and should be available for this job.

You may not be aware of it (although you ought to be), but from the moment of my first approach on this deal you're being evaluated. The myriad of small impressions that flash across my mind in the course of the transaction will ultimately amalgamate into an overall judgment on your abilities. This isn't cause for paralysis; you don't have to feel you're "on stage" at all times; but it's a fact worth keeping in the back of your mind.

And the first thing I'll notice is your reaction to my initial query: "Good morning, Ellen. I've been told you might have some time available. There's a public offering for Vehicle in the works; I was wondering if you could help me out. We've never had a chance to work together, and this might be a good opportunity." Your reply—more on this later[1]—can set the whole tone of our professional relationship. Then, assuming you do sign on, the enthusiasm with which you approach your duties will also be observed. The public offering is an interesting and important task for me, and I'd want to believe it's the same for you; to put the thought another way, it would be irritating to receive the impression that you're doing me a favor.

Once we get started, I will exhibit real interest in the diligence with which you apply yourself to the project.[2] Shepherding a public offering to market in a brief interval is a difficult and time-consuming task; there are few shortcuts. Even if we can enlist the aid of a junior associate, I would anticipate that you will be spending some nights and perhaps weekends in the office, to meet the accelerated time schedule. And I will certainly consider it odd if, in the middle of Vehicle's offering, I find you've gone to Pittsburgh for two days on a deposition for another client. If you have other matters that can't be postponed or transferred to another associate, bring them to my attention and we'll try to work something out—but otherwise, I will assume you're working full-time on this project.

As your work begins to take shape in the form of a draft prospectus, in addition to analytical and writing skills, I will be observing the accuracy of your presentation, the thoroughness of your approach, the care you take with facts.[3] Are there significant omissions? Have you appropriately indicated points remaining unresolved? Are words and terms used in a consistent manner? Do the cross-references check out? Are there obvious, glaring, typographical errors? In short, does the document display a disciplined or slip-shod approach?

As things become more complex, and we get into meetings with Vehicle's executives, its accountants, and the underwriters, I will be looking for signs that you are well-organized.[4] Do you have the necessary documents at your fingertips, so that when I ask for, say, the company's loan agreement, it's in my hands within moments? Are you on top of this mass of information, or have you let it overwhelm

---

[1]   See Section 4.2.
[2]   See Section 4.3.
[3]   See Section 4.3.
[4]   See Section 4.4.

you? Do you have a sense of priorities—an appreciation of which problems have to be solved before the next step can be taken?

Moving into the home stretch, I'll be cognizant of your productivity,[5] your ability to churn out documents and prose which can be circulated to the working group—not merely having something in the works but actually placing it on our colleagues' desks. This is a results-oriented business; a great many pieces of paper must be produced in the course of a public offering. And produced, moreover, within established deadlines; the concept of productivity subsumes the notion of on-time work.

Inevitably, as in every public offering, the pressure is going to mount as the deadlines approach. I can't help but notice how you react to such pressure.[6] You may have been sailing along up to that point, but all of a sudden the company's time requirements are absurd, the underwriter's demands become unreasonable, the problems loom insurmountable, tempers flare, I'm unavoidably absent—how do you handle all that? Do you rise to the occasion or sink beneath the weight?

So, here we have a number of interrelated aspects of legal practice that they don't teach you in law school, all to be exhibited by you in the course of a single assignment, and which in their totality will form an indelible impression of your abilities in a partner's mind—as well as in the minds of the client and other professionals involved in the project.

4.2. THE ENTHUSIASTIC SELF-STARTER

Perhaps the simplest, but often the most elusive, of these qualities is enthusiasm. I'll say this: taken alone, enthusiasm may not get you all the way home, but it pays real dividends. I can recall meetings where partners were discussing the sub-par performance of a particular associate, and then someone reminded the assemblage of the tremendous zest the associate brings to every project—how powerfully motivated he or she appears to be—and we often end up deciding to give the associate another chance. In any choice between otherwise equal, competent associates, the presence or absence of enthusiasm inevitably enters into the balance.

The reason for this is obvious, once you make an effort to put yourself in the partner's place. This legal stuff you're fooling around with—hey, that's his life's work. You may be uncertain as to whether it will be yours, but while you're at the firm, you may as well give it a shot. I'm not talking about phony enthusiasm either; "faking it" is

---

[5] See Section 4.4.
[6] See Section 4.4.

often easy to spot and may be worse than merely passive behavior. The enthusiasm I mean takes the form of a genuine interest in the law and facts at issue, in the personalities involved, in being helpful to the harried partner, and in solving whatever problems may arise.

In most cases (at 3:00 A.M., I'll admit, it's hard), taking an interest shouldn't be so difficult. Most of us *don't* work on a legal assembly line, fitting in a certain covenant or tying on a single warranty to the same interminable product. Isn't the avoidance of an intellectual rut one of the main reasons we become lawyers? At least in the early years of practice, each matter you undertake has fresh aspects, presenting different intellectual and practical challenges, varying personalities, new uncertainties to be encountered and resolved. You should relish the opportunity to try out fresh negotiating gambits on a clever adversary, to come up with creative solutions to problems. There's nothing more fascinating than to figure out how someone's mind is working and what will motivate him. If you approach your tasks with gusto, your relationships with partners (and ultimately with clients) will be stronger than those of lackadaisical associates.[7] I operate on the premise that, for an inquisitive associate who's eager to learn a profession, the proper mood should be relatively simple to achieve. If you find it difficult, then maybe you ought to find another field more conducive to your interests.

So now we're back to that initial reaction, when the partner first approaches you with a new assignment. What a difference there is between the associate whose response is: "Well, I've got a hell of a lot of other things on my calendar. I just don't know if I can work it in. Isn't there someone else you can get?"—does that sound familiar?—and the associate in the next room who replies: "That sounds like an interesting job, and one I'd like to be involved in. I do have a few other matters I ought to complete first, so it might take two or three days to clear my desk. Will it be all right if I can get started on your job this Friday?"

Inevitably, there will be times when you're really much too busy to take on a major new matter, in which event you should turn it down; the negative impact of a poor performance, whether due to the press of other duties or otherwise, is always much worse than a declination to become involved in the first instance.[8] Even in this situation, how-

---

[7] See Section 10.3 on the partner's responsibility to convey this same zest to associates.

[8] See Section 4.4 on the difficulties of serving two masters. If the project suggested by the partner is a small one, however, you should probably strain your schedule to try to fit it in. We partners are always prepared to be told you can't take on a major project; but frankly, it's bothersome to get turned down on a minor matter that you seemingly could have squeezed in with a little extra effort.

ever, the way you handle matters can be important. Is it so difficult to suggest that you *would* have been interested in taking on the job if circumstances permitted? Pretend for a moment that *you* are the partner; which of the following responses would you rather hear from an associate?

—"I'd really like to handle that acquisition for you, but it's just a bad time for me. I'm working for Ed, Paul and Donna on three different projects, and that's been taking up all my time. I hope—although I can't be sure—that they'll be finished in about three weeks; and if there's anything I can do on your matter at that point, I'd be happy to help."

—"I'm too busy."

There's a term I often hear floating around the office to describe a highly-motivated lawyer: he or she is known as a "self-starter". I'm not sure I can define self-starting for you, but partners know it when they see it—and they're cognizant of its absence.

At the beginning of his or her legal career, most of what an associate does comes under the category of specific assigned tasks—write this memo, research that point of law, draft an agreement. The associate is simply reacting to instructions from on high. But as the associate attains more seniority, the marching orders tend to be more generalized—take care of this transaction, find out what's bugging that client—and opportunities for discretion and initiative increase. Basically, self-starting has to do with how effectively the associate handles these opportunities to implement the partner's objectives.

The high point of an associate's day should occur when the partner calls him in and says: "Now, in connection with that Smith matter, did you think to interview Stevens?" "Yes, I did," replies the associate; "we got his affidavit last week." "But," continues the partner, "I bet you didn't look through that '76 prospectus to see if there was any mention of the agreement." The associate is ready: "We not only did that—which came up empty—but we also looked in the '75 proxy statement and found some things right on point." Believe me, that's impressive! The partner has to come away with a positive view of the associate's initiative. Contrast this with "Have you done X?" "No, I was waiting to speak to you." "What about Y?" "I didn't think of that."

It doesn't all just drop in your lap. Get off your hindquarters and decide what you can do to advance the ball *before* the partner gets around to telling you. Let's say the partner has asked you to draft an acquisition agreement for a client of the firm. You do so and send it to the partner. His secretary, however, informs you that the partner is really under the gun on other matters and probably won't be in a position to review your draft for several days. It follows, you realize, that he won't be able to start assigning you other projects in connection with the acquisition. You could just leave it at that and sit on your hands; after all, you've completed your assignment in a timely manner, and it's not *your* fault that the partner doesn't have time to review it or advance you to the next step. Or, you *could* compose a letter from yourself to the lawyer on the other side, requesting copies of all material documents of the seller corporation that you know you'll have to review; and you *could* place the letter on the partner's desk with a note (which his secretary is instructed to bring to his attention) saying: "Do you mind if I send this out to get things going on the acquisition?" Which approach do you think the partner will appreciate more?

4.3. DILIGENCE AND THE ELEMENT OF DUE CARE

Let us now praise the most mundane of all lawyerly qualities—diligence, industriousness, thoroughness, meticulous attention to detail. Carved out in this fashion, these suggest nothing so much as the earnest plodder, the cautious dullard—plugging away for hours without any flair for the work or spark of creativity. And to be sure, possession of these qualities without more won't take you very far. Yet, if these traits are lacking in your professional personality, all your other prime attributes can come to naught.

Being a lawyer is damned hard work. There are few simple tasks. To accomplish anything worthwhile not only takes brains and creativity, but it also takes time—no matter how brilliant you may be. This is particularly true for an associate, who has to read all the documents, analyze the authorities, dig out the facts, and so forth. Shortcuts should be viewed with extreme caution; many an associate's career has been marred due to one crucial overlooked precedent.

Although most of your work is performed outside of the partner's presence, there are a number of ways by which partners can assess how diligently you're applying yourself—and I don't mean by means of a stopwatch. An experienced attorney has a mental benchmark of how long the drafting of a certain agreement should take and will note this when the draft shows up on his desk. If numerous documents must be perused before a particular event can occur, whether or not you've accomplished this will be noticed when the partner checks on your progress. Your diligence—or lack thereof—will show up.

In this regard, the question is often asked: how many hours should I be working? Even the most industrious associate in a law firm could work a little harder—by coming in an hour earlier or staying thirty minutes later at night or taking some additional documents to peruse on the commute.[8a] Where do you draw the line—that fine line between applying yourself assiduously and yet not blotting out the remainder of your life?

There's no simple answer here. Most lawyers manage somehow to strike their own particular balance. Some young associates make a great show of working at night or on weekends, always careful to come in earlier and stay later than the partner to whom they report. To my way of thinking, true diligence doesn't consist of such optics, nor in the recording of any magic number of billable hours. Most partners I know don't care what time an associate comes in or what time he goes home, as long as he gets his work done in a reasonable fashion.[9] Any mathematical view of industriousness misses out on the crucial qualitative features; we all know lawyers who can accomplish more in ten minutes than some of their colleagues can manage in an hour.

The thoroughness and care which you bring to your practice, the accuracy and appearance of your written work—although requiring diligence, these are not necessarily co-extensive with that quality. Some extremely industrious, hard-working lawyers tend to be rather careless. Painstaking attention to detail is undramatic and not especially ripe for analysis, but it's basic. Making sure that written work has been proofread and doesn't contain errors; checking that correlative provisions are worded consistently; remembering, when something is deleted in one part of a document, to make the appropriate cut elsewhere; what can I say? If the *presence* of this kind of careful lawyering isn't always properly credited, its *absence* can be devastating.

I do want to leave you with one thought in this area, which I call the absence of quantitative features in the concept of quality work. In other words, the little job you're given to do can be just as important as the big ones. Sure, the minor task is easier to do well—but as a

---

[8a] The classical tale in this regard concerned James Byrne and his apprentice, Harrison Tweed. Byrne demanded to know why a memorandum wasn't ready; Tweed answered that he hadn't had time to finish it. Byrne glared at him. "What time did you go home Friday night?" Tweed replied: "Three in the morning." "What about Saturday night?" "Two A.M." Byrne pressed, and Tweed confessed that the next evening he'd departed the office at 11 o'clock. Byrne pounded his desk and said: "Don't tell me that you didn't have time to finish that memorandum. Tell me the truth—that you wanted to go home early Sunday night." As quoted in M. Mayer, *The Lawyers* (1966), at 330.

[9] If, however, a certain partner habitually places a call to your office at precisely 9:30 A.M., it's not good judgment to arrive each day at 9:45. And never, never depart on a vacation leaving a project in midair, without having fully briefed the partner or another associate so the matter can be picked up where you left off.

corollary, you look much worse when you blow it. And that negative impact can blunt an awful lot of good work on major projects.

So, when you start to get those nagging reminders—"Have you formed that Delaware sub yet?" "Did you check out that tax point?" "Where's that letter to the irate stockholder?"—get off the stick and finish the job. And, by the way, if you hear nothing about it, *don't* assume that this small job is as deep in the recesses of the partner's or client's mind as it is in yours. Assume rather, that it's a constantly festering sore.

I will let you in on a secret. In the councils of the partners when an associate is being evaluated, once the major statements have been made by those partners with whom the associate works most closely, one of the other partners will frequently chime in with: "Well, all I know is that he did a small job for me—I'll admit it was no big deal—and I had absolutely no complaints"—which, if the bulk of the prior discussion was unfavorable, can often go a long way toward keeping that associate with the firm (on the theory that he has the talent but just hasn't been applying himself). And conversely, I've heard glowing reports of associate success on major projects seriously marred by the dissenting view of a partner who reports: "Well, she hasn't worked for me much, but I asked her to write one short memorandum back in April and I'm still waiting for it." So, don't procrastinate; overcome inertia; get it done.

4.4 THE WELL-ORGANIZED, PRODUCTIVE, DEADLINE-MEETING ASSOCIATE

In this section, I want to talk about a species of somewhat more sophisticated, overlapping traits: organization, productivity and timeliness.

So often I hear the subjective appelation of "well-organized" applied to one of the promising young lawyers in the firm; on the other hand, lawyers who receive poor marks are not infrequently described as "disorganized." One begins to wonder whether the characterization possesses some independent significance—or is it just a result-oriented, shorthand description of other abilities? Am *I* well-organized? If the term implies cutting through red tape and having a sense of priorities—if it starts to verge on being productive and meeting deadlines and such—then I may be on the right track. But if organization is what I fear—a quality with its own distinct essence of good order, fine-tuning and the like—then one look at my hopeless desk, the littered byways of hastily scribbled notes and deferred actions and unfinished business and unread periodicals and whatnot, forces me to face up to the fact that whatever it is, I ain't. So, in the absence of a clear role model, these next few paragraphs can be taken to represent wishful thinking.

What a delight for a partner when an associate has a matter so well in hand that the partner is convinced nothing's slipping through the cracks—and that accordingly, the case doesn't require his total attention. The well-organized associate who has all the relevant documents in files where he can locate the one you want at a moment's notice; who has checklists of items to be discussed and marks them off as they're accomplished; who works out schedules and timetables of events and actually follows them—this individual leaves impressions that go far beyond narrowly-based concepts of legal skills.

I don't mean to imply that this is a cosmetic quality—a demeanor one can adopt at will for the occasion. It's real—it works—for I have seen with my own eyes several good lawyers transformed into excellent lawyers by the rather simple application of some hard-nosed organization into their professional lives. Disorganization not only hampers your work but creates negative impressions; get yourself organized and you solve both problems.[10]

Avoiding the previously noted dilemma of serving two masters simultaneously comes also under the rubric of organization.[11] The practice of law in a firm requires a number of delicate juggling acts; associates frequently find themselves handling several cases for different partners at the same time. The well-organized associate, retaining a sense of priorities and refusing to let himself be torn in two, attempts to head off the confrontation that can develop when one partner, who thinks the associate is working on *his* project, finds out he's busily engaged somewhere else.

So, if a second partner asks the associate to interrupt his project for the first partner in order to take on a crucial short-term matter, the associate—who would like to oblige the second partner[12]—makes a point of going to the first partner to report what has been asked of him. (Surprisingly enough, in actual practice this *doesn't* always happen.) If the time pressure of the first job is not that tight and the first partner is satisfied that the associate's attention can be diverted temporarily, well and good. If there's a need to complete the first job promptly, then the two partners will just have to work out the priorities between themselves—but the associate doesn't allow himself to be squeezed in the middle.

Questions of priority can also arise in the context of working for one partner on a single project. You've completed and sent out the

---

[10]   Organizing one's professional life is not unlike the substantive organization of a document through outlining and such, as discussed in Section 3.2.2.

[11]   See, e.g., Section 4.2.

[12]   See Section 4.2.

basic acquisition agreement; do you turn now to the document creating an escrow for part of the purchase price or the employment contracts for the seller's key executives? Sometimes it doesn't matter, but often it can. The seller's president may be leaving town in a few days, and your client would like him to see the employment contract before he goes; if you're working on the escrow, you might miss connections. Often you can determine the relative priorities on a strictly logical basis (break the eggs first; *then* make the omelet). In other cases, you may need (and should seek) direction from the partner[13] or client.

Here's how I approach the subject of productivity. We're not being paid for our jurisprudential or philosophic musings. Almost everything we do represents some sort of problem-solving, of coming to grips with a real issue. (The scientific analogy would be to applied technology, as contrasted with basic research.) And this inevitably requires us to turn out work, usually in the form of pieces of paper—our stock in trade. So I'm always very conscious of whether an associate actually produces usable work. It's not enough for the wheels to spin; nothing really counts until the document lands on the other fellow's desk. Having a draft of the agreement almost finished, at a time when the partner wants to send it to the client, just isn't good enough; it has to be *ready* to go. And in this regard, it matters not whether the hold-up is due to forty items or a single omission.

In the prior chapters[14], I've stressed the need for *thinking* about a project before starting in on it. Productivity commences at the point when you *stop* thinking about the project and start *doing* something about it. If you're writing a memorandum based on legal research, there comes a point when you have to conclude the research and begin to write, even though there are other possible avenues you're tempted to pursue. Similarly, the investigation of factual matters can —but shouldn't—go on forever. The practice of law is an imperfect science. Almost nothing is ever complete, or neat, or pat; there will always be open holes and caveats and uncertainties and imperfections. Don't become paralyzed with inaction.[15] Sense when the point has

---

13   For the partner's role in this, see Section 10.3.
14   See, e.g., Sections 2.1, 3.2.1, 3.2.2, 3.3.1 and 3.3.3.
15   In this regard, see the discussion about the importance of initially getting your thoughts down on paper—no matter how unstructured or unpolished they may be—in Section 3.2.3. Sometimes, *too much* knowledge can induce the same kind of writer's block. I am reminded of the probably apocryphal story that used to circulate about one of our college instructors, reputed to be the world's leading authority on some arcane subject, who was simply unable to write his Ph.D. thesis—ostensibly because his overabundance of knowledge gave rise to an exception for every assertion, an unruly specific for each generalization, and so forth.

come to announce or prepare your conclusions. If you feel they're tentative, then label them as such.[16] But you simply must bite the bullet.

The key to productivity is the ability to overcome roadblocks in the way of completing work. There are countless ways to skin almost any cat you encounter—all in the interests of avoiding frustrating obstacles to progress. I've selected a few examples to illustrate what I have in mind.

A partner has asked you to investigate and determine whether certain actions taken by one of the firm's corporate clients constitute an unfair labor practice. Although the partner omitted to set a deadline for your memo on the subject, you detected a note of some urgency in the assignment. You perform your factual investigation, interview participants and witnesses, and check the applicable law. Your tentative conclusion is that no violation of law has occurred. The only gap in your analysis is that one important witness has been on vacation and will be unreachable for another four or five days. Although theoretically her testimony could jeopardize your conclusion, you have picked up enough evidence through hearsay and otherwise to be reasonably assured that her story won't upset the applecart. Should you: (i) do nothing until she returns, then interview her promptly, and write your memo; (ii) draft the memo now (with a hole for her testimony), wait for her return, interview her promptly, and complete the memo; or (iii) do the memo now and give it to the partner?

Under these circumstances, I would opt for alternative (iii). It seems to me the partner is entitled to know where you stand, just as soon as you believe you have things under control. Of course, the memo should contain a paragraph alluding to the missing testimony and the outside chance it could change the result, plus an undertaking to update the memo when her testimony can be taken. Alternative (i)—the do-nothing approach—is clearly wrong. The problem with alternative (ii) is that the partner is just as much in the dark as to the outcome of the matter as if you chose alternative (i), or hadn't otherwise almost completed your investigation. Look at it from *his* vantage point, which might well include the necessity to respond to a phone call from the client inquiring as to where the investigation stands. Don't hesitate when you're so close to the mark.

Now let's say you are analyzing for a client a proposed series of securities transactions which involve, among other things, the purchase and almost immediate resale of a block of stock. After spending some time on the project, you have learned all the relevant facts and have analyzed the matter fully, except for one thing—you still don't know whether the seller of the block could be deemed a

---

[16]   See Section 3.2.8.

controlling person of the issuer, in which case your client would have to acquire the block under investment letter and would be restricted in making the contemplated resale. Another law firm has promised to furnish you information on this point in a few days. Should you at this point render legal advice to the client? Clearly not. The issue on which you lack facts is such an integral element of the entire analysis that without such knowledge you would simply be going through a hypothetical—and perhaps dangerous—exercise.

All right. Several days pass and you learn that the seller is *not* in control of the issuer. You proceed with your analysis, and are ready to deliver an advisory letter on the matter to the client, when it suddenly occurs to you that you have never seen the stock certificates evidencing the block of shares. It's just possible (although none of the other facts has pointed in this direction) that the certificates could bear on their face some restrictions upon transfer which would be binding on the recipient. A quick check reveals that the shares are locked in a vault, with the sole custodian out of town for several days. Should you hold up your letter until he returns? Definitely not. Your letter ought to indicate that you haven't had an opportunity to physically examine the certificates, that the possibility exists of their bearing restrictive language, and that they should be examined before any transaction takes place (or the client becomes contractually committed). But you're ready to give your advice *now*, and this particular detail—especially where you've had no alarm signals to put you on guard—ought not to detain you.

One of the firm's corporate clients has been discussing a joint venture arrangement with another company. The president of your client—the only executive in the place who's familiar with the matter—briefs you on the details and asks you to draft an appropriate agreement. The president is anxious that the other company understand he is serious about this deal, which the draft agreement will accomplish; and since he's about to go overseas for two weeks, he authorizes you to send it to the other side without his review.

In drafting the agreement, you realize that you forgot to ask the president one important question: since the joint venture participants will be obligated to invest up to $1,000,000 each in the deal over the next 12 months, and inasmuch as the other party appears to be financially unstable, should the parties place the full amount of the funds in some sort of joint escrow account at the outset, to insure that the money will be available as needed? It would be easy enough to insert a provision to that effect in the draft agreement; however, the other party might take offense at the implied suggestion that he wasn't financially responsible—the word "escrow" does possess an unusual capacity to make blood boil—which is a risk you hate to run without your client's advance blessing. Unfortunately, the client is now unreachable. On the other hand, if you say nothing about the escrow, and your client later decides he *does* want some such arrangement, it may be more difficult to introduce into the negotiations—the other side using the initial omission as a concession on your part. Do you (i) put the provision in, (ii) leave it out, or (iii) hold up the agreement until the president returns?

My solution to this not atypical dilemma would be to send out the draft agreement with all other provisions in place and, at the point where the escrow would otherwise appear, a statement along these lines: "[Here insert provisions, to be discussed between the parties, relating to the funding of the moneys being invested in the venture.]" This raises the issue sufficiently so that if your client wants to take a hard escrow line, no one can accuse you of having waived anything; at the same time, the other party cannot possibly take offense at this point, since you've specifically noted that the details of the "funding" (a nice neutral word, less potentially explosive than "escrow" and therefore appropriate for these purposes) remain to be discussed between the parties. Most important, you didn't let the problem keep you from advancing the ball—which was exactly what your client had in mind when he left.

A word about deadlines. By now, I'm sure you've all realized that there are deadlines and then there are deadlines. Some can be quite artificial, imposed for no other reason than to instill a sense of urgency in the people working on the transaction; a lawyer's reaction to these should be characterized more by flexibility than slavish adherence. On the other hand, there are real deadlines—the date by which briefs are due, the last day for filing registration statements, and so on; and the ability to meet these deadlines in timely fashion should never be minimized. An associate who repeatedly fails to meet deadlines—no matter how plausible each individual excuse appears—ends up with a black eye.

Part of the trick of meeting deadlines is learning to pace yourself. As you perform particular tasks for the second and third time, you begin to develop a sense of how long certain jobs take. Once you've done a first draft of a typical acquisition agreement, you're in a pretty good position to gauge how many hours the next one will require. Upon receiving the assignment, ask the partner when he needs to receive the first draft. If the date he selects seems within your capacity, you can pace yourself handily during this period to turn the work out on time. Alternatively, figure out yourself how long it will take and say to the partner: "Look, I estimate I'll have this done by late afternoon Thursday. Is that satisfactory for your purposes?" Actually, this is preferable from your point of view, because it allows *you* to fix the timetable—whereas the partner might be tempted to push things ahead to a date somewhat earlier than what you had in mind.

Finally, a word about handling pressure. Writing from the depths of a pretty high-powered Manhattan law firm, I recognize I might have an exaggerated notion of the pressures on attorneys engaged in business law and related litigation. Nevertheless, it's no secret that practicing law is not a nine-to-five occupation. There *are* deadlines; there *are* pressures; and the ability to work under stress is an important characteristic of a good lawyer. Rising to the occasion is clearly more impressive than wilting under the load. This quality of grace under pressure, so over-romanticized in other aspects of life (athletics, politics, etc.), is no less apt in a law office. I'm not going to attempt an analysis, or suggest how to attain it; for all I know it's not an acquirable trait. If you find you're one of those people who don't perform well under stress, then you should consider shifting into an area of law where the pressures are less noticeable, and a more orderly process holds sway.

CHAPTER 5

DEALING WITH PARTNERS
AND OTHER COLLEAGUES

Up to this point we've been examining a quiver of skills for an associate to tote through his practice—with the emphasis on the skills rather than the practice. However, lawyers don't operate in a vacuum, but among real people—partners and other colleagues, clients, adversaries and regulators—and your relations with those people are as crucial to your future as the level of your operating skills. These relations form the subject matter of the next three chapters. This chapter touches primarily on the partners,[1] with additional material on relationships with other associates, those within corporate and governmental legal groupings, and practising law on your own.

5.1. DEALING WITH PARTNERS

5.1.1. Adapting to the Partner-Associate Relationship.

The structure of the typical law firm—partners on the one hand and associates on the other—places considerable emphasis on the associate's relationships with the partners as a group. Unlike the situation in the usual pyramidical hierarchy, the ultimate decision on the associate's future—his admission to partnership—will be made by the partner group. Over the years, the associate will have an opportunity to work for a number of the partners who call that ultimate shot. So, the focus here is on how the associate should handle partners—and don't mistake the fact, there is some handling involved.[1a]

---

[1] One notable omission in these pages on various collegial relations is the relationship between partners themselves—representing the boundary at which my good sense overcame a striving for comprehensiveness.

[1a] For a discussion of the ambivalence in the self-image of associates—the difficult problem of professional people who are still employees—see E. Smigel, *The Wall Street Lawyer* (1964) [hereinafter cited as "Smigel"], at 230 and 296 *et seq.*

Our starting point is that no two partners are alike, and each calls for individualized treatment. Generalizations are hazardous. I can conceive of partners with messianic tendencies, where typical associate overtures might be construed as unwarranted garment-hem-touching, and the safest course is to lob memo missiles in from a discreet distance. Or partners who have never departed Siwash U. in spirit, where failure to begin each day with the old fraternity handshake constitutes a material omission. Still, most partners turn out to be human beings, with minimal ogre features.

Oh, I'm sure there are firms where the conventional wisdom is that the partners comprise a classic "in" group, jealously guarding their domain and feeling threatened when an associate distinguishes himself. And there are individual tales of woe—"I didn't become a partner because old Jarvis didn't like me" (spoken so as to imply that *I* was normal and competent while Jarvis' behavior was bizarre and irrational). I would never proclaim total fairness for the system or deny the existence of circumstances where individuals have been wronged. But my experience has been that, in the overwhelming number of cases, merit is appropriately rewarded.

You may feel that this is partner propaganda I've been hired to spread, but the plain fact is that the typical partner—even if he doesn't let it show—*is* interested in having you succeed. For a number of reasons, the better you perform, the happier he is. First and foremost, if you're any good, he can depend on you; this lifts a heavy load off his back. So long as you remain as an associate, however, there are limits to what you can take over for him; partnership confers the added stature needed to permit him to substitute you in his place with increasing frequency. Conversely, your lack of success presages little respite for the partner, who will be acutely uncomfortable leaving you on your own.

Then too, your advancement creates a number of potential ego satisfactions for the partner. If he played a role in hiring you, it tends to confirm his initial judgment. Your success supports his self-image as a good teacher and role model; he feels his message has gotten across. And never forget, that in order for this partner to start slowing down in his sixties and ultimately to retire, free from concern over repayment of his capital and other moneys due from the firm, he will be looking to you and your peers as the source of such bounty. So partners realize practical and personal benefits in having you join their ranks; and in my experience, few partners are so jealous of their clients or so insecure within the firm as not to root for your ultimate success.

This theme of associate/yesterday-partner/today, or associate/today-partner/tomorrow—the law firm analogue to West Point's long gray line—is central to the partner-associate relationship. We tend to focus on a particular moment in time; but the *process* is also important and provides a frame for our discussion. For example, the tone of your relationship with the partner may differ substantially as between a situation where you're a senior associate and he's a junior partner (who only two years ago was your fellow associate), and the case where you're the most wide-eyed of associates and he's the senior partner of the firm. I leave these nuances to your own good judgment—with merely a suggestion that where a senior partner is involved (and here I refer less to status than to age), even one who has adopted a posture as "one of the boys", certain formalities should be observed, with some deference to his position being definitely in order.

I firmly believe that, without sacrificing your integrity or sublimating your brains, you can and should make an effort to adjust yourself to the style of the particular partner with whom you're dealing. His style may not be yours, and yours may be infinitely preferable; but he is entitled to his way of doing things—he's earned it—and at this moment in time, your stylistic rights haven't vested. Later on, when you become a partner, the roles may well be reversed, with some upstart associate chafing at the need to fall into line behind you—but my position then would be consistent: *you're* entitled to call the shots. Oh, I suppose some iconoclasts and curmudgeons—driven by the need to constantly assert their own individuality—can make it to partnership and beyond on ability alone; but if you're like most of us, with a less exalted sense of self and normal organizational leanings, then it's worthwhile making an effort to get into step with the man or woman for whom you work. Save your individuality for matters of substance—analytical ability, fine writing, good judgment—rather than of style.

In deciding how to handle a particular partner, the first thing to do is study his habits—guidance in this regard will undoubtedly be forthcoming from other associates—and devise a mental checklist of his particular quirks. Is this partner, for instance, the type who wants the associate to report to him with every question of any significance, to make no decisions on his own, to render constant status updates, and the like? Or would he be pleased for you to handle routine (and maybe even some less-than-routine) matters by yourself and only come running when something significant happens? Does the partner prefer his communications with the associate to be oral or in writing—and, if written, is there a certain format he has encouraged you and others to use? Does he wish to personally undertake all of the dealings with the client, or with the other lawyer, or with the SEC—or would he just as soon not be bothered? When you send out correspondence, is it sufficient to send him a copy, or should he see the letter before it leaves the office? If another associate senior to you is working on the matter, does the partner want you to communicate through the other associate, or should all roads lead directly to him? How much initiative does he expect you to display?

Once you've sized up the partner, then adjust your style accordingly. You might feel perfectly qualified to send a certain letter to the client on your own, but if your reading of the partner is that he'd like a crack at it first, let him have it. If after several such forays you are reasonably confident that the partner will be satisfied with your correspondence, then send him the letter in final form with a note, saying: "I'm about to send this out. Please let me know if you have any problems." If, on the other hand, he's the kind of partner (I suppose I would fall into this category) who feels strongly about nuance in other-than-routine matters, and so is likely to put his own imprimatur on such letters, then send him a double-spaced draft with plenty of room for his own interpolations—that final-form method will just serve to antagonize him.[2]

Let's assume you're a relatively new associate, somewhat unsure of yourself, who would like to have the comfort of a partner's blessing before making even minor decisions or taking inconsequential actions. You find yourself working for a partner who is running all over the place, with few spare moments and a reputation for not wanting to be bothered with trivia.[3] Hard as it may seem, if you don't want to end up in the doghouse, you simply must bite the bullet and make those small decisions. Presumably, you can obtain some assistance from more senior associates. But it's just not prudent to accost that partner on his way to the elevator in order to raise a trifling point.

When a partner is being handled well by an associate, the partner usually doesn't notice it—or to put the thought another way, the absence of awareness on the partner's part that the associate is striving to adapt himself to the partner is a good barometer by which to measure the associate's success in the venture. It's *mishandling* that raises the partner's consciousness. And what bothers the partner most is for an associate, *knowing* the partner's presumed desires, to

---

[2] Two further suggestions: when you've slightly modified a long draft, mark the changes so the partner doesn't have to wade through the whole thing again; and when a letter or memo refers to a key case or contractual provision or whatever, attach a copy of the case or original document so the partner can examine it if he so wishes.

[3] Here's a body language clue. If the partner is writing as you enter his office, and when glancing up to receive your message he *doesn't* put down his pen, make your report brief and get the hell out of there.

do the opposite. For example, let's say a certain client has instructed me to send a personal cover letter with his monthly bill, as a means of insuring that I've personally reviewed the amount of the charge. So I've adopted the practice of attaching a one-sentence note. ("Enclosed please find . . ."). However, I forget to tell this to a new associate, and he sends out a routine bill to the client without my cover letter. Since an unaccompanied bill isn't unusual, I can't get too mad at the associate. If, on the other hand, I had *told* the associate that I wished to append a one-sentence cover letter to this client's statements—even if I had neglected to advise the associate of my reason and he put it down to eccentricity—and *then* the associate transmits a bill to the client without one, I would get sore as hell. The associate may have considered the cover letter superfluous, but that just wasn't his decision to make; rather he should have adapted himself to my ways, however foolish they may have seemed.

Associates ought to realize that a partner tends to extrapolate from an associate's behavior toward *him* just how the associate will handle a client under similar circumstances. If an associate displays a consistent indifference to instructions of the partner, then even if the partner would be inclined to overlook this vis-à-vis himself, he begins to wonder whether this same attitude carries over to the associate's handling of clients. Or when an associate becomes sarcastic or abrasive with a partner in the course of a discussion over the proper way to handle a corporate disclosure, the partner may well think to himself: if we were involved in a public offering, and the associate was in a prospectus-drafting session with company executives and the underwriter's team, could this same abrasiveness—ordinarily out of place in such a setting—rise to the surface? And clearly, if a senior associate consistently abuses his juniors, this will be considered indicative of how he might act toward associates generally as a partner.

5.1.2. Reports, Questions, Problems and Bad News.

In this section, I want to discuss a variety of situations whose common theme is that *you* are initiating the contact with the partner. Perhaps you have a status report to make;[4] or a question has arisen that you think requires the partner's attention; or a problem needs solving; or you're the bearer of some news (hopefully good news, more often bad). And the first issue to be addressed—which goes to the core of the whole partner-associate relationship—is how often and in what manner should the associate initiate these professional contacts.

This is not an easy question to answer, but as with most things in

---

4   See Section 3.3.1 on oral reporting generally.

life, the two extremes are equally untenable. An associate who constantly barges in on the partner, interrupting the latter's schedule with a myriad of reports and questions and problems of varying degrees of importance, becomes a real irritant. Central to your perceptions of the associate-partner relationship should be the realization that, while the particular case on which you're exclusively working occupies unrivaled importance in your personal lexicon, the partner may have three other matters of equal magnitude demanding his attention, as well as a dozen less significant diversions—and he must divide his time and attention accordingly. But the other extreme can even be worse: where you never approach the partner on your own, where every contact between the two of you is initiated by the partner who wants to know how things are going, what problems are coming up, etc.. Your lack of initiative may be no less conspicuous than the ubiquitous presence of your overbearing counterpart.[5]

So, this is one of those areas where you have to exercise judgment and pick your spots. Even in the absence of burning issues, you should let the partner know you're alive by voluntary appearances at appropriate intervals (preferably, at moments when the partner appears to be under minimum pressure—a state of affairs on which his secretary can provide useful input), to deliver a brief status report on significant matters you're handling for him. If possible, key your reports to *changes* in the status of the matter, although if much time passes without any development, you might still want to pop in or send a note to indicate you're on top of things. If you're in doubt whether a development would be considered significant enough in the partner's mind to warrant a report, one useful technique is to introduce it in this fashion: "Just in case Farnsworth [the client] should happen to mention something about this to you, I thought you ought to be aware that. . . ."

Approaching the partner with questions or problems presents a more difficult issue. You should always make a conscious decision as to whether a particular question or problem is one that the *partner* will perceive as appropriate for you to bring to him.[6] As between sins of commission and omission in this respect, there's simply no contest; it's far worse *not* to consult a partner on a matter that he believes you should have, than to bother him unnecessarily with a problem he feels you should have solved yourself.[7] So, any doubts ought to be resolved in favor of running the issue by the partner.

---

[5] On initiative and self-starting generally, see Section 4.2.
[6] On the subject of sensitivity to a partner's quirks in this respect, see Section 5.1.1.
[7] For an analogy to the commission-omission dichotomy in writings, see Section 3.2.8.

It's impossible to be comprehensive on what constitute proper (or improper) matters to raise with the partner, but let me put a little flesh on the bones of this principle by several illustrative situations that I believe fall on one side or another of the line. In each of these, let's assume that you're an associate with four or five years' experience, who has been assuming gradually increasing responsibilities.

1. Ten days ago you filed a registration statement with the SEC for a corporate client's proposed public offering of securities. Today an SEC staff attorney calls you on the telephone.

a. He says that, contrary to the implication in your filing cover letter, your client *will* need updated financial statements in the final prospectus. Proceed instantly to the partner; do not pass "Go"! This news can be devastating to the proposed time schedule for the offering, and the partner should immediately be apprised of the staff position in order to lobby for an administrative change of heart or accelerate compliance by the client.

b. The staff attorney advises that he wants certain items to be filed as supplemental information. The inclusion of one of the listed items suggests to you that the staff might be considering some additional comments on the filing that could prove troublesome. On balance, you should report your suspicions to the partner, although haste is probably unnecessary. Even better: *before* approaching the partner, ascertain from the staff attorney the reason behind this request. If your inference then proves incorrect, I wouldn't bother the partner with the document request.

c. The sole reason for the staff attorney's call is to alert you to the fact that the SEC will require a consent from the mining engineer whose name is used in the prospectus. No need to bother the partner here; pass along the information to the company—or if you're dealing directly with the engineer, handle it yourself.

2. You represent the purchaser in an acquisition. Negotiations over your first draft of the merger agreement have resolved most of the points at issue. You prepare and send out to the seller's attorney a second draft, revised to incorporate the results of these negotiations. You then receive a call from the seller's attorney.

a. He hasn't had a chance to go over your second draft carefully, but he did notice Section 2(a) (regarding an escrow of part of the purchase price), which he feels completely misstates the understanding of the parties on the point—and since the matter is so basic, he just wanted to call that to your attention without delay. By all means, relay this quickly to the partner—after telling the seller's lawyer, of course, that he's all wet. Prompt action could be important in solving this problem, which will probably also involve a business decision on the part of the client.

b. In reviewing your draft, the seller's attorney noticed that you had omitted a representation on the part of the purchaser regarding its SEC filings—a representation that the seller's attorney claims to have specifically requested in the negotiations, without objection from your side. In fact, you and the partner had discussed this very point in preparing the second draft. The decision was made that since the seller's request was a little vague ("Just tell me that what's available publicly is true . . ."), it wouldn't constitute bad faith for the second draft to limit the purchaser's warranty to its published financial statements. It was clear to you both, however, that if the seller demanded a representation on the full-blown SEC filings, he was entitled to it. I don't think you have to rush to the partner with this news. When and if the opportunity presents itself, I'd let him know that your little ruse didn't work, and the seller was demanding what you feared he might.

c. The seller's attorney has been working on the schedules to the agreement and he noticed that the second draft omits any "Schedule 5" (although there is a "4" and a "6"); also, there doesn't seem to be any schedule provided for him to list the patents you've asked him about. Don't bother the partner with this; you can work out the details and point out any changes necessitated at the time of the next revised draft.

3. You represent a publicly-held corporate client, which is in good financial shape. The company has a sizeable term loan agreement with its major bank. The financial vice president of the client calls you.

a. He says that, on the basis of some quarterly numbers being prepared by his accounting people for distribution in a few days, the company may be in technical violation of the net quick assets test under the loan agreement, due to a quirk in last month's operations. It's no big deal, says the vice president, but he just wanted his law firm to know. Tell the partner immediately. Any violation, however technical, of a company's principal debt instrument can be a serious matter—possibly touching off other cross-defaults, reporting requirements and the like. This can probably be headed off by getting a waiver in advance. Let the partner call the shot.

b. The vice president says that the company is considering taking a certain action that he realizes will require bank consent. It won't happen immediately, since it requires Board approval; and the company does intend ultimately to seek the necessary waiver. No need to go flying in to the partner here. In due time, he should be informed; but it sounds quite routine, and you'll probably be able to handle the whole thing yourself.

c. The vice president asks whether, if the company were to take a certain action, it would violate the agreement and thus require a consent. A similar question came up several years ago, at which time you and the partner had concluded that consent was required. Don't say: "Wait, I've got to check this with the partner." If you're sure what the document says, don't even say: "Wait, I've got to check the document." Give him the answer right off the bat; show you're on top of his affairs. Clients like that kind of treatment.[8]

One footnote, with importance in psychological terms: try to avoid the trap of only initiating contacts with the partner when a serious problem occurs or there has been an adverse development. I've seen this happen, with a resultant negative tone to the whole partner-associate relationship. The partner, seeing you coming, involuntarily cringes—knowing you're the inevitable harbinger of some bad news or on the verge of serving up a new knotty problem for him to solve. If this seems to be happening, make a point of interspersing among the downbeat visits a "good news" call or two—or at least a neutral status report—so that the partner doesn't come to view you as the local Cassandra.

The most salient thought I can leave with you on this subject is as follows: when you do come to the partner with a question or problem, proffer your own proposed answer or solution for his ultimate determination.[9] Remember, you've known about this long enough to reflect on the merits; the partner is getting it cold. It's much easier for a partner to react to a proposed solution than to devise one himself from scratch. More importantly, this is your golden opportunity to display initiative.

In fact, I would go so far as to say that, unless the partner is one of those irrepressible "Please-mom-I'd-rather-do-it-myself" types, don't wait for his response to the problem but offer your proposed solution first. If he tends toward the instantaneous reaction, you can introduce the subject as follows: "A problem has come up that I think I know how to solve, but I just wanted to get your reaction to what I propose to do." This puts him on notice that you'll be tendering a possible solution; it would almost be churlish of him to deny you the opportunity to strut your stuff.

There is one rather sensitive area in which you as an associate can be of great value to the partner: namely, in serving as his eyes and ears vis-à-vis relations with the client. Often, officials of a client company—particularly those in the second echelon—will be more candid about such matters with the associate than with the partner. On other occasions, an alert associate can sense the presence of irritants in the

---

[8] More on this in Section 6.3.
[9] The partner should encourage this also; see Section 10.2.2

relationship that could stand an application of balm. Your prompt report on the subject to the partner will be much appreciated.

However, a ticklish situation can develop when you discover that the client's unhappiness is specifically directed at the *partner* for whom you're working. Let's assume this is not just an inference on your part; the client has let his hair down to you on the subject—and you're reasonably certain that the partner is unaware of the client's dissatisfaction. What do you do? Should you ignore this as none of your business, and assume that either it will blow over or the client will let the partner know directly? Or should you risk the fate of the Hellenic bearer of bad tidings?

I can't give you one answer that fits all situations, but I will say this much. So often in these cases, when you cut through the camouflage, the client's unhappiness boils down to one fact: he feels the partner isn't paying enough attention to him. The partner is off on other matters, leaving you—an associate—to carry the ball; and this is the client's way of letting the firm know how he feels about the slight. It seems to me that when you sense this lies at the root of the problem—notwithstanding the client's apparent focus on more substantive issues—you ought to tell the partner what's going on. There's no need for embarrassment on your part. Be diplomatic, of course; don't linger over the details of the client's diatribe, but merely state your view that the situation can be readily rectified by the partner devoting some additional time—"and I *know* how busy you've been"—to the client's affairs. As long as you don't appear to be gloating over the partner's discomfiture, he should ordinarily be grateful for your insight. It's a problem he can probably solve with a phone call or two; and yet, if you hadn't advised him, he may have been too busy or inattentive to realize what was happening.

If the client dissatisfaction with the partner stems from something more serious than inattention—such as where the client believes he's been misadvised—then your problem is more acute. My rule of thumb here is that if you disagree with the client's negative judgment, or if the situation is otherwise soluble by the partner, then you ought to let the partner know—in your best diplomatic fashion—so that he can have a shot at fixing things up. One face-saving technique here is to put the matter to the partner in terms such as: "Apparently Tatum [the client] didn't understand you and *thought* you had advised him that. . . ." On the other hand, if the partner *was* wrong and it's too late to rectify, or if you sense that the client just doesn't like the cut of the partner's jib, you're probably best advised to stay out of the situation.

5.1.3. Disagreements with the Partner

The thorniest of all issues arises when the associate finds himself in disagreement with the partner over a professional matter. Should the associate yield quietly, or should he stand up to the partner? How can the associate handle the dispute so as to avoid creating an irreparable breach between them?

In dealing with this issue, I find it helpful to make a threshold distinction between whether the disagreement arises over a question of legal analysis or a proposed course of action. Let's start with the legal analysis. You've presented your views on the subject to the partner, and he announces his disagreement with your conclusion. Well, the first thing for you to do is reexamine your conclusion. After all, the partner has been at this legal business longer than you, and it's dangerous to underrate the possibility that he just may be right—that you've overlooked a case or a regulation or taken a wrong turn in your reasoning process. If after such review, however, you still think you're right, my advice is to stick to your guns. If the partner wants to overrule you and sign the opinion letter (or whatever) adopting a legal position with which you disagree, that's his prerogative—but he should realize that you're not in accord with his determination.[9a]

You may be able to head the partner off from going over the edge. First, be sure to strive for the correct tone to your disagreement. The dispute should be purely on a professional basis—never descending to a personal level—with a tacit acknowledgment on your part that this is a matter upon which intelligent men of goodwill can differ. Assuming the right tone exists, with some partners it may be possible for you to say: "Why don't we run this by Bernie [another partner with some peripheral connection to the engagement], just to get a third view on the matter?" This is a little ticklish, however; that suggestion really should emanate from the partner.[10] If it seems inappropriate, but you're concerned that the firm may be issuing an incorrect opinion, then seek out a senior associate whose judgment you respect, relate the problem, and see how he reacts on a substantive level. If he comes out your way, he might also be a good source of advice as to how best to proceed.

Let's assume neither of these approaches is feasible. Well, knowing

---

[9a] "Disputatious behavior on the part of an employee in most bureaucratic situations would be considered nonconformity. Disputation on the part of the lawyer in . . . large firms is conformity. Traditions of the legal profession require it. . . . [D]ispute helps the associate keep his professional independence. The partners are able continuously to sharpen their legal minds, and the client receives the benefits of the free give and take." Smigel, *supra* note 1a, at 322.

[10] See Section 10.5.2.

when to stop on a disagreement is a matter of good judgment; and in most cases, once you've reiterated your position strongly, the matter will probably end there. But what if it's a significant issue which could cause harm to the firm? Should *you* take the additional step of going to another partner? This can backfire if you're wrong on the substantive issue. But if you know you're right, then I say to go. Pick a partner with whom you enjoy good relations. Don't go into the gory details of the disagreement between you and the first partner; just put the legal question to him. If he comes out the first partner's way, then forget the whole thing. If he comes out your way, thank him for his help and leave—still without getting into your delicate problem. Then tell the first partner that you mentioned this issue to the second partner over lunch as a hypothetical (without revealing it was the subject of a difference of opinion), and he came out the same way you did. This should certainly give the first partner pause. If he nevertheless perseveres, then I think you ought to go back to the second partner, tell him what is happening, and let him head off the first partner from issuing the opinion. This is an awful position to find yourself in, however, and you should pull out all the stops to avoid ending up there.

On the other hand, if the question is one of pursuing a practical course of action (as contrasted with legal analysis), it seems to me that once you've indicated to the partner your disagreement with his contemplated course, have explained the reasoning behind your views, and have made sure he's not relying on any mistaken assumptions—and still haven't gotten anywhere—the better part of valor is to yield gracefully. I have in mind here such matters as developing a negotiating strategy, deciding whether to send a document to the other side before your client has seen it, delaying a filing to include some last-minute information, and so on. Matters such as these involve essentially subjective judgments; and it's his shot to call. He might well be wrong, but this is the kind of mistake a partner ought to be allowed to make.

No matter what kind of disagreement the partner and you may have between yourselves, a united front should be presented to the client and adversary. Avoid second-guessing and back-stabbing in public —and in the firm, too—much as you might be tempted. This seemingly uncontroversial advice, however, is not without problems; for example, what should you do if, in the middle of a meeting with the client (or with your adversary), the partner makes a statement that you know is incorrect? Here's a situation which calls for extreme sensitivity in handling.

Once again, I see an important threshold distinction turning on the *kind* of incorrect statement which the partner has made. If his error relates to a factual matter, there's nothing particularly offensive in your speaking up—respectfully, of course—and noting that he may be mistaken on the point. "I believe, Phil, that the date of the meeting was February 23rd, not March 2nd." "Phil, I think it was Oswald who made that remark, not Warren." It's not a big deal; anyone can recall a fact incorrectly. If the error is immaterial to the rest of the discussion, don't even bother to stop and correct it.

It's quite a different matter, however, if the partner adopts an erroneous position on a legal issue during a meeting with clients or other lawyers. Even if you're pretty sure he's mistaken, try to avoid contradicting him in front of the others. Wait for your first opportunity to speak to the partner privately—taking care that the fact of your private conversation doesn't signal anything to the others—and then let him know you think he was wrong. This gives the partner an opportunity to devise a clever means of backing off his position—if, in fact, he was mistaken—without having to improvise a hasty and embarrassing retreat in front of all the others.

What about the rare situation when a partner proposes to you a course of action that you consider unethical? Under pressure, each of us can temporarily lose our ethical bearings, while cooler heads—further removed from the emotions of the matter—retain greater perspective. Well, first of all, be very sure of your ground here; no one likes to be told that his suggestion is unethical. If you're sure, then you should definitely raise it with the partner—suggesting, in as tactful a manner as possible, that "others could consider there to be a possible ethical impropriety," and citing your rationale. If the partner persists, then I think you must talk to someone else in the firm about the matter.[10a] Again, pick the partner to whom you're closest—someone who will treat your information as "off the record"—and tell him what's going on. (Here, a hypothetical approach would probably be unavailing, so you may have to go into the actual details.) If the second partner thinks the proposed action is ethical, make every effort to keep news of your visit from getting back to the first partner. If the second partner thinks the action is unethical, then it's up to him to decide on a means of getting that message across to the first partner—without implicating you directly if possible.

The point I want to stress here is that, although these are terribly difficult situations to find yourself in, a law firm is not an SS unit. No one should just take orders—you're a professional and you ought to think for yourself.

What if you just can't seem to get along with the partner for whom

---

[10a] If the firm has an ethics committee, this would logically be the place to go—but that might escalate the matter to a too formal level prematurely.

you're doing the bulk of your work? God knows you've tried, but there's just an irreconcilable personality conflict. Although it's a difficult step to take, I feel that in the long run you're probably better off asking the firm to let you work for another partner. This shouldn't be done lightly; you can easily get a reputation as someone who's hard to get along with—particularly if the other partners don't realize how impossible this one partner is to work with!—and *his* feelings toward you are unlikely to be overly charitable. But the conflict is probably affecting your work; the partner's evaluation of you is probably lukewarm at best; and ultimately, your career has to suffer. So, make the best of a bad situation, with the hope that you can make up lost ground under a new mentor. Before taking this step, however, subject yourself to a rigorous analysis—could it be *your* fault? how do other associates get along with this partner?—and have a senior associate friend (or better still, another partner with whom you're on good terms) confirm your view.

If the problem is not a lack of rapport with the partner, but rather that (after a lengthy trial run) you're unhappy with the sort of work he's involved in, once again I feel you must ultimately try to get out from under. Doing work that you don't like isn't conducive to optimum performance. Your future is at stake. Make a fresh start.[11]

5.2. DEALING WITH OTHER ASSOCIATES

So much for partners. We turn now to associate-associate relations. To the extent a senior-junior theme emerges here, many elements of the partner-associate relationship are applicable, but with some subtle differences. Inter-associate relationships can be significant. Newer associates in a large firm tend to work much more directly for senior associates than for partners; as a result, the initial evaluations will primarily emanate from these seniors. And if you're a senior associate supervising junior associates, the manner in which you discharge this responsibility—your ability to delegate and review work, to keep things moving smoothly—will be one very logical basis on which you are judged for partnership.

5.2.1. Working for Seniors.

Much of the material applicable to the relationship between associate and partner—the necessity to develop a personality profile, the question of when to report and which questions to bring up, and so on—is equally relevant to the goings-on between junior and senior

---

[11]   For a partner's perspective on these matters, see Section 10.5.2.

associates. Generally, however, this takes place in an atmosphere of informality—perhaps even camaraderie—between associates that can differ substantially from some of the artificial dictates of partner-associate relations. Expressing disagreement with another associate, for example, is certainly a less ticklish experience than where a partner is concerned. And, of course, in the inter-associate realm, you always have a court of last resort—namely, the partner.

I think many of the problems of the junior in the senior-junior associate relationship can be classified under the rubric of your joint relations with the partner. For example, are you—the junior associate—doing all the work while the senior is getting the credit? The partner has asked the senior for a draft of a certain agreement. The senior calls you in, tells you what's expected, and asks you to take a first crack at it. You produce the document for the senior. He makes a few minor changes and submits it to the partner. Assume it's a first-rate draft agreement: does the senior associate get credit for it or do you? If you suspect that this particular senior associate is not giving credit where it's due, how do you handle the situation?[12]

By the way, credit isn't the only commodity bestowed around a law firm. What about the corollary situation—where something originating with the senior associate has gone wrong. Take that draft agreement, for example. When the senior gave you the project, he expressly said that the indemnification provision should be phrased in terms of several—not joint and several—liability; that's the way you drafted it, and that's the way it ended up (after the senior's review) on the partner's desk. But the partner had never said anything on that subject to the senior. It was strictly the senior's idea, and the partner thinks it was a bad one ("Let *them* ask for that!"). But how will the partner know who in fact was the source of the idea . . .?

I don't mean to sound sinister, and in my experience the vast majority of senior associates never resort to dirty tricks. Yet the broader problem created by the senior's need to excel in the partner's eyes may sometimes influence the senior's appraisal of the junior's performance, as communicated to the partner. From the junior's viewpoint, it makes sense to try to be present in the room with the senior associate and partner when the matter is under discussion. If you're there when the subject of praise or blame arises, credits or debits will tend to be assigned where they belong. The junior associate should attempt to maximize his contacts with the partner for other reasons also: to let the partner appraise him directly; to view the partner in action and form a better idea of his likes and dislikes; to become more a part of the situation, less an isolated

---

[12] An example of this kind of problem can be found in "A Tale of Two Associates" in Section 9.4.

appendage. There's no reason why the junior associate shouldn't sit in on these internal lawyers' meetings.[13] But you can't depend on either the partner or senior associate to remember to include you; take the lead yourself by asking the senior associate whether you can attend—a request difficult for him to deny.

Actually, no alternative solution to the problem posed is particularly agreeable. Confronting the senior with the facts directly is embarrassing and not calculated to win friends—and remember, the senior may be evaluating your performance for the benefit of partners. An end run to the partner to complain about the senior associate is worse, to be reserved only for dire situations. You might consider raising the point in oblique terms at the next periodic review by the firm of your work ("I don't think I'm getting the requisite contact with partners . . ."). Or you could do nothing—especially in the failure-to-get-credit situation—on the premise that it will all come out in the wash some day.

If you disagree with a senior associate on a substantive point of law or even on a practical approach to a matter, and you think it's important that your views be taken into account by the partner, then you should make sure the partner knows where you stand. You can let the senior do it for you, although it's generally preferable to state your own views to ensure they receive their due.[14] The partner is entitled to hear your separate viewpoints. If the senior associate is so insecure as to block your views from being presented to the partner, I would doubt he's fit to pass judgment on other matters.[15] Legal questions rarely admit of a single answer; different points of view—both on substance and style—can exist in any complex transaction. I can recall a number of occasions when two associates have come jointly to my office and, often with unselfconscious jocularity, reported their differing views on a matter—leaving it to me to make the final determination.

The other side of the coin is that, assuming you have a good relationship with a senior associate, try not to undercut him with the partner. You may be in a situation where you think you're a lot smarter than the senior associate. The senior will be very cognizant of how you handle this; a certain amount of delicacy is called for on

---

[13] For attitudes on this from the viewpoints of the senior and the partner (including possible reasons why the junior may be excluded from meetings involving the client or the adversary), see Sections 5.2.2. and 10.2.1, respectively.

[14] On this point generally, see Section 3.3.1.

[15] Under these circumstances, you should probably write the partner a brief memorandum which, without denigrating the senior, indicates that another possibility exists here—which you happen to believe is the right one.

your part. To the extent you backstop the senior associate, it will obviously be appreciated and will stand you in good stead when the time comes for him to assess your performance for the partners.

5.2.2. *Supervising Juniors.*

Now *you* are the senior associate, supervising the work of other associates who are junior to you. In many ways, this is similar to the situation dealt with in the final chapter of the book, directed to partners in their dealings with associates. But there are certain nuances of senior-junior associate relations that deserve separate analysis.

Let me start out with the most basic point, one that I find myself constantly stressing to senior associates. The senior is responsible for the work product of the junior—just as the partner is ultimately responsible for what both of them produce, and the firm is answerable for the final product. You can't hide behind the fact that the junior did the real labor. As far as the partner is concerned, he's looking to *you*—he may not even know that the junior is involved in the matter.

Now, the *wrong* way to react to this axiom is to do everything yourself—an attitude of "What the hell, if I'm on the hook anyway, I might as well handle it." The temptations in this direction will be manifold: the feeling you can do the task better and faster, an unwillingness to take time out to instruct the junior, impatience with his learning process. But doing the whole job yourself may not be the best use of your time; perhaps you shouldn't get bogged down in writing the initial draft of board minutes or handling basic research. Keep yourself available to take on the more responsible matters—drafting the key documents, dealing with the client and the other lawyer, and so on. A law firm functions best when each attorney is performing at his own level of competence—each junior working up to his abilities at that moment, the seniors not required to handle work for which they're over-qualified.

The *right* reaction to the principle of hierarchical responsibility is to learn how and what to delegate, and to make sure you review the result before it goes to the partner. Mastering the proper delegation of work to turn out a respectable and efficient product is one of the more difficult aspects of practicing law—but an essential skill to develop as you attain seniority within the firm. Let's face it, this is great on-the-job training for becoming a partner, a function not overlooked by those who evaluate your progress.

Of course, you have to pick the right tasks to delegate. You can't ask a junior to handle an important call to the SEC; if he errs badly, it may not be rectifiable. Rather, select those matters which are either well within his capacity to handle on his own (a routine letter to the client) or, although possibly too advanced, will be subject to your review before anything irrevocable happens (the first draft of an important agreement).

Then too, you have to get the junior off on the right foot. For example, if the partner initiating the assignment is the type who gives brusque, fragmented instructions[16]—and then expects you to turn out a fine-tuned product, pulling together all the loose ends—you can't just dump this in the junior's lap as is. Use your knowledge and experience as to what the partner typically expects in order to flesh out the problem for the junior. Or where the productive avenues for a research project aren't self-evident, suggest to the junior some leads for further exploration.

As for reviewing the junior's work, a fine line exists between doing the whole thing over again yourself and failing to probe deeply enough to uncover latent shortcomings. If the job is wretched, I suppose it's easier—although rather dispiriting to the junior—just to start over; but in most cases, you can preserve a portion of what the junior has done. I'm aware of the wrench many a senior associate experiences in passing along to the partner a piece of work that's not quite the way he would have done it had he started from scratch; but this is an unfortunate aspect of the collective practice of law which we all learn to live with. If you can remove all the *substantive* kinks from the job, the fact that the style isn't your own shouldn't concern you unduly.[17]

The key to reviewing is to put yourself in the position of the partner receiving the document from you. Try to do the partner's work for him; otherwise, he'll wonder why you didn't. If a particular sentence is unclear to you, make sure it's clarified; presumably, the partner would react similarly to the failure to root out the ambiguity at an earlier stage of the process. Where research has been done, you don't have to go back and read all the cases and authorities cited; but if there's an obvious leading case, interpretation of which is critical to the conclusion, you should certainly analyze it for yourself. If you discover the key case hasn't been handled well, then you probably have to check into the other authorities as well. Learn to cross-examine the junior on his findings; how well he stands up to your interrogation will help determine your confidence level in the conclusions expressed.

Don't be reluctant to get your own fingers dirty in this process. If the junior is laboring badly with the work—his research is at a dead

---

[16]   A subject discussed in Section 10.3.
[17]   If you're disturbed nevertheless, you can include a notation to the partner that what you're forwarding is basically the junior's work, which you have reviewed and modified for substance but not for style.

end, he doesn't know how to begin the draft—then step in and help him over the hump.

While you're at it, make sure that the junior doesn't end up spending too much time on matters of relative insignificance. Either the partner[18] or you should appraise the importance of the assignment in terms of the junior's dedication of effort. He might, for example, be engaged in a piece of research on a clearly peripheral matter—the kind of question where, if the answer doesn't present itself within the first few hours after hitting the books, you sense the partner would be inclined to discontinue the effort. This takes on more practical importance in situations where the firm won't be able to bill for unproductive lawyers' time. The partner may be too far removed to observe whether the junior associate's hours are well spent; you have to act as the partner's eyes. Develop a feel for how long various kinds of projects take and keep close tabs on the junior in this regard. But some wasted motion is unavoidable—there's always learning time when young associates are involved—and you shouldn't let it deter you from delegating. Just keep the slippage within bounds and make sure the partner is apprised of what's happening.

When you've made extensive revisions in a junior associate's work product, try to sit down with him and go over the changes. Tell the junior *why* you made certain revisions, in order to avoid repetitions of the same mistake. If there's time for this critique right on the spot, do it then—that's best. If not, make an effort later on. The junior will appreciate this feedback, in which you're acting as a surrogate for the partner.[19]

Always make a conscious effort to have the junior associate feel he's part of the team. Bring him into contact with the partner and client as much as possible. The partner may overlook this;[20] so when he calls you in for a meeting, just take the junior along. If the meeting is with the client or the other side, ask the partner if you can bring the junior along; let the partner be the one to make the exclusionary decision.

Take an interest in other aspects of the junior associate's professional life.[21] For instance, be alert to an overwork situation developing, where the junior is staying at the office every night of the week until past midnight, and working all weekend. If it's not within your power to alleviate such a situation, then go to the partner and solicit additional associate help. Similarly, if you see a young associ-

---

[18] See Section 10.3.
[19] For a discussion of feedback by partners to associates generally, see Section 10.4.
[20] But he shouldn't; see Section 10.2.1.
[21] For the partner's role here, see Section 10.5.1.

ate who has spread himself too thin by taking on more assignments than he can handle, help him resolve the crush by interceding with the other senior associates or partners involved; don't just leave this monkey on his back. Conversely, it's wrong to monopolize a particularly capable junior associate; let others view him in action, to further his career.

Your appraisal of how well the junior associate performs is important and ought to be imparted to those in authority at regular intervals. When he or she does a particularly good job on a matter, let a partner know about it while the impression is still fresh in your mind. If you're supervising a junior who is goofing off, and you've exhausted all efforts to motivate him, it's in the firm's best interest for you to bring this to the attention of the partners. Perhaps a partner can speak to this junior and get him back on the track. If not, then he's probably not long for the firm. But the point is that the partners may never realize the problem exists unless you bring it to their attention.

Just this final thought. It's one thing for a partner to give orders to an associate;[22] the partner's status may adequately compensate for deficiencies in his supervisory technique. But it's quite another matter for one associate to give orders to another associate. There's no status symbol behind the senior; you're both professionals in an unclear hierarchy. As a result, it's necessary to develop more subtle techniques. Demands should be phrased as requests; a dressing down ought to be couched in the more neutral tones of constructive criticism; and so on. Make an attempt to be courteous and sensitive. From time to time, we hear a negative report on how a senior associate has mishandled some juniors; it doesn't sit well. Incidentally, the same advice can be given in terms of your dealings with non-legal personnel in the office, such as the office manager, paralegals and secretaries. Don't get a reputation as one who abuses his position.

5.2.3. Dealing with Peers.

This is the shortest subsection in the book, because there's only one point I want to make about the peer situation. There will be times when you're working at close quarters with another associate who isn't clearly senior or junior to you. All I can say is that for an associate to develop a reputation as one who can't work well with his peers ranks as a real negative. Sure, we all know competition exists in the associate ranks, and the temptation to outdo your colleagues can be appealing, but it's not suitable for open display. The suspicion that

---

[22]   See Section 10.5.1.

one associate is backbiting or undercutting another can more than cancel out plaudits achieved for superior work.

Now, if you can handle the competition in ways that are more subtle, so that the partner never knows what hit him—well, if you like to play this sort of game, that's your business. In the long run, class will tell; if you've got it and your peer hasn't, that fact will ultimately emerge, without any questionable assists on your part. And remember, for a partner to report to the firm that the two peer associates on a certain project got along very well, divided up the work, supported each other, and achieved real teamwork, is indeed a high accolade. If you can accomplish that, and still come out on top, more power to you.

5.3. OUTSIDE THE LAW FIRM

5.3.1. Corporate Counsel's Office.[23]

The emergence of corporate law departments within large companies has been one of the notable developments of 20th century American legal practice—a response to the increasing need of corporate executives for daily counsel on legal intricacies in a complex, regulated business environment. In other words, doing business nowadays isn't so easy, and the traditional relationship of executive

---

[23] As I have never been employed in a corporate counsel's office, this section is necessarily derivative. I have, however, talked with a number of corporation lawyers who have provided helpful information, and I have utilized several articles on the subject, including the following: Hickman, "The Emerging Role of the Corporate Counsel," 12 *The Business Lawyer* 216-228 (1957) [hereinafter cited as "Hickman-1"]; Hickman, "Corporate Legal Departments Revisited," 43 *New York State Bar Journal* 391-393 (1971) [hereinafter cited as "Hickman-2"]; Szabad and Gersen, "Inside vs. Outside Counsel," 28 *The Business Lawyer* 235-251 (1972) [hereinafter cited as "Szabad"]; "Special Problems of Inside Counsel," 33 *The Business Lawyer* 1433-1473 (1978) [hereinafter cited as " 'Special . . .' "]; Hershman, "Special Problems of Inside Counsel for Financial Institutions," 33 *The Business Lawyer* 1435-1451 (1978) [hereinafter cited as "Hershman"]; Forrow, "Special Problems of Inside Counsel for Industrial Companies," 33 *The Business Lawyer* 1453-1467 (1978); Rast, "What the Chief Executive Looks for in his Corporate Law Department," 33 *The Business Lawyer* 811-815 (1978) [hereinafter cited as "Rast"]. See also *Model for a Corporate Law Department Manual*, developed by the Corporation Law Committee of the Young Lawyers Section, in cooperation with the Corporate Law Departs Committee, Corporation, Banking and Business Law Section, American Bar Association (1971) [hereinafter cited as "Model . . ."]; Hand and Gang, "The Practice of Law in a Corporation," in *Practicing Law in New York City* 111-115 (J. Fishman and A. Kaufman eds. 1975); J. Donnell, *The Corporate Counsel a Role Study* (1970) [hereinafter cited as "Donnell"].

and outside counsel—the lawyer being consulted on special occasions when significant problems or opportunities arose—has given way to the need for more garden variety legal advice, which can often be handled most efficiently inside the company. I have seen estimates that 50,000 or so attorneys fall into this category today—over 10% of all U.S. lawyers; and apparently the ranks are swelling more rapidly than among their brethren in private practice.

Perhaps even more significant is the increasing professional recognition accorded corporate counsel in recent years, reflective of their higher standards of professional competence, their more active roles in bar associations, and the like. As one observer[24] has graphically chronicled, the inside lawyer has emerged from the derisive connotations of "kept" counsel (who sold his professional independence for a monthly paycheck) in the earlier part of this century, through the "house counsel" status of the 30's and 40's (implying relegation to legalistic housekeeping tasks in lieu of complex legal problems), to the present day top-ranking corporate counsel—often the company's general counsel, usually an officer, perhaps on the board, and (given the right circumstances) a party to the corporation's innermost councils.

I assume that many readers of this book are inside counsel at corporations, and that others may contemplate such work in the future. Although most aspects of legal practice that we've discussed elsewhere are equally applicable in a corporation, sufficient distinctive factors exist to call for some special comment. I've divided this section into four somewhat overlapping topics: the nature of corporate practice; relations between lawyers in the legal department; the inside lawyer's relationship with his "client"; and dealings with outside lawyers (from inside counsel's viewpoint).

Nature of the Practice

Let's skip over the substantive types of work that inside lawyers perform in corporations; the range is broad—antitrust, claims, contracts, labor relations, litigation, patents, copyright and trademarks, real estate, tax, etc.—and published material is available on the subject.[25] In public companies, the legal department invariably has to deal with securities regulation—usually in conjunction with outside counsel, but with a good deal of the reporting requirements handled internally. In a company closely supervised by a particular regulatory body, the corporate legal department would tend to specialize in that field of regulation.

---

[24]   Hickman-1, *supra* note 1.
[25]   Szabad, *supra* note 1; *Model* . . ., *supra* note 1.

I'm interested more in the *subjective* distinctions of practice in a corporation. For example, inside lawyers tend to view themselves as more activist—less contemplative—then outside counsel. Legal departments don't spend as much time researching questions of law as a law firm might; if the problem calls for extensive research, the department will probably call on outside counsel. Inside lawyers pride themselves on their ability to anticipate legal problems and suggest means of working them out, as contrasted with good library skills.

In large companies with sizeable legal departments, individual lawyers specialize quite a bit—the old postulate of a developed skill creating disincentives for rotation. In smaller legal departments, however, individual practice tends to be more generalized than within a law firm. And the necessity to deal with a great variety of matters makes it difficult to remain current in each field. Drafting one prospectus every two years isn't a steady enough diet to keep an inside lawyer up-to-date on registration statement developments—in contrast to his law firm counterpart whose investment banking client is churning out a new prospectus every other month.

Then too, many company lawyers travel a great deal, attending internal conferences, flying to the scene of problems with the key executives. Being on the spot is beneficial for client relations and problem-solving, but it does detract from the quiet study of the law. The situation is exacerbated by the relative lack of legal support facilities within a company—fewer skilled secretaries, less of the paralegal assistance that firm lawyers are increasingly receiving—and the traditional understaffing of many law departments.[26]

One commentator[27] has pointed to three unique advantages enjoyed by the corporate counsel. First, he's ideally situated to practice preventive law. If (as should be the case, but isn't always) he's consulted early in the planning and development stage of corporate projects, the inside counsel has the maximum opportunity to anticipate trouble, to counsel a change in the program to avoid problem areas. This role is more difficult for outside counsel, who is commonly consulted only *after* legal obstacles have arisen; it's much easier to pick up the phone and summon a knowledgeable inside lawyer in the same building than to hire and educate an outside counsel with respect to a problem that hasn't yet arisen.

Second, corporate counsel is in a position to be certain of his

---

[26] Although the staffing may be adequate for six months of the year, there can be real pressure during the other six months, causing the company to turn to its outside counsel—good management technique perhaps, but questionable in terms of legal practice.

[27] Hickman-1, *supra* note 1.

facts[28]—to develop prompt, accurate and comprehensive information on a situation. His full time is devoted to the affairs of a single company, so he generally knows what's cooking and can tap any source within the corporation as a matter of routine. He can also accurately appraise his colleagues who supply the information—sorting out the objective ones, the optimists, the executive inclined to slant his presentation to produce a predetermined answer. Outside counsel, on the other hand, with fewer close contacts inside, possesses less knowledge about the company and the foibles of its officials—in fact, his very presence on the scene may arouse fears, producing a cover-up response within the organization.

Third, corporate counsel has a very real timetable advantage. Timing is crucial to many corporate decisions. Unless the sales representative, for example, can get legal advice about price discrimination within a matter of hours, the sale may be lost to a competitor. Inside counsel, presumably current on the relevant Robinson-Patman decisions, is in a position to respond promptly to a question regarding the legality of a proposed sales gambit. Assigned to a project at inception, corporate counsel sits in on the initial discussions and becomes conversant with the factual background and personalities involved, thereby facilitating a rapid reaction cycle. But most corporations are reluctant to retain outside firms to absorb background before the legal problems surface; and the ultimate call for help to outside counsel has to compete with pressing assignments from his other clients. By contrast, the inside lawyer, always available for the company's work, can marshal his time to give priority to the most urgent problem.

Relations with Lawyer-Colleagues

I was surprised at the seeming paucity of written material on this subject. It's clear, however, that no structure exists within corporate law departments akin to the partner-associate dichotomy of law firms. Legal departments tend to be structured along hierarchical lines, reflecting the general organizational pattern of the corporation itself.[29] There's no magic dividing line—the law firm dynamics of today you're an associate, tomorrow you're a partner (and presumably set for life) doesn't exist in big business.

I also get the distinct impression that in a corporate law office,

---

[28]   The importance of facts has been discussed on several occasions; see, e.g., Section 2.3.

[29]   As a result (and in common with most hierarchical structures), such details as the size of the office, the number of windows, and the presence or absence of a couch can betoken status; and at some companies, legal secretarial salaries are tied directly into the status of the boss—much like possessing a governmental G.S. number. See Section 5.3.2.

much depends on the individual who heads it up—the general counsel (or his equivalent) of the company. What status does he enjoy within the organization? How strong an individual is he? Does he protect his lawyers, insulating the law department from corporate politics? At some corporations, the general counsel is "one of the boys"; at others, he's a more removed, less accessible figure, with offices in the executive suite—more a counselor to the higher levels of the organization than a part of the company's legal apparatus.[30]

In most corporations, a young lawyer's performance apparently receives much less in the way of critical review than would be the case in a firm. As the atmosphere at companies tends to be somewhat less professional than at law firms, less of a professional judgment is rendered on an attorney's performance. The sensation of someone looking over your shoulder is often lacking—you're the pension expert, and there's no one around to evaluate whether you know your stuff or not.[31] Awareness of this relative lack of surveillance can adversely affect your work product, stifling the incentive to achieve the kind of high gloss for which outside lawyers strive.[32]

I get the distinct feeling that many corporation lawyers have closer relations with the executives than with lawyer-colleagues. Their primary bailiwick is a designated area of responsibility—either in terms of subject matter (such as products liability) or of structure within the company (such as legal advisor to a particular division)—and their principal contacts are with the non-legal personnel similarly involved.[33] Some company lawyers bemoan the lack of companionship with other lawyers which is so evident in a law firm context—the ability to talk over problems, discuss professional developments, and the like.[34] This partial isolation, however, is in-

---

[30]   Donnell, *supra* note 1, at 51.

[31]   As a result, it may be easier to hide in a corporate environment—to go through the motions—as contrasted with law firms, which are painfully conscious of individuals who don't pull their share of the load.

[32]   A related phenomenon remarked upon by company lawyers is that the pressure to turn out work often overrides considerations of quality. To an executive, volume of product is impressive and more easily evaluated than excellence—which can also lead to a lack of thoroughness on the part of corporate counsel.

[33]   In other cases, the inside lawyers are closer to the outside lawyers they work with on a regular basis than to others within the corporate law department.

[34]   Of late, corporation lawyers have increasingly sought to combat this isolation by forming professional organizations on a national (e.g., American Society of Corporate Secretaries), state (e.g., Association of Corporate Counsel of New Jersey) or local (e.g., Westchester–Fairfield Corporate Counsel Association) level, with working groups in such areas as securities and anti-trust law.

versely proportional to increased "client" exposure, which serves to distinguish company practice from the more protective atmosphere in a law firm.

Relations With the Employer-Client

Turning now to the relations between the corporate lawyer and his employer-client (for our purposes, the executives of the company[35]), the varying views all do seem to mesh on one point: that it's often a quite different relationship than that between client and outside lawyer. Perhaps the best way to approach this subject is to examine typical client expectations with respect to the inside lawyer. Here, for instance, are the nine criteria which one chief executive says he looks for in his corporate law department.[36]

First, he expects the law department to provide top executives with the kinds of answers to legal questions upon which they can act—preferably clear-cut "yes" or "no" answers. He's not interested in a legal treatise; to run his business, he wants objective legal opinions, cast in an action framework—even in gray areas.

Second, the chief executive desires the advice to be both professionally sound and practical, to combine legal expertise with business experience. Corporate counsel must have an understanding of business in general and this employer's business in particular—not only to render pertinent advice but to shorten substantially the requisite fact-finding process.[37]

Third, he wants the legal staff to recommend courses of action and actively participate in the decision-making process, volunteering opinions on operating matters *to the extent they draw on professional knowledge*. The negative inference: stay out of areas which don't have a sizeable legal element. The extent to which an inside lawyer should concern himself with business problems evidently touches a live nerve, evoking quite disparate reactions. In one sense, a corporation has *only* business problems; its interest in legal topics is solely as

---

[35] I don't intend to discuss some of the "higher loyalty" questions of inside counsel's obligation to the board of directors and ultimately the shareholders; see, e.g., Hershman, *supra* note 1, at 1439-1440, and "Special . . .", *supra* note 1, at 1469 *et seq.*
[36] Rast, *supra* note 1. In a role study of corporate counsel, the key qualities (from the client's view) were listed in order of importance as follows: 1. Professional competence; 2. Understands the business; 3. Positive attitude, imagination; 4. Prompt service; 5. Clear-cut advice; 6. Accessible; 7. Doesn't try to dominate client; 8. Easy to talk with, a good listener; 9. Comprehensible language; 10. Not a "nit-picker"; 11. Takes initiative. Donnell, *supra* note 1.
[37] The observation has been made that the lawyers who go furthest within corporations have healthy doses of business background; an MBA is a valuable tool for a lawyer planning this kind of practice.

they relate to business questions. However, legal risks can't always be completely eliminated and must be weighed against business risks and gains: should the lawyer participate in striking the balance necessary to the decision? The willingness of counsel to volunteer "business advice," and the corollary receptivity of clients, appear to vary widely, based on the predilections of the individuals involved. Needless to say, young corporation lawyers should be alert to this divergence of view and tread gingerly.

Fourth and fifth, we've previously discussed: the chief executive looks to the legal department for advice in preventing problems from arising and for expertise in the major special disciplines that impact the company. Sixth, while he expects his lawyers to be loyal, he doesn't want a legal department of yes-men. In his words, a lawyer's objectivity is his "most priceless asset"; when objectivity is sacrificed in an effort to please, the advice is useless. More on this later.

Seventh, he expects his lawyers to suggest alternative courses of action. Eighth, they should handle relations with outside counsel (discussed under the next topic). And finally, he looks for his lawyers to have a high sense of honesty and fairness, of even-handedness — serving (along with other officers) as the keepers of the corporate conscience.

Well, that's a mouthful of goals for any law department to live up to. Let me try to cut through the loftier ideals and offer my impression of certain frequently reiterated themes. We start with the proposition that the company generally expects its law department to be an advocate of company policy as laid down by its chief executive and board of directors, rather than an institution sitting in judgment on that policy.[38] The general counsel's office is not an independent censor but a member of the company team, actively participating in implementing the company's goals.

So the corporation attorney who usually fares best is a "can-do" type — possessing the imagination and creative ability to come up with legal ways of achieving a proposed plan of action. Concomitantly, negativism is perceived as the deadliest of all inside lawyer sins. After all, the lawyer — occupying a role somewhat akin to the bearer of ill tidings — is seldom the most popular figure in the corporation.[39] He is presumed to represent restraint on freedom. The executive, while understanding the need for the lawyer's role — and not averse to an occasional sprinkling of holy water — still chafes under the necessity to clear his proposal. When the attorney poses seemingly insoluble problems, without offering constructive alternatives, this merely compounds the problem.

---

[38] Hershman, *supra* note 1, at 1435.
[39] Donnell, *supra* note 1, at 61 n.6.

As you might expect, this has to affect the attitude of the company lawyer. He's aware of the officers' desire to feel he's "on their side"; this causes pressure on the lawyer to find a way of achieving company goals—of maximizing the bottom line. And this strong tendency to be a team player highlights the most difficult problem facing the inside lawyer: the matter of independence.[40] How do you deal with high-powered top executives who possess the powers of retention, advancement and the purse?[41]

When inside lawyers speak for publication on this subject, they reject the notion of any shackles on their independence. For example, in one counsel's words, "freer men I have never known."[42] Lacking sales quotas or production targets, he notes, they alone within a corporation can stand up against wrongful business pressure; and if possessed of judgment, they will be listened to as the one voice in the corporate family which is detached, analytical and objective—raised with the corporation's overall and long-range interests always in mind.[43]

But when you put down the articles and actually talk to corporate counsel, you can't escape the feeling that practicing law for an employer does generate some real differences in terms of independence. An inside lawyer has difficulty in achieving a status equivalent to an outside partner. As a result, it's not that easy to speak up boldly without fear of losing job, pay, or favor.[44] A chief executive's pressure, even if unspoken, can be very real. If the presi-

---

[40] The issue of lawyers' independence is explored in "A Matter of Opinion" (Section 9.5). An even more disturbing issue (but thankfully much less frequent in occurrence) can arise when the client disregards the lawyer's advice and commits criminal-type acts (such as affirmative misrepresentation in disclosure documents or deliberate concealment of continuing price-fixing violations). At the risk of oversimplifying this most troublesome of situations, just as the outside attorney should resign the engagement under such circumstances, the inside lawyer can't live in that kind of environment and must move on to other employment.

[41] It should be noted that, as contrasted with outside lawyers whose dealings are often with high level executives, inside lawyers must frequently cope with the middle managerial level, who are inclined to treat attorneys with a greater degree of deference and respect. Independence problems apparently don't surface much in this context.

[42] Hickman-1, *supra* note 1.

[43] In Hickman's view, the great danger to the corporation lawyer's professional independence lies within the individual himself: he may *choose* to subordinate his professional judgment to a commercial one; he may *forget* that he's the lawyer, not the businessman.

[44] Needless to say, the longer an attorney remains with a company, the more his stock options and other benefits build up, the harder it becomes to voluntarily resign or take stands which could lead to forced resignation.

dent wants a strong, independent view, he'll set the tone and let you know; but if he's not looking for rugged individualism, the inside lawyer will sense that also—and it's very difficult not to respond in kind. After all, pleasing the boss is a respectable American tradition, and it takes a hardy soul to step between a division president and the profit he needs to beat the prior year's results.

Still, this framework of potential coercion shouldn't keep you from speaking your mind. You just have to be a little more wary; cover your tail; be sure your position is correct; and sound constructive. State the problem, but then attempt to *solve* it. Sure, you'll have to be more goal-oriented, and you may not achieve an outsider's degree of detachment; but with luck, this will be balanced by your more active role in the decision-making process.[45]

Relations with Outside Lawyers

We will shortly be examining relations between outside and inside counsel from the outside looking in;[46] here, let's see how this looks from within the company. Contrary to what one might expect, the impression I derive is that corporate counsel are quite content with the periodic presence of outside attorneys—that life would be much tougher if law firms didn't exist. The various areas in which the outside lawyer's input can be crucial have been chronicled elsewhere;[47] principal among these are delicate internal situations (such as the chief executive officer's employment contract) which call for the institutional blessing of the law firm;[48] the review of sensitive documents (which may be drafted inside) designed for distribution to the public; handling litigation and time-consuming matters of that nature; working on big deals, particularly where the negative impact on the company could be severe; and backstopping the inside lawyer on the hard questions—especially where the answer is "no."

Inside counsel are of the view that their presence has resulted in more effective utilization of outside lawyers.[49] They say that the law firm attorney couldn't move freely on his own within the corporate

---

[45]   This role seems to vary from company to company, depending on the executive and how he uses his lawyers. Some corporation counsel feel they don't really participate in setting the direction of policy. It may also depend on the lawyer: those who are more interested in the business aspect of problems—who in fact are very conscious of lateral moves they might make into the business side—would tend to participate more; others prefer to maintain their uniqueness and professionalism.

[46]   See Section 7.2.3.

[47]   Szabad, *supra* note 1.

[48]   This is strictly a "no win" situation for inside counsel, forced to choose between representing the interests of the corporation or his boss.

[49]   Hickman-2, *supra* note 1.

structure; people's guards were up, lest something be discovered that would reflect adversely upon the executives involved. It's different, though, when the corporate legal department is interposed. These lawyers are insiders, part of the corporate team; they *know* where the bodies are buried. They're employing the outside counsel as *their* advisors and colleagues. The two complement each other rather than compete.

However, inside lawyers very much want to set the tone of this relationship; since the company is paying the bill, they feel the outside lawyer should be responsive to their needs. To be sure, once the insider is convinced of the outsider's competence, then in many cases the outsider need only keep the insider generally advised with respect to a matter he's handling, such as litigation. But this is for the insider to decide, and some opt for more involvement in a significant lawsuit (regardless of the outsider's competence). Generally speaking, the insider wants to serve as the interface for the outsider in dealing with the executives of the company, since the insider is convinced he's in a better position to reach the right people, obtain the needed information, etc.[50]

Finally, here's some advice from inside counsel which is specifically directed to the outside *associate*. Always keep in mind that you start off at a disadvantage, since the partner has undoubtedly convinced the client that *he* is the only lawyer in the land equipped to handle the company's problems. Now, all of a sudden, he's introducing you—the associate—into the matter, and taking a partial powder himself. This can be a tough act to follow—the line you have to walk between blandness and arrogance may be fine indeed. Just remember: the inside counsel knows who you are, and what your status is in the firm. He's able to judge your competence better than businessmen can, and his feedback on your performance to the partners of the firm—positive or negative—is taken seriously indeed. He's not just another lawyer, or another client; he's a lawyer-client, who requires some adroit handling.

5.3.2. The Government Agency.[51]

One of the largest repositories of legal talent in America is the government. Lawyers proliferate throughout the many branches of the federal, state and municipal bureaucracy. Surprisingly, however, little seems to have been written about their lot; and since I lack per-

---

[50] But see the discussion in 7.2.3 about the dangers this might entail for the outside lawyer who feels his message isn't getting through.
[51] Section 7.5 covers dealings with government agencies from the vantage point of the private practitioner.

sonal experience, what follows reflects the observations of former federal attorneys.

At the outset, let's distinguish between two broad categories of governmental lawyering—a distinction rather basic to certain aspects of the practice. In an organization like the Justice Department, on the one hand, almost everyone is an attorney. A young lawyer works for other lawyers; he reports to them, undergoes their critiques and evaluations, is recommended for promotion by them, and so on. In an agency like the Securities and Exchange Commission, however, although in organizational theory a fledgling attorney may come under the aegis of a divisional chief counsel's office, in practice he may well be working for a branch chief who isn't a lawyer—but who observes and evaluates more of his work than the counsel's office, and who plays a very influential role in his advancement.[52]

As you might imagine, most government offices are structured along rigidly hierarchical lines. You're tagged with a G.S. number and treated very much in the civil service tradition. Everything's carefully organized—advances up the ladder, specified pay hikes—with nothing approaching the relative freewheeling of the two-tier partner-associate law firm system.

In terms of attitude, working for a governmental unit such as the Department of Justice generates in many lawyers a staunch feeling of idealistic pride in representing the United States.[53] Professionally, it can't be beat—if the compensation were only a mite more generous. Concomitantly, government lawyers are very conscious of operating under significant statutes and enforcing the laws—less concerned with what executives euphemistically refer to as business realities.

Perhaps the leading incentive for a young lawyer to cast his initial lot with the government is the prospect of taking on a good deal of responsibility rather quickly—probably much faster than would occur in a law firm, and in terms of more significant assignments than in solo practice. It's also an ideal place to learn a specialty, without professional distraction. As a result, the attitude of "get in, get educated, and get out" isn't uncommon. In fact, the government depends on bright young lawyers who ultimately leave for greener pastures. A number, however, end up staying—at least until they face

---

[52] This is not unlike the corporate law department attorney who works more closely for certain executives (e.g., handling the legal affairs of a particular division) than for the general counsel himself. See Section 5.3.1. Although the lines of authority run to the general counsel, the lawyer's success may well be measured principally by how well he services these "clients."

[53] For those at the SEC, the client is the investing public—amorphous perhaps, but with much the same overtones.

the inevitable financial crunch; the sense of affecting broad policy issues, of wielding real power, can be immensely satisfying. Unfortunately, not all who stay measure up; and since it's difficult to fire a government attorney on grounds of incompetence, the workload for able lawyers is correspondingly augmented.

The big problem comes when you bump up against the top of your grade, and your salary starts to level off—a situation existing throughout government. Less obvious but equally troublesome is functional blockage: a lawyer who wants to advance to another level may have to abandon active litigating (or some other legal skill he's mastered) in favor of an administrative or managerial type job. The latter isn't to his taste, but may represent the only path of advancement.

Access is a hurdle for the young government lawyer. There may be forty partners in a law firm, and an associate can anticipate working for—and with luck, impressing—a fair number of them. In the government, however, you work almost exclusively for the next fellow up the line; so there's plenty of jostling for a position where the top brass can see you in action. Special projects, which usually involve working with the upper echelon, are a common means of attracting front office attention.

In government, you have to guard against over-specialization. A lawyer in the SEC's Division of Corporation Finance isn't equipped to handle an enforcement action, and never gets to write a brief. In the Antitrust Division of the Justice Department, if you develop an expertise (say, in a commodity such as steel), you tend to stay involved in steel cases. The principal impetus to move around has to come from you. But be careful not to give the impression you're simply trying to beef up your resumé; the government doesn't like to think of itself as a post-graduate course. A search for additional challenges is likely to be more warmly received. Broadening the point, the quality of self-starting, so valuable in the law firm context,[54] is particularly effective (perhaps because it's somewhat rarer) in the governmental agency.

The government provides for feedback on your performance, although its effectiveness usually depends on the individuals involved. In the Justice Department, which tends to be more professional and law firm-oriented than most agencies, critiques are plentiful; less of this may exist in other agencies, where lawyers and non-lawyers are commingled. Continuing evaluations are common, however, with the lawyer having access to the resulting paperwork.

Many governmental lawyers feel that the private bar views them as second class citizens—working for the government because of

---

[54] See Section 4.2.

inability to find a job in private practice, never forced to meet a payroll, and such. While the government lawyer doesn't usually resent the sizeable incomes earned on the outside, there is considerable sensitivity towards being talked down to by private practitioners. This perception—however inapposite to the particular circumstances—is one which private lawyers would do well to keep in mind.

Contrary to popular belief, most government lawyers *don't* adopt a holier-than-thou, how-can-you-represent-such-a-crook attitude toward the private bar. Still, some distrust exists. The government lawyer views the private attorney as an advocate whose primary concern is his client; thus he can't be expected to wax objective in his presentations to the agency. As a result, government lawyers approach their private counterparts with some degree of cynicism, consciously distinguishing between lawyers who possess credibility and those who don't.[55]

Need I say that what most irks a government attorney is to be leapfrogged in the decisional process, to watch in anguish as the matter lands on the desk of a political appointee—or to receive, hard on the heels of an adverse decision he's made, a questioning letter from some Congressman. These are sure ways to stifle government cooperation; any pressure that the private lawyer seeks to bring to bear in this manner works against him. Rightly or wrongly, the government lawyer believes that the private attorney must at this point be attempting to cover up rather than dealing with the matter on the merits.

5.3.3. Hanging Out a Shingle.

Up to now, we've focused on the practice of law within an organization—a law firm, a corporation, a government agency. But a lawyer can ply his trade wherever he hangs his hat, and many of our brethren operate strictly on their own (or with a colleague or two). The bulk of the matters we've discussed are equally applicable to the single practitioner; still, some points deserve special mention. In particular, since the life blood of any solo practice is the clientele, we'll devote some time to the subject of obtaining clients.[56]

---

[55] For example, a private practitioner who, for no apparent reason, is unwilling to put something in writing upon request, engenders real suspicions in the government lawyer.

[56] We won't, however, go into the mechanics of setting up an office—plush quarters vs. modest accommodations (without tarnishing the success image)—the economics of the practice, and such questions as whether to hire a secretary or to share space in return for legal services. Two good introductory books on the subject of starting a practice, from which I've drawn much of the material in this section, are J. Foonberg, *How to Start and Build a Law Practice* (1976) [hereinafter cited as "Foonberg"]; and S. Gillers, *I'd Rather Do It Myself* (1977) [hereinafter cited as "Gillers"].

The strongest incentive to go out on your own is the apparent exhilaration of independence—accomplishing things by yourself rather then depending on other people. The prospect of working for a boss within an organization just doesn't sit right with some people.[57] Law firm partners achieve a measure of independence, but this takes time—and even then you have to operate within organizational confines. Other reasons to take the plunge include client contact occurring at a much faster rate; more practical on-the-line training; the prestige of having your name on the door—and then there's the involuntary choice: frustrated in finding the right kind of job at a firm or company, you opt for this practical alternative to put shoes on the kids.

Individual practitioners differ on the timing of the move. Some believe you should open your doors for business as soon as possible—before developing a taste for the finer things in life.[58] Others consider a lawyer fresh out of law school incapable of practicing law. (He might know what the law *is*, but not how to *practice* it.) The appearance of confidence, so essential to a successful lawyer, simply can't be conveyed when you have little notion of what you're doing. So they suggest going with a firm for awhile, to gain experience before starting out on your own. (Those holding the first view counter by observing that early experience gained in a firm—minor court appearances, the preparation of lesser documents, insignificant client contact—may not be all that helpful.) For what it's worth, I tend to the wait-a-bit view. It seems to me that while you're learning your trade, you shouldn't have to be worried about finding clients, paying the bills, and such. Those first few years in a firm are a good time to collect your resources—mental and financial—for the solo plunge. But you do have to avoid the trap which ensnares so many, particularly in government or corporate life—that combination of the perquisites building up and inertia setting in tends to stifle movement.

Should you start out with another lawyer? The negative view has been summed up in these terms: "As a general rule, two new lawyers getting together will accomplish very little except to prove that two can starve to death at least twice as fast as one."[59] But solo practice can be wearying, with no one to cover for you during crises or

---

[57] Gillers, *supra* note 1, at 6-9. In his view, the benevolence and protectiveness of large organizations can be dangerous—undermining your spirit and sense of freedom to the point that you begin to think of yourself mainly in terms of the organization.

[58] Foonberg, *supra* note 1.

[59] Foonberg, *supra* note 1, at 12. On the subject of taking on partners, see also Gillers, *supra* note 1, at 127 *et seq*.

vacations. And if you each have experience under your belt in different substantive areas, "the firm" has that much more expertise to sell, with a correspondingly reduced learning curve.[60] Once you take on a partner, though, a number of issues require resolution—not least of which is the age-old problem of splitting the pie.[61]

The most obvious difference between firm and individual practice is the matter of clients. The young law firm associate knows the bread will be on the table; he needn't worry about bringing in new clients at the outset. By contrast, solo lawyering requires the production of clients through one's own efforts—a challenge which anyone contemplating the move should feel capable of undertaking. But don't be disturbed by the absence of a *present* clientele, since the opportunity for exposure in a firm is limited—and you never know where clients will come from.[62]

Have you ever thought about why someone hires you as a lawyer? Sole practitioners think about it all the time.[63] It's *not* because you're a nice guy—a jovial companion on the links. Prospective clients want to feel that you can do something for them—that you can offer them first-rate professional advice.

Now, to be sure, there are many ways you can bring yourself into contact with prospective clients; after all, this is your livelihood and there's no sense in hiding your light under a bushel.[64] You can develop your name through lecturing and writing. You can promote business deals that require lawyering. You can build relationships, be on the lookout for situations, join groups.[65] The best sources of

---

[60]   If possible, your partner should not only complement you in this regard, but also in terms of circles of acquaintanceship which can be expected to lead to new business.

[61]   Gillers, *supra* note 1, at 134 *et seq.*

[62]   One source from which you might *expect* some business—your former law firm—may not come through as handsomely as anticipated. This seems particularly true for corporate attorneys; most lawyers just aren't anxious to refer corporate matters. Litigators may fare better in this regard—taking with them cases they've been handling in the firm and getting future referrals where conflicts exist or multiple representation is involved.

[63]   As one told me recently, he's constantly reflecting on the larger questions, such as "Where is my practice going?" and "Am I doing things better this year than last?" There's a sense of taking perpetual inventory that seems to occur more often than in the firm setting.

[64]   Gillers, *supra* note 1, at 57 *et seq.*

[65]   If you join an organization solely to get clients, however, you'll probably be wasting your time and money; the other members will see right through you. If, on the other hand, you belong to an organization because you sincerely believe in its purposes, and you work hard for it, then the other members will be impressed by your efforts and your sincerity—and then perhaps they'll come to you for their legal work.

fresh business for you will probably be other lawyers and individuals who have observed you in action handling prior matters. Above all, don't sit by the phone, hoping it will ring with a new retainer. Time is your most valuable asset; don't let it go to waste.

Although the impulse to take every case offered to you will be great, an intelligent lawyer knows what cases and clients should be turned down.[66] Viewed affirmatively, marginal matters you would be inclined to take on include those providing an opportunity to become involved in an interesting new field of law,[67] or introducing you to a client in an attractive new "market" where you're not well known, or referred to you by someone of significance who will appreciate your involvement, or simply involving a client you like and an issue you believe is important.[68] Viewed negatively, here is one lawyer's list of definite no-thank-you's:[69]

1. When you're the second or third lawyer on the case (indicating either a non-meritorious case or an uncooperative or non-paying client);

2. Hurt feelings cases (lacking provable special damages);

3. Landlord-tenant cases (unless you're paid in full in advance—these apparently rivaling divorce actions for vindictiveness, with resultant dissatisfied clients);

4. Divorce cases for people heavily in debt (unless paid in advance);

5. Criminal cases (unless paid in advance);

6. Slipfalls unless the damages are substantial (since they're hard to settle short of trial);

7. Bankruptcies (unless paid in advance—it's embarrassing when your client amends his bankruptcy schedule to include the unpaid balance of your fee!);

8. Clients who proclaim loudly that you can have *all* the money recovered—they're only interested in the *principle*;

9. Clients who want to use your telephone, secretary and offices to conduct their business;

10. Clients who ask for a loan of money against their case;

11. Cases where the client claims his adversaries will settle right away "because they can't afford the publicity of litigation" (and where, in fact, the other side typically waits until the U.S.

---

66   Abraham Lincoln is reputed to have advised a new lawyer: "Young man, it's more important to know what cases not to take than it is to know the law." Foonberg, *supra* note 1, at 51.
67   But see *infra*, this section.
68   Gillers, *supra* note 1, at 44 *et seq.*
69   Foonberg, *supra* note 1, at 51-54.

Supreme Court denies *certiorari* before opening settlement discussions);

12. Cases totally without merit.[70]

Since the best source of legal work is repeat assignments from existing clients,[71] it's important for you to stay in close touch with them. Here are some example of follow-up work commonly neglected by lawyers:[72] sending out a reminder letter prior to the required annual meeting of a corporation or with respect to the annual statements of corporate officers to be filed with the Secretary of State; calling your client's attention to lease options for renewal or purchase; reminding the client by letter, some years after execution of his Will, that a periodic review would be appropriate; sending a letter prior to a judgment becoming unenforceable; and contacting a minor (for whom you've worked) prior to his becoming an adult, at which point certain legal relationships will attach.

For the most part, your clients will probably differ from big firm clients, tending to be smaller companies or individuals of relatively modest means. You lack the manpower to service a multi-national company—but you may be consulted by a large company on a specific question, especially if you've developed a specialty and reputation.[73] There is always a risk of becoming overly dependent on one or two substantial clients, which not only portends a real crisis should you lose them but threatens your independence as a lawyer to some degree. Some clients have a penchant for leaning on you pretty heavily ("I'm your biggest client; drop everything else and handle this for me."); others are more forebearing. If possible, you should never let a big client know how important he is to you. In the last analysis, independence will stem from your own strength of character.[74]

---

[70] In addition, doing business with friends and relatives can often give rise to unhappy experiences. No matter how difficult the effort or how favorable the result, the friend or relative thinks he did the lawyer a favor by giving him the "experience"; as a result, he considers almost any fee an overcharge. You should strive in these situations to develop a professional relationship, getting the client into your office (away from the kids) and with a clear understanding on billing. Foonberg, *supra* note 1, at 29.

[71] Don't neglect the principle of reciprocity here. Some clients or potential clients who have their own service business—say, a broker—will send you business only if they think you'll return the favor.

[72] Foonberg, *supra* note 1, at 34-36.

[73] You're actually in a good position to receive a referral of this kind from a large firm, which won't be worried about you taking away the totality of the business.

[74] For a hypothetical test of character, see "A Matter of Opinion" in Section 9.5. See also Section 5.3.1 on the question of independence as applied to a corporation's law department.

We will discuss at length the servicing of existing clients in a firm,[75] and the same goes in solo practice—but in spades. Here, the client is yours—there's no senior partner interposed between you and him, inhibiting the establishment of a one-to-one relationship. Always keep in mind that the client wants to see *efforts* on your part. Results are fine, too, but he also wants to know you're putting forth effort on his case. So let him see what you're doing, by sending him copies of each document you produce or review, returning his calls as soon as possible,[76] billing monthly, making house calls (including visiting clients at their places of business), informing them of new cases or statutes affecting their affairs, and so on.

Because your clients may be unable to afford large fees, your legal services have to fit into an appropriate framework.[77] Don't neglect those measures deemed necessary to protect your client—but you can't afford to spend 20 hours looking up rather esoteric peripheral points. You have to scrutinize each matter for the key items, and avoid becoming mired in minutiae. It's a question of getting a feel for the situation and then coming to a reasonable conclusion. To be sure, some risks exist in practicing this way; and these may have to be made clear to the client for a practical decision—i.e., I have to advise you there's a collateral question here, which to research in depth would be rather expensive; here are the risks and opportunities; what do you say?

Most single practitioners would prefer to practice only in the particular legal areas where they excel, but this rarely happens. It can be risky to venture outside your expertise; the possibilities of doing an inadequate job (especially if the client won't pay for your education) and having it take longer than expected cannot be ignored, and you'll probably end up writing off a good portion of your time. Still, many lawyers will tell you to take the good cases as they come, even though not falling into your prime domain. You'll end up being a better all-around lawyer—and probably part businessman, also. To be sure, you lack the backup of a big firm. When I have a tax question, I can turn to my tax partner; but you might have to *know* the answer. Lawyers in private practice are also adept at developing a web of relationships

---

[75] See Chapter 6.

[76] Some lawyers, working on a client's case in the evening or on a weekend, will call the client at his home to ask a question—thereby letting him know that the lawyer's "personal" time is being devoted to the client's matter.

[77] It's generally a mistake to sell legal services by cutting billing rates. Among more obvious drawbacks, it suggests to the client that your skills aren't adequate to command what other lawyers charge. If price is a critical factor to the client, convince him that your expertise in the area will save him from having to finance your education or the training of junior attorneys.

around town, learning to pick experts' brains for guidance (a/k/a research by telephone)—at least to obviate those initial hours needed to focus the issue or to get a handle on the mechanical details (What's the procedure here? What documents do I need?).

The concomitant of no supervision is the absence of any critique or evaluation of your performance. No one tells you how bad you are! This tends to retard improvement, and unless you're careful, can portend a drop in quality. I've heard careful lawyers remark that when they probe the work of a typical small practitioner—which might appear on the surface to be competent—they find rather large gaps. There's no magic solution here, but what's basic is continual and critical self-analysis of your abilities—the absence of any delusions as to your own state of perfection.

The other side of the coin is that, in a one-person firm, you're often over-qualified for the work at hand. One attractive aspect of a properly functioning large firm is that everyone operates at his own level of expertise; the partner rarely does first drafts, the senior associate can delegate the initial research, etc. But the sole practitioner has to do everything, and he may well be too good for corporate minutes. Sure, he may turn out a better set of minutes, and there's no problem of quality control;[78] but is it really efficient? Viewed from a different perspective, however, few of the big firm inefficiencies exist—all that talking back and forth, writing memos, the duplication inherent in a number of people looking at a single document. Is the incremental difference in result achieved by all that massaging justified by the additional effort? Besides, sole practitioners claim that they really like to do everything themselves— read each document, know each aspect of the deal from top to bottom; they feel better prepared than the partner who merely reviews someone else's work.

The most ironic problem the sole practitioner has to face is his own success. With business booming, it's tough to stay on your own—unless you're willing to turn down good business, which most lawyers seem constitutionally incapable of doing. The pressure to expand begins to build. Guilt feelings abound as clients are inadequately serviced. And what often results is that another lawyer is brought in or you combine with an existing firm.[79]

One solution for the single practitioner who wants to stay small is to upgrade his clientele. Typically, law firms don't discard paying

---

[78]   In this regard, see Section 5.2.
[79]   If, for example, you're a non-litigator seeing a lot of potential litigation business which you hate to turn down, you might opt for consolidation with a firm having that expertise. It's probably more difficult to bring someone in and train him to litigate; then too, he might turn out to be the wrong person.

clients; rather, they pass the smaller clients down the line for servicing by recently hired junior personnel. The sole practitioner's ability to render legal services, however, is finite; and the price of not taking on associates may be the necessity to upgrade. This, though, may be easier said than done. It's no picnic to tell one of your earliest, most loyal clients that you no longer can handle his affairs because he won't be able to afford your new billing rate—even with the excuse that you've decided to limit your practice to a single specialty. But if you're game, this might be the only businesslike way you can preserve the independence you've come to enjoy.

CHAPTER 6

HANDLING CLIENTS

This chapter is all about my favorite subject: clients. Not that we haven't previously alluded to their presence and won't be dealing with them later;[1] it's just that certain thoughts on the topic don't seem to fall into other categories.

6.1. CLIENTS: COLOR THEM INDISPENSABLE

I'd like to be able to sum up in a few well-chosen words the key to obtaining new clients, but I simply don't know the words. I've had clients develop out of the most unlikely prospects around—while, conversely, a number of "sure things" have failed to materialize. Pure chance plays a role—a remark dropped in passing can often be the difference—as well as the vagaries of the market, timing and other imponderables outside your control.

I have a feeling that the days of landing clients on the thirteenth tee are largely behind us (if indeed they ever existed), although it's clearly worthwhile to enlarge your circle of friends and acquaintances—spreading bread on the water, so to speak. Nowadays, however, clients come to a lawyer because they've heard good things about him or her professionally, or they've witnessed the lawyer in action representing another client. If you give efficient, intelligent service, the word is going to get around. So we tell our young people not to worry too much about *how* to go about attracting business; we say "Do a first-rate job and the clients will seek *you* out."

One prime distinction between employment as an associate in a sizeable law firm and practice as a sole practitioner,[2] is that the

---

[1] See, e.g., Sections 2.3, 3.2.6, 3.3.1, 3.3.2, 3.3.3, 5.1.2, 7.2.3, 7.3.9, 8.3, 8.4, 8.5, 8.6, 9.2, 9.5 and 9.6.
[2] For a discussion of attracting clients in individual practice, see Section 5.3.3.

associate isn't required to bring in new clients for the firm. In fact, some firms may even discourage him from doing so. The theory is that he's been hired to service the existing and anticipated clients of the firm. Still, even where there's no pressure to produce clients, and associates lacking the velvet touch are nonetheless admissible to partnership, a favorable perception of your potential abilities in this regard can be one factor in your advancement.

More important to the partnership deliberations, however, is the perceived ability of the associate to *service* existing firm clients. The care and servicing of clients is no less important a factor in a large firm than the ability to produce clients is in a small firm. I have the distinct feeling that some associates—swamped by the intricacies of legal problems, awash in the pressure of turning out work—aren't nearly as sensitive to this point as they might be. They tend to forget that without clients there would be no firm and few interesting projects; you can't pay the bills by solving hypothetical problems.

The skill of servicing clients satisfactorily isn't solely a matter of subject matter competence; it's also a question of the proper attitude toward people. One of the first issues an associate should face up to, in deciding whether to make his future with the firm, is whether he enjoys dealing with clients generally, and with the clients of *this* firm in particular. Some lawyers discover, after an initial trial period, that they just don't cotton to the notion of working for clients. They may love the law—be fascinated by the intellectual challenges presented—but would prefer performing in a less chaotic arena, without the pressures created by the attorney-client relationship. Or perhaps it's just the *firm's* clients that turn the associate off; they may be too aggressive for his taste (or not dynamic enough), or the firm's practice is too business-oriented for an associate who seeks work on matters with redeeming social value.

Well, the firm's clients are the raw material for your labors while you're there. If you don't like working with clients, then you're better off in some other aspect of law—perhaps employed by the government, or teaching, or writing for a legal publication. If your distaste is for the firm's client roster, and feelings of disrespect or disinterest begin to interfere with the practice of your profession, then you're unlikely to be an effective lawyer in the client's behalf; and you might be well advised to look elsewhere for more congenial employment.

6.2. A CLIENT RELATIONS PRIMER

But there's more to clients than just indispensability. Notwithstanding the headaches involved, your relationships with clients can produce some of the most substantial satisfactions you achieve as a practicing attorney. Once you get to the point where you're truly functioning as a counselor—the person to whom the client turns for advice when he has a *problem*, which may not necessarily be purely legal—you can experience a sense of personal accomplishment equivalent to the pleasure of devising a creative solution to a complex substantive issue.

As an associate, your role vis-à-vis each client will depend in large measure upon the partner for whom you're working. Some partners insist on their total continuing involvement with the client—consigning the associate to a strictly back-up role and severely restricting his ability to create close client relationships. Other partners are pleased to have the associate assume the leading role with certain clients, the partner's availability being limited to major questions that arise. Most partners fall somewhere in between these extremes, making their judgment on the basis of client expectations and associate ability in handling clients.

To the extent you have any choice in the matter, I urge you to seek out situations conducive to the fullest range of client contact. Avoid being stigmatized as a lawyer who can't be trusted with clients—the proverbial closet attorney, relegated to drafting indentures in the dark of night, to be submitted to the client by another, more presentable lawyer upon reappearance of the sun. By the way, this happens to be a prime area probed by intelligent interviewers, if and when you're changing jobs. How much responsibility have you held with particular clients? Are you capable of handling a matter on your own with only indirect and sporadic supervision by a partner? Firms aren't interested in hiring experienced lawyers who need constant surveillance.

It goes without saying that, as previously discussed in the context of dealing with partners,[3] you have to take into account the client's idiosyncrasies and attempt to adapt yourself accordingly. Does he like to communicate in writing or would he prefer an oral report? Is he a stickler for the timely response, even if your conclusion is accordingly tentative; or is he less interested in how fast the reply arrives and more concerned that it be definitive? And so on. Perhaps at some point you will become a renowned senior partner, whose foibles clients are willing to overlook; but until then, you should make an effort to satisfy each client on his own terms. The partner in charge of the client can be extremely helpful to you in this regard, and his counsel should be sought.

Clients can be unrealistic at times, offering the lawyer a Hobson's choice of either swallowing hard and remaining silent, or gritting the teeth and advising the client his expectations can't be met. Take a

---

[3]   See Section 5.1.1.

situation where the two businessmen—perhaps in alliance with the lawyer on the other side—have proposed a totally quixotic timetable for the transaction. Should you speak up to say that the job simply cannot be accomplished in the time period projected, at the risk of appearing to be unable to keep up with everyone's pace—though you're just as diligent and efficient as the next person? I'll concede there have been times when I've remained silent under such circumstances—hopeful that when things inevitably lagged behind expectations, factors other than my own performance would be viewed as the primal cause. Generally, however, the better course is to speak the words no one wants to hear, along with a convincing factual demonstration as to why the schedule is unrealistic (multitudinous documents to be prepared and reviewed, third parties to be dealt with, etc.).

In a similar vein, you'll undoubtedly encounter the client who's outraged at what some scoundrel has done to him and eagerly awaits your advice that he has an open-and-shut case. You'd certainly like to oblige, but unfortunately—viewing the situation from all angles with lawyerlike perspective—you realize that your client has been a bit of a scoundrel himself, while there appear to be some mitigating circumstances on the other side. Here's a delicate balance to strike—giving an objective evaluation without coming across as lily-livered and non-supportive. Under these circumstances, it may be helpful to remind the client that you wear two hats. If and when you're to be cast in the role of advocate, you will present his side of the case as vigorously and aggressively as possible. However, you also owe him your best thinking as a more dispassionate advisor, in order to help frame the optimal course of action.

You will note that most of my client examples involve situations where your services are being provided on a continuing basis to regular clients of the firm. There's a reason for that. If you're involved in strictly a one-shot deal, you do what is required and don't become involved in the broader picture of the client's affairs. With a continuing client, however, in order to give really good service, you must anticipate matters, initiate phone calls ("How is that draft quarterly report coming?"), bring recent developments to the client's attention, and so on. This embraces the quality of self-starting or initiative we spoke about earlier[4]—the difference between merely responding and actually originating.

6.3. THE DECISION TO ADVISE OR DUCK

Here's a common situation that can be troublesome. An associate is asked a question by the client (on the telephone, let's say); and the

---

[4]   See Section 4.2.

associate has to decide whether to advise the client at that point or defer any answer until he's had a chance to talk matters over with the partner in charge.[5] The conservative position would be to duck all but the simplest of questions—on the theory that any advice given, regardless of the fact it originates with an associate, is deemed to represent the viewpoint of the firm, with potentially serious repercussions for all concerned. However, the price paid for such waffling is to confirm the client's suspicions that the associate is no more than a flunky, which seriously inhibits the associate's chances of developing an independent relationship with the client.

Let's begin by eliminating those situations where to venture a response would simply be foolhardy—as a matter of fact, the *partner* would be equally imprudent to shoot from the hip were the question directed to him. When a client asks a complex question that will require a good deal of analysis or research or examination of documents or investigation of facts—or where the matter at stake (complex or not) is of great importance to the client—then clearly, the associate should not volunteer a response on the spot. The client doesn't really expect an immediate answer, and proffering one may tab you as an immature gunslinger not given to measured reactions and learned judgments. Moreover, if you sense that the client *expects* the question to be answered by the partner—where the client is using you only as an intermediary, because the partner is presently inaccessible and the client wants to place the issue before the firm—then you must go to the partner for his judgment. To offer an answer in such a circumstance would place the client in the embarrassing position of having to reply that he *still* wants you to bounce it off the partner.

The issue is squarely raised where the question (i) doesn't involve a critical matter for the client, (ii) requires no additional investigation of facts or research of law to arrive at a solution, (iii) is answerable in terms you're comfortable with, and (iv) is directed to you for a response. This last consideration is perhaps the most important of all. You must judge whether the client perceives his question as one to which a good lawyer would have a ready answer. If you sense he does, then (all other things being equal) you should try to oblige. When your antennae signal that the client expects further research or thought, it's much easier to decline an authoritative response.

---

[5]   Aspects of this issue are also discussed in Sections 5.1.1 and 5.1.2 (relations with the partner) and in connection with the treatment of deferring judgment in Section 8.3. In this section, we will confine ourselves to the narrow question of whether the associate should advise the client or defer to the partner. The answer to the question posed can vary on the basis of the position within the client hierarchy occupied by the questioner; for purposes of this section, we'll assume that one of the top executives is involved.

To illustrate some of these aspects, let's examine the issue in the context of two hypothetical situations—one, a client question which is primarily legal; and two, a client question which, although having legal overtones, essentially involves a practical course of action. In both cases, the partner in charge isn't around at the crucial moment, although there's a chance you can track him down in his travels. You're an associate with four years' experience, who knows both callers reasonably well.

In the first case, Mr. Reed, the president of Repurchase Corp., a medium-sized public company whose stock is traded over-the-counter, calls to ask you whether the company need apply to the SEC for permission (in the form of an exemption or otherwise) in order for the company pension fund to go into the open market and buy shares of Repurchase stock at this time.

In the second case, your client, Merger Incorporated, a mini-conglomerate whose stock is listed on the American Stock Exchange, has just entered into an agreement in principle to acquire a privately-held company. The Merger press release announcing the deal, which went out earlier in the day, contained no mention of the price to be paid. Mr. Merritt, president of Merger, now telephones you to report a call he received ten minutes earlier from a reporter for a well-known financial publication. The reporter inquired about the purchase price for the acquisition, since this would affect their news judgment in terms of whether to run an article or not. Mr. Merritt wants to know whether, in your view, this information should be disclosed to the reporter.

We start with the premise that it would have been a good idea for you and the partner to have discussed in advance the possibility of such a situation arising, and to have established some ground rules for your handling of the matter. Partners may differ widely on such issues; one may be quite satisfied for the associate to field these questions, while another would prefer being consulted.[6] We'll assume, however, that no preliminary discussion has taken place, and you're not really sure how the partner would react.

One practical factor with significant bearing on this decision is whether the client is likely to take immediate action on the basis of your advice—thereby risking an irretrievable situation if you're wrong—or whether the matter involves only longer range considerations. For instance, in the case of the reporter, you can assume that in order to meet the publishing deadline, the client will act quickly—which might give you some pause if there is any doubt about your response. Had Mr. Merritt's question been phrased in terms of a possible problem that might arise over a press release

---

[6]   See Section 5.1.1.

scheduled for next week, you might be more tempted to give the advice, recognizing that it could still be revoked at a later time. In the situation involving the buyback of shares, if Mr. Reed is thinking of having the pension fund go into the market today, any lingering doubts on your part would make you less likely to give him a green light, since once the purchases are made the fat's in the fire. If, however, Mr. Reed is merely hypothesizing about the pension fund making future purchases, you may be more inclined to take a whack at an answer. When time is on your side, incorrect advice—while embarrassing to you personally—doesn't cause irreparable harm.

You've probably surmised that another practical factor here is which way your answer is likely to come out. Take the buyback situation. Assume you know that Repurchase Corp. has an outstanding issue of publicly-held warrants, and you're aware of the SEC's position that this constitutes a continuing distribution of the shares issuable upon exercise of the warrants; thus, an exemption under Rule 10b-6 would be required for purchases by the company. Although your memory is a little vague on the point, the logic of this position would seem to extend also to purchases by a company pension trust. So your answer to Mr. Reed will probably be that Repurchase ought to apply to the SEC for an exemption, although this is a relatively *pro forma* step which shouldn't present any substantive problem. Well, that's pretty safe advice; and if it develops you were wrong, the extent of the harm is to delay the pension trust's buying program by several days and to relegate to the wastepaper basket the draft of the exemption letter you've begun. If, on the other hand, Repurchase had no warrants outstanding and you weren't aware of any other distribution of securities on its part, your advice might be that nothing is needed from the SEC—a potentially more dangerous position, since the client could be expected to go right ahead and cause the pension trust to make the initial purchases.

These two situations also illustrate another relevant distinction. On the one hand, the Rule 10b-6 matter involves a legal question where some research may well be in order. No one could fault you for giving the following response: "Well, in view of your warrants, you would need an exemption for purchases by the company. I have every reason to believe that the SEC's position also extends to purchases by the company's pension trust, but I would just like to check that out before giving you a final answer." It sounds like you know what you're doing. By contrast, the reporter's question is one to which you either have an answer or you don't; there's really nothing to look up. If you want to establish that *you* are a competent alternative legal advisor for Merger Incorporated in the partner's absence, then you ought to provide an answer on the spot.

Familiarity with the client's affairs might also be a factor. If Repurchase Corp. is a regular client of the firm on whose matters you've been working for several years, a certain familiarity should be presumed. With a new client, or where you're a newcomer to the engagement, it's somewhat easier to punt ("I just want to check whether the company has applied for any Rule 10b-6 exemption letters in the past.").

Finally, a distinction can be drawn in terms of how the partner might react to your assumption of his role. The Rule 10b-6 question is a pretty straightforward one, which doesn't require too much judgment[7] (as contrasted, for these purposes, with legal knowledge); either you have to go to the Commission or you don't. But the reporter question is much more a matter of subjective judgment, in which the criteria affecting your ultimate decision aren't necessarily legal. And in such a situation, the interplay with the client becomes more important. How badly does Mr. Merritt want an article to appear in the paper? What reasons did he have for not disclosing the price in the first instance? Disclosure is more meaningful when the price is included; at least readers can get a quantitative handle on the deal's dimensions. But once you decide to disclose the price, isn't the next question going to be—so as to put the price into perspective—what are the revenues, earnings and net worth of the company being acquired? And is Mr. Merritt prepared to go that far? Well, the partner just might want to be part of the interrogation and give-and-take involved in these more judgmental matters.[8]

All right. Now let's assume that you've decided to advise the client, but you'd also like him to have the comfort of the partner's judgment. The following method is *not* recommended: "This is my judgment on the matter . . . [elaborate] . . . but if you like, I will confirm it with the partner." I feel that this puts the client in a somewhat awkward position. He might very much like to hear the partner's views, and yet feel concerned that you'll consider an affirmative response as implying lack of confidence in your judgment. The better way is to give the advice, then tell the client that you intend to check it with the partner and—assuming you can reach him—get back to the client as soon as possible. In effect, you're acknowledging a basic fact of law firm life: that the client is entitled to receive the best advice from the highest authority available to him within the two-tier structure of the firm. You didn't duck—and assuming your advice is confirmed, this will count in your favor in similar future situations—while at the same time you haven't created an awkward problem for the client.

---

[7]   A quality which is the subject matter of Chapter 8.

[8]   See Section 8.5.

If you're less sure of your answer but still feel a reply is appropriate, the best way to handle the situation is to say that your "tentative answer" (or your "initial reaction" or "gut feeling") is such and such, but there are certain aspects you want to check out—to which you can add (although not necessarily) that you would like to run the question by the partner if he's available. At least you've reacted; nobody can put you down as a total dummy. Yet the client is on notice that he shouldn't act on your advice, in view of its preliminary nature. If the check-out process causes your advice to be reversed, the client will undoubtedly be relieved that you didn't state your views more definitively and thus induce reliance on his part. And particularly in the judgment area—such as with the reporter's question—there's little loss of face in reporting back that the partner disagreed with you for several, mostly subjective, reasons.

When you do render advice without consulting the partner, unless it's trivial, you should inform the partner after the fact. If you're concerned, go to see him personally as soon as possible, tell him what you've done, and ask if he feels (i) that the advice was correct, and (ii) that you were justified in giving it on the spot. With a more routine matter, you might just drop the partner a short memo, stating: "On [date] I advised [client] to the following effect: . . . [describe] . . . Please let me know if you have any problems with the advice given." This doesn't even require a reply from the partner if he agrees with your position.

6.4. A POX ON HYPOTHETICALS

In law school, all problems—even the real ones found in reported cases—were essentially hypothetical. The essence of the learning process involved tinkering with one or more elements in an assumed set of facts to determine whether this altered the analysis and perhaps the ultimate outcome. Well, my hearties, bid fond farewell to law school days; there's little room in the practice of law for jousting with hypotheticals. No one's paying the firm to solve the problem that interests *you*. It's the *client's* problem you have to address, however more complex (simple), favorable (unfavorable) or interesting a set of facts you can dream up. And your job is to find out what those real facts are—not to proceed down irrelevant primrose paths.

Let's examine this point in the context of (gasp!) a hypothetical. (They're all right in *books*. . . .) As part of a larger problem for John Client, the partner has asked you what corporate actions Client can block as a stockholder of Limited, Inc. You know that Client holds a substantial block of Limited stock, but aren't sure of the precise amount. Under the applicable law, Client's capacity to block

Limited's actions may well vary, depending on the number of shares he owns. For instance, if he holds 40%, he can veto those actions which under corporate law require a two-thirds vote, but not those for which a bare majority will suffice. With 30%, his rights are correspondingly lessened, but he could still play havoc with an attempted pooling and perhaps a tax-free reorganization. And so on. Don't you think it might be a good idea to find out how many shares Client actually owns?

And yet, far too often in this kind of situation, I've received memoranda to the effect that *if* Client has 40%, then he can do thus-and-so; but *if*, on the other hand, he only has 30%, then . . . etc. How frustrating! I call the associate into my office. "Why did you write the memo in this hypothetical fashion?" I ask. "Because," says the associate, "I don't know how many shares Client has." "Well," I reply, "could you have found that out—say, by a simple phone call to Client's accountant?" "I guess so." "Why didn't you?" "I don't know; I didn't think of it." Let's mercifully depart this conversation; I think you get the point.[9]

There's another side to this coin, by the way; where possible, you should avoid answering purportedly hypothetical questions posed by your client. My experience is that the client isn't just passing the time of day dreaming up interesting situations to satisfy his curiosity. No, he's much more likely to have a scheme in the back of his mind, but for some reason—perhaps to avoid the loss of face from having suggested actions which you might deem unethical or which possibly possess overtones of white collar crime—he doesn't want you to know that the matter is under actual consideration.

The problem here is that you can't trust the client to put before you all the relevant facts on a hypothetical basis. He may be omitting key points, either inadvertently through ignorance or designedly to position your answer. (When caught red-handed, he will justify these omissions by pointing to the "what if" basis on which the question was posed.) But it's the *real* facts on which he'll ultimately act; and if you've given him the answer he wants on the sanitized version, you can bet your boots that the critical distinction will totally escape him.

So, pass by the hypothetical and solicit the actual facts; base your views on the complete situation. For instance, a client happens to mention to you: "I know a fellow who holds stock in a company. He

---

[9]   A similar kind of situation could occur where you're trying to decide on the optimum form of an acquisition transaction, which may depend on whether the acquired company holds its assets directly in divisions, or through subsidiaries. For God's sake, make a call and find out. See also Section 3.3.1 for an analogy to the client's interest in results and not bravura displays of brain power.

didn't buy it from the company, and he doesn't control the company. He wants to sell. Are there any problems?'' Don't venture an answer to this one. Control is an elusive concept; do you trust your client to appreciate all the nuances? Perhaps your client (excuse me: ''the stockholder'') would be deemed to be part of the control group of the company and therefore holding securities whose resale is restricted. Or he might have purchased them from a controlling person, with varying consequences depending on the nature of the transaction. There's no substitute for inquiring into all the facts.

6.5. SOME TRICKS OF THE TRADE

It would be unusual to work at anything as intensively as we lawyers approach our dealings with clients without amassing some tricks of the trade that make life a little simpler. I'm sure everyone has his own list. Let me share with you a few of my own.

An undoubtedly apocryphal anecdote has made the rounds in recent years, concerning a businessman who, having decided to change accountants, proceeded to conduct interviews with representatives of each of the major firms. The total interview consisted of his asking the accountants a single question: ''How much is two and two?'' The replies were relatively predictable; and it wasn't until the final interview that the businessman found the firm he wanted to hire—the one whose representative answered: ''What number did you have in mind?'' I know it sounds like professional heresy, but I maintain it's important for a lawyer to know how his client would *like* him to come out on the question the client has posed, or what the client's preferences are with respect to possible courses of action.[10] If the desired response isn't obvious from the content and phrasing of the client's question, the lawyer should make an effort to ascertain it, either subtly or—given the right relationship—via a more direct approach.

Now, before you round up a posse to haul me before the bar association, let me hasten to add that the reason for desiring this knowledge is *not*—as the implication runs in the accountant anecdote—that it can or should affect the *substance* of your answer or reaction, where a legal issue or some other objective manifestation of your views is concerned. You're not worth your salt as a lawyer if you provide phony

[10] There's a contrary school of thought on this, which maintains that you can be more objective in your advice when you *don't* know your client's preferences. I have heard of one renowned attorney who, taking this philosophy to its extreme, required his associates to prepare a brief on the *other* side of the proposition he was attempting to support, in order to test out the worth of his thesis.

answers to please a client. You have to call 'em as you see 'em, no matter what the consequences; it may be painful at the time, but in the long run your client will respect you for this and value your advice all the more.

On the other hand, knowing how the client wants to come out can be very important to you in deciding on the manner in which you reply—the *style*, as contrasted with the substance—and on shaping any practical advice you might offer. Take the following example. You receive a telephone call from your client, Hotseat. He announces to you (everyone has at least one client who does this sort of thing) that you're on the speakerphone in his office; that Worker, a key employee, is sitting there with him; and that Hotseat wants to know if the company can issue Worker shares of stock, which Worker will pay for with promissory notes.

Now, the way that you handle this question can be influenced significantly by whether Hotseat actually *wants* to issue Worker some stock for notes, or whether Hotseat's just going through a charade—using you as a whipping boy—for the benefit of Worker. If you determine that Hotseat isn't really interested in issuing the stock, you can emphasize the legal difficulties which do exist under the applicable state law when you use notes to pay for par value shares—to say nothing of the unfriendly scrutiny such a transaction would receive from stockholders, other employees, and so on. All of this is good, sound counsel; you're not deceiving anyone—although you would undoubtedly feel more comfortable if Worker's own lawyer were present. On the other hand, if you sense that Hotseat very much wants to issue the shares, then your litany of difficulties would be somewhat more muted, with a smooth transition into a constructive analysis of how the transaction *can* be accomplished—by securing the note, charging bona fide interest, and so on.

By the way, ascertaining Hotseat's real interest here may not be so easy—and *tomorrow*, you should let him know what an uncomfortable position he put you in, with a warning against future repetitions. But there *are* ways to proceed. For openers, don't answer right away. Get Hotseat talking; he's likely to drop a clue (such as, "I told Worker this was a very difficult thing for a public company to do . . ."), which you can then pick up on.

Take another example. A client company has been involved in negotiations looking toward its acquisition by a large public company. The parties had been discussing a deal worth about $3,000,000, payable in shares of the purchaser's stock. Your client telephones to say that the acquiring company has just suggested switching from stock to a cash deal, but has dropped the consideration to $2,500,000. He pauses to await your reaction. If you sense that he's interested in the cash, you would presumably launch into an examination of the differences between the two types of deals, their relative pros and cons in terms of tax considerations, his liquidity, and so on. But if your client is really unhappy about this development, and you start talking about the pros and cons, he may feel you're not reacting with proper indignation to the rotten deal they've offered him. Much better that you share his outrage at this blatant welching on the part of the purchasers, and begin immediately to explore your rebuttal position in the negotiations. So, before jumping in, test the water. Say: "And what did you tell him when he made that suggestion?" The client's reply should give you a fair indication of the direction in which he's heading. Remember, the client's state of mind is a fact like any other—much more important than most—and you might as well know it cold.

When you suddenly encounter a serious problem in the course of a professional engagement, I find it's usually good practice to inform the client of its existence *while* attempting to work out the resolution. Don't keep him in the dark; let him follow your progress. After all, it's his money on the line. If the obstacle proves insurmountable, you've prepared him for the worst—rather than springing the bad news on him abruptly and with finality. There's a collateral benefit for you, too. When you manage to solve a problem that the client never knew existed, it's no great shakes—somewhat in the nature of an historical footnote to the deal. But when the client has shared the anguish of your real concern over the outcome, then the victory is all the sweeter—and redounds much more directly to your credit.

Oh, by the way, there's one major exception to this last piece of advice—where the problem which arises is of your own making. For instance, you neglected to file a certain form for the client on time. This causes annoying complications but is basically curable. By all means, cure it first; *then* make your report ("Oh, by the way . . .").

Recently, we were preparing a friendly tender offer for a client company to pick up the remaining minority shares of a subsidiary located in a remote jurisdiction. Several other firms of lawyers were also involved. As we neared completion of the necessary papers, one of my associates advised me of a possible technical problem in complying with the local blue sky law, due to a somewhat ambiguous provision in the statute. After analyzing the problem, I could tell that we were unlikely to have a definitive answer for 24 hours. I made the decision to advise the client immediately that we had uncovered this possible problem, were looking into it, and would get back to him as soon as we had an answer.

The reason for my call here was slightly different than above; and were an answer expected within the hour, I might have refrained from calling the client in hopes that it was a false alarm. But frankly, I was concerned that one of the other lawyers involved in the transaction would discover the existence of the problem before we had resolved it, and would announce his discovery to the client—leaving us with egg all over our face and a client skeptical of our protestations that we were already engaged in finding a solution. It's the "getting there first" principle; when you discover an unresolved problem or conceive of what may be a brilliant idea, get it on the table before anyone else can—even if it's not fully resolved or in final varnished form. In the long run, the credit you'll receive for being Johnny-on-the-spot (though some problems prove insignificant, certain ideas pedestrian) will outweigh any negative impact from premature exposure.[11]

As your self-confidence and judgment increase, don't be afraid to play Jeanne Dixon once in awhile. If you have a hunch about something, make a prediction to your client. It might prove very useful to him in anticipating trouble and taking preventive measures. I remember a case where I felt that the lawyer representing the seller in an acquisition was attempting to sabotage the deal. I said so, to general disbelief. It turned out he was. People recalled my warning. I've also expressed a number of predictions that never materialized. But these are rarely remembered and never held against you—after all, they're only suppositions. Once you're proved right a few times, however, you can gain a reputation for prescience that you'd never enjoy if you kept your hunches to yourself.

Finally, a few words on the gentle art of covering one's tail. You're in the big leagues now, playing for keeps. No contract binds the client to you, and any number of applicants for the post are lying in wait. You have to be concerned not only with what's happening today, but also with how your words or actions will look two years from now—particularly if you and the client are then no longer on speaking terms. So, protect yourself. When you give important oral advice, follow it up with a letter (if that's appropriate), or at least a file memo for record purposes. Include all the caveats that were contained in your advice, but which the client will no doubt omit when he's busy misquoting you down the road.[11a]

---

[11] The general topic of throwing out ideas for discussion, at the risk of being shot down, is discussed in Section 8.6. A particular application of the getting-there-first principle occurs in dealings with administrative agencies (discussed in Section 7.5). It's always better to be the one who brings the problem to the agency—even if you lack all the salient facts—rather than to have them discover it on their own. You're in an area here where good faith is important, and your initiative will stand you in good stead. The recent SEC voluntary program on sensitive payments was based in large part on just this principle.

[11a] For a similar admonition in the area of dealing with the client's auditors, see Section 6.7.

There is also the question of responsibility. If something is your responsibility, then do it. If it's not, then make damned sure everyone is aware it's *not* your responsibility—because if you don't, you can bet that someone will attempt to put the onus on you. A letter or a phone call to set the record straight may do the trick. Suppose you're held up in drafting a certain document while awaiting some data that the company's comptroller has promised to supply. Is the company president aware of this? Make sure he knows the reason why things are not progressing. Otherwise, he'll probably assume you're falling down on the job.

6.6 THE CLIENT COMES FIRST

Particularly for lawyers who practice in the business area, it's impossible to ignore the businessman's popular conception of a lawyer as a breaker, not maker, of deals—and thus to be avoided if at all possible.[12] This unfortunate reputation as obstructionist—prone to talking but not doing, given to raising more problems than we solve—plagues us in all our endeavors.

So, always make an effort to stand back a little and ponder how you *appear* to the client. Not how you *are*—because no one goes out of his way to be non-constructive—but how you're being perceived by the party in interest who doesn't appreciate the obstacles to be overcome. Is it possible that most of your remarks during the course of a lengthy meeting could be construed as throwing up roadblocks in the way of the client's desired goals? Have you served solely as the bearer of bad tax tidings, the Paul Revere of regulatory problems, the harbinger of protracted litigation? Look at yourself through the client's eyes; and if you don't like what you see, then change the image.

Be constructive. When you raise a problem, don't dwell on its magnitude but move quickly to a discussion of possible solutions. Be practical. Get off the theoretical plane and down to your client's level of reality. Don't give him the runaround. If the client asks a question, try to answer it—limiting yourself to such caveats as are absolutely necessary. Focus on the bottom line.

Servicing a client also calls for something else. You can call it hand-holding—and to some of our intellectually arrogant brethren it may appear to have that demeaning quality—but whatever the name, it signifies your consistent availability to the client. He may want you

---

[12] An advertisement for R. Ringer's bestseller, *Winning Through Intimidation* (1974), put the case in these terms: "Have you ever had a deal blow up solely because of an attorney? . . . [Y]ou must face the reality that attorneys have been, are, and unfortunately, probably always will be a major obstacle in just about every significant business transaction that takes place."

to answer questions, to reassure him that what he's doing makes sense, or just to serve as a sounding board. But hey, man, that's what he pays you for! He's *entitled*. You may think it's not the highest and best use of your valuable time, but don't tell that to *him*. If it weren't for his ilk, you'd probably be out selling insurance. . . .

Remember, too, that the corporate client is not necessarily faceless and unitary. Companies are composed of men and women who don't always communicate, much less agree or get along. Sometimes they're playing politics, jockeying for position. They can be touchy about protocol in situations where you're unaware it exists. So, use common sense and don't get caught in the middle. Avoid reporting only to A at the risk of miffing B. Don't seek answers from C to questions more properly directed to D. Never assume that E is passing on your pearls of wisdom to F. It takes some effort to insure that everyone is on the same wavelength—a few extra calls, copies of letters, and so on—but be sure you touch those extra bases.

Finally, don't ever allow yourself to reach the point where the client has disappeared from your consciousness and you're out there performing in his role—making business decisions and other judgments that are properly the client's bailiwick. Oh sure, you should *help* with those decisions. When asked for your views, don't just reply: ''Well, that's a business decision'' and leave it at that. You can outline the alternatives, show how certain assumptions may affect the answer, and so forth.[13] But even if you're certain how the client will come out on an issue, you should always let *him* make the decision.

You'll soon develop a technique for handling this in a way that neither impinges on his primacy nor requires you to seem stupid or indecisive. For instance, on a relatively simple issue you might say to the client: ''I assume that you're agreeable to the interest being paid quarterly'' (as contrasted with saying either ''When do you want the interest paid?'' or ''We'll pay the interest quarterly''). And don't forget that in negotiating with other lawyers[14]—except over something legalistic like your opinion—you should always qualify any agreement reached among attorneys as being subject to your client's acquiescence. Similarly, when sending the other side a draft document that the client hasn't seen, make sure to state in writing that it hasn't been reviewed by the client, who may want to make changes (even if you don't think he will). Gestures such as these are designed to firmly establish your agency status in all matters concerning your principal.

---

[13] There's more on this aspect of decision-making in Chapter 8, particularly Sections 8.4, 8.5 and 8.6.
[14] A subject discussed in depth in Section 7.3.

6.7. INTERACTION WITH THE CLIENT'S OTHER PROFESSIONALS—PARTICULARLY ACCOUNTANTS

In the course of representing most business clients, you will have occasion to come into contact with other professionals who render related services to the client. Your effective interaction with these people can significantly impact the outcome of your assignment. There's another dimension, too; you're under constant scrutiny by these other professionals, whose views on your performance can be expected to carry weight in the client's overall appraisal. Let's face it, when the client's prestigious investment banker advises him that the company's lawyer isn't up to par—the banker having observed several other attorneys recently who would better serve the client's interests—your days may well be numbered. On the other hand, the increased exposure can be professionally rewarding and may lead to other relationships.

By way of example, let's take a closer look at the investment banker, in his role as a member of the corporate team on a particular project (such as an acquisition)—advising the client, assisting in the negotiations, and so forth.[15] Of course, if he has brought you into the matter, many of the same considerations to be later discussed in connection with sponsoring lawyers[16]—making your sponsor look good, keeping him informed and invited, etc.—are equally applicable to the investment banker. We'll assume, however, that this isn't the case; you're just two independent professionals who happen to be working for the same client.

Now, although others might disagree, I take a positive view regarding the role of investment bankers in a matter such as an acquisition. In some instances, their participation can even be vital to consummation of the transaction. What appears to disturb some businessmen and lawyers—namely, that the investment banker generally has a substantial fee riding on consummation of the deal—doesn't bother me; these people are entitled to compensation for their services, and the size of the stipend has to make up for beatings they've taken on other aborted transactions. The contingent fee furnishes a real incentive for the investment banker to play an ac-

---

[15] The investment banker as underwriter occupies a somewhat more arm's length position, raising different considerations—some of which are explored in Section 7.2.4 on parallel representation. A variant of the theme under discussion (but beyond the scope of this section) occurs when you are the lawyer representing the *investment banker* in circumstances such as a merger or takeover; i.e., where you're on the same side as the company and working in its interests, but your primary responsibility is to the investment banker.

[16] See Section 7.2.1.

tive, constructive role in attaining the goal. And this is his real forte: cutting through red tape, keeping things moving, resolving the knotty impasse.[17] Investment bankers can bring a broad fund of experience to bear on the situation, and their talents mesh neatly with the lawyer's particular attributes.[18]

For these reasons, it's a good idea for you to be present when the client meets with his investment banker. Major decisions are made during these encounters, which you may only discover after the event. Things can move fast in a business deal; being one day behind can put you completely out of touch. Then too, you should be alert for the occasional investment banker who practices law without a license. This fellow has participated in so many deals that he exudes a patina of expertise on corporate, securities and tax matters—to say nothing of accounting. This can appear quite convincing to the client, who may accept such advice as holy writ if you're not around to provide a rebuttal or cautionary signal.

Conversely, be careful not to tread too heavily on the investment banker's turf. I would suggest a measure of discreet non-intervention on matters of price and other financial details that represent his bread and butter. You can assist in developing the strategy and participating in negotiations designed to achieve the goals set by the client and investment banker—if invited. But some investment bankers prefer to handle these matters strictly on their own, viewing lawyers as not particularly helpful at such moments; and if the client sees things the same way, then you're probably better advised to stay uninvolved.

Perhaps even more so than the client—and particularly where the investment banker has engineered the deal—the investment banker may view the lawyer as a potential hindrance and nay-sayer. So, exercise some care to be (and to *appear*) constructive when this fellow is around. Avoid making even off-hand negative comments about the deal to the investment banker; these simply confirm his suspicions and will be duly reported back to the client *sans* caveats—with the predictable result that you're promptly tabbed as a negative thinker. If you're unhappy over some aspect of the deal, tell the client directly —in a way that highlights the constructive nature of the questions you are raising.

---

[17]   I'm assuming here that the deal is one which *should* get done, but has run into temporary roadblocks. Watch out, however, for the occasional investment banker who pushes too hard for accommodation when your best judgment says "stick on this point."

[18]   Less helpful are those investment bankers who stand off from the fray, refrain from playing an active part, and only pass on questions of fairness and such. See Section 13.3.2 of *Anatomy* regarding the two hats worn by investment bankers—the institutional role of passing on fairness and the advocate's role in negotiating the price—which can often come into conflict.

Another frequent figure on the scene is the client's public relations advisor. A talented specialist in this area can be quite helpful in drafting press releases, preparing annual and quarterly reports, and dealing with the press and investment community. He furnishes a dimension which many lawyers (who come across as too legalistic) and executives (whose literary efforts often lack distinction) don't otherwise supply.

However, this particular bottle is marked "Handle With Care." You should never allow an important press release, drafted by a public relations consultant, to be disseminated without your prior review. He won't necessarily be alert to your concerns. There may well be restrictions, rules, questions of policy and matters of judgment upon which you should pass. So, by all means, obtain the public relations input, but exercise a veto if you sense trouble brewing. This may land you in a brief flap with the client; but my experience is that sophisticated public relations people back away from confrontations of this kind, and the client usually ends up following your recommendation when it's based on sound legal judgment.

There are a number of other professionals (and semi-professionals) we could discuss, but I think it would be more productive to examine one such relationship—the most potentially complex of all—in some detail. I have in mind here your interaction with the company's public accountants.

In modern day corporate life—with so much emphasis placed on financial results by corporate executives, the SEC, analysts and the investing public—the outside auditor is an important, ubiquitous figure. He doesn't *create* anything; he's more a reviewer than an advisor; but his blessing and imprimatur count for much. And because accounting is less of a science than accountants would have us believe, the client-accountant relationship is rarely cut-and-dried.

Unlike other professionals who service the client, the outside accountant plays a curiously ambivalent role. Although the accounting firm is hired by the company, paid by it, reports to its board and can be fired at will, the firm as auditor must maintain a degree of independence far beyond what's expected of a lawyer and most other outsiders. This isn't limited to financial independence;[19] it also means maintaining some distance in terms of subject matter. The auditors must form an independent judgment as to the appropriateness of the accounting principles and practices utilized by the company. If, in their judgment, these fall short, then they so advise the

[19] Accountants can't own stock in or have other financial interests related to the company they are auditing, which would be deemed to compromise their independence and render their audits unacceptable in filings with the Securities and Exchange Commission.

company, with a view to the adoption of permissible principles.[20]
If the company ultimately refuses to change its principles or restate its
numbers, then the report issued by the accountants must be
qualified—stating, in effect, that the financial statements do not measure
up in this respect to applicable criteria.[21] The resulting brouhaha is not
simply semantic; companies with qualified reports can find themselves
in trouble with the stock exchanges and the SEC, thwarted in their efforts to issue securities, accomplish mergers, and the like—a heavy load
to bear in the pragmatic world of business.

Although grasping the concept of auditors' independence intellectually, as a practical matter the client often becomes frustrated when
the accountant actually stakes out an independent position—by insisting
that the client treat an income item in a certain way, or take a reserve
to which the client objects. This is a major source of client/accountant
friction. If a lawyer disagrees with his client over a particular course of
action which isn't unlawful or unethical, it's ultimately the client's call;
and the lawyer will presumably swallow his pride and go along if he can't
convince the client otherwise. But an accountant can't knuckle under
quite so readily, and relations between the client and his accountant can
become rather stormy.

Now, lawyers often find themselves unwittingly drawn into these
accounting controversies. And this may result in an awkward situation
for the attorney. On the one hand, he does represent the client, and must
have his best interests continually in mind; on the other hand, a lawyer
with any depth is likely to form his own judgments, rather than simply
doing the client's bidding. Actually, however, this status can be helpful in negotiating a resolution of the client/accountant dispute, since
the auditors may be inclined to give the lawyer's semi-detached views
more weight than the client's predictable response. If you detect a
situation where you may be able to resolve a contretemps between
client and accountant—or if you sense that the client would appreciate your involvement—then by all means, step up and take your shot;
you could become a hero, and there's little downside (since the client
has presumably been unable to make progress on his own).

One dispute, however, that I would avoid like the plague concerns
the amount of the accountant's fee. When the client complains to me
how much his auditors are charging, I moan along in sympathy—although not too loudly, inasmuch as I might be next in line

---

[20]   In this regard, the recent proliferation of audit committees—generally
composed of outside directors on company boards—has increased the potential influence which accountants can bring to bear on management.
[21]   Financial statements are expected to be prepared in accordance with
generally accepted accounting principles, consistently applied, and should
fairly present the finanacial position and results of operations of the company.

for the same treatment! But I won't volunteer to approach the accountant to negotiate a decrease, just as I wouldn't want him butting in where my firm's charges are concerned.

The real problem for a lawyer who becomes involved in a dispute between client and accountant occurs when the dispute contains a legal element—that is, the accounting problem will go away (or at least become manageable) if the client can adopt a certain legal position vis-à-vis a third party (such as a plaintiff or government agency). At these moments, auditors love nothing better than to seek comfort from lawyers, to solidify their record of reasonable reliance.[22] And so, the focus of the dispute can often shift from client/accountant to accountant/lawyer—with the accountant asking the lawyer to go out on a limb, the lawyer queasy about his ability to do so as a professional matter, and boom!—you're right in the middle of a pickle, with the client now disturbed at *your* seeming intransigence.

Obviously, this is a situation to be avoided, which may be easier said than done. When you sense such a clash developing, you ought to approach the client *first*—before the accountant arrives—with the news that the accountant is seeking an opinion you're professionally unable to render. Then, make every effort to avoid a confrontational mode with the accountant. Advise him, even before he asks, that "Obviously this is *not* a matter we can opine on"—but that perhaps comparable assurances can be derived from certain representations or undertakings by (or to) the company, together with some more limited advice on your part. . . .

By the way, lawyers can and should turn the tables on the auditors. There may well be specific matters of a financial nature, arising other than in connection with an audit, on which the company could use some comfort. Don't be bashful; ask the accountants for a letter on the subject. For instance, if you're concerned whether the company's proposed repurchase of shares may interfere with its ability to account for a subsequent acquisition as a pooling of interests,[23] have the accountants go on record at the time the repurchase transaction is occurring—while there's still a chance to reverse gears if the desired conclusion is not forthcoming. Never wait until after the fact to ask for the auditors' view, thereby risking a "you should have consulted us earlier" reaction.

Don't get me wrong; I have a healthy respect for auditors and their function. If they didn't exist, the lawyer's policing role would be well

---

[22] For one approach to handling the disputes that can arise over auditors seeking comfort from lawyers, see American Bar Association "Statement of Policy Regarding Lawyers' Responses to Auditors' Requests for Information," 31 *The Business Lawyer* 1709-1745 (1976).

[23] See Section 4.4.2 of *Anatomy*.

nigh unbearable. When you're not on such close terms with a particular client, and a trifle unsure of developments behind those corporate walls, you can derive a marked degree of comfort from the continuing presence of a reputable accounting firm.

So, lawyers and accountants serve complementary roles; and except for occasional conflicts, they can and should interact constructively on a well-tuned client team. If you're going to practice corporate or securities or tax law (or for that matter, almost anything that touches on business), much that concerns you as a lawyer will revolve around the company's financial statements. And in order to deal with auditors effectively, the lawyer must have a working knowledge of accounting. Unless you can speak to accountants in their own language, it's difficult to understand the significance of the problem at hand.

To paraphrase Clemenceau, accounting is just too important nowadays to be left solely to the accountants. There's nothing automatic about what accountants do. When the auditors insist that unless a certain level of reserve is established they'll have to qualify their report, but the client is unwilling to set up the full amount of the reserve, there's usually a point somewhere between their respective positions at which the qualification will be dropped. You can be helpful in this process—provided you understand what the issue is all about, what factors are relevant to the auditing determination, and how much flexibility the accountants possess.

So bone up on accounting. If you don't understand something that seems important, ask the auditors for an explanation. Accountants are delighted to educate you on the intricacies of their profession—after all, it's not the kind of patter that's much sought after at cocktail parties! Accountant friends whose judgment you trust should be highly prized. You can address questions to them on matters not involving their firms; this can serve as a useful check on the client's accountant who's giving you a hard time. In addition to advising you whether the particular issue is one involving a rigid principle or containing room for maneuver, your friend can also direct you to the relevant literature and provide precedents from his own shop.[24]

Now, in dealing with accountants, there are a few facts of life that you ought to know.[25] First (and not surprisingly), many accountants do not

---

[24] Nowadays, the large accounting firms all have internal legal staffs. You should also become acquainted with some of these people. On occasion, they can be very helpful in dealing with matters you have with that firm—or for that matter, with another firm—because they speak *your* language and can better understand the lawyer's particular problem.

[25] Obviously, the characterizations which follow do not apply to all accountants equally; but on the basis of first-hand observation, I do consider these traits to be sufficiently typical to make for useful generalizations.

use the English language with as much precision as mathematical notation. Yet accountants do considerable writing—the footnotes to the financial statements being the most notable example.[26] So it behooves you, if provided the opportunity, to review these notes before they're set in stone, making sure they're clear and unambiguous.[27] Moreover, the notes often lack a "PR" sense, shall we say; the unfavorable information may not be communicated in as harmless a fashion as possible, consistent with the facts.[28] Perhaps some minor rephrasing on your part will render the matter less seemingly onerous.[29]

Of course, inasmuch as these notes are the joint product of the company's internal accounting staff and outside auditors, a light touch in suggesting non-substantive changes may be advisable. But I've found that where the lawyer notes an ambiguity or suggests a desirable revision, his recommendation is usually accepted. Provided, that is, the suggestion is made at a sufficiently early point in the cycle. On the night before the financial statements are slated to be delivered to the SEC, accountants—like most of us in similar situations—will tend to resist change.

Your client's accountant may not be skilled in the arts of persuasiveness. He's not used to having to perform as an advocate. Perhaps you can supply the missing element. For example, let's say a meeting is taking place at the SEC to discuss the manner in which the client

---

[26] The auditors are fond of telling you that these are the *company's* financial statements and footnotes—they only audit them. That may be so in theory, but to anyone familiar with the actual process, it contains a strong element of fiction. Sure, the operating results themselves are the company's; but the manner in which those results are stated—the sophisticated judgments involved—are as much the auditors' as they are the company's. So when that hands-off formulation is used to duck a question, your client should insist that the auditors come to grips with the issue. For instance, the auditors may consider a financial institution's proposed loan loss reserve to be inadequate; the company has to increase the amount or suffer a qualified report. In such an instance, the company shouldn't have to guess what will satisfy the auditors—"You name a figure and we'll audit it"; rather, the company is entitled to receive the auditors' best judgment and advice.

[27] (Conciseness is a virtue I wouldn't be too concerned about in this particular context.) Most auditors would actually *like* you to review these notes, particularly those involving matters with a legal context.

[28] A consideration discussed in Section 3.2.7.

[29] For example, the footnote might state: "When the note became due, the company defaulted. The payee sued the company. The company defended on the ground of the payee's non-performance." Assuming the non-performance issue is a genuine one which caused the company to refuse payment, and assuming no cross-defaults have been triggered or other dire consequences ensued, this could be rewritten to state: "When the note became due, issue was joined on whether the payee was entitled to payment in view of his alleged non-performance; the matter is currently being litigated." Much preferable, I would think—though still accurate.

proposes to handle a certain major accounting issue.[30] Don't rely solely on the auditors to persuade the staff that the client's position is correct. They may be unable to formulate convincing rationale for sound substantive points. Prior to the meeting, speak to the accountant; get the facts; understand the issue. Then lend a hand in working up the presentation—even though it might ultimately be made by the auditors (especially if the principal staff representative is himself an accountant).

When faced with a problem or impasse, it's not always easy for an accountant to conceive of ways to side-step the issue or adopt a fresh approach.[31] I recently encountered such a situation, where I felt the auditors were being overly conservative on an issue, to the detriment of our mutual client. I wasn't sure, however, how to deal with the problem. Here's where that accountant friend—preferably one with a lively imagination—can come in handy. I reviewed the matter with him; he suggested some fruitful avenues to pursue. I brought these back to the client's auditors, and the story had a happy ending. But the accountants required some nudging in the right direction; and to handle the chore, *I* had to be primed first.[32]

When left to their own devices, accountants do not always move at a lightning pace[33]—a charge, I might add, that's also leveled at attorneys with some frequency. The time element can be frustrating when it's necessary to file documents quickly, conclude agreements that depend on finanacial statements, etc. Some prodding may be necessary, although this is best handled directly by the client (to whom you've passed the word); after all, he's paying their bill and responsible for annual rehiring—not you!

It's a good rule never to leave accountant assignments open-ended as to time. There should always be a due date for receipt of the materials being prepared. And the best method to handle this—equally valid in dealing with other professionals and executives—is to let the auditors select their own deadline. Of course, you can assist a bit in the process. For example, you might say to the accountant (preferably, in front of the client): "Can you have that

---

[30]   For dealings with government agencies generally, see Section 7.5.

[31]   In fairness, since the accountant's aim is to represent economic reality, he rarely views his role as a creative one—in fact, "creative accounting" is a term of derision in the industry. This constitutes a major contrast with lawyers, who frequently *must* be creative to overcome a weak position and prevail.

[32]   By the way, I could never have brought the second accountant into the situation openly; this would just have stiffened the resolve of the first firm. But coming from me—a non-competitor—the suggestions didn't threaten them quite so much.

[33]   This may be due more to our lack of understanding of the accountant's function than to any dilatory aspects in their nature. Auditing by its very nature is a meticulous process, and things always seem to take longer than one anticipates.

financial information prepared by a week from this Friday? That would seem reasonable." If he says, "Yes," then he's adopted the date. (It may be a trifle difficult for him to say "No," in view of the message you've conveyed to the client.) But don't push too hard; assuming you've provided some leeway in your date selection (as you should have), let him suggest an alternate target that both of you can live with.

Accountants should always be asked to review any documents—including press releases and other matters of lesser dignity—that contain references to matters within their bailiwick. It's awkward to have an accountant (or any other professional, for that matter) read something after the fact and say: "If I had seen this before it went out, I would have made the following comments. . . ." Remember, accounting principles are abstruse, and accountants have a jargon all their own. Don't take it upon yourself to pass on these matters.

Moreover, the outside auditors should be kept advised of significant developments at the company. It can be extremely troublesome when they discover something that hasn't been communicated to them—raising suspicions over whether the client has been withholding information. On the other hand, assuming no emergency, you needn't bring the auditors into a matter prematurely. Try to get a handle on the legal, factual and practical dimensions of the problem by the time you're ready to consult with them, so that the difficulty isn't blown out of perspective through inadequate knowledge.

You should always assume that the auditors are taking notes on whatever you say.[34] I have little doubt this memorialization occurs simultaneously when your conversation is over the phone; I would also bet that any significant personal contact is followed by a debriefing file memo. The auditors are building a paper record, and you may be very much a part of it. Therefore, if your observations or advice contain important caveats,[35] it may be safer to communicate with the auditors in writing, to ensure that the caveats aren't disregarded. At the very least, make your own contemporaneous memo of what you've said. Don't rely on *his* notes. I can recall seeing one of those auditors' memos, taken from notes of a phone call with me. I was horrified to read what I purportedly had said. All the subtleties were excised; everything was stated in absolute terms; forms of expressions were put into my mouth that I would never have countenanced. Most of the time you never get to see these memos; but they're sitting in the auditors' files—and should litigation ensue, you'll be stuck with them.]

---

[34] This may be understandable in view of the plethora of lawsuits directed against accountants in recent years.
[35] See Section 3.2.8.

In re-reading this section, I'm aware of a slightly negative tone—have I been too hard on the accounting profession? If so, I apologize. The problem is, of course, that the *positive* aspects don't give rise to the kind of conflicts that need concern attorneys. As a matter of fact, some of my best friends are accountants—and if I had a sister. . . .

CHAPTER 7

DEALING WITH OTHER LAWYERS

7.1. A FEW PRELIMINARY OBSERVATIONS

Up to this point, the *other* lawyers who have peopled these pages have been primarily located in your own firm—partners, seniors, juniors, peers. It is now my sad duty to advise you, Virginia, that yes indeed, there is an A.B.A.; and clustered out there in the great beyond are literally thousands of attorneys who don't work in your office but with whom you must learn to deal—which happens to be the subject matter of this chapter.

Let me begin by stating what should be obvious: namely, that your ability to handle the attorney on the other side of a transaction or case is a prime measure of your progress as a lawyer. Just as the partner's growing confidence in your abilities makes him comfortable leaving you alone with the client,[1] it's equally important for the partner to feel he can propel you solo into an adversary situation—without concern that you'll concede a vital interest of the client or fail to achieve rightful protections and appropriate advantages. *Note:* it's the partner's *perception* in this regard that counts, which may not necessarily be on all fours with whether you actually possess the necessary skills.[2]

As contrasted with, say, legal analytical skills (on which you've cut your teeth during three exhausting law school years), a novice lawyer doesn't emerge fully equipped to deal with other lawyers. In professional relations, there's no substitute for experience. You must observe carefully what your supervisory partner says to his opposite number (and, even more important at times, what he *doesn't* say). You need to think through such questions as: what do I want to achieve from this negotiation; and what is my adversary really wor-

---

[1] See Section 6.2.
[2] See the discussion in Chapter 1 on the optics of your performance.

167

ried about? And no instant formula exists for achieving the flexibility, the sensitivity to nuance, the ability to peer into another person's mind, the capacity to create effective compromises, that are the hallmarks of a sophisticated attorney.

It all takes time and requires your attention—but it's time and attention well spent. And don't make the mistake of assuming that your particular area of legal practice doesn't require this skill. An attorney who handles trusts and estates, for example, might have relatively little contact with other lawyers on an adversary basis; and yet, when the day comes that his corporate partner—involved in a messy struggle for control of a company having certain trusts as major shareholders—calls upon him to "sell" some dubious trust law theories to the adversary lawyer in order to position the ultimate settlement, he should be prepared to do battle. Similarly, a tax lawyer, who is often removed from the rough and tumble of negotiations, might feel no need to sharpen his hortatory talents; but when he finds himself down in Washington at the Internal Revenue Service office, attempting to obtain a favorable tax ruling from that I.R.S. agent—government regulators being one of the subspecies of the adversary breed we'll be examining here—he had better be persuasive and possess other prime qualities basic to lawyer-to-lawyer dealings.

Since I'm sure my personal attitudes toward this subject will show through (rigid impartiality never being one of my strong suits), let me say at the outset that this discussion touches on matters which are quite individualistic, as to which no "correct" modes exist. Your style in handling an adversary is composed of many elements—most notably, your own personality; and unless you're a consummate actor (a worthwhile skill to possess, incidentally), switching personalities for this purpose isn't an easy task. Nevertheless, you ought to be conscious of how your traits of character affect your performance. If you're generous to a fault, for instance, satisfy your magnanimity in philanthropic endeavors; big hearts are out of place in hard-headed business negotiations. If you're an unreconstructed, table-pounding male chauvinist at home, don't try to pull your usual act seated across the conference room table from the underwriter's female securities lawyer. The talented attorney varies his style constantly to suit the combination of his particular adversary and the situation.

Obviously, the extent of your responsibilities and freedom of action in negotiating and otherwise dealing with other lawyers will be substantially affected by your supervisory partner's degree of involvement. Having the partner present can be quite inhibiting.[3] Even when

---

[3]   See Section 10.2.2 for a discussion of this very real Catch-22: the associate is loathe to negotiate when the partner is sitting in the room; yet it's only when the partner is present that he can observe the associate's negotiating skills.

you're there on your own, the question arises: has the partner delegated the matter to you, or are you dealing simply as his surrogate?[4] Since the essence of this chapter is the inter-lawyer relationship, and inasmuch as partner-associate problems are handled elsewhere,[5] we'll assume for purposes of this chapter that (unless otherwise indicated) you've been authorized to handle the other lawyer on your own.

To assist in our analysis of this subject, I suggest we distinguish among four major categories of relationships with other lawyers, listed in ascending adversarial order.

Category One—which we'll call "joint representation"—covers the situation where you and another lawyer (from outside your firm) are working together on a matter, representing the same client. Insofar as the client is concerned, your interests and those of the other lawyer are co-extensive. This arises most often when a corporate client has inside counsel with whom you work on a cooperative basis, either as regular outside counsel or special counsel for a particular deal. Or, your firm might be general counsel for a client in a situation where a specialist—perhaps an expert on patents and trademarks—has been brought in to assist on a certain transaction. Or vice versa: *you* may be the specialist. Joint representation can also arise where the engagement requires some advice from a local lawyer, in addition to the lawyer who is in overall charge.

Category Two—let's call this "parallel representation"—involves matters in which you and the other lawyer are working together in a common effort, but representing different clients. Attorneys representing co-defendants in litigation, who aren't claiming against each other, fall into this category. Another good example of parallel representation occurs in the complementary roles that counsel for the company and the underwriter play in connection with a public offering of securities. Other than negotiating the underwriting agreement and the technical terms of any senior securities being offered, their principal efforts are essentially cooperative—directed to drafting and clearing the prospectus and getting the issue in shape to be sold. It's a joint endeavor to ferret out the facts about the company, to deal with the SEC, and so on; and yet, their respective outlooks can't help being molded by the somewhat different interests which their clients possess. With business transactions becoming more and more complex, the number of times lawyers find themselves in this parallel representation category has increased noticeably.

---

[4]   Working out in advance with the partner how much freedom you have to cede points and swap concessions in the negotiations is one of the topics contained in Section 7.3.4.

[5]   Primarily in Chapters 5 and 10.

In Category Three—we'll dub this "friendly adversaries"—you and the other lawyer are on opposite sides of the table, although working towards a common goal. Corporate acquisitions are a classic example of this genre. One of you represents the seller, the other the purchaser. Their separate interests are directly in conflict, but the parties have decided to link the two companies. They recognize the necessity of achieving agreement on a document that will protect their respective interests—contracts being at the core of most friendly adversarial dealings. Although there are bound to be some clashes as conflicting goals get ironed out, a commonality of interest exists; after all, no one's *forcing* the two parties to get together. They've made their own decisions to negotiate, and either side can pull out with impunity before the contract is signed. Real estate transactions partake of much this same character. Labor negotiations do to some extent, although with important differences: the parties aren't totally free to walk away—some elements of coercion are involved—and the frequent bitterness of the exchanges can elevate this close to the Category Four level. In most commercial transactions, however, you will be dealing with friendly adversaries.

Finally, Category Four—let's call this one "hostile adversaries"—reflects situations where you are locked in combat with the other lawyer. The obvious example here is litigation, with one of you representing the plaintiff and the other the defendant. Another instance occurs when one company has made a hostile tender offer for another. The two lawyers may be personal friends, and may even remain on good terms throughout the contest (a feat not always easily achievable, as the rhetoric heats up and the client's blood boils); but except when the talk turns to settlement, there is no common goal here (as in a merger). One side is going to win and the other will lose; and to make sure which is which, the lawyers are apt to knock each other's block off in the process.

Many aspects of your dealings with other lawyers turn on the category of relationship in which you find yourself. The following subsection will deal with the rather subtle shadings of Categories One and Two—joint and parallel representation. A large portion of this chapter is devoted to the friendly adversaries of Category Three, a relationship offering unique challenges and opportunities. The hostile adversaries of Category Four are then used as a springboard for a broader-based discussion of various aspects of litigation and the courts.

There is another important category of lawyer—possessing quite distinctive characteristics, attributable more to position than to personality—with whom you'll be called upon to deal. I refer to regulatory officials, who possess the power to grant or deny items of real significance to your client. Knowing how and when to approach them—asking the right question of the right official, making the optimal presentation, and obtaining the best possible answer—is a separate skill to which we'll devote the final subsection.

7.2. JOINT AND PARALLEL REPRESENTATION

In case you didn't notice, we're currently poised in the age of the lawyer. The New Yorker cartoon depicts a stylish woman and a Wall Street attorney-type conversationally engaged at a Manhattan cocktail party—and she is saying: "How did I guess you were a lawyer? Simple. *Everybody* is a lawyer." We have managed to construct a society of such convoluted laws and regulations that legal advice is needed to accomplish the most basic transactions.

So, one of the facts of life in today's legal practice is that, no matter what you're doing, there are bound to be plenty of other lawyers around—not only members of your own firm and adversaries, but a sizeable number who inhabit your side of the transaction, representing either the same client or one whose interests parallel those of yours. Which brings us to the subject of cooperative lawyering. *Not*, how do I beat the other side's brains out, but how do I communicate with my colleague. *Not*, how am I coming across to the judge, but how do I appear to a common client.

A significant recent development in business-related law has been that more and more large corporations—formerly dependent for all their legal advice upon a single outside law firm acting as general counsel (with a partner usually sitting on the board of directors)—now charge an inside general counsel with the responsibility of parceling out the company's legal work. Much of it will be performed internally by a staff of lawyer-employees; and the tasks requiring outside counsel may well be allocated among several different law firms—even in a single transaction. Increasingly, the principal criterion for selection is becoming: which law firm or lawyer is best qualified to handle this particular job or aspect?

All of which makes a great deal of sense. After all, the kinds of transactions handled externally are usually those requiring some special expertise not possessed by the inside lawyers—so why not hire a firm that has that very expertise? If a company requires sophisticated tax advice on an international transaction, is it smart to engage a firm with a so-so tax department whose focus is exclusively on domestic matters—even though the company enjoys quite satisfactory relations with this firm in other areas, and might even be using them for the corporate aspects of the deal? Should a company pay its regular firm to educate itself on how to accomplish a complex real estate financing, or should someone be retained who knows the ropes? You might feel differently if you're the lawyer displaced—but this is basically a sound development, encouraging a merit-oriented approach to the selection of counsel. And that, after all, is one of the main points of this book: if you fashion yourself into a really good lawyer, clients will seek you out.

In any event, as a result of this evolution, you are now likely to encounter some rather subtle relationships among attorneys: relations between inside and outside counsel; between expert and generalist; between regular outside counsel and special counsel brought in for this transaction by (i) regular outside counsel or (ii) by someone else; and between lawyers representing different clients whose interests coincide in most (but significantly, not all) respects. These relationships often call for skills which extend beyond the merely adversarial into the realms of psychology and gamesmanship; but it's crucial that you recognize the niceties and make the necessary effort.

7.2.1. Joint Representation: The Reluctant Rivals.

The proper goal of joint representation should be to coordinate the talents and energies of the two lawyers in order to most effectively benefit the mutual client. But, to be candid, the fact is that this relationship—at least between two sets of outside lawyers working on aspects of the same transaction[6]—often degenerates into a contest for the client's favor. Destructive competitiveness of this sort between lawyers is not in the client's interest and demeans the professionals involved. I'm not suggesting for a moment that you shouldn't strive to be perceived as superior (or at least equal) to other lawyers involved in the matter, but the manner in which you go about achieving this result can be almost as important as the result itself.

At the threshold of any discussion of this subject is a very basic distinction: how did your firm happen to come into the picture? As an associate assigned to the matter, this is one of the first morsels of information you should elicit. There's a world of difference between, on the one hand, being hired by the client because he heard your firm was proficient in this particular area—and there you are, face to face with a sullen, regular outside counsel, who is prepared to second-guess, needle, backbite, and otherwise demonstrate to the client why he needed no help from you in this situation—and, on the other hand, having been brought in at the *instance* of the regular counsel, who has recognized the need for your particular knowledge. At the risk of stating the obvious, allow me to enunciate the principle applicable to this latter situation: when you're introduced into a matter

---

6   Problems of inside vs. outside counsel are discussed in Section 7.2.3.

by another lawyer (let's call him your "sponsor"), you owe that law-yer a special obligation—not merely to refrain from overt attempts to woo the client, but to use your best efforts to make your sponsor look good in front of his client. In one sense, your *real* client here is your sponsor.

So, always make sure that your sponsor is invited to be present at all meetings between you and your mutual client, unless your sponsor has explicitly advised you that he's not interested in attending. If your sponsor wants to continue to serve as an interface with the client, he should be allowed to do so—assuming it doesn't diminish your ability to advise the client and obtain the client's judgment on matters of significance. The flow of information to your sponsor about what you're doing and what's going on should be constant. Wherever possible, he should be given the opportunity to sit in on meetings with the adversary or other third parties. Don't spring major new ideas on the client or adversary without having discussed them first with your sponsor. And when the idea is a good one that your sponsor endorses, submerge your ego and present it to the client as a mutual offering. If your sponsor wants you to get the sole credit, he'll make that fact known to the client; remember, the sponsor probably went out on a limb with his client to get you hired in the first place, so he's also interested in your looking good.

Take a minute to appreciate what's going on inside your sponsor's mind. You might have no aggressive designs on his client whatsoever; and yet, as you begin to develop a close relationship with the client—as the client starts to look more to you for advice than to your sponsor—your intentions can appear questionable to your sponsor. So, avoid giving the impression of having developed a wholly inde-pendent relationship with the client—one which has the effect of ex-cluding your sponsor. If this restriction inhibits the warmth and depth of your relations with the client, that's just the price you have to pay for the referral. This point is particularly sensitive for you as an associate; the line between developing a good client relationship (which the partner hopes you'll do) and not overstepping your bounds vis-à-vis the firm's sponsor is exceedingly narrow.

Now, when *you* happen to be the sponsoring lawyer, you'll do well to have a heart-to-heart talk with your designee *before* he embarks on the job. Not to say: "Hey, stay away from the client, he's all mine," but to indicate the degree to which you expect further involvement in the matter, in terms of attending meetings, consultations, receiving reports, and the like. This helps to clear the air prior to the onset of any misunderstandings.

This may all appear as a bit of a minuet, but believe me, quite prac-tical ends are at stake. The sponsoring lawyer is apt to have matters in the future with other clients requiring your type of expertise. If, in addition to your legal acumen, he's also impressed by your adroit handling of the relationship, he's likely to turn to you again. Moreover, he'll tell other lawyers about you, enhancing your reputation as the right person for this sort of referral. But if you treat your sponsor poorly, then all your substantive smarts will count for naught; there are plenty of other, more sensitive fish in the sea (remember the woman in the cartoon: "*Everybody* is a lawyer!").

On the other hand, if your entry into the engagement was other than through the regular lawyer's auspices, this particular pressure disappears. I suggest, however, a relaxed attitude toward your colleague. Your future relations with the client are less likely to depend on any competitive edge you've established (or snow job you've engineered) during the deal, but rather on how effectively you've been able to operate as a lawyer. Avoid the infighting, if possible; it's so unprofessional. The client is entitled to your full energies—which doesn't include petty bickering among counsel.

Some time ago, our firm was engaged by a new client to assist in a large acquisition. The idea was that the various tasks in this complex deal would be divided between us and another law firm which had a traditional relationship with the client. On each document of importance, one of us would be assigned the primary responsibility, with the other firm (as well as the client's inside legal staff) functioning in a review capacity. The main agreement was our responsibility. We prepared a first draft and circulated it for comment to our team.

The regular outside lawyer decided to highlight which firm really knew its stuff by marking up our draft with numerous comments in a thick black ink (I remember thinking there must be a special blunt-tip pen for just such occasions), and then sending *his* marked draft to the inside counsel, the client, and all others concerned. Although this struck me as a somewhat unorthodox way to proceed, I gave it little thought until I began to notice a repetition of the process with each re-draft. As the agreement became more refined, the regular lawyer—in order to amass a suitable quantum of black ink—would often reiterate remarks a second or third time, notwithstanding prior joint discussions with the client rejecting the thought. Perhaps he felt that the client wasn't actually *reading* the marked comments, but would judge our product by their bulk. Although this began to gall, I was reluctant to question the regular lawyer's style or motives.

Eventually there came a point in the deal when the regular lawyer did the initial draft of another document and distributed it to all concerned. We had a number of comments to make. The temptation to give him a dose of his own medicine—perhaps in green ink, or maybe with a crayon—was quite powerful. We decided, however, not to rise to the bait. We called the regular lawyer, offering him our comments directly, for incorporation in the next draft; and we advised the client and inside counsel that we had done so, without characterizing the importance or quantity of our comments. I would like to think that self-restraint is not only the proper way to handle this kind of situation, but is also appreciated by the client; however, I doubt whether most clients are even aware of such undercurrents.

I've discussed this mainly from the viewpoint of the incoming lawyer because I'm less familiar with the position of the regular lawyer who suddenly finds himself involuntarily supplemented by a new face. I can appreciate the damage this can inflict on one's ego; deep down, I suppose, most of us feel we can do most things as well as or better than the next fellow. But the addition of someone with expertise can be viewed as a blessing—freeing the regular lawyer from having to perform in those areas where he's least qualified, enabling him to concentrate his efforts on familiar turf. And to the extent there's an overlap, well, two heads . . . etc. No one demands that the new lawyer be welcomed with open arms, but the fact is that he's there; and all things considered, it's best to keep the relationship as cordial as possible, with the stress on mutual effort for the client's benefit.

In a jointly lawyered deal, it's important that you operate effectively within the context of the entire transaction. You can't just ignore the other aspects which aren't your responsibility; true severability is rare and most matters impact at various points.[7] So, there's need for effective communication between the various lawyers. Those involved in the transaction should know what everyone else is doing at any given moment. Coordination of this type is particularly significant at the point when a particular document is about to be sent to the other side. It's no small feat to assemble the necessary inputs from all sources without unnecessarily delaying matters.

This coordination aspect is a natural for the younger lawyer to handle, working through his counterpart at the other firm. The partner will have other concerns demanding his attention and precluding him from orchestration of these undramatic but necessary activities. Moreover, the associates may be free of those hang-ups about status and role and impressing the client which often weigh down their seniors.

So, if you engage in (or observe) a discussion with the adversary lawyer in which something important is said, pass this information along to the other lawyers on your own side. When you receive instructions from the client, fill in your colleagues so that everyone is operating on the same frequency. Make sure you're receiving

---

[7]   More on this in Section 7.2.2 regarding experts.

adequate communication from them, too; when things are too quiet, call up to inquire what's happening. If you feel you're being kept in the dark on purpose and your attempts at encouraging coordination fail, then you may have to let the client know you can't operate effectively without full information—but this should happen only as a last resort.

7.2.2. Joint Representation: The Care and Feeding of Experts.

Just a few words about so-called experts. Although the legal profession has waged an unending struggle against the exploitation of expertise, *apparent* expertise has a way of getting its nose under the tent. And in an age of increasing specialization, the client feels reassured to have the views of an expert in the field. If *you* are the expert—that is, if your firm has been brought in on a matter because of the client's perception of the firm's expertise—it's a splendid entrée onto the scene. Not only is everyone looking to you for advice, but they're predisposed to believe you know your stuff. You achieve a sort of instant cachet, without the need to prove your mettle in the first instance.

On the other hand, especially where a sullen regular counsel is lurking about, it's not difficult to lose that edge rather quickly. A few mistakes can put you right behind the eight ball, with a tougher path to recovery than if you hadn't disappointed those advance expectations of salvation. This darker side of expertise can work a hardship on the associate who is not yet as expert as his seniors but is held to the same high standards. At the very least, it tends to keep you on your toes; for example, you're more likely to look up a relevant point of law *before* the meeting in order to have a ready answer.[8] If you get in a little over your head, don't rush to concede the deficiencies. Whatever your informational shortcomings, the others probably know *less* about the subject than you do—an imbalance which, with small doses of skill and bluff, you may still be able to parlay into acceptable expertise.

Turning the coin, here's a word of advice to the *recipient* of the expert advice: take it all with a big grain of salt! One reason is the reputed expert who's faking it; this can happen, and you must be alert to the possibilities. But the more common problem occurs where, although the expert does possess special knowledge in his own field, this constitutes only one of several important facets of the transaction. The expert, unfamiliar with the client and not completely comfortable with the other interacting disciplines, lacks the big picture; his advice and judgments are based solely on the dictates of his own field. Never assume that the expert has in mind any other points of view; rather, presume he's reflecting what's best from his narrow van-

---

8   See Section 8.2 with regard to this kind of preparation.

tage. By the way, in most cases that's all I *want* the expert to do. I'll handle the other inputs; the expert's views are most helpful undiluted, provided they're approached with the proper degree of caution.

Put another way, although the expert's technical input ought to be respected, he isn't necessarily an oracle. To appraise a troublesome situation fully, you must have a grasp of the expert's reasoning, which may require some interrogation on your part. Try to ascertain the degree of disadvantage from his perspective if the transaction were slightly altered to better suit *your* other purposes. You may be pleasantly surprised to learn that this creates only a marginal additional risk for the expert, while solving a number of your problems (which the expert was unaware of when proposing the original scheme).

This often arises with regard to tax input into a corporate decision. Since the tax laws have an annoying habit of elevating minor matters of form into appalling substantive ramifications, tax expertise is essential. If you find yourself handling a complex corporate transaction in which your firm lacks real tax expertise, you should reach outside to an expert. Let's say you do just that, for an acquisition intended to qualify as a tax-free reorganization. The tax expert comes in and recommends a structure for the deal that, in his view, will assure that treatment. The trouble is, though, that while his prescribed format is optimal from a tax perspective, it presents grave corporate and business problems—obligations may be accelerated, consents from third parties will be needed, a number of additional complexities are introduced. Resist the tendency to treat the tax advice as scripture. Unlike your own tax partner, this outside expert may be viewing the deal in highly parochial terms, oblivious to *your* problems in proceeding his way. Talk to him about it. Perhaps you'll find that his suggested structure is far from absolute, that it's capable of absorbing substantial modification—including a transmutation which, while not precisely covered by a published ruling, is safe enough tax-wise and solves your other problems.[9]

Regardless of how many experts dance on the head of a transactional pin, the overall legal responsibility for the deal is still yours. Don't abdicate that responsibility just because a learned authority has arrived on the scene. Familiarize yourself sufficiently with his area of expertise in order to suggest possible alternatives. Any corporate lawyer worth his salt should know enough about tax considerations to realize when he has a potential tax problem, to ask the right questions, and to devise other options. He may not know quite as much about, say, trademark law, since he doesn't encounter such questions that often. When a corporate generalist suddenly finds him-

---

[9]   See the discussion in Section 2.5 on breaking out of the assumption mold initially imposed on you by the client's wishes or your own predilections.

self involved in a transaction where trademarks are paramount, he should not only bring in the specialist but ought to absorb some basic trademark knowledge himself—through article or treatise—in order to understand the significant considerations and be positioned to probe the expert's thinking.

7.2.3. Joint Representation: Inside and Outside Counsel.

The most common instance of joint representation occurs where your firm is outside counsel to a corporate client which has its own internal legal staff.[10] The status enjoyed by corporate counsel can vary greatly from company to company, making it somewhat difficult to generalize; but it's safe to say that the relationship between outside and inside counsel is basic to the smooth functioning of most transactions.

There is an unfortunate tendency on the part of some outside counsel to consider themselves a lot smarter and more experienced than inside counsel, with the result that—at least in matters where the insider isn't responsible for the outsider's presence—inside counsel's views are given short shrift and his participation in the transaction is discouraged. I'm convinced this is the wrong approach. The situation doesn't call for arrogance but for a melding of talents. Whatever the capability of corporate counsel (and, like their brethren on the outside, they range widely in terms of professional competence), the insider brings to the table several distinctive features which outside attorneys rarely possess.

First, the legal department generally has ready access to the individuals within the corporate organization who are the decision-makers—the right persons to approach for information or a quick reaction. After all, an inside lawyer has to deal with these people on a regular basis; and such matters as lines of authority, pecking orders and the like are the grist of his daily mill. He can also keep you posted on developments within the company, to which your outside antennae may be insensitive. As a result, even a corporate attorney with no substantive input can be extremely helpful to you in formulating strategy, expediting matters, and reaching final judgments.

But I have found that inside counsel is usually able to make contributions of substance also. Remember, this is his full-time occupation. He's likely to be much more familiar with the intricacies of the company's business, operations and structure than you are, and can prove an invaluable source of information in this regard. His general factual knowledge, plus your expertise in the area of concern, should

---

[10]   Section 5.3.1 discusses the practice of law in a corporation law department, including relations with outside counsel from inside counsel's viewpoint.

form a more potent combination than either of you working on the project alone.

On a very practical level, you ought to assume that the inside lawyer is likely to play a major role next time around in the selection of outside counsel. Regardless of your competence, he is unlikely to choose someone with whom he feels uncomfortable. None of us is irreplaceable. Most inside lawyers are anxious to make a personal contribution. The corporate attorney should be made to feel an integral part of the team that is handling the problem. This is particularly appropriate, of course, in a case where the inside lawyer is responsible for your firm's representation; and the same considerations applicable to the treatment of a sponsoring outside lawyer are equally pertinent here.[11]

Occasionally, however, you run up against a situation where the inside general counsel interposes himself between you and the client to such a degree that the attorney-client relationship suffers; you miss the feedback and fear your messages aren't getting through. This politicized genus of inside general counsel wants to appear to the corporate executives as the lawyer who's calling the shots—with all that fancy, high-priced outside help reporting to *him*. Well, a little posturing on the part of corporate counsel is all in a day's work; but it can become troublesome when communication is impeded.

There's no simple way out of this spot. Begin by using whatever ruses are at your disposal to make the communication more direct; references to the need for your firm to ultimately issue an opinion, for example, can often work wonders. If your performance continues to be hampered, however, then be forceful with the inside general counsel, insisting on an audience with the president or other key executive (with the general counsel present, of course) in order to ask specific questions and put certain issues directly to him. If this still doesn't get results, then you have to take the drastic but unavoidable step of going over the general counsel's head directly to your client. In the last analysis, that's where your responsibility lies; and you won't be able to excuse your performance later by claiming the impediment of an interposed general counsel—unless the corporate executives have responded to your predicament by announcing that they prefer to deal through an intermediary.

Along with varying degrees of competence and organizational status possessed by inside counsel—and perhaps linked to such characteristics—are major differences as to their degree of autonomy. The spectrum extends from those who function virtually as if they were outside attorneys—taking exposed positions, debating the merits of management suggestions, standing up for what they believe—to

---

[11]   See Section 7.2.1.

those who are closer in spirit to employee status—their opinions and
actions reflecting what's expected of them within the organization.
The typical inside lawyer is somewhere in between, with his own
autonomy the product of (i) how assertive an individual he is, and
(ii) how overpowering a personality the chief executive officer
possesses.

It would be naive to believe that the answer you receive from inside
counsel is always dictated solely by the legal parameters of the
problem. Other influences can be (and often are) brought to bear upon
him. His willingness to render a certain opinion may not amount to a
totally disinterested determination on the merits, but can be tilted
somewhat—at least off dead center—by institutional expectations.
So, if your client is anxious to close a transaction today, and a
problem arises which appears to impair your ability to give the
necessary legal opinion, and the inside counsel tells you, "Don't
worry, everything's all right"—my advice is to worry a little. Assume
that he's under pressure from his superiors to overcome this hurdle
and get the deal closed; reserve for *yourself* the final judgment on the
matter.

But, while you shouldn't ignore this possibility, don't be too quick
to judge the inside counsel on the basis of his susceptibility to
pressure. Try to appreciate the position he finds himself in—with
someone exercising direct control over his present and future employment—and recognize that he has to work effectively within these
limitations. You, too, have to work within limitations of a sort,
vis-à-vis the partners of the firm; you're not completely free to call
each shot exactly as you see it. We all report to some higher
authority—it's just more noticeable with the inside general counsel.

At times, you may be able to mitigate the problem. For example, if
you anticipate that a certain issue will be arising within the organization, you can advise the inside counsel as to your negative position on
the matter in advance. Then, when the issue does come up between
the president and inside counsel, the latter is less likely to
be mousetrapped into an initial affirmative response—so difficult to
retract later—to comport with the president's evident leanings. Moreover, inside counsel will be in a position to avoid the brunt of the
president's displeasure by leaning on your views.

7.2.4. Parallel Representation: Separate But Equal.

Many of the issues involved in parallel representation are similar to
those discussed under joint representation, but with some significant
differences. Since you and the other counsel are representing separate
parties whose interests generally—but not always—coincide, you

have to be alert to whether the particular matter before the house is a mutual or divisive-type issue. Should you be in an adversarial mode or not? In the classic parallel representation situation of a securities underwriting, when the subject matter under discussion is the underwriting agreement, your interests (as counsel for the company) and those of counsel for the underwriters clearly diverge; friendly adversarial negotiations usually ensue. But when the two of you are attempting to draft a difficult section of the prospectus, your interests in full disclosure and the avoidance of ultimate liabilities are roughly similar—and an adversarial manner is rarely appropriate. So, the posture you adopt often depends upon the topic then engaging your attention.

Unfortunately, things aren't always so clear-cut. Issues which don't appear to divide two parties on the surface may contain subtle strains requiring reconciliation of their interests. Take that underwriting situation, for example. Let's assume that the issuer's president would like to avoid making a certain disclosure about the company's business in the prospectus—not because it would scare away potential investors, but because this information could give certain competitors an unfair advantage, which in turn could penalize the company's business several years down the road. You wrestle with the issue—it's a close question on materiality—and finally acquiesce in omitting the disclosure; admittedly though, if your client wasn't so concerned, you might well duck the hard decision and simply disclose. The underwriter's counsel also recognizes this as a toss-up issue; but reflecting *his* client's more immediate concern with whether the prospectus fairly describes the company's *present* business, he will probably opt for more (rather than less) disclosure—taking the position that future speculative adverse effects on the company aren't really his concern. Although the wrangling between the two of you over this issue will be cast in terms of whether disclosure is required under the securities laws, it's not hard to see how the parties' diverging interests might affect your respective viewpoints.

In matters where the parties' interests coincide for the most part, try not to let the adversarial aspects overwhelm the cooperative ones. Without shirking your duty as an advocate, you can still avoid creating roadblocks in the path of effective coordination. It's not facetious to suggest scheduling your time so as to separate out the issues; on certain days, you deal only with topics of mutual self-interest, postponing those which divide the parties in order to minimize residual bad feeling.

Communication and coordination are as important here as under joint representation. If you (as company counsel) have been in charge of dealing with the SEC, for example, you should advise your opposite number representing the underwriter promptly when significant regulatory developments occur. If you're about to confer with the staff on a crucial issue, consult underwriter's counsel in advance on your intended position; among other things, this makes it more difficult for him to second-guess your approach after the fact. New happenings of note at the company should similarly be relayed. The associate will find himself playing a key role in these activities.

If you've been brought into the picture by your opposite number at the parallel client—which often happens in the conflict of interest situations discussed in the next subsection—not only should you steer clear of *his* client, but you probably shouldn't have any long-term designs on your *own*. In other situations, however, the clients are generally fair future game; and many a permanent client relationship has developed out of such exposure. However, I suggest you avoid getting too cozy with his client in the middle of *this* transaction. For example, don't start giving his client advice when the lawyer's not present; in addition to provoking criticism from the absent lawyer, this can also miff your own client, who's paying you to watch out for *his* interests.

Complete parallelism rarely works, and it's generally desirable for one counsel to carry the laboring oar. So, in most underwritings where the company is adequately represented, counsel for the company will take the lead in writing the prospectus, with counsel for the underwriter serving in more of a review capacity.[12] In litigation, there is usually a lead counsel among the various defendants' attorneys—generally the attorney representing the defendant with the most to lose, or at least the deepest pocket—so that questions of law aren't researched two and three times and other unnecessary duplication is avoided. Where the lead lawyer isn't clearly earmarked by the situation, the mantle will fall on either the one possessing the most ability or the one who makes the most aggressive move. Be aware of the extent of your responsibility in this kind of a situation.[13] And I'd be somewhat cynical over whether someone else's lawyer can fully protect my client's interests.

7.2.5. Parallel Representation: Conflicts of Interest.

The most difficult parallel representation problems arise in what may be termed the conflict of interest area. Consider the following

---

[12]   In addition, of course, to the special responsibilities of underwriters' counsel in such areas as the underwriting agreement, any required indentures and blue sky compliance.

[13]   As discussed in Section 6.5, be sure to cover your tail. Assume that, unless you're alert, you will be blamed for whatever mishaps occur, you will be pointed to as the source of all delays, and so on.

situation. The chief executive of a company you represent decides he deserves a new, richer employment contract, and the board of directors is responsive to his mood. The executive should be separately represented in negotiating the terms of that contract, while you continue to represent the company. You can't carry water on both shoulders. Yet, once the contract is signed, you'll be right back working for that same chief executive, which makes your situation somewhat awkward—not unlike the daily pressures on inside company counsel.[14] To resist the unreasonable portion of the chief executive's demands in good grace and without disturbing your ongoing relationship is a tricky piece of diplomacy.

Another instance illustrating the problem occurs where you have been representing both a company and its 65%-controlled, publicly-owned subsidiary. Now the two corporations have decided to merge. You will be counseling the parent in the transaction; another lawyer will be brought in to represent the subsidiary. This isn't so easy; among other things, you probably have developed many friends at the subsidiary. A similar situation arises where a charge of self-dealing has been lodged, and separate lawyers now represent the company and its independent directors. All of these circumstances call for extreme delicacy in the handling—yesterday's client is today's "adversary"; today's adversary is tomorrow's retainer.

My two bits of advice on these transactions are short and simple, and—although perhaps appearing so at first blush—not inconsistent. Point number one: no matter what pressures (real or imagined) are applied to you, never permit something to occur that you consider unfair to either party. Neither past relationships nor future potentialities provide any possible justification for such impropriety. Point number two: notwithstanding the first exhortation, remember that there's almost always a range of fairness on any issue; and within that range, you should hesitate to impose *your* standards of what's appropriate on the businessmen involved. Presumably, if you've gained the clients' respect, your views will be sought out and given weight. Once these views have been rejected, as long as the ultimate position cannot be deemed unfair or over-reaching, my advice is to acquiesce quietly—don't get carried out on your shield.[15] Who's to say that your concept of fairness is entitled to any more weight than that of your client?

In conflict situations like this, it's very important that the lawyer "on the other side" be someone with whom you're able to develop a close working relationship. I don't mean to suggest that either of you ought to "sell out" to the other; but for the sensitivities of this

[14] See Sections 5.3.1 and 7.2.3.
[15] Make sure, however, that the company is fully protected, by bringing in independent experts to bless such determinations as valuation.

representation, you don't want an opinionated ass across the table—a
table-pounder who takes up the cudgels over each minor point, adopting non-negotiable positions and giving fits to all concerned. If you
can arrange to select (or at least approve) that other lawyer yourself,
make every effort to do so.[16] Don't ever pick an individual you feel
isn't competent, or someone who'll be inclined to surrender
everything you want. What you should aim for is an intelligent lawyer
with judgment, who can jointly focus with you on difficult questions,
to discover that fine line which fulfills both the dictates of fairness and
the parties' desires.

7.3. THE FRIENDLY ADVERSARY[17]

In a business-oriented practice, the bulk of a lawyer's dealings with
other lawyers outside his firm can be categorized as friendly adversary relations. Two individuals or entities want to do something
together, which involves an agreement between them. It takes two to
tango—a sale requires both a willing seller and a willing purchaser—but
each party has different goals in the transaction. So their counsel
joust with each other, attempting to accomplish the deal in a manner
that retains maximum advantage for their respective clients.

A number of lawyerly skills enter into this process: the more substantive ones (such as analytical ability[18]), the intangibles (such as
industriousness[19]), the capacity to communicate[20] and coordinate
with other counsel,[21] and so on. The primary skill isolatable in the
friendly adversary context, however, is the ability to negotiate. And it
is to this subject, the central theme of this section, that we now turn.

7.3.1. An Introduction to Negotiating.

I had always assumed that negotiating was an acquired skill—that
good negotiators were made, not necessarily born. After an incident
that happened last summer, I'm not so sure.

I was playing backgammon at our beach house with my two sons,

---

[16]   In that chief executive employment contract situation, for example, if
you haven't recommended the lawyer who represents the chief executive, he
will probably have designs on the client for later deals—and thus may do his
best to make you appear stingy.
[17]   Portions of the material in this Section appeared originally, in somewhat
altered form, in Chapter 2 of the author's book on acquisitions, *Anatomy of a
Merger* (1975). Most of the examples utilized in this Section, however, were
newly conceived for this book.
[18]   See Chapter 2.
[19]   See Section 4.3.
[20]   See Chapter 3.
[21]   See Section 7.2.

Erik (11) and Tom (8). We play for stakes: if they win, it's measured in dimes or (the ravages of inflation!) quarters; if I win, I become the recipient of a number of "services" (such as sweeping sand off the deck or mixing a vodka-and-tonic) which they'll be called on to perform over the next few days. At the end of one game, Erik mentioned how delicious a batch of chocolate chip cookies would taste; a quick search of the pantry, however, revealed none in stock. Whereupon my younger son (Tom), who at the time owed me seven services, announced that he would be willing to bike down to the grocery store for the cookies, but it would cost me a three-service credit. "No," I declared in a quite positive—one might even have termed it supercilious—tone; "That's only worth one service—perhaps two if it were raining out." There was a pause. "If you want me to go," replied Tom with carefully measured cadence, "it will cost you three". A great deal of will power seemed to lurk behind his words.

I looked over at Erik, my older son, who returned my glance. I could tell that he agreed in principle with my stand: a quickie run to the grocery store could in no way rise to the level of a three-service credit—for the same stipend, Erik had once sawed an entire supply of logs for a cool evening. And yet, we both wanted those cookies badly, with neither of us willing to go ourselves. Tom—whose iron will appeared unshakable—was available, though the cost was high. I blustered around for a while but eventually yielded; the bargain was made.

Later that day, Erik and I rehashed the matter. Had Tom been bluffing? If I had held firm at, say, two services, would Tom have ended up on his bike? He did state his position in unequivocal terms; and the boy has an independent streak to his personality—he's definitely not cowed by his father or older brother. From our years of experience with Tom, it seemed unlikely he would have weakened. On the other hand, Tom wanted those cookies, too; realizing (as he undoubtedly did) that neither of us would raise ourselves for the task, and that two services wasn't such bad pay for a minor errand, perhaps he would have accepted the assignment on a two-service basis if we'd been firmer. Erik and I concluded that we were just a couple of easy marks, not prepared to go to the wall for a principle, but anxious to end the suspense and latch on to the cookies.[22]

Upon further reflection, I realized there was another possibility. If the basic impasse had lasted for a while, with neither of us backing off our position, perhaps I could have offered a face-saving compromise. For example, Tom would be entitled to the full three-service credit if

----

[22] When I related this tale to one colleague, his reaction was: "Dummy! At the very least, you should have gotten Erik to chip in 1-½ services to the pot. . . ."

he would both get the cookies and then, upon returning, pour us glasses of milk to wash them down. I think Tom might have gone along with that, since it didn't involve too much extra effort. It wouldn't have required him to retreat from his three-service position, while I—getting more bang for a buck—could avoid the dilution of value from awarding a sizeable credit for a modest chore. But even that compromise might not have worked if Tom, recognizing my last-ditch attempt to save face, had decided I'd ultimately yield without the milk.

I mention this incident because I'm now convinced that the seeds of negotiating ability are implanted within us at an early age, though we do little to nurture them. I can hardly remember the subject of negotiating even being mentioned in law school. After a brief apprenticeship, I found myself in the midst of transactions which placed a high premium on this particular skill. I'm sure I floundered; I had no training, no theoretical platform to fall back on. There were no black letter instructions to memorize. My seniors focused on substance, rarely pausing to instruct me on tactics and the like.

And so, as I began to negotiate, I made what (in retrospect) were a number of clear mistakes. I ceded points when I didn't have to, receiving nothing in return. I became stubborn on issues that didn't rise to the requisite level of importance. Against a patient negotiator, I wasn't as persistent as I might have been. I ignored significant clues that might have suggested paths of favorable compromise. And so on.

One moment stands out particularly in my mind—a sort of watershed to the realization that negotiating was a skill in its own right, and not just a necessary means to a preordained end. As an associate, I was assisting a partner in acquisition negotiations on behalf of a corporate client. The president of the client, who actively participated in the proceedings, was himself a savvy negotiator. During one all-hands meeting, a seeming impasse arose over a particular issue (the nature of which I've long since forgotten); our client took a position to which the other businessman appeared diametrically opposed. As I listened to the debate, however, it struck me that the two viewpoints weren't really opposites; that there was probably a failure of communication between the parties; that they were really talking about different aspects of the same problem—and I suddenly saw, with crystal clarity, a compromise solution that would preserve for my client the protection he was really concerned about (although not in the sweeping terms that his position embraced) without unduly burdening the other party.

Without hesitation, I barged into the fray, waving my solution as the panacea for all ills. I paused to await the reaction. The lawyer on the other side remarked that it sounded like a good idea. Our client looked out the window for a while, then suggested that we pass this issue for now and take it up again at a subsequent time.

Later that afternoon, I was called into the partner's office and received a stern dressing down—which I now realize was fully deserved. Our client was furious. He had known exactly what he was doing in the negotiations—polarizing a conflict that didn't really exist, confident that his adversary would ultimately cave in and cede the point. My compromise, which suffered from the defect of being too logical to generate counter-argument, denied him that extra measure of protection. By speaking out of turn without consulting my client, I had allowed my ego-satisfaction over devising a solution to get in the way of good judgment. It was a lesson I shall never forget.

Gradually, I stopped treating negotiating as a legal stepchild, and began to view it as something worthy of serious consideration. Because negotiating tends to be somewhat free-form, it doesn't lend itself easily to this sort of thing.[23] As a result, many lawyers simply don't bother. They just let it happen, trusting their instincts; and as you might expect, those with good instincts usually turn out to be quite competent at the bargaining table.

But the sad fact is that a large number of otherwise skilled lawyers are mediocre negotiators at best. They become so immersed in difficult substantive questions that they rarely stop to analyze how best to achieve their goals. They neglect to size up their adversary, to peer inside his mind and discover what's really troubling him. They seem to lack adeptness at devising effective compromises. Their inventiveness is reserved for matters of substance—new ways to structure a deal for tax purposes and the like—while the equally creative and necessary task of circumventing a difficult sticking point remains ignored.

Yet lawyers are the logical persons to handle negotiations in these kinds of transactions. A legal mind is invaluable for clarifying situations—for example, to identify the cause of a seeming disagreement as a simple failure to distinguish between separable issues. Lawyers possess the training and experience to ask the hard questions so crucial to the bargaining process. It's usually the attorney who realizes that the parties' minds haven't really met on an issue which is seemingly resolved. For instance, the parties to an employment contract may *think* they've reached agreement on a cash bonus formula

---

[23] A number of books have appeared in recent years, couched in terms of pseudo-scientific jargon, which attempt to raise negotiating to the level of a science—or at least an art form. Frankly, these treatments have always left me cold—a little too removed from reality and the simple application of intelligent common sense.

based on the company's net earnings—but wait a minute, should that bonus be based on the company's net earnings *before* or *after* the bonus itself? The parties never thought about this, but the question needs to be asked; and more often than not, it's the lawyer who raises the query.[23a]

7.3.2. A Balanced Theory of Negotiations.

Most of what takes place in the course of negotiations can be characterized as either attempting to get a leg up on your adversary or striking a compromise between your respective positions. I firmly believe that the key to effective negotiating lies in achieving a functional balance between these two seemingly inconsistent aspects. If all your efforts are directed toward gaining advantages over your adversary, you will undoubtedly come on too strong; and where the parties possess relatively equal bargaining power, with freedom to consummate the transaction or not, you may cause your client irreparable harm—such as losing the deal. On the other hand, if you don't push a little—if you never strive for advantages in drafting or stake out positions that invite rebuttal—then your client is unlikely to achieve his share of obtainable rights and protections.

This balancing act has various applications. For example, a skilled negotiator should mix equal parts of persistence and perspective. Bargaining sessions often spill over into the wee hours, with points conceded that need not have been, were the parties relatively fresh. If you have the stamina to persist, more often than not you'll come out on top. But a failure to temper that persistence with perspective cuts down on your effectiveness. After all, you're not going to prevail on *all* the issues that arise in a negotiation, so save yourself for the big ones—let the other fellow win a few also. Don't become mired in the pursuit of trivia, losing all sense of what's significant and generating bad feelings that make it harder to obtain concessions or reach compromises in areas of real importance.[24]

Having adopted this principle of balance, you will come to realize that the non-negotiable-demand school of bargaining is quite inappropriate. In my experience, very few points are really non-negotiable; *some* movement is usually possible—cosmetic if not

---

[23a] And the query—unfortunately—sometimes sours the deal. "It is by universal misunderstanding that all agree. For if, by ill luck, people understood each other, they would never agree." Charles Baudelaire, *Intimate Journals* (C. Isherwood trans. 1887), at 99.

[24] Benjamin Disraeli expressed a similar thought in these terms: "Next to knowing when to seize an advantage, the most important thing in life is to know when to forego an advantage." As quoted in G. Nierenberg, *The Art of Negotiating* (1968).

substantive—from the position originally advanced. Refusing to negotiate around even the periphery of a complex point is less a valid bargaining technique than the absence of technique. This is why many of us find negotiations with a bank over a commercial loan so frustrating. The institution and its lawyers adopt a series of non-negotiable positions, justifying their stance with "This is how we always do things" or "That clause is in all our agreements". It's like banging your head up against a stone wall. No matter how much sense you make, your adversaries aren't really listening—and besides, the person to whom you're talking probably lacks the authority to make the requested changes.[25] A similar phenomenon often occurs in attempting to negotiate with landlords on behalf of tenants when rental space is scarce.[26]

Don't get me wrong. There will be times when an important issue has been whittled down to its bare essentials, and you feel the need to take a stand; in such a case, by all means do so. Just make sure it's a basic point for your side, perhaps even a deal-breaker. Don't act out of pique or a lust for power. And be sure you've adequately communicated this sense of importance to your adversary, so he knows what he's up against.

The balance theory also renders obsolete what I term the martial arts of negotiating: threatening to call off a deal, blowing up over a point, stalking out of the room, and other assorted brinksmanship techniques from the hairy-chested school of confrontation. As a rule, this sort of thing just doesn't belong in ordinary commercial negotiations.[26a] There are other means than packing up your yellow pads to impress an adversary with the seriousness of your position. And if you do take a walk, again make sure it's over a real deal-breaker and not some trivial side issue.

At times, though—and in my case, I must concede, perhaps too often—a momentary flare-up may be almost requisite, as a narrowly focused expression of disapproval over an unpardonable depredation by your adversary. If the lawyer on the other side has been reiterating a point *ad nauseam*, you might feel terribly frustrated but you shouldn't blow up. However, when he tries to retract a concession previously granted, that's another matter. Similarly, when your adversary suffers a convenient loss of memory or misquotes you, he deserves a dramatic memento of his bad faith; and a brief but convinc-

---

[25]   On this point, see Section 7.3.9.

[26]   On the other hand, when space is abundant, landlords can be extremely accommodating.

[26a]   Remember: "Indignation is the seducer of thought. No man can think clearly when his fists are clenched." George Jean Nathan, "Indignation," in *The World in Falseface* (1923).

ing display of your indignation will signal that he's heading down a
dangerous road.

7.3.3. A Leg Up in the Documents.

Well, let's begin with a look at some techniques for getting a jump
on your adversary. And the best place to start is with the written
agreement itself. Simply stated, the trick here is to gain your advantages without the other lawyer knowing he's been had. If he realizes
what you're up to, the issue will be openly joined and the matter ripe
for accommodation; but if he fails to focus on the point or appreciate
its full significance, you're home free without the necessity to bargain.

For example, consider an indemnification provision, drafted by the
lawyer for the party to be indemnified (Mr. Aggrieved), providing that
the indemnitor (Mr. Dontsweat) will indemnify Aggrieved against
virtually everything. Dontsweat's lawyer realizes the provision is
broad—he expected that—but he fails to realize that its reach extends
to certain prospectus information supplied by Aggrieved *himself*.
There obviously ought to be an exception for this—and were the
point raised, Aggrieved would undoubtedly be agreeable. But it's not
the job of Aggrieved's lawyer to bring the matter to Dontsweat's attention.

That's failure to focus. Consider a further provision in the same
clause, granting Aggrieved a right of setoff. Dontsweat's attorney will
undoubtedly *focus* on this clause; but he may miss its *significance* if he
fails to realize that certain other monies will be coming due to Dontsweat from Aggrieved in a few months—thereby giving this provision
real bite down the road. With this knowledge, Dontsweat's lawyer
might have bargained for protections applicable to disputes over the
amount or propriety of the offset; without it—facing what seems a
purely theoretical issue—he might not bother.

For an offensive-minded lawyer, the obvious starting point is to
seize the opportunity to draft the relevant documents. There are so
many options available in drafting an agreement—so many choices in
the introduction and phrasing of concepts, the purposeful omission of
particular language, the deliberate use of ambiguity, and so on—that a
fair number of the draftsman's edges are bound to slip by the critical
gaze of the reviewing adversary.

So, representing the purchaser of a business, you ask the seller to
warrant that, in addition to all the specific information he's provided,
he knows of nothing significant that might affect the assets, liabilities,
operations, etc. of the company being sold; and into that litany you
drop unobtrusively (perhaps somewhere in the middle) the word
"prospects", hoping the seller's lawyer will miss it—in which case

your client has bought himself an insurance policy against reasonably foreseeable future harm. Or, in drafting an indemnification "basket" clause (which provides that the first $50,000 of claims are non-indemnifiable), you choose language which will enable your purchaser client to allege that if the claims rise above $50,000 (say, to $60,000), he's entitled to collect the full $60,000, not just the $10,000 excess—in hopes that the seller's lawyer will fail to see that possibility.[27]

Remember: the other lawyer can't read your mind. He doesn't necessarily know which points are troubling you; and by drafting around your concerns, you can often achieve a certain result without your opponent's awareness. For instance, assume that you represent the purchaser in a merger transaction, where the selling company is almost as large as the purchaser and its stockholders are receiving the purchaser's stock. You have a hunch that no matter what representations you seek from the seller in your first draft of the merger agreement, the seller's attorney will come back with a demand for symmetry—requiring your purchaser client to make exactly the same representations to the seller. You're aware that your client is having some trouble with collectibility of its accounts receivable, while accounts receivable are not a significant factor in the seller's business. So, in preparing the original draft agreement, you omit asking seller for the usual accounts receivable representation, with the hope that seller will limit his symmetrical demand to what's already there in the draft—which, after all, sprawls over 15 pages—and won't pry further into purchaser's business.

In certain transactions, an etiquette has developed over who handles the initial drafting: landlords draft leases, financial institutions draft loan agreements, and so on. In an acquisition, the purchaser's lawyer drafts the basic agreement—which makes sense, since most of the protective provisions are for his client's benefit. In other situations, the appropriate draftsman may not be clearly defined. All I can say is, if the opportunity presents itself, make every attempt to seize it. Even in a transaction where the other side does the basic preparation, there may still be opportunities for you to volunteer for drafting; e.g., when a particular compromise that you've suggested is agreed to in principle. By the way, some client education may be required here. A client who thinks he'll save on your legal fee if the other side handles the drafting has to be persuaded that your control of the document will redound to his benefit.

Most experienced lawyers are aware of this advantage, so you can

---

[27]   The subject of indemnification in an acquisition context is discussed at length in Chapter 10 of *Anatomy*.

expect some opposition. But others don't think about it, or are too busy, or are just plain lazy, or feel they're smart enough to catch any hookers that might come their way—so you'll get your chances. Remember, though: in a wide-open situation, if your adversary thought that your drafting worked to his disadvantage, he'd be forced to volunteer himself. So, it behooves you to introduce the subject in a way that doesn't betray your desire—for God's sake, don't make it look as though you're salivating for the opportunity. Your posture should be that, as between the two of you, you're willing to undertake this necessary evil. If possible, a simultaneous suggestion that your adversary take on the drafting of something else—perhaps a disclosure document, possessing less of an adversarial nature—may provide a useful framework. "I'll tell you, Jack," you remark, as if the idea just happened to fly into your head a moment ago; "Why don't you do the proxy statement and I'll handle the agreement?"

In this same vein, learn to appreciate the value of subtlety in shepherding a beneficial provision through your adversary's review. Hit him over the head and he's bound to react; yet many lawyers can't help being tendentious in pounding home a point. Here's the way I look at it: I would much rather that my 75%-perfect provision remain in the contract intact (because it's never contravened) than that my 100%-perfect provision get watered down to 50% (as a result of hard adversarial bargaining). So be a little oblique. For example, in a relatively informal contract, you might be able to whisk a certain representation by the other party; but if you insist on gilding the lily by providing that breach of this representation gives rise to indemnification, and including a plethora of "hold harmless" provisions—the effect of which could largely be obtained through the representation plus general principles of contract law—you risk raising your adversary's dander and losing the point altogether.

Now, let's view this from the vantage point of the lawyer who *receives* the draft agreement. Needless to say, you have to pore over it quite thoroughly—particularly with a view to what provisions of surface innocence might be onerous to your client and what omissions need to be rectified. Ponder what your adversary may have had in mind. This usually requires some facts from your client—which points up a major recurring blunder in this area.

The lawyer examines the contract on his own, with legal but not factual inputs. The client goes over the contract by himself, with plenty of factual background but without appreciating the various points of legal significance. If you don't want important matters to fall between the cracks, you and your client should get together—*before* meeting with the other side—to coordinate your review. I have in mind a session where, in effect, the client says to you: "We have the following operational problem . . . [describe] . . . Does it present a problem?'' You then evaluate it for him. Later, you say to him: "If you have the following factual situation . . . [describe] . . . then there might be a problem under the contract.'' And he can tell you whether the situation exists or not.

Typically, your response to a draft agreement takes the form of orally detailing to your adversary the changes you wish made, and negotiating their resolution; the agreement is then revised accordingly by the original draftsman. If you have numerous or lengthy changes to suggest, it may be appropriate to embody them in a memorandum—perhaps with some suggested language for the more complex points—delivered to the other side in advance of a meeting. Unless the other lawyer is a hapless draftsman, however, don't take it upon yourself to completely revise his draft contract. To make stylistic changes is considered bad form in the friendly adversarial universe, serving only to infuriate the initial draftsman. Save yourself for the substance. The contract you end up with is unlikely to be enshrined in the National Archives. Negotiated agreements rarely resemble models of draftsmanship or generate intellectual pride; more typically, a complex contract ends up as a hodge-podge document, with substitutions and additions cropping up in unlikely places, detracting from the careful organization embodied in the initial draft.[28]

7.3.4. More Legupsmanship: Timing and Swapping.

At this juncture, I want to discuss two interrelated phenomena in the bargaining area: timing and swapping. You ought to develop a sense of timing in any negotiation—a feeling for where you are at any given point, what you hope to achieve, and where you'd like to be at the end of the day. Once achieved, this timing sense regulates such matters as selection of the optimum juncture to raise a certain point. To the extent you control issues of timing, you can obtain a real edge in the negotiations—since the precise moment that certain subjects surface may be almost as important as their substantive content.

So, for example, the purchaser's lawyer in an acquisition learns that he's better off not to introduce an onerous point—such as the necessity for a strong non-competition covenant—in the early stages of negotiating the deal, when the key element is to obtain the seller's commitment to dispose of his business with a minimum of second thoughts. Or, should you detect that your adversary is in a charitable mood today, wisdom suggests that you assemble and put forth all re-

---

[28]   This admittedly differs from my attitude toward written work prepared *within* the office, as discussed in Sections 3.2, 5.2.2 and 10.2.3.

quests forthwith—whereas if the gentleman (like Richard III) is not in a "giving vein" just now, then you, good Buckingham, are best advised to parade your petitions another day.

Although timing is a matter of feel, you can't always leave it to the instinct of the moment. Some advance planning may be in order. For example, if you anticipate an imminent discussion that's likely to worry the other side, try to get certain collateral questions resolved in your favor *before* the troublesome point poisons the air. Take the seller of a business for cash, who is determined that no part of the purchase price will be escrowed—he wants to get paid every cent at the closing. It seems to me he's well advised to raise that point affirmatively, take his firm position, and obtain the other side's agreement in principle, *prior* to other matters surfacing which reveal how shaky the seller is in some of his representations—thus underscoring the purchaser's potential need for just such an escrow. (Conversely, purchasers are well-advised not to concede the absence of an escrow until satisfied that the risks of the deal are minimal—but more of that when we come to swapping.)

I'm always a little startled when the other lawyer says, at the beginning of a major negotiating session: "Okay, let's start at page 1 and work our way through the agreement page by page"; and he then proceeds to take up big points, small points and typographical errors as they appear, with no attempt to tie together related issues or concentrate initially (while the client is present) on the significant topics. This kind of approach might make sense to wear me down, or to underplay a few nuggets secreted among the dross. But in most cases, it makes more sense to start out with a plan of battle or game plan—much like a general or quarterback. Obviously, things might not go exactly according to plan—who ever expected Rommel to appear on the right flank, or the free safety to blitz, or the purchaser to zero in on the value of the inventory?—so you have to stay flexible; but at least you have an overall idea of where you're heading, what's significant, which areas to probe, which to avoid, the optimum order of presentation for prime effect, and so on.

Let's assume that your adversary's draft agreement contains a troublesome provision which you'd prefer to dodge. With some advance planning, a sidestep may be possible. For example, the purchaser in an acquisition has asked your seller client to represent that all machinery and equipment is in good condition. In fact, it's not in such great shape; although no serious breakdowns have yet occurred, some problems could surface in six months or so. If the representation remains in the contract, you'll advise your client to disclose this state of affairs to the purchaser—first, because you'd feel uncomfortable ethically sponsoring a specific factual misrepresentation, and second, because the mechanical breakdown might trigger the indemnification provisions of the agreement to your client's financial discomfort. Yet, early disclosure might tempt the buyer to renegotiate the purchase price downward. You have no reason to believe the other side suspects your problem; as a matter of fact, the purchaser's experts have examined the equipment without batting an eye. This is just a standard clause in this type of agreement. If you proceed through the contract with your adversary and, coming to this provision, ask for its removal, you're unlikely to prevail; no matter what ostensible reason you supply, he'll suspect the seller's equipment is in disarray and pass the word on to his client.

So, in order to remove the representation from the contract, some strategy is in order. One possibility might be as follows. Assume that the equipment representation is one of a number of warranties relating to the sellers' assets. At the point in the bargaining session when you reach the first of these—which has nothing to do with the condition of equipment, but might relate, say, to inventory—you interject this thought:

> "Look, Bill, I've got an idea. There are a whole bunch
> of asset representations here, the terms of which we could
> negotiate for three days. Rather than go through that
> ordeal, what do you say we simply compress them all into
> a single warranty, to the effect that the seller's assets are as
> stated on its most recent balance sheet—and I'll even
> throw in a representation that they have an aggregate
> market value at least equal to what's on the books."

Now, the purchaser might not buy your scheme, for reasons unrelated to the condition of your equipment—he might, for instance, feel the need for abundant detail concerning inventory—but you can never tell; and volunteering the warranty that aggregate market value exceeds book value, which he hadn't even *asked* for (but which you can afford to give because of the substantial depreciation taken on the equipment, plus some appreciated real property still carried at original cost), makes it more of a real swap. If he goes for it, you're home free. If he doesn't, you still haven't revealed the equipment problem, which you can decide how to handle when it comes up in the normal course.

Does that illustration bother you a little? Are you troubled by the element of deception involved? Well, I guess this is as good a place as any to mention the phenomenon I call "creative motivation"—the role of euphemism in the negotiating process. You can't misrepresent facts to your adversary, that's clear; but a certain lack of candor as to the reasoning behind requests and refusals is not at all unusual. Most lawyers operate on the premise that they're under no obligation to let an adversary see the inner workings of their mind. Now, you might feel uncomfortable being less than candid with respect to motives; and if that's the case, then by all means, don't dissemble. (In addition to your moral qualms, you undoubtedly won't be very good at it!) Nevertheless, it would be foolish to assume that your adversary is equally scrupulous. Almost as a reflex action now, I tend to question all ostensible rationale and speculate on my adversary's real motivations. Examine any unusual requests very closely, and constantly ask yourself: what is this guy up to?

The quintessential timing issue is whether, when called upon to make a concession you're able to grant, you should cede the point right then or hold it back for later disposition (such as a trade for something *you* want). Some lawyers are masters of the technique of saying "no" without seeming overly negative. They listen to your points; they encourage you to think there's some possibility of give in their positions; you're certain that they don't feel strongly about a number of the issues and *could* gracefully yield; but at the end of the day, you're right back where you started—with nothing. There's been a dazzling array of talk about "going back to my clients" or "running it past my partners," but you haven't gained a single meaningful concession. You know you're in for a tough time; anything you end up with down the road will have to overcome agonizing reluctance. Other lawyers call things more as they see them, don't worry about hoarding away nuts for the winter, and let an adversary know where he stands. How should you line up on this scale?

Before answering that question, there's a major threshold issue: just how much authority have you received from the partner in charge to agree to changes and make concessions?[29] It's terribly frustrating to negotiate under wraps, where you aren't authorized to exercise any discretion—to say nothing of how unappetizing this is for your adversary.[30] If the partner wants you to function simply as a note-taker, then you ought to announce that fact to the other side before the session begins, so you can avoid squirming when you'd like to be ceding. But always try for the partner's blessing on using your judgment to some extent—sure, you'll save the big issues for him, but there's plenty of stuff you can handle too. For purposes of the discussion which follows, let's assume that you have the necessary authority.

---

[29]   See Section 5.1. Let's assume that the issues here are legal-type matters that you don't need to take back to the client for decision (as discussed in Section 6.6).
[30]   See Section 7.3.9.

All right. It's difficult to provide any generalized guidelines on this subject, but let me offer a few suggestions. Take the case where you've done a first draft of an agreement, and now your adversary comes back at you to ask that certain provisions be changed. My philosophy here (not necessarily shared by all lawyers) is that when the other side requests a perfectly plausible change—to correct faulty draftsmanship or mitigate an unintended overreaching effect—it's a mistake not to make the concession on the spot. Look, you should be striving for a mood of sweet reasonableness in these negotiations. There are going to be plenty of sticky points to come, in which you'll want your adversary to act in a responsible manner. If you react to this obvious point by muttering: "Well, I'll have to think about it," you come across as a hard-nose who ultimately deserves a dose of his own medicine. Of course, you have to exercise a little care; be sure there are no hidden traps in what appears to be a straightforward request. If you spot a possible clinker, then by all means label your concession as tentative, indicating your desire to check whether the change adversely affects your client—so at least your adversary knows he's not dealing with the proverbial dog in the manger.

How about the situation where there *is* room for argument on the point, although as a practical matter you're willing to concede it? Well, the key question for you to address here is: what else is coming? If this is the only concession of any substance to be sought, then perhaps you ought to cede it gracefully—or at least propose a slight variation that your adversary will have no trouble in accepting.[31] On the other hand, a request that's only the first in a series of desired indulgences is less deserving of a gracious response. You're better off to wrap the points up in a bundle—giving on some, sticking on others, and offering to compromise the rest.

But how can you tell what else is in store at the point of the first request? If you suspect a litany of suggested revisions, one useful technique is to advise your adversary that you want to hear *all* his points before you react positively or negatively to any of them. You can justify this posture by pointing out that many issues in the fabric of an agreement are interrelated; you're concerned that a concession on one point might unwittingly affect your position on another; therefore, you want the totality of his objections in front of you in order to formulate intelligent resolutions. Actually, you don't *need* a euphemism; just tell him that's the way you want to play the game. What's he going to do—demand instant decisions on the spot?

When in doubt, my advice is *not* to cede the point. There will be plenty of opportunity to do so later, and with a modicum of

---

[31] This is useful in establishing for the record that what you had originally proposed wasn't *so far* off base.

cleverness you can usually swap it for something running in your direction.

7.3.5. A Negotiating Tactics Sampler.

I'm going to restrain myself, with some difficulty, from saying too much about negotiating tactics—partly because each individual ought to experience the satisfaction of discovering techniques that work, and partly because whatever I say will come back to haunt me one day in a bargaining session! This is where you get your kicks, matey; I'll never forget the first time I was able to hoist an adversary on his own petard—and *realize* I had done it (i.e., abstract the principle from the specifics of the situation). There are so many tricks of the negotiating trade; and if you practice in an area of the law where hard bargaining occurs with any frequency, you can't consider yourself a complete lawyer until you've mastered a few of your own.

"Wait a second," I can hear some of you saying: "Tricks? Gambits? What role does all this have in my professional life? Here I've spent three years in school learning about the majesty of the law, and you're telling me to think deviously. . . ." Well, I hate to be the one to break the news, but someone has to. The worlds of business and law are literally peppered with gaming elements—which is just what makes it all so fascinating. I know clients who are more pleased at winning a small point through your clever ploy (which you've alerted the client to in advance, so he can watch you in action[32]) than at prevailing on larger issues through bargaining muscle or the ineptitude of the opposition. Most clients enjoy having a clever lawyer on their side—provided, of course, that this cleverness is tempered with brains and judgment and integrity and diligence and all the other desirable professional qualities. The psychological benefits of accomplishing a successful ruse shouldn't be underestimated. And the rewards may not be insignificant: just as an astute litigator can gain victories in cases that by all rights deserve to be lost, there's no question that a party's degree of protection, parcel of rights, and outside limit on obligations can be substantially affected by the bargaining ability of counsel.

Let me start by stating the obvious: there are as many different styles of negotiating as there are participants in the game, and consequently no pose is the "right" one for anyone to adopt. You must feel comfortable in what you're doing. Adopt an artificial style and the falseness will soon show through, causing you to lose credibility—perhaps the most important asset in any negotiation. But

---

[32] This is analogous to alerting the client to a pending problem, discussed in Section 6.5.

within your individual range of comfort, there will undoubtedly be a variety of tactics from which to choose.

For instance, no matter what your predilections, you really can't afford to pass up the opportunity to foil your adversary right out of his own big mouth. Lawyers tend to be verbose, making unnecessary statements that, though innocuous at the moment, return to plague them at a later time. And their clients, who may not be so glib, are also less aware of the significance of their utterances—a shortcoming which often lands them in the soup. Sometimes this sort of opportunity just falls into your lap; at other times, a little stage managing is in order. An intelligent line of questions can work wonders here, so long as your interrogation doesn't suggest cross-examination and place your adversary on his guard. You have to plan ahead a bit—principally in order to know, prior to your adversary figuring it out, just where you want to end up. And, of course, you probably need a dose of old-fashioned dumb luck.

Take a simple example. Your client, Forsyth, has been negotiating the purchase of a used truck from C.B. Smokey. Unfortunately, Forsyth has to be out of the country for a few days, and has asked you to conclude the deal for him.[33] There has been tentative agreement on a price of $5,000. Forsyth's inspection had revealed that some work was needed on the transmission. Smokey has been down-playing this problem, but your client suspects it may be fairly major. Now, you *could* take the position right from the outset that Smokey should get the transmission work done before the transaction takes place; but he might well refuse, and then there's no telling where things will end up. After all, Smokey never warranted to your client that he was delivering a truck in perfect condition; and to your knowledge, there were no discussions about Smokey taking steps to put the truck in tip-top shape.

The better tack to take, I would think, is *not* to disabuse old C.B. of the idea that it's Forsyth who'll have to contract for the necessary work. The inference you want Smokey to draw is that, assuming you can be satisfied as to the insignificance of the defect, this won't stand in the way of striking a deal at the $5,000 price. And so you patiently lure Smokey into the trap. He begins to go to great lengths— flaunting his vast mechanical expertise—to convince you it's not really a major job. Finally, he puts a $100 estimate on what it should cost. At that point, you have him. "Okay, C.B., I want to deliver a clean truck to my client—not a truck that he has to take into the garage for repairs the very first day. *You* get the transmission fixed, and I'll increase

---

[33] Your suggestion to Smokey that he might wish to be advised by counsel in dealing with you was greeted with a loud snort.

the purchase price to $5,100." Ten-Four. Smokey is in a difficult position to dispute your compromise, since he made the estimate himself.[34]

Here's a different kind of tactic. Let's say you're trying to make your stubborn adversary change a contractual provision he has drafted. To make progress, it can help to show how inappropriately the proposed clause would operate under a particular set of facts. And the more you can dramatize the point, the better. Enter, the absurd example—a key weapon in your negotiating arsenal, designed to tighten up over-broad draftsmanship. Dream up a preposterous situation to illustrate how the provsion could lead to clearly unintended, improper results. Your adversary may reply that this was obviously *not* what he had in mind, but you continue to heap ridicule on his position, thereby laying the groundwork for a favorable compromise solution. For example, this is the ideal device to introduce a materiality standard into a contractual provision (such as the typical condition of a deferred closing agreement that requires all representations to be true as of the closing):

> "You mean that if I forget to tell you about the supply contract for our water cooler, you can walk away from this multi-million dollar deal? Absurd? Sure—but that's exactly the way you've drafted it. Come on, Joe, you've got to be kidding. In order for you to avoid your obligation, the misrepresentation has to be *material. . . .*"

That technique calls for a dose of bluster. Other ploys require more in the way of subtlety. Let's say that you represent the prospective purchaser of a business for eight million dollars. The seller has asked your client for a typical "basket" or "cushion" provision; i.e., in the event of misrepresentations by the seller which are discovered by the purchaser after the closing, the purchaser will not seek indemnification unless the total damage exceeds the basket amount. You've agreed to the basket in principle, but have deferred any bargaining over its amount until all other points have been resolved.

Thinking ahead, you wonder what number you'll ultimately suggest. You could kick off the bidding with a ridiculously low number—say, $10,000—but you know this will only lead to interminable bargaining;[35] and as a matter of fact, unless you pull it off with a

---

[34]   *N.B.* You *didn't* say that you would increase the price by the *actual* cost of the repair (which could presumably be a lot higher), but rather by Smokey's own estimate. Your remaining concern will be that Smokey's garage doesn't do a half-hearted job—the old $99.95 special.

[35]   If I were on the other side, my reply to the $10,000 figure would be in the $250,000 range, just to establish a proper spread between the bid and the asked.

smile, your adversary might question your good faith. Your best bet is to select a figure that your client finds comfortable—let's say, $50,-000—which has enough of a reasonable ring to cause the seller, in the spirit of good fellowship (and convinced that *any* indemnification will be unlikely), to accept it on the spot. But you're concerned that if you wait and simply trot the number out cold, your adversary will wax indignant ("Hell, buddy, that's only a few bucks more than ½ of 1% of the entire deal!") and the auction will commence at too high a level.

Well, one technique to obtain some advance input into this decision *before* making the offer is to maneuver yourself into a situation where, in discussing the operation of the indemnification sections with your adversary, you illustrate your point by use of an example containing a hypothetical number for the basket. Something like this: "Now, let's assume we had a basket of, say, $50,000, and two different claims were made which in the aggregate . . .", etc. Note the reaction to this number which you dropped ever so casually into the proceedings. Are any eyebrows raised? Has anyone made a caustic remark about your penuriousness? Does the other side actively participate in discussion of the example, utilizing your figure? Use the number hypothetically a few more times if you can. If the signs are right, you may have neatly paved the way for its ultimate introduction into the bargaining.[36]

By the way, if you're the *seller's* lawyer and your adversary pulls this kind of $50,000 stunt, it behooves you to speak up and make clear that, although you're willing to indulge his mathematical computations using that figure, the ultimate basket will undoubtedly be a fancy multiple of that sum. Never let another lawyer infer that your silence signifies assent.

7.3.6. Two-Thirds Up Pike's Peak Ain't Bad.

So much for getting a leg up. Now let's talk about the other side of the negotiating coin—compromise—which may be even more important. Deals just don't get done unless you achieve solutions to divisive issues acceptable to both parties—solutions which accomplish your client's purposes without making the adversary so un-

---

[36] The corollary to this proposition is probably too obvious to require stating but I'll do so anyway: *never, never* use a figure for hypothetical purposes that exceeds what you're ultimately willing to settle on. If you do, then no matter how you later twist and turn, the other side will extrapolate from your presumably subconscious use of the number that you're prepared to go at least that far.

happy that he walks away or proceeds with permanent scars.[36a] This involves a search for what may be termed the favorable common ground; and believe me, it often takes some imagination and planning to arrive there in one piece.

But arrive you must. Because in the kind of voluntary two-party transaction under consideration here—an acquisition being a prime example—you can't afford the luxury of standing up and shouting "Take it or leave it" or dismissing an obstacle with "That's *his* problem". Always remember: the guy on the other side doesn't *have* to do the deal. If, for instance, *his* tax problems appear insurmountable—every way you twist and turn results in a whopping tax bill that he refuses to pay—then he's likely to terminate the discussions; so his tax problem is your deal problem, and unless you can figure a way to make the transaction palatable to him, you're nowhere.

At the very root of the friendly adversary relationship is the implicit assumption that both parties and their lawyers basically want to reach agreement. Sure, each will hold out for terms he deems desirable (or at least can live with), but the ultimate goal is mutual. As a result, they work together in solving the structural and legal issues—in a merger, for instance, the tax questions, the accounting aspects, the considerations of corporate and securities law—that populate the landscape. Even working together, these are difficult enough to resolve.[37]

When the parties and their attorneys really want a deal to happen, and strive jointly for its accomplishment, almost all issues are ultimately soluble. Once you cut through the rhetoric—your own, as well as that of your adversary—so many questions which appear to possess philosophical overtones boil down to dollar issues, solvable by moving piles of money around. If the dollars aren't enough, perhaps an additional face-saving device is necessary, to provide the party who has taken a firm negotiating stand enough room to back off without embarrassment.

[36a] "*Compromise,* n. Such an adjustment of conflicting interests as gives each adversary the satisfaction of thinking he has got what he ought not to have, and is deprived of nothing except what was justly his due." Ambrose Bierce, *The Devil's Dictionary* (1881-1911).

[37] In at least one instance in my experience, however, the lawyer for the other side, while professing a business-as-usual approach, was trying his damnedest to sabotage the deal. And you can't believe the fresh parameters of complexity and confusion this opened up. New problems appeared daily; problems having apparent solutions remained as problems because of his unwillingness (cloaked behind some euphemistic rationale) to take the path of obvious resolution; and so on. His capacity for mischief was unlimited, and he almost managed to abort the deal until everyone finally woke up to what was happening and new lawyers were brought in to put the pieces back together.

You're representing Cashcow Inc. in negotiating an employment contract with S. Glick, one of its key vice presidents. Glick has taken the position that his remuneration should be at least equal to that of any other Cashcow vice president. It seems that one vice president, Jones, makes $150,000, and Glick wants to keep up with . . . sorry. Cashcow originally offered Glick $120,000 and has grudgingly increased the stipend to $135,000. Although Cashcow's president, Chexoff, values Glick's services and wants him to stay with the company, that's as high as Chexoff is willing to go. You suspect that Glick would like to settle at the $135,000 figure; however, he has stated that most-favored-nation principle so often that he's backed himself into a corner, where accepting the $15,000 differential would constitute a significant loss of face. What do you do?

Well, one possibility is to suggest a provision that gives Glick, in addition to his $135,000 salary, a $15,000 bonus if his division achieves a certain level of annual earnings that, deep down, both you and he know—although neither mentions the fact—is beyond the division's capacity. Sure, it's not quite the same as non-contingent equality; but at least it's a cosmetic step by Chexoff in the direction of the principle Glick's been espousing, permitting the latter to climb out of the trap he's erected.

But let's assume this Cashcow is a public company, where the *actual* remuneration received by the highest paid officers is set out in the proxy statement. This is what Glick has been worried about all along; and for this purpose, the contingent $15,000 he's unlikely to receive won't solve his problem of appearances. So it's back to the drawing board. Then it dawns on you. Several years ago Cashcow loaned each of its vice presidents $200,000 in order to buy Company stock. Interest at 7% per annum has been accruing on these loans, but Cashcow has never collected it, and has no present intention of doing so.[38] The solution is obvious. You tell Glick: "All right. We'll pay you a $150,000 salary, but now we're going to collect the $14,000 annual interest on your loan." Regardless of the fact that his net remuneration will be about $136,000, Glick is happy because the $150,000 number will show up in the proxy statement; and Chexoff is happy, because Cashcow's out-of-pocket cost has stayed at about the level where he determined to stick. And that, in a nutshell, is the theory of a successful compromise.

7.3.7. A Practical Approach to Impasse.

The path to compromise is not always clearly marked, and some

---

[38] Make sure, of course, that in these days of emphasis on "perks", this situation has been adequately disclosed in the company's filings.

creative ability is required to discover the ground on which the accommodation will be based.[38a] As a practical matter, the most important single weapon in your compromise arsenal is the ability to
divide up a seemingly indivisible issue, so that you satisfy your adversary's *real* concerns (which are generally narrower than those he
has expressed) while at the same time protecting your client's *essential* interests (which are generally narrower than those you've previously advanced). To do this well, you have to peer deeply into the
minds of both your client and your adversary. But rather than
generalizing further on the subject, let me illustrate its application
with a few examples.

You are in the midst of negotiating an acquisition agreement on behalf of the prospective purchaser of a private company. The seller's
first fiscal quarter is due to end shortly, and unaudited financial
statements for the period will become available prior to the closing—although after the agreement has been signed. The section of
the agreement containing the seller's representations and warranties
contains a specific reference to the quarterly statements, indicating
that when delivered these will carry the same warranties as to conformity with generally accepted accounting principles, consistent application and fair presentation as the audited year-end statements
already delivered. All contractual representations will survive the
closing and give rise to indemnification claims if errors are later discovered.

The seller is opposed to making this representation. He says: "I
don't like to warrant something that's being prepared in the future—a
document that I don't have in front of me at the time I sign the agreement. If the deal were otherwise ready to close, you wouldn't wait for
the quarterly statement; why should it be different just because the
schedule has been set back a month." And so on. All of which makes
your client extremely uneasy. Is the first quarter a disaster? What's
the seller up to? The parties appear adamant. If you don't find some
way to cut through this issue, you may have a deal-breaker.

So, you stop and try to examine this from your adversary's point of
view. What's he really worried about? And from various things that
have been said and other clues, you're convinced that the seller's
lawyer is afraid of the internally-prepared unaudited statements
because they're not as complete as audited ones, lacking the careful
footnotes and supporting data—and accordingly they constitute a ripe
prospect for potential future claims under the indemnification
provisions if the business later turns sour. And that, after all, is *not*
what your client is after. He's satisfied to rest his long-run indem-

---

[38a]   In this regard, Section 2.5 on cracking the assumption mold—seeing
things in a fresh light—is particularly relevant.

nification potentialities on the year-end audited financial statements. The significance to him of the figures for the quarter, on the other hand, is to ensure that they don't reflect a drastic downtrend in earnings before he's even bought the business.

And then you realize that this is a divisible issue, capable of compromise. The quarterly numbers need not be the subject of an ongoing representation,[39] but they can and should form a condition to the purchaser's obligation to close. The agreement would provide that if the quarterly figures aren't at least as good as those of the comparable quarter of the prior year (or whatever other standard you require the seller to meet), then your client can walk away from the deal. Since the seller doesn't anticipate any problems, this isn't such a difficult provision for him to accept. If your client is concerned with the reliability of the numbers, he can insist that the seller's auditors review them and issue a comfort letter. But if the purchaser then decides to close, the seller won't have to stand behind the unaudited figures down through the ages. You've split up the issue, giving the unaudited statements enough contractual significance to suit your client's needs without unnecessarily crowding the other side.[40]

Let's take another example. Suppose that you're representing the seller in an acquisition structured as an earnout—that is, a portion of the purchase price will be contingent upon the earnings which the seller's company (as a subsidiary of the purchaser) is able to earn over the five years immediately following the closing.[41] Extensive negotiations ensue on the various questions arising out of the need to make provision for the future. Twin themes are sounded: (i) the seller's paranoia over the purchaser taking actions adversely affecting the seller's earnings and thus reducing the ultimate purchase price, and (ii) the purchaser's insistence on the right to ultimately call the shots for his newly-acquired subsidiary. The purchaser is willing to let the seller exercise day-to-day control, but the purchaser's board can't shirk its responsibility to the stockholders by delegating total responsibility to a subsidiary official. The seller, on the other hand, is a 'amant that unless he's allowed to run his business free from interference and in the manner that he deems most fruitful, he won't be able to make his earnout. All of which is standard bargaining procedure, but thorny nonetheless; and solutions to the various sub-issues must be found or the deal will founder.

---

[39] Even without a contractual representation on the numbers, if they later proved incorrect—and assuming materiality, scienter, reliance and the transfer of securities—your client would have a claim against the seller by reason of Rule 10b-5 under the Securities Exchange Act of 1934.

[40] The matters discussed in this example are explored in more detail in Sections 5.3, 7.1 and 7.4.2 of *Anatomy*.

[41] Section 6.3 of *Anatomy* contains a lengthy discussion of earnouts.

One particular area of dispute involves the seller's concern that the purchaser will force the subsidiary to enter new sales territories or introduce new products during the earnout period against the seller's better judgment. The seller can visualize the negative impact on his earnings of such start-up costs, even though benefits may ensue in later years not included in the earnout formula. And so the seller demands a veto right over territorial expansion and new products. The purchaser, however, is unwilling to cede such power to the seller. The purchaser knows that any such decisions will be made not on the petty basis of attempting to reduce the seller's price, but rather in an effort to expand operations for the overall good of the business. The parties reiterate their positions with vigor, and the developing impasse is causing increasing tension.

Well, you can cut through this type of deadlock by the same device of dividing up the issues. The purchaser is really interested in controlling the business decision, not in limiting the size of the seller's earnout; the seller is concerned with the size of his earnout, less so with who makes the expansion decision (assuming he'll ultimately yield, as most sellers do, on the several control issues). So you whack it up in this fashion: the purchaser gets the final say as to whether the business will be expanded; but if the seller doesn't consent to the move in advance, then the results attributable to the expansion won't affect his earnout. Put another way, if the purchaser wants the seller to go into a new state over seller's objection, then the results of seller's operations related to the portion of his business conducted in that new state—whether profit or loss—will simply be ignored in computing his earnings for earnout purposes. To be sure, this principle is easier to state than to apply; allocating overhead and other indirect items to separate portions of the business is always difficult. But it does get the parties over a critical bargaining hump; and after all, how likely is it that the provision will even come into play in the years ahead? Meanwhile, the seller's concern over his earnout and the purchaser's interest in controlling his new business have both been adequately protected; and you can move on to the next item.

7.3.8. Laying the Groundwork for Compromise.

Negotiations are rarely an exercise in naked power. Rather, they are generally conducted in a spirit of give and take, with the lawyers and the parties striving in relatively good-natured fashion to resolve all issues to everyone's satisfaction. An atmosphere of reasonableness should prevail: you win this point, I get that one, we split the next.

In this milieu, the attorney should support his positions in the most rational possible terms. Requesting the addition of a certain representation, you should present plausible proof of your client's need for the protection; if you seek to be indemnified against a certain potential liability, tell your adversary why it's logical. Your opponent will attempt to dispute your views—showing why you don't need the protection or why he can't afford to give it—in terms which vie with yours for the cogency trophy. And not infrequently, the more logical the arguments you advance in support of a point, the greater your chances of successfully compromising the issue on terms satisfactory to your client. If you're fast on your feet, and have been over this particular ground before, you ought to be able to produce valid arguments on the spot. But some advance preparation can often be important—especially when you're unwilling to expose to your adversary the *real* reason behind your position,[42] since this would cause him to refuse your request.

Let's take an example to illustrate the marshaling of arguments in support of a position. You represent the seller of a business in a proposed cash transaction. The purchaser's first draft of the acquisition agreement provides that the purchaser's obligation to close is subject to his ability to obtain the necessary financing for the purchase price. Wait a minute, Charlie, hold it right there! This provision, you stammer, turns the whole deal into nothing more than an option for the purchaser. If he doesn't receive his financing, then he doesn't have to do the deal, and your client has no recourse. Assume the purchaser later decides that, for other reasons, he doesn't want to go through with the acquisition; all he has to do is "arrange" for his bank to decline putting up the money.

The purchaser's attorney replies that his client can't commit to the deal absolutely without knowing whether he'll get the funds. Just to assure you there won't be any monkey business, however, he's willing for the purchaser to undertake a "best efforts" obligation to obtain the financing. "And counselor," he adds, somewhat patronizingly, isn't it obvious that the purchaser is motivated to get the financing? Otherwise, why would he be entering into this deal in the first place?

Well, you ask in a suspicious tone, then why doesn't his client just take a walk down to the bank right now, get his financing commitment, and we can proceed to sign the agreement without the condition? To which Charlie candidly replies that the bank is more likely to finance the acquisition if shown a signed contract—even a voidable one—than with an oral deal that's easier to nip in the bud. Look, he says (in his most engaging manner), "trust me" that it's in our clients' *mutual* best interests to adopt this somewhat unusual chronological order. If

---

[42]   See Section 7.3.4 for a few words on "creative motivation."

you insist on deleting the condition, counselor, then we'll just have to go to the bank first; but, believe me, that's riskier—it's far preferable to position the lender with the executed agreement.

At this point, you stop to take stock of your situation. Charlie just might have a point here, and certainly your client doesn't want to lose this deal. Your client trusts the purchaser; still, you hate to tempt your adversary's baser instincts by granting an absolute withdrawal right. If the bank *really* doesn't go along, all right—there's no way to deal with that; but what you need is a built-in disincentive against the purchaser deciding to abort the deal and using the bank as his cover. In order to succeed here, however, you have to pound a little more on the point to soften your adversary up for the ultimate compromise.

C'mon, Charlie, you know "best efforts" has no meaning in and of itself. For instance, what if the bank insists on an interest rate pegged at two points over prime? Would the purchaser's refusal to accept this violate the best efforts undertaking? And how about the other terms of the loan—the payback, the default covenants and such? You know, Charlie, if we start to define what constitutes "best efforts" under these circumstances, the bank will spot the definition in the agreement and know the parameters within which the purchaser is willing to negotiate.

After playing with this for a while, you then work on eliciting informal statements from the purchaser as to the unlikelihood of the bank turning him down—statements you will use against his interest at a later point.[43] At this point, you shift ground and plow into the real heart of the matter—the potential harm to your client from this manner of proceeding. You have to make the purchaser appreciate that you have some real problems with which he can empathize. Your main point is the damage that could be caused by announcement of a deal which might not take place. Once public disclosure is made upon signing of the agreement, the competitors, suppliers, employees and customers of your client all know his business is for sale; and everyone looks at it in a new light. If the deal should abort, no matter what the ostensible reason put out for public consumption, everyone will assume it relates to something non-kosher discovered by the purchaser in his investigation. "When this deal is announced," you state with some force, "my client wants to know that it's going to get done—subject, of course, to the purchaser's investigation confirming that the company is what we say it is. We want the purchaser *obligated.*"

Now you're in position to spring your compromise—which is basically a liquidated damages provision if the deal expires because the purchaser fails to secure financing. The purchaser can live with

---

[43]   See the discussion of petard-hoisting in Section 7.3.5.

this, since he knows the extent of his liability (which, in the absence of the financing condition, would otherwise be open-ended). Actually, he's hard-pressed to beg off, since he's already told you the bank approval is so likely to be forthcoming; in fact, if he refuses the damage provision, then I'd call his bluff and send him to the bank in advance. And your client can live with it,[44] since the purchaser is unlikely to manipulate the bank if he knows it will cost him the liquidated amount. The arguments you pulled together, however, were essential to arriving at the right result.

If you want to stick on—or close to—a particular position, you must convince your adversary that you have a good reason for being unmovable; otherwise, he'll assume that if he hammers away at you long enough, you'll fold. Say that a dispute has arisen about a prospective finder's fee. The finder is claiming, on the basis of somewhat ambiguous documentary evidence, that he is entitled to $200,000 if the deal goes through. (He recognizes, of course, that *any* fee is dependent on the transaction taking place.) Your client is only willing to pay him $75,000.

As long as the finder believes that your client wants to make this acquisition come hell or high water, the finder will be tempted to press ahead for the $200,000. In order to get him to listen to reason, he has to be worried about whether the deal will get done at all—and has to believe that the size of the finder's fee itself is a factor in your client's ultimate decision. One method of accomplishing this would be to convince the finder that payment of the $200,000 would have such a negative impact on current earnings,[45] it would make no sense for your client to do the deal. This is an argument the finder can understand; and he might be more inclined to opt for the $75,000 bird in hand—which he can probably push up to $100,000—rather than to shake the bush and find it empty.

Your timing is also important here, as in so many bargaining matters. You have to negotiate this particular finder's fee *early* in the game, before you take other steps (such as going to your board of directors for approval of the deal) that indicate your client views the deal favorably and is likely to proceed no matter what the outcome on the fee. Remember, once the finder believes you're committed to the deal, your argument on the earnings impact is muted—and he'll tend to hold out for his $200,000. In order for your strategy to work, it

---

[44] Unless he's been convinced, by your rhetoric, of the harm befalling him should an announced deal be terminated!

[45] In an acquisition accounted for as a pooling of interests, the finder's fee and other expenses are charged against current earnings, which can have a devastating effect. See Section 11.1.1 of *Anatomy*.

must take place early enough for the finder to be persuaded of the genuine possibility that he'll lose his fee altogether.

The broader timing principle at work here is that, assuming you have devised a possible compromise, you must be careful not to introduce it into the bargaining prematurely, thereby running the risk of your adversary's reflexive rejection—at which point your purported solution becomes your new bargaining position, and the ultimate compromise will require further concessions on your part. It's often necessary to bite your tongue, continue to polarize the deadlock, and then proceed in a roundabout way—often by posing a series of questions—in order to lay the groundwork for your solution. I have included in Section 9.6 a lengthy example of this principle at work, in the course of negotiations over a joint venture agreement.

7.3.9. The Friendly Adversary Has a Client Too.

It's easy to lose sight of the fact—especially when you're pounding away at each other—that the lawyer on the other side also represents a client. He's not a completely free agent. You may persuade *him* your cause is just, but if his client's not buying, you haven't advanced the ball. Conversely, when the other lawyer turns obstreperous, his client can sometimes turn out to be your best ally. In this section, I want to talk about several aspects of the relationship between friendly adversarial lawyers that involve the other attorney's client.

At the very core of this discussion is the observation which I'm sure each of you has made at times: that the presence of your adversary's client in the conference room (or his absence) can be a major factor in your adversary's attitude and the general progress of the negotiations. Not that it always cuts in a certain direction; the possibilities are varied, as we shall see. But for better or worse, this is consistently an element of some importance.

For instance, there are some issues that are generally best negotiated lawyer-to-lawyer, with no clients around. The content of the legal opinion to be delivered in a business transaction is a good example.[46] Clients don't necessarily understand these matters, and it's usually a mistake to have them peering over the lawyers' shoulders while opinions are under discussion. There are rather refined sorts of professional judgments involved in the rendering of opinions, which don't lend themselves to lay oversight. A lawyer's unwillingness to opine can too easily appear as intractability, when in fact it represents a more subtle form of discomfort.

---

[46]   See Section 8.4 of *Anatomy*, with regard to negotiating legal opinions in acquisitions.

However, on relatively rare occasions, when you believe your adversary is acting in bad faith in refusing to give a customary opinion, you might just want to position things so that your adversary's client is present—the idea being that if *he* can see what his lawyer is up to, how unreasonably he's acting, perhaps you'll be able to generate some pressure towards compliance with your reasonable demands. This is clearly the unusual case; and in most instances, I am firmly opposed to generating pressure on another lawyer to give an opinion through manipulation of his client.[47]

When dealing lawyer-to-lawyer on issues other than legal opinions, the first estimate you must make is whether your adversary has the authority to make decisions. Can he, acting alone, grant the requests or concessions you seek? If you're in a position to speak for your client, but he can't commit his, you may find yourself in the worst kind of one-sided negotiation. All the concessions flow from your end of the table; he's just sitting there, gratefully accepting whatever you have to offer and proffering nothing in return. The solution here is simple: don't allow this to happen. As soon as you realize he lacks authority, I suggest you break off the negotiations and tell him to produce his client on the morrow.

Taking a broader focus, you should always attempt to identify the individual on the other team who is really calling the shots. It's not always the person nominally in charge; perhaps it's a key executive with good judgment, or the long-time lawyer who plays a trusted role extending beyond mere legal matters. But whoever it is, that's the person to whom you should direct your most serious attention.

Try to exercise some control over the invitation list for the bargaining session. If matters have proceeded to the point where only a few tough problems remain and the purpose of the meeting is to resolve these, then the decision-makers have to be present. There's nothing more frustrating than for a couple of lawyers to sit there and bargain hypothetically, helpless to reach accommodation in the absence of their clients. There are times, however, when you would prefer hav-

---

[47]   I am *not* opposed, however, to playing my adversary's client off against him on other kinds of business-related issues—a horse of quite a different color, which we'll deal with later in this section. But legal opinions are different. For instance, I find quite reprehensible the sometime inclination of lawyers for financial institutions to ask borrower's counsel for outrageous opinions that they simply can't give, and then to bring pressure to bear on counsel by having the banker tell the borrower that the latter's lawyer is holding up the deal. The borrower, who needs the money and doesn't understand the technicalities of the legal opinion question, calls his lawyer up and tells him to "give the bank the damned opinion, for God's sake!" It's all highly unprofessional.

ing several bites at the apple; and an initial lawyer-to-lawyer pitch might just pay ultimate dividends.

Let's assume that your adversary's client is there in the room. When your adversary makes a blustery speech or takes a rigid negotiating position, you have to speculate that he may simply be posturing for the benefit of his client. Some lawyers thrive on this kind of showboating—raising unnecessary objections, introducing hypothetical problems, and the like. The poseur's client, having no idea whether the points possess substance, assumes they do. This lawyer, apparently laboring so mightily to overcome horrendous obstacles, really gives him his money's worth. Well, this is the converse of the lawyer who lacks authority. If you sense you're in this kind of a situation, just relax; don't worry about resolving things that day; wait for an opportunity to corner your adversary alone, when there's no client around to generate the pyrotechnics.

When your adversary's client is in the room, you should always be alert to the possibilities of speaking directly to him over his lawyer's head. This calls for a great deal of subtlety and is not recommended for the tyro attorney—your adversary might take serious umbrage at a clumsy attempt. Not infrequently, however, you will want to get a message across to your adversary's client, which you can't expect your adversary to transmit in its most effective form. After all, you would tend to put your request or refusal in the best possible light, marshaling persuasive rationale to back it up—whereas your adversary can be expected to view your motives more cynically, adopting a negativistic approach that can cause automatic rejection by his client.

So, after staking out your position vis-à-vis your adversary in essentially legalistic terms, you might pause and say: "Let me just put this point into everyday language so that the businessmen can understand what we're talking about." Ostensibly, you're doing it for your own client's benefit, but the real thought is to get the message across to the other party in your most persuasive tones. Needless to say, the corollary here is to be alert to instances where an adversary is trying to talk over your head to your client. Intercept those kinds of transmissions before they can do you any harm.

By the way, when the other party is represented by counsel, you should never negotiate with him in his lawyer's absence, except under unusual circumstances. The other party, having taken a liking to you, may deem your presence useful to help the principals clarify their thoughts, even though his lawyer is out of town. But he and your client don't necessarily appreciate your ethical problem in this regard. If you find yourself being drawn into such a session, always try to reach the other lawyer to tell him what's happening and obtain his consent to that arrangement. If he doesn't consent, then get out of the room. If he does consent, make a real effort to be a clarifier and compromiser. Don't play an advocate's role; if you put a few over on the other party, you can bet your adversary will answer you in spades when he arrives back in town.

No matter how heated relations become between the parties, it's essential that the lawyers maintain their cool and keep communicating. Even if the clients cease to have direct contact, there is still hope for the deal if the lawyers can work together. But once the lawyers stop talking, the death knell is sounded. Now, it would defy human nature for a lawyer not to become somewhat agitated in the middle of a heated negotiation and adopt his tone from his client to some degree. If the client feels aggrieved, the lawyer had better act in consonance, or the client will quickly find himself a more sympathetic counselor. But the lawyer ought always to strive for a measured response to the exigencies of the situation. Once the dramatics of the meeting are over, he should be able to sit down with the lawyer on the other side and, in a rational manner, work things out.

Above all, the lawyer must keep things in perspective. Often, toward the close of a difficult deal, minor points become magnified out of all proportion to their importance. What would have been a simple concession to make at the outset of negotiations suddenly becomes a deal-breaker. The lawyer is often the only person who can advise his client that this issue shouldn't be exalted to an hysterical level—that it's only the lateness of the hour and the pressures of the deal that distort reality. Such coolness on the lawyer's part can often salvage a troubled deal. If, on the other hand, you let yourself become caught up in the machismo of those final minutes, you only serve to exacerbate an already critical situation.

7.4. LITIGATION AND THE HOSTILE ADVERSARY

It's a sobering task for a corporate-type lawyer to compose an essay on litigation—the nature of advocacy, pre-trial procedure, court papers, judges and juries. The plain fact is, though, that a healthy percentage of practising lawyers do this sort of thing for a living; and any book on lawyering without some material on the subject would certainly be incomplete. Moreover, in the context of this chapter on dealings with other lawyers in various capacities, it's difficult to examine the hostile adversary without some appreciation of his usual bailiwick. And in terms of "other lawyers," could we possibly ignore the pride of the species—the judge? So, after several useful sessions with experienced litigators, and having perused some helpful material on the topic[48]—and not without considerable trepidation—I hereby offer up a sprinkling of secondhand pearls.

7.4.1. Some Reflections on Advocacy.

Although the experts agree that each trial lawyer must "be himself" and shun imitative characteristics,[49] it is equally axiomatic that a good litigator must be an effective advocate. He has, after all, a point (or two) to make, and he ought to bend every effort to do so—even if he's not fully convinced of its soundness.[50]

Most lawyers from time to time (especially at cocktail parties) are assailed with variations on the "How can you defend a man you know is guilty?" theme. Somehow, the presumption of innocence—while legally impeccable—doesn't quite suffice. The added concept that the law is what the judge says it is can seem a trifle sterile.[51] More difficult to articulate—but right on the money—is the fact that a hallmark of the effective advocate is his belief in the rightness of his

---

[48] See L. Stryker, *The Art of Advocacy* (1954) [hereinafter cited as "Stryker"]; M. Mayer, *The Lawyers* (1966, 1967) [hereinafter cited as "*The Lawyers*"]; Lasky, "The Essentials of Successful Trial Advocacy," 6 *The Practical Lawyer* 89-94 (1960) [hereinafter cited as "Lasky"]; Solomon, "A Concise Guide to Courtroom Craft," 6 *Juris Doctor* 37-41 (1976) [hereinafter cited as "Solomon"]; Summit, "Conducting the Oral Deposition," 1 *Litigation* 22-26 (1975) [hereinafter cited as "Summit"]; Wesely, "Pretrial Development in Major Corporate Litigation," 1 *Litigation* 8-12 (1975); Zoeller, "Plotting Basic Strategy in Corporate Litigation," 1 *Litigation* 13-16 (1975) [hereinafter cited as "Zoeller"]; Gold, "Pretrial Management of the Big Case: A Plaintiff's Perspective," 3 *Litigation Journal* 8-12, 51 (1977); Levitt, "Managing Psychological Factors in Trying a Case," 7 *The Practical Lawyer* 73-78 (1961) [hereinafter cited as "Levitt"]; Walzer, "Misconduct of an Attorney During Trial," 7 *The Practical Lawyer* 92-98 (1961); Keefe, "Advocacy and the Criminal Trial Judge," 13 *Trial* 43-44 (1977) [hereinafter cited as "Keefe"]; Connolly, "Civility in the Courtroom: The Judge's Obligation," 1 *Litigation* 14-17 (1975) [hereinafter cited as "Connolly"]; Brandschain, "Preparation and Trial of a Labor Arbitration Case," 18 *The Practical Lawyer* 17-42 (1972) [hereinafter cited as "Brandschain"].
[49] "Trial lawyers are of all styles: the brisk and crisp, the silky smooth, the circuitous and indirect, the patient builder of the carefully articulated and monumental, the precise adherent to exact truth, the cavalier addict of the momentary advantage, the architectonic and the artful, the theatrical and the pedantic." Lasky, *supra* note 48, at 89.
[50] An observation that hasn't escaped the gaze of leading satirists. Witness Swift, in *Gulliver's Travels*, offering his lowly opinion of lawyers: "A society of men bred up from their youth in the art of proving by words multiplied for the purpose that white is black and black is white according as they are paid." As quoted in Keefe, *supra* note 48, at 43.
[51] But not in the hands of Samuel Johnson who, when asked by Boswell what he thought about supporting a cause which he knew to be bad, replied: "Sir, you do not know it to be good or bad, till the judge determines it. I have said that you are to state facts fairly; so that your thinking on what you call knowing a cause to be bad, must be from reasoning, must be from supposing

cause.[52] Witness the following colloquy taken from the transcript of a recent court proceeding:

> "*The Court:* Well, some days [Counselor], you are on the plaintiff's side of the case and then the next day on the defendant's. Apparently, you don't have to have any strong moral position as to what is right and what is wrong.
>
> "[*Attorney*]: Well, your Honor, I just am of the view that whatever position I assert is the position of my clients, and they are with very few exceptions the ones who have the stronger moral position."[53]

Some litigators will tell you that the effective advocate has to start out with something less than a completely open mind—definitely tilting in the direction of the conclusion which best serves his client's interest. And before he can set out to persuade others to agree, the first person to convince is himself. However skeptically the litigator begins, by the time he's arguing the case in court, his belief is total and absolutely sincere. In the words of one advocate, "You cannot very well keep your tongue in your cheek while you are talking."[54] Others differ on this point, emphasizing the need to be fully aware of the weakness in a case in order to operate effectively.

Nothing is cut and dried about a lawsuit. Surprises abound, tough decisions must be made, opportunities can be seized or irretrievably lost. And, though clad in the garments of a search for truth, trials are also very much an exercise in salesmanship. As one astute observer of the trial scene put it: "The end is not to convince but to persuade, not to appeal to the mind but to move to action."[55]

---

your arguments to be weak and inconclusive. But sir, that is not enough. An argument which does not convince yourself may convince the judge, to whom you urge it; and *if it does convince him*, sir, you are wrong and he is right. It is his business to judge; and you are not to be confident in your own opinion that a cause is bad, but *to say all you can for your client*, and then hear the judge's opinion." Stryker, *supra* note 48, at 275.

[52] Brandeis put it this way: "As a practical matter, I think the lawyer is not often harrassed by this problem partly because he is apt to believe at the time in most of the cases that he actually tries, and partly because he either abandons or settles a large number of those he does not believe in." *Id.* at 44.

[53] Transcript of hearing in *Telco Marketing Services, Inc. v. Irving Abramowitz*, at 12 (Del. Ch. C. A. No. 5649, July 12, 1978).

[54] Charles P. Curtis as quoted in *The Lawyers*, *supra* note 48, at 34.

[55] Lasky, *supra* note 48, at 91. Allow me to quote further on the point from this pithy source: "The first task of the trial lawyer, therefore, is to make the judge want to decide in his favor. The second is to give him the rational basis on which to do so. The former without the latter is a fraud; the latter without the former is likely to be a failure. Between these two poles of fraud and failure, the trial lawyer must hover, avoiding the one for the sake of his integrity, and the other for the sake of his client." *Id.* at 92.

A successful trial lawyer needs both a theory and an image for his case.[56] The *theory* (or legal premise) seeks to logically compel a certain result by intermeshing applicable principles of law with a particular collection of facts. The *image* is the picture of the case the lawyer wishes the judge and jury to have. It should be simple and uncomplicated—no matter how complex the facts, no matter how abstruse the legal theories.[57] The proper image can color the evidence, affect the perception of witnesses' testimony, and even accomplish an end run around a pesky rule of law. In the well-tried case, theory and image combine—the litigator skillfully utilizing an appealing image to dramatize a sound theory.

To accomplish this, one school of thought advocates finding and then piercing through to the jugular vein of the case—reducing the undigested, diffuse mass of facts in every controversy into neat categories, culling out irrelevancies—a crisp and candid presentation. Other successful attorneys take another tack, building slowly and laboriously to an impressive conclusion.[58] Each advocate tries a lawsuit in his own way—which may not even be the same in each lawsuit *he* tries. But whatever the style, the successful effort bears a common trademark:

> "Every case should be so tried that, when it is concluded, no one will compliment the winner on his skill but all will wonder why the loser ever had the temerity to bring the case to court at all. The cause should seem to have done the pleading, not the pleader."[59]

7.4.2. The Hostile Adversary.

In dealing with your adversary on the other side of a lawsuit, the first question to address to yourself is: what attitude should I adopt in this case to best serve my client's interest? It's important for you to answer this right at the outset of the litigation, since the whole tone of the adversarial relationship may be set at this time. And although the variants are innumerable, there are really two basic choices here: antagonistic or amicable.

---

[56]   *Id.* at 92-93.

[57]   There may be times, however, when it's to your advantage to *complicate* your case; e.g., to persuade a judge that the matter is too complex for him to grant preliminary or summary relief to your adversary.

[58]   "They are like pointillist painters, using innumerable and seemingly disconnected blobs of color, all daubed on the canvas in apparently helter skelter fashion, but causing a vivid picture to emerge by the end of the trial." *Id.* at 94.

[59]   *Id.*

One type of lawyer believes he performs optimally (and his client's interests are thus best served) by adopting a bellicose style toward his adversary. He wants the lawyer on the other side to think of him as a tough guy, perhaps in hopes of being able to dominate his foe. So he refuses every request, declines minor accomodations, espouses inflexible positions.

If you come up against one of these belligerents, your best bet is to use the court system to advantage. Pugnacious litigators are bound to take unreasonable positions (in terms of arranging schedules, refusing extensions of time, and the like) that are unlikely to be supported by a judge. When your opponent makes such a move, your response is simple: "All right. I'm not going to argue with you about this. Let's go down and see the judge."[60] Your adversary, made to look somewhat ridiculous in the courthouse, may become more reasonable.

By the way, we've just touched on one of the marked differences between hostile and friendly adversaries. The latter, engaged in private ordering, are forced to work out agreements between themselves; there's no intervening third party—such as the court—to settle their differences. What's called for is a spirit of accommodation and come creativity in devising workable compromises—or else there just won't be a deal.[61] But as between hostile adversaries, there's always someone peeking over your shoulder—the judge (or magistrate) who can resolve these kinds of questions.[62] If you think your opponent is acting unreasonably, you have a place to turn to—no need to endure the adversary who takes outrageous, frustrating, non-negotiable positions.

For the average lawyer, however, an antagonistic attitude neither suits his basic behavior pattern nor serves him well. It's rather rare for one litigator to be able to dominate another, requiring a certain weakness of spirit in the latter that just isn't typical of the breed. In fact, a contentious posture frequently just serves to make the other lawyer madder than hell—much like a red cape waved in front of a bull. And that won't help you down the road when—inevitably—you'll need the other lawyer's cooperation.

The initial contact between hostile adversaries at the outset of the lawsuit is generally a call from defendant's lawyer to plaintiff's lawyer, asking for more time to answer or move against the plaintiff's

---

[60]   Need I say that you shouldn't suggest this course unless you *are* prepared to visit the judge. Crying wolf is a notably ineffective tactic in dealing with a hostile adversary.
[61]   This subject is discussed at length in Section 7.3.
[62]   Many local court rules provide that attorneys *must* attempt to reach a resolution of their differences, and court papers seeking relief have to recite those attempts.

complaint.[63] This usually occurs near the end of the prescribed period, at a point where enough time remains to visit the judge should the plaintiff deny the defendant's request, but not so early that the plaintiff's lawyer can question the need for additional time.[64] Among the litigating fraternity, it's considered discourteous to deny this request for more time in the typical lawsuit where time is not of the essence[65]—a practice underlined by the realization that the court upon request will invariably grant the defendant additional time.

If you represent the plaintiff—and particularly when you have no previous acquaintance with your adversary—the way you handle this request can set the tone for the rest of the lawsuit. Take a hard position on a simple matter like extension of time and you'll probably act the tough litigator in the forthcoming depositions—one who tries to scare answers out of the witness, rather than relaxing him into babbling what you want to hear. You can't "love a witness to death" once you've antagonized his lawyer by your unreasonable refusal of simple requests.

Also at stake here is the matter of your reputation. You're going to be handling a large number of cases within the legal community over the years; you'll probably be dealing with this lawyer again in other matters—perhaps even on the same side in a joint or parallel representation situation.[66] How would you like to be known? Some lawyers generate reputations as so tough and unpleasant that other attorneys shun professional dealings with them; such ogres not only obtain few referrals, but are consistently denigrated when the subject of attorney retention arises. On the other hand, no one wants to be considered a milquetoast. Perhaps the best type of reputation to possess in this regard is as someone who gets along well with others, but can only be pushed to the point where it makes a difference—cordial and reasonable, but not conceding any essential client interest.

---

[63] The defendant's lawyer normally makes the first contact, since the plaintiff's lawyer presumably doesn't know the identity of the lawyer who will be representing the defendant.

[64] Generally, you ask for an extension "to answer or move." The question may arise, when you call to ask for an extension of time to *answer*, whether to mention that you're considering making a *motion*. If you say nothing, then using the additional time to move could be considered somewhat underhanded—not the ideal way to establish rapport and trust with your adversary. If the subject comes up (or if your words could be construed negatively on this point), you probably should make the plaintiff's lawyer aware of your intention. If the defendant's lawyer says nothing on the subject, the plaintiff's lawyer is certainly entitled to ask whether a motion is coming or not.

[65] Of course, in the event of an emergency situation (e.g., where key assets are being removed from the jurisdiction), the usual courtesy would give way to a more hard-headed decision.

[66] Discussed in Sections 7.2.1—7.2.5.

A reasonable attitude is particularly important during pretrial discovery.[67] Many hours will be spent negotiating with your adversary the scope of document production, the content of interrogatories, and the conduct of depositions. Busy judges become easily irritated by discovery applications; moreover, rulings by jurists unfamiliar with the complexities of a case may not help either side. You and your adversary are in the best position to work out sensible solutions to discovery disputes—with a consequent saving of your time and your client's money.

As far as I can tell, this constructive-reasonable approach is the one most favored by experienced litigators. Sure, you're locked in combat; and over the course of a lawsuit (particularly during trial) there will necessarily be moments of outright hostility; but you ought to attempt to keep matters under control. Judges don't react favorably to comments between snarling counsel. Be subtle: rather than call your adversary a liar, destroy him by more oblique means. And whatever hostility has been generated in the heat of combat—turn it off at the end of the day. Never make your judgments out of pique, but rather on the basis of rationality.[68]

The tone of your relations with a hostile adversary will often be influenced by the client. This makes sense at the strategic level, since the client's interests may suggest adoption of a certain attitude. Particularly in corporate litigation, the goal of victory may actually be secondary to other objectives. For instance, if the parties have important ongoing transactions—as where your client is forced to litigate against a good customer who's really only a nominal party (e.g., a suit by the customer's property damage insurer against your client in subrogation)—then it's important to keep bitterness out of the trial. Litigation with an agency is necessarily affected by the client's need to function under its regulatory thumb over the years ahead. On the other hand, the client may want to keep the litigating pressure on an adversary who has been stealing salesmen from his employ. But that's all in the realm of *strategy*; you shouldn't let the client direct your *tactical* moves involving the other lawyer.[69]

As an associate, another influence bearing on you is the style of the partner in charge.[70] When you're working for a partner who has

---

[67] A subject discussed in Section 7.4.3.
[68] See Chapter 8 on making professional judgments generally.
[69] Some litigators would go so far as to suggest that when the client's ire has pressured you into being discourteous to your opposite number, you should adopt a means of letting your adversary know that you don't think he's *really* an s.o.b. (though you're calling him that to mollify your client).
[70] As noted in Section 5.1.1., the associate should properly take account of the partner's quirks.

developed antagonism into an art form, you're probably well-advised to lay aside the more amiable approach you would adopt if handling the case on your own. Since you're functioning as an adjunct here, consistency in the way of tactics is a necessity (unless the two of you have consciously decided to adopt a good-guy bad-guy parlay). Try to avoid being second-guessed by the partner. Presumably, he has an overall strategy for the litigation fixed firmly in mind. Your courtesies might not fit into his belligerent scheme; or conversely, pugnaciousness on your part might be jarring to the reasonable chord the partner has attempted to strike with his adversary. In the absence of partner pressure, however, associates on opposite sides of a case (as in other substantive areas[71]) can keep the lines of communication open, free from some of the ego and other hangups affecting the partners who head up the respective teams.

There are two factors you must always assess in dealing with a hostile adversary: (i) how much control he has over his client (or, put another way, how much authority he possesses to deliver the goods); and (ii) whether he's worthy of your trust. Actually, the authority point is probably more important in the negotiating realm of friendly adversaries.[72] In litigation, for the most part, lawyers do exercise control over the subject matter. If you sense, however, that the other lawyer is operating under wraps, then the situation may call for some different handling.[73]

The element of trust, on the other hand, affects many of the day-to-day decisions you're called upon to make in litigation. For example, although in New York litigators tend to reduce everything to writing,[74] I understand that in other locales where trust exists, various stipulations (such as for an adjournment) are often handled orally in the first instance. You can turn confidential documents over to another lawyer whom you trust (particularly if your two firms have continuing relationships), on the understanding that you'll work out a stipulation governing their use; however, with an untrustworthy lawyer, you would undoubtedly obtain a protective order first. It does seem to me, though, that the judgment to forego putting an agreement in writing should probably *not* be made by a young associate. From his point of view, it's preferable to get things down on paper; no one will ever fault him for requesting a written stipulation, but he runs a

---

[71] See, e.g., Section 7.2.1.

[72] See Section 7.3.9.

[73] This can come up, for instance, in the labor field, where it is generally understood that a basic rule of the game is to avoid putting the union leader in an untenable position—a factor in the litigating equation which can affect relations between adversary lawyers.

[74] By court rule, agreements between attorneys in New York are unenforceable unless in writing.

real risk of being second-guessed if a matter he's handled on an informal basis doesn't work out.

7.4.3. Pre-Trial Proceedings.

Before getting into pre-trial proceedings, I think a word about pre-*lawsuit* days is in order.[75] Defendants by definition are involuntary participants in an action. But as a prospective plaintiff, the option not to sue is always available. And the lawyer bears the responsibility of explaining to his client all the potential negatives of litigation—the necessity for a number of key individuals (chosen by the adverse party) to testify at lengthy depositions, the opening of his corporate or personal files to produce large quantities of documents (including personal items such as executive pocket diaries), the substantial expenses to be incurred, and so on.[76] Of course, the client should not conclude from this tale of woe that you're negativistic or lack the stomach for a good scrap. You're ready, willing and able; but he has to understand what's involved—to avoid that "why didn't you tell me what I was getting into" speech when he seeks to bail out in midstream.[77]

All right. The litigation has begun. The trial itself is months or years away. Dramatic results at that trial can only spring from painstaking advance planning. And although the denouement of a big case is often a negotiated settlement, it's still essential that you plan and prepare fully for trial; much of your effort will be requisite to proposing and evaluating the settlement terms. So, you throw yourself into the crucial pre-trial phase of the case.

Much of the skirmishing here revolves around the discovery process—depositions, document discovery, interrogatories. Young litigators are more likely to be involved in this process than in going to court, so let's take a closer look—particularly at the oral deposition.

Just a word about interrogatories, which are likely to be used extensively in major corporate litigation. Experienced practitioners feel that interrogatories require proportionately more work and expense relative to the return than any other discovery device. Yet there are issues that can be developed most effectively in this way—identifying persons and documents, ascertaining dates, obtaining statistical data.

---

[75] For a discussion of the initial client interview, see Section 3.3.2.
[76] Zoeller, *supra* note 48, at 14-15.
[77] The necessity for this lecture on the expenses and discomfort of the discovery process is especially marked when foreign clients are involved. Our friends from o'er the sea are often aghast at the wholesale invasion of private files and confidences that takes place in an American trial. Moreover, they don't seem to realize that there is seldom, if ever, any right in American courts to recover attorney's fees.

Interrogatories also give you the "corporate answer," which no single witness may be able or willing to provide during depositions. However, the answers are prepared by lawyers in an effort to *avoid* making significant admissions—and, as a result, are often unsatisfactory. At the very least, the questioner can ask the recipient to specify every document which relates to a particular subject, and to name each person who was a participant in the matter at issue. The documents are then discoverable, and the individuals make prime candidates for depositions.

Documents are obviously crucial in any corporate lawsuit. Your initial request for document production should be issued early in the litigation, since the balance of your discovery may well be shaped by the documentary information unearthed. The necessity of working out agreements on privileged and work product documents, as well as matters which are sensitive and confidential,[78] points up the need for a reasonable approach to your hostile adversary.[79] As a litigator, you can never ignore this elemental fact: that with so many people participating in a corporate decision, companies are hard put to avoid creating documents which reflect recommendations or action taken. And pieces of paper are the stuff on which litigation thrives.

The oral deposition[80] can be the litigator's most useful tool in the discovery phase of a big case—not only for developing the facts crucial to the lawsuit but also for its significance in any possible settlement. As with most of the topics we've discussed, careful planning is requisite here too. The analysis begins with a clear identification of the examiner's goals in the deposition; these may extend beyond fact development to creating a record of the witness's views in support of a motion, or to delve into possible collateral issues. To limit one's self to the obvious questions suggested by the pleadings—the casual approach to depositions—does little justice to the opportunities.

Next, "get to know" the witness prior to your encounter. Pertinent background information—is he controlled in his speech or loquacious?—can be helpful. Identify the witness's precise relation to the case,[81] particularly with respect to documents. In addition to

---

[78] By agreement, a privileged document which is inadvertently delivered can, under certain circumstances, be considered as not having been produced; and documents turned over may be limited in use to litigation purposes only (with particularly sensitive documents limited to the eyes of counsel). A comparable protective order is necessary only if such an agreement cannot be reached.

[79] See Section 7.4.2.

[80] The Summit article, *supra* note 48, is particularly helpful on this subject, and much of the following material has been based on it.

[81] It's good practice to attempt to distinguish between the "record" role and actual role of a witness. Some chief executives, for instance, insist on taking

reviewing any papers he is known to have authored or received, check out other documents which—based on his position and role—logically should have emanated from or paused on his desk, but as to which his participation is still unclear. And then go a step further, attempting to visualize what relevant documents *ought to* exist (but apparently do not); after a while, you'll be able to spot events or subjects that have probably been the subject of a writing. Try also to assess the witness's attitude or motivations with respect to the case—which may not be the obvious ones. Think of him in relation to the other persons involved. Was his role a natural one for him? Or was he, for example, a resentful subordinate who was overruled on some critical questions?

The specific tasks involved in getting organized for deposition day—organizing files, isolating topics for witness testimony, preparing fact sheets, compiling lists of each mention of the witness by other persons or in documents—are beyond the scope of this section; but I do want to touch on the matter of questioning. Many experienced lawyers shun prepared questions for the witness. They feel that any set pattern of questioning tends to make the examiner predictable, which allows the witness to become more comfortable. Spontaneous examination, on the other hand, keeps the interrogator alert to the fine shading of each answer—less likely to overlook a follow-up question, keenly attuned to whether the hoped for results are being achieved. Spontaneity also generates a more briskly paced dialogue (as contrasted with the cautious responses induced by prepared questions), encouraging the witness to forget his adverse relationship to the questioner.

Nevertheless, even experienced litigators do prepare some lines of questioning;[82] and for the younger attorney, a bit hesitant and unsure of himself, this kind of preparation can be helpful—so long as he realizes that the written questions furnish only a starting point, and

---

full responsibility, but in fact have little involvement with the disputed matter; conversely, individuals who prefer the background shadows may have played a crucial part.

[82] Advance preparation of questions may be desirable to force an admission, or where a number of documents must be referred to, or for hypothetical or technical questions, or to lead a witness likely to be evasive or dishonest in a direction he's trying to avoid. See Summit, *supra* note 48, at 24: "An obvious example is where the witness wants to establish his ignorance of certain facts. If you attempt to establish that he is ignorant of certain insignificant facts, he may defend himself and show his total command of those facts. Having demonstrated that he is an astute perfectionist on these matters, he will be reluctant to claim ignorance of critical facts. Achieving this result requires careful advance wording of each successive question."

that the *answers* possess the real significance.[83] If you don't prepare specific questions, then use a checklist of the topics you intend to cover in the deposition; this, together with the fact sheets you have prepared for each topic, should assure a thorough and comprehensive inquiry.

Now you're in the deposition room, which you have selected and prepared carefully.[84] A usual method of examination is to begin with a lot of background information to determine the witness's role, and then to ease into the substantive questioning—perhaps on a semi-chronological basis. But you may not want to let the witness get too comfortable—the sudden plunge into a critical line of questioning, before a nervous witness can relax, may be very effective ("Name?" "Address?" "When did you first see [the backdated document]?").

Remember, a deposition isn't a trial; and whatever your technique, you just can't obtain too much background information. Even lines of inquiry seemingly unrelated to the facts in dispute may provide insight into the organization or individuals with whom you're dealing. Some litigators even suggest asking an adverse witness questions that elicit narrative answers; since the purpose of the deposition is to obtain admissions and information, confining the interrogation to material in the documents may result in omission of valuable information. Others warn strongly against permitting an adverse witness to ramble, particularly one who appears well-prepared.

The examining attorney must always determine whether it's advantageous to make the witness feel at ease. A witness who gives the impression that he's trying to be candid and complete in his answers is a good candidate for this treatment; what is there to gain by making him nervous? On the other hand, a witness whom you've treated with courtesy and respect, and who reciprocates with incomplete or evasive answers, is another matter entirely. Here, you must assert control: sharpen the tone and substance of your questions; adopt a more peremptory manner; repeat the same questions until the witness answers them satisfactorily.

With a witness who is lying, and whose lies can be exposed through documents, you face an important decision (on which it's difficult to generalize without specific facts): should you demonstrate the falsity promptly, or save your fire for the trial or settlement discussions? Keep in mind that where the falsity can't be established conclusively

---

[83] On the topic of being a good listener, see Section 3.3.2.
[84] For instance, Summit (*supra* note 48, at 24) advises placing the reporter at the head of the table, with you and the witness occupying the seats adjacent to him and across from each other. This forces adversary counsel out of the witness's line of sight, and permits you to have direct eye contact with the witness.

and extensive questioning is required, you may succeed in embarrassing the witness but probably won't produce a very usable record for trial. One word of advice if you do decide to go after him: don't barge right in, but wait until unrelated subjects have been covered. The lying witness has a strong consciousness of his perjury; and just as he's relieved when you move on to other topics, he'll be all the more chagrined when you return to the critical subject—which may assist you in arriving at the truth.

A common deposition character is the witness who can't seem to recall any matters of importance. One method of dealing with him is to cover other matters taking place within the same time period or similar in nature, and then try to accumulate (in a single question, if possible) all that he can recall during that period—followed by a pointed summons to explain the evident lapses in his memory. Make his failure to remember conspicuous and embarrassing, so as to shame him into giving you an honest recollection—at least on other matters. And ask him to identify any document or person that might assist his memory—with your side fully prepared to call for immediate production of any such documents or witnesses—so as to preclude the possibility of a credible recapture of his recollection between deposition and trial.

In terms of preparing your own client for the other side's deposition, the key lies in your ability to forecast the questions your adversary is likely to ask. Compose a set of questions for your client as if you were the adversary, and take him through them one by one. Ideally, at the close of the deposition, the witness should turn to you and say: "I felt very comfortable. I was ready with the answer to every question asked." In this regard, although group preparation might be more efficient, you should generally prepare your witnesses separately; it's more thorough and avoids your adversary's argument that the witnesses collaborated on their testimony to avoid inconsistencies.[85].

The pre-trial phase of the case also involves considerable drafting of documents—answers, demands, motion papers, briefs and the like. Pre-existing office forms can be helpful; but just as with agreements and other documents prepared on the corporate side of the office,[86] don't be overwhelmed by models. Copying a form is no substitute for researching the law and checking the form against the facts of your case. And to borrow from a book of adjudicated forms can be

---

[85] In corporate litigation, the chief executive officer and his top associates may be less fully prepared than subordinates, because they consider their time too valuable to be preempted by lawyers. As a result, more spontaneous answers may be forthcoming from them than from middle management.
[86] See Section 7.3.3.

dangerous; these are often so ambiguous or poorly drafted that an appellate court decision was required to determine their meaning or legal sufficiency.[87] ,

Here's some good advice from a judge about memoranda of law.[88] Don't use string citations; they're unnecessary if you have a case or two in point and won't help if none are relevant. Don't talk about "hornbook law" or "black letter law" or say that the law is "clear and unequivocal"; all that usually means is you're in a difficult position. Cites from legal encyclopedias aren't much help either (except perhaps on procedural matters). And don't relate what the court *said*; give the facts of the case and tell what the court *did*. A case stands for its facts and its holding, and the holding is limited to the facts; you can't tell what the case holds without stating the facts.

In every document seeking to persuade, the temptation always exists to say more than you should. Try to curb this natural impulse. Sure, if it's really essential, then don't hesitate.[89] But try not to rehash the entire case every time you submit a writing; focus instead on the main issue demanding attention.

In connection with papers, you'll be dealing with clerks of the court,[90] who are an integral part of the permanent court structure. Most lawyers treat this group with extreme deference. The feeling seems to be, at least around these parts, that these worthies take special relish in whittling big-time lawyers down to size. So, if you prepare a pleading the way the book tells you to, but the clerk says it isn't right, don't get into an argument with him as to what the law is and such—that's inviting more trouble than you need. Relax and do it his way, even though you know you're right. Clerks can be helpful in terms of what form to use, etc.—but they can also turn against you. Your own managing clerk will be helpful in dealing with them, and you might consider taking him along when you're down at the courthouse on business.

---

[87] This, however, isn't invariably the case. When Simon Rifkind was a federal judge, a defense lawyer objected that the complaint was frivolous because it was copied word for word from a complaint in another matter filed with the court several months before. Rifkind asked from the bench: "Was it a good complaint that he copied?" And when the lawyer admitted it was, Rifkind remarked drily: "You wouldn't want him to copy a bad complaint, would you?" *The Lawyers, supra* note 48, at 43.

[88] Solomon, *supra* note 48, at 39.

[89] Even where, for instance, the rule makes no provision for you to go beyond a reply brief, you will probably be able to put the extra information in somehow—in the form of a letter or other supplemental piece of paper—unless you have reason to believe that it may antagonize this particular judge.

[90] To be distinguished from judges' law clerks, referred to in Section 7.4.4.

Finally, a few words on the settling of cases—the moment when hostile adversaries become, in effect, friendly adversaries, although against a litigation backdrop.[91] I'm assuming for our purposes that the lawyers do the settling; on occasion, however, the clients get into the act—unencumbered by the baggage of the litigation, knowledgeable at striking deals—and manage to reach a workable accomodation.

The most critical aspect here is the timing; in fact, the question of *who* makes the overture is probably not as important as *when* it's done. Obviously, you don't send up signals for a settlement at the point when your adversary has just taken a powerful deposition. There will be propitious moments, though, and you should wait to select one of these. Perhaps the most opportune time is when the litigation is going nowhere—a state of affairs which has become obvious to both sides.

Of course, any initiation of settlement discussions should be handled in a way that doesn't suggest any weakness in your case, or imply your unwillingness to go through with a trial. A good neutral opener is, "What are your thoughts on disposing of this matter?" To which a constructive response might be, "I'm not authorized, but $5 million [clearly too much] ought to do it." Your reply ("I was thinking more in the area of $1.5 million") might evoke a "Well, we already have a lot of dollars into this case," and so on—by which point you're well into the negotiations.

There's no firm rule about whether, when talking settlement, you should hold up the litigation or move ahead. Your overall strategy is determinative here. For instance, let's say it's the threat of your taking his client president's deposition—where you're likely to probe such sensitive areas as executive perks—that has goaded your adversary into a settling mood. If you take the pressure off by postponing the deposition, there's less immediate reason for him to settle, but the ultimate leverage still exists. On the other hand, once you go ahead and take the deposition—the worst now being over—there may be less incentive for your adversary to settle at all. So you just have to adapt to the particular situation.

7.4.4. *Your Day in Court.*

Except for the occasional jury trial, the big test for a litigator today is how well he performs in courtroom appearances before a judge. And although young attorneys are unlikely to be trying substantial

---

[91] In this regard, see the material on negotiating in advance of an expected lawsuit, contained in "The Case of the Welshing Art Collector" (Section 9.3).

cases on their own, they might well be arguing motions or handling procedural matters before the bench.[92]

For inexperienced lawyers, a courtroom appearance can be a disconcerting experience. That man in the black robes inspires no little awe.[93] It's easy to forget that he was also a practicing lawyer—that he understands your problems, that the two of you can relate on both intellectual and practical levels. And at times, quaking as you may be in your boots, you simply have to stand up to the majesty of the law in defense of what you believe is right.[94]

So, let's assume that you're in court, arguing a procedural matter to a judge. You should never assume, however, that just because you're in court on a relatively narrow aspect of the case, the judge will restrict himself to that single issue. He might say: "All right, that's fine in terms of the deposition schedule. Now, counselor, what about that statute of frauds problem?" And should that happen, you ought to be ready with a reply—because the best moment to secure this judge's sympathetic hearing of your side of the case is when *he* is interested. So

---

[92] The threshold question as to the desirability of oral argument on a motion or other such matter is beyond our scope. Obviously, if the judge requests it, you should always make the offer; but on a simple case with a good judge, you're likely to be satisfied submitting on the basis of papers. And in New York Supreme Court, for example, where there may be three hundred motions a day, the judges would rise up in arms if the attorneys wanted to argue each one. It is a fact, however, that the opportunity to capture the judge's attention in the oral argument may be unavailable through a written brief.

[93] One lawyer, about to appear before a formidable jurist, fantasized over delivering the following opening remarks (but lacked the nerve to do so): "Your Honor, I hereby stipulate that you know more law than I do, that you are more conscious of the implications of this action than I am, that you are better acquainted than I am with the customs of my client's industry, and indeed that you understand his cause better than I do. Now will you please permit me to earn my living?" As quoted in *The Lawyers, supra* note 48, at 498.

[94] In this regard, I was impressed by an incident (reported by Connolly, *supra* note 48, at 17) that occurred before a circuit court panel which included Orie L. Phillips, a federal judge for over forty years. "A young court-appointed lawyer was arguing against the denial of a writ of habeas corpus which sought to challenge a state court conviction. Thirty minutes a side are allotted by rule for oral argument in that circuit. After five or six minutes, the presiding judge interrupted the young lawyer to say, 'Haven't you sufficiently made your point, counsel?' The young man responded with determination, 'I have accepted my assignment as a matter of duty,' he said. 'I have conferred with the petitioner and consulted with his family. I know what hopes they have for this day in Court and I would have them have it by the completion of my argument.' He was permitted to proceed and, at the completion of his argument, Judge Phillips said in compliment, 'Young man, I have never been prouder of the profession of law than at this moment.'"

be prepared. But if you're ignorant on the subject—lacking the broader perspective of the case or uncertain as to the partner's litigating strategy on the point—then don't bluff.[95]

Similarly, when the judge asks you a question about some aspect of your argument that you haven't yet raised but intend to, it's not good practice to reply: "I'll cover that later." In contrast to the way you might handle this kind of interruption in an oral report to the client,[96] where a judge is involved you're well advised to stay flexible and proceed right to the point he's mentioned, while you have his attention.

When arguing before a judge, try to speak your piece as quickly and effectively as possible—especially if your adversary argued first and rambled on at great length. Perhaps the most difficult skill for a lawyer to master is knowing when to shut up. And in court, the right moment to terminate your remarks is when you sense the judge leaning your way. Every seasoned litigator will trot out for you his version of this semi-apocryphal tale: the plantiff's lawyer finishes at last, after droning on for hours; the judge turns to the defendant's lawyer who remarks briskly "I have nothing to say"; whereupon the judge pounds his gavel, declaring "I find for the defendant." The plaintiff's lawyer hadn't made out a case; the defendant's lawyer, knowing he had won, realized that anything he might say would have been superfluous.

Don't treat judges as fungible. Pitch your argument to the particular jurist who's sitting today.[97] If he's never heard of a proxy statement, then you just have to invent the wheel. Try to assess his level of sophistication; when you're talking over his head, you're getting nowhere. Conversely, with a shrewd and knowledgeable judge, you risk losing his attention (or worse) by too simplistic or basic an approach. And when the judge isn't listening—a state of affairs you should detect unless mesmerized by the sound of your own voice—then you just have to come up with something that will grab his attention.[98]

Don't interrupt while your adversary is speaking—even if he's making misstatements. There will always be time for a reply. Listen carefully and take notes on his erroneous statements. Then, if they're

---

[95] If, for instance, the judge asks you to agree to a stipulation on the deposition schedule, don't be ashamed to say that you have to check with the partner or client.

[96] See Section 3.3.1.

[97] If you don't know the judge before whom you'll be appearing, it's a good idea to go down to court several days before and observe him in action.

[98] Of course, among litigators—where speculation in such matters is always rife—the judge's lack of attention could also be a good sign; i.e., since he isn't even bothering to hear what you have to say, he must have already decided to rule your way.

significant, weave into the fabric of your own points the matters where your opponent has misled the bench. But don't call your adversary names over something trivial; judges don't go for that sort of thing.

If you've turned in papers that cover a lot of ground, you can afford to be more selective in your oral argument, referring to the brief for elaboration on the other issues[99]—perhaps asking the judge if he wants you to address yourself to any of these.[100] Oral argument is always more effective when focused on a few key issues—although again, if the judge has a different notion as to which are the key issues, you should take cognizance of his concerns.[101]

Just a word on contacts with judges out of court. There appear to be substantial differences in approach on this subject in various parts of the country—also depending upon the size of the community. In New York, for instance, you would rarely call a judge's chambers to speak directly with the judge, whereas in some parts of the Southwest such *ex parte* contacts apparently occur quite frequently.[102] In all cases, however, an attitude of deference to jurists is in order. I have it on good authority that they actually like to be called "Judge" or "Your Honor," even by long-time acquaintances. The judge should be permitted to set the tone for any extra-judicial contact. And refrain from discussing a pending case with a judge or his law clerk out of court.

Speaking of law clerks, here is a group of individuals—recent honor graduates of law school—with no official authority in the federal courthouse structure (unlike clerks of the court[103]), but who are quite

---

[99] If no brief has been filed, and you cite a case during oral argument, you ought to have a copy with you to hand up to the judge—with a copy to the other side, of course. Watch out, however, for the judge who was on the bench when former Justice Robert H. Jackson, as a young lawyer, cited in his support a newly decided Supreme Court case and handed up the advance sheets to prove his point. The judge handed them back, glared, and snapped, "I don't take no law from no magazines." As quoted in *The Lawyers, supra* note 48, at 497. Incidentally, in citing cases, always try to select authorities that this particular judge has written; Lexis makes this rather easy now.

[100] Of course, this is based on the notion that the judge has *read* your papers—something you should try to ascertain by the judge's comments or questions. In this regard, some appellate benches are known to be "hot" and some "cold."

[101] Some judges won't let you say anything but merely answer their questions; needless to say, you should be prepared to perform under these difficult circumstances.

[102] A good general rule is never to go to chambers to see the judge without an appointment. Always call first and express your desire for an audience. And unless it's essential, speaking with the judge over the phone is simply not a good idea.

[103] Referred to in Section 7.4.3.

important because of the help they furnish judges in writing opinions.[104] For a judge who has little time to research the law, the views of his law clerk can carry a lot of weight. Obviously, this is not a group which savvy litigators treat with arrogance, since they can be helpful—or extremely harmful—to your cause.

With respect to jury trials, here is a subject on which the great (and would-be great) pillars of the bar have waxed eloquent over the years.[105] From the opening address, where you "draw the robes of your own character about the shaking shoulders of your client"[106]; through cross examination, which many barristers feel is the true test of their profession[107]; to the summation, where the attorney culls the critical points from weeks of facts and documents—a trial epitomizes law at its dramatic zenith. I shrink from the task of compressing into a few pages the art (and craft) of great advocacy.

Let me rather confine these brief remarks to some basic psychological factors that create an additional litigation experience when a jury is empaneled.[108] What is it that converts a hostile jury into a friendly one, striving to accept your contentions and reject those of the other side? Conversely, what causes the jury to decide against you?[109]

In the first place, you and your clients are under constant observation by the jurors. You should endeavor to show your understanding of the seriousness and solemnity of the occasion. Any loudness or frivolity—whether or not connected with the events of your

---

[104] They also hold conferences, set schedules, etc. The state court equivalent is the law secretary, but his function tends to be more ministerial and less substantive.

[105] See, e.g., Stryker, *supra* note 48, who wrote with great feeling on the subject.

[106] *Id.* at 59.

[107] Professor Wigmore, for example, wrote that the art of cross examination "requires the greatest ingenuity, a habit of logical thought, clearness of perception, in general; an infinite patience and self-control; power to read men's minds instantly, to judge of their character by their faces, to appreciate their motives; ability to act with force and precision; a masterful knowledge of the subject matter itself; an extreme caution; and above all the instinct to discover the weak point in the witness under examination." As quoted in Stryker, *id.* at 73.

[108] Levitt, *supra* note 48.

[109] The makeup of the jury and background of the jurors is an entire subject in itself. Every seasoned litigator has weathered some eye-opening experiences on this score. For instance, listen to the Iowa lawyer, reminiscing about a case he didn't think he'd lose: "After I'd lost it I watched the jury walking out, and I noticed that an old farmer was missing three fingers of his left hand. He looked pleased with himself; he hadn't gotten any money when the threshing machine got him, and my client hadn't got any money either. Since then, I always look at their hands." As quoted in *The Lawyers, supra* note 48, at 481.

case—might leave an adverse impression. Even your dress can be harmful; it's well to avoid displays of affluence and other superficial indicia possessing negative potential.

You have to instill the jurors with your confidence. Fumbling for exhibits, being unsure in your presentation—these leave the negative implication that you didn't feel the case was worth your serious consideration. Let the jury see that you've worked long and hard on this matter, that you've mastered the evidence and adopted a coherent—although not too "smooth"—approach.

The jurors will make a judgment about you as well as your case—a judgment that directly impacts their ultimate appraisal of your client's honesty and sincerity. It's important, for example, that from the outset the jury considers you fair and considerate. This may call for some tact in the substance and style of the questions you ask. When you've destroyed a witness, don't continue to assault him; the brilliance of your cross-examination may be negated by the jurors' perception of your seeming cruelty.[110] Conversely, if you appear hurt by a witness's testimony, the jury will assume that your case is going badly—so cloak your feelings.[111]

And learn when to stop. When you've really scored a direct hit, forget your other points and sit down. Don't spoil all you've accomplished by asking that one last fatal question.[112]

Finally, in terms of appellate advocacy, I'd like to pass on to you the ten precepts of John W. Davis, contained in a notable Bar Association address.[113]

---

[110] On the other hand, there are times when deflation of an arrogant witness may well be in order. The jurors will give less heed to his testimony if you can make them laugh at him. The famous Edward Carson once cross-examined such a witness, asking in his thick and charming Irish brogue, "Are you a drinking man?" "That's my business," the witness haughtily replied. "And have you any other?" Carson shouted. The jury roared. The witness was demolished. As quoted in Stryker, *supra* note 48, at 93.

[111] It has been suggested that you always smile and thank the court when your objection is overruled, to avoid appearing harmed by the ruling. Levitt, *supra* note 48, at 76.

[112] "A rather pompous lawyer was once cross-examining a witness in an assault case. The charge was that the defendant had bitten off the complainant's ear. A stupid and reluctant witness had testified that he had seen the affray but that he did not see the incident in question. With unction, the defendant's counsel rose to cross-examine. 'Well, my good man,' he said, 'you have told us that you did not see my client bite off the complainant's ear; now, just what did you see?' 'Well,' the witness drawled, 'as I was coming along the road I just happened to see him spitting the complainant's ear out of his mouth.'" Stryker, *supra* note 48, at 95.

[113] Stryker, *supra* note 48, at 239 *et seq.* Davis allowed as how there was "no mystical significance in the number ten, although it has respectable precedent. . . ."

1. "Change places, in your imagination of course, with the court." Try to imagine what you, as a judge, would first want to know about the case—how, and in what order, you would want the story told.
2. "State the nature of the case and briefly its prior history."
3. "State the facts." He went on to say that "in an appellate court, the statement of the facts is not merely a part of the argument, it is more often than not the argument itself. A case well stated is far more than half argued." The Davis safe guide to stating the case was comprised of the three C's—chronology, candor, and clarity. But, he added significantly, "No statement of the facts can be considered as complete, unless it has been so framed and delivered as to show forth the essential merit, in justice and in right, of your client's cause."
4. "State next the applicable rules of law on which you rely."
5. "Always 'go for the jugular vein.' " He cited one well-known lawyer who, before appellate courts, addressed himself customarily to but a single point, often speaking for not more than twenty minutes but with compelling force. When he had concluded, it was difficult for his adversary to persuade the court that there was anything else worthy to be considered.
6. "Rejoice when the court asks questions." Not only does it show that the panel isn't comatose, but a question affords the advocate his chance to penetrate the mind of the court.
7. "Read sparingly and only from necessity." A speaker doesn't hold the attention of his audience for long without looking it in the face.
8. "Avoid personalities." Keep the mind of the court on the issues at hand without distraction.
9. "Know your record from cover to cover."
10. "Sit down." The mere fact that you've been allotted an hour doesn't "constitute a contract with the court to listen for that length of time."

7.4.5. The Labor Arbitration: A Study in Contrasts.

Let's close this section with a few observations about the labor arbitration case, which differs substantially from the rest of litigation and provides some interesting contrasts.[114]

At the outset, labor arbitration should be distinguished from commercial arbitration, which usually results from a breach of agreement

---

[114] See Brandschain, *supra* note 48.

between parties and emphasizes damages or other remedy for such breach.[115] Labor arbitration, which represents one episode in an ongoing relationship, is designed to assure the continuance of overall union/management harmony despite the claim that a contractual provision has been breached. In the words of the U.S. Supreme Court:

> "In the commercial case, arbitration is the substitute for litigation. Here arbitration is the substitute for industrial strife."[116]

As a result, labor arbitration should not be carried on in the spirit of adversary litigation, utilizing tactics which could seriously damage the basic relationship. Past resistance has largely disappeared, and there is now almost unanimous acceptance of grievance procedures and binding arbitration as a means of forestalling work stoppages caused by minor shop disputes. Most of labor arbitration is concerned with grievances—complaints by employees that the employer hasn't treated them as required under the agreement. Disciplinary acts by the employer—discharging or suspending employees—are in the forefront, as well as such matters as seniority rights, pay scales, assignment of employees to job classifications, crew sizes, job duties and the like.

As befits this difference in philosophy, labor arbitration proceedings are marked by a high degree of informality. The arbitrator and opposing cousel might not even be lawyers. There are rarely formal pleadings or written statements of the issue, other than an unpolished grievance in non-legal form prepared by the aggrieved employee or his union representative; often no attempt is made before the hearing to define the issues to be decided, as lawyers commonly try to do in litigation; and the hearing can be an amorphous and free-wheeling affair, characterized by unorthodox arguments and presentations, in which the legal rules of evidence take a definite backseat.

The selection of an arbitrator—think of it: picking your own judge!—is a subject possessing obvious significance. It's less common now for the parties to sit down by themselves and agree upon a mutually satisfactory arbitrator; the more general technique is to employ the procedures of the American Arbitration Association or Federal Mediation and Conciliation Service, which make available lists of candidates for joint selection. The arbitrators need not be attorneys—many are college professors or equivalent—although a number are ex-practicing labor lawyers. Since the unions may be good

---

[115] Actually, some of the same considerations apply, since the parties generally are involved in continuing contractual relationships.

[116] *United Steelworkers v. Warrior & Gulf Navigation Co.*, 363 U.S. 574, 578 (1960).

clients of many of the arbitrators, lawyers representing the employer must be extremely careful in their choice—by-passing candidates who may have hidden relations with the union or whose background, prior decisions or other history indicates a bias adverse to the employer's position.

The arbitrator may well be uncomfortable about deciding cases on the basis of legal principles or rules of contract construction. Rather, he places great weight on what he believes the parties intended in the contract, as well as their past practice—all in the context of his perception as to how the parties should behave to promote good personnel practices and healthy labor/management relations. And so, your efforts to persuade the arbitrator have to go beyond the strictly legal proof and deal with such points as are contained in the following quoted listing[117]:

— "Fairness, justice, and equity to your side demand the result you are urging.
— The imposition of the other side's view will be oppressive to your side.
— The theory or effectuation of the labor contract and the collective bargaining process requires the result that you advocate.
— Great damage could result not only to your client, but also to the collective bargaining process and the relations between parties by the other side's success.
— The spirit of the entire collective bargaining contract compels acceptance of your view.
— It is a fair construction of the contract that the claimed right or duty was retained in the contract, or granted by implication, if not expressly, in the bargaining of the parties.
— The other side is trying to impose duties on employees or the employer that it does not have the right to insist upon as a result of the contract it negotiated.
— The other side is asking the arbitrator to rewrite a part of the contract or to write into it a term that was rejected in negotiations—actions that the arbitrator is without power to award. (This is a frequently used argument.)
— The union (if you are on the company side) is trying unduly to restrict the employer in its right to manage or to operate efficiently, and to maintain or establish fair work rules.
— The company (if you are on the union side) is trying to damage the union's prestige and oppress it and the employees."

---

[117] Brandschain, *supra* note 48, at 32-33.

If you represent the employer, your opponent may not be a lawyer, but rather a business representative of the international or local union. He will probably utilize tactics and unorthodox procedures with which you're unfamiliar. But don't underestimate this breed; some are very effective at getting across their message—and usually they're not only well-versed in arbitration but acquainted with the arbitrator. Your adversary will undoubtedly attempt to introduce a plethora of extra-judicial evidence and testimony, most of which will be admitted by the arbitrator. You'll probably find that many of your objections are directed less to keeping material out than to alerting the arbitrator that he shouldn't·credit such testimony or written material as evidence.

As in any litigation, however, thorough preparation is required in an arbitration case; don't feel you can play it by ear because of the informal procedure. You should visit the work premises to get a better idea of what is involved, review the employee's previous record (where the case involves a disciplinary issue) in the context of comparative records of other employees, familiarize yourself with other grievances and arbitration decisions involving similar situations in the same plant as well as reported cases from elsewhere, and master the specific terms of the contract.

Above all, never succumb to the notion that there's no room for you—the classical attorney—in all this. The lawyer's training, experience, and self-discipline can help to bring order into the frequently chaotic world of labor arbitration—to substitute reason and logic for the emotionalism and sloppy thinking that infect many arbitration proceedings (as well as some of the decisions). But here the lawyer has to rise above the status of a mere technician. He should be something of a labor philosopher and statesman, with a feel for solving industrial relations problems—which, at bottom, are nearly always human problems. And above all, he must refrain from trying to win the battle "at any cost," for that may lose the war.[118]

7.5. THE REGULATORY OFFICIAL.

7.5.1. An Agency Primer.

We turn now to a special category of lawyer with whom you'll undoubtedly come into contact—the regulatory official, employed by the federal, state or local government and charged with overseeing aspects of your client's business or affairs. Needless to say, as life in the twentieth century has grown increasingly complex, agencies of government have multiplied geometrically to the point where they im-

---

[118] *Id.* at 42.

pact upon almost every area of a lawyer's practice (a circumstance not entirely overlooked by the profession, to its infinite financial satisfaction!). In contrast, however, to your usual adversaries who appear on behalf of mere private parties to transactions or lawsuits, the regulator views himself as representing "the public"—a symbolic burden that often sits heavily on narrow bureaucratized shoulders.[119]

For purposes of this discussion, I am excluding the overtly hostile adversary relationships that develop when a government agency initiates an investigation or proceeding against your client; these situations are closer to those in the fourth category (discussed above[120]). I am interested here in less dramatic confrontations involving informal, lower key contacts: asking an agency (such as a state commissioner) to permit your client to take some action (for instance, where an insurance company would like to pay a large dividend to its holding company parent); or seeking from another agency (such as the Internal Revenue Service) its imprimatur on a contemplated transaction (for instance, a favorable tax ruling on a proposed recapitalization); or expediting the processing by an agency (such as the Securities and Exchange Commission) of client documents (for instance, a registration statement which the SEC has to order "effective" for securities to be sold); or attempting to persuade government officials (such as the lawyers in the Justice Department) to refrain from doing something adverse to your client (like initiating an anti-trust complaint).

In dealing with these agencies, much of what you do is devoted to persuading the regulator that your position is correct—that the ruling ought to issue. This concept of a "right" solution also comes into play in your dealings with private lawyers—but there it's all mixed together with such matters as negotiating muscle, the parties' desire to effect a transaction, creative ability to structure around a problem, and so on. With a regulator, these kinds of considerations are essentially extraneous; you have to focus directly on the narrow issue before him. As a result, your ability to make judgments on such matters as which issues to bring before the agency, what individual in the department is in the best position to make the decision, how the presentation should be made, and the dimension of the answer sought—all can be crucial to the ultimate outcome.

The particular agency I am most familiar with is the Securities and Exchange Commission, and my remarks on this general topic are undoubtedly colored by this experience. In many respects, dealings with the SEC are representative of agency practice in general, and thus the

---

[119]   For a discussion of legal practice in the government, see Section 5.3.2.
[120]   See Section 7.4.2.

points made should have broad applicability. I recognize, however, that in other respects the SEC experience may not be entirely typical, to wit:

—The SEC is one of the most professional of governmental organizations, far less politicized than many other agencies. You can nurture contacts on the Commission staff; you can develop relationships that enable you to get a telephonic response to your problem; but you don't get—and shouldn't ask for—favors from the SEC.

—The SEC administers its legislation with a great deal of discretion. There's nothing simple or cut-and-dried about the federal securities laws; the Commission provides tone and content to what's on the books. As a result, the staff of the SEC is constantly available for consultation on a wide variety of subjects. Unlike certain other agencies (where contacts are limited to the more formal aspects of the petitioning process), the SEC is a responsive agency, where the contacts are plentiful and informal answers are readily forthcoming.

—The SEC's major function under the securities laws is to ensure full disclosure. The philosophy is: "We're not telling you what action to take, but we want to make certain you tell the investing public whatever you know." Although a few areas administered by the Commission involve substantive questions such as fairness or approved rates (and are therefore more analogous to regulation by other agencies, I'm more at home with issues that touch on disclosure.

For the balance of this discussion, I am assuming that you alone are handling the contact with the agency. It goes without saying that on important regulatory issues calling for some discretion, you ought to consult with your supervisory partner. Experience plays a major role here, and presumably he will have been down some of these roads before; he might want to handle the contact himself, which he should be given the opportunity to do. In conversations with the partner, you should make an effort to show your appreciation of the nuances involved in dealing with agencies—that communication with the SEC, for example, is not strictly a matter of mechanics or rote response. As he comes to realize that you do understand what's involved, he'll be more likely to let you handle the agency contacts on your own.

7.5.2. Ask Me No Questions. . . .

I begin with the proposition that, in situations where choice exists, a lawyer's judgment as to which questions should be or should not be referred to an agency is as important as any single aspect of regulatory contact. I'm thinking of a case where no specific agency approval is required by statute, and the agency hasn't initiated the contact (so that your role would be essentially reactive), but rather where your client is about to adopt some course of action that might violate a law administered by the agency—and the question is whether or not to seek the agency's blessing in advance.

Implicit in even posing this issue is a fact of life well known to experienced practitioners: namely, that certain questions should probably *not* be addressed to an administrative agency, because of the high likelihood of a negative reply.[121] Once you've asked and been put on notice as to the adverse position of the agency staff, your client may be acting at his peril in proceeding. On the other hand, if you don't approach the agency in the first instance but move ahead on the basis of a legal opinion, the client is pretty well insulated from any criminal taint (the opinion furnishing evidence that he didn't intend to commit a crime), and the agency's position on the particular matter is unknown—obviously a preferable state of affairs should the agency decide to come after your client.

To be sure, there are certain questions that most lawyers would prefer to take to the agency in the first instance, rather than shooting from the hip. Many agencies possess wide discretion in administering the laws under their jurisdiction. The statute gives little guidance; no rules specifically cover the situation. The penalties for violating the law may be enormous. In a case where your client is unwilling to take the action unless he's certain it won't be attacked, then pre-clearance with the agency is probably requisite. And it may just be, in this kind of situation, that the agency's reaction to your proposal would be more adverse if they caught you in the act than if you voluntarily appeared as a supplicant seeking their permission to take the same action.

Assume you represent the potential purchaser of a control block of stock in an insurance company. Having struck a deal with the holder

---

[121] Those of you who peruse SEC staff "no-action" letters have undoubtedly winced (along with me) upon running across the occasional question-that-should-never-have-been-asked, which furnished the staff with an opportunity to adopt a newly restrictive position on a subject that the rest of us had been treating with considerably more liberality in our practice. In regard to the broader question of what to put into writing and what to keep oral, see Section 3.2.9.

of the block, your client very much wants it reduced to a written agreement before any public announcement is made. The applicable state statute, however, provides (as some do) that you can neither buy control nor enter into an agreement to buy control of an insurance company without the prior approval of the Insurance Commissioner. If you follow the apparent thrust of the statute and apply for Commissioner approval *prior* to signing an agreement, news of the proposed deal[122] might attract other potential purchasers, who would attempt to outbid you for the block; and since the seller would not be contractually bound, he could pick and choose among the lot. At best, the block could become more expensive; at worst, you might lose it altogether.

Understand: this is *not* a case where you're thinking to bypass the Commissioner; the *closing* under the agreement will be made expressly subject to his prior approval. Since he'll have his shot at the transaction, why should it matter if a conditional agreement is executed to protect the purchaser against the seller changing his mind in the face of well-heeled third parties? And yet, by signing up the seller first, you would be violating the plain—albeit misguided—statutory language. Sure, in other states with a similar provision, the administering authority has interpreted the statute sensibly (i.e., that a prior agreement which is expressly subject to and conditioned on the necessary approval doesn't violate the law). But since *this* statutory provision is of relatively recent origin, there has been no such determination in your state; and none of the lawyers involved is aware of the present Commissioner's thinking on this score.

This strikes me as the kind of situation where, just before the parties are ready to sign the agreement, you (or a lawyer who regularly practices before the insurance department) would want to go to the Commissioner (or his deputy or legal counsel), tell him what you propose to do[123] and why, and obtain his informal blessing[124] to signing the conditional agreement subject to his ultimate approval. My reasoning runs as follows. The statute directly prohibits what you

---

[122] This could result either from a required press release by the parties or through a notice to interested persons by the Commissioner.

[123] If you are concerned about a leak emanating from the Commissioner's office, you might consider stating the proposition anonymously. I find, however, that this often sets the wrong tone—it looks like you're up to something fishy—and if you anticipate a quick decision and reasonable security, revealing the actual names is probably preferable.

[124] You might feel more comfortable if the Commissioner expressed himself in writing; but if asking for a letter would run the risk of imperiling the favorable result—for instance, if the Commissioner were reluctant to take a public position on the issue—then it's sufficient to make a memorandum of his verbal assurances.

propose to do; if you went ahead without consulting anyone and were attacked on this ground (by the Commissioner himself or perhaps a competitive bidder), you would lack the kind of defense that ambiguity breeds. You're going to be forced to deal with this Commissioner in any event—both in terms of getting his approval for the purchase, and then (if you succeed in taking control of the company) over the years, as you try to merge out the minority interests and so on. It makes a lot of sense to avoid stirring up an antagonistic Commissioner, one who suspects you of flouting his authority. The proposition you're putting before him is entirely reasonable; presumably you can show him favorable precedents from other jurisdictions to further influence his decision. If he says yes, you're on sound ground with him, and the seller is locked in. If he says no, you're no worse off than if you had taken the conservative path in the first instance; and you're better off than if you had gone ahead without his blessing, thereby provoking a negative reaction that might adversely affect his ultimate judgment on permitting the purchase.

The tax area furnishes perhaps the clearest example of dealing with the agency in advance. Large corporate transactions involving numerous stockholders and many millions of dollars are commonly referred to the Internal Revenue Service for advance rulings on the resulting tax effects. No legal necessity exists to apply for advance rulings, and many transactions are done on the basis of tax opinions by lawyers. But when, for example, the form of acquisition transaction contemplated is not entirely cut-and-dried under the Internal Revenue Code—containing some added fillips that distinguish it from published rulings—and where a lot is riding on the outcome, most lawyers are unwilling to go on the line. Even when the attorney feels his position would hold up in court under challenge, he can't opine as to what position the IRS will take in interpreting its own statute; and no one wants to incur the wrath of thousands of stockholders, crying: "You didn't tell us in the proxy statement that the IRS would attack this transaction!"

At the other end of the spectrum are the instances where you don't go to the agency because the answer you will get is quite clear. The statute says thus-and-so, and the agency can't help you out since it has no power to deviate from the statute. With luck, the matter is clear in your favor. If the statute and published rulings say that a particular transaction is tax-free, and the lawyers are comfortable, and the exposure is minimal, and time is of the essence (IRS rulings take a long time), then you go on your own. Or it can be a case where, although you know the answer will be negative, you're nevertheless prepared to go to the mat. You don't *ask* the Justice Department to approve a Hertz-Avis merger; you don't ask an agency to deviate from its own published rule (that you think exceeds its powers) or ruling (that you consider incorrect). The matter is just going to have to be fought out in the courts.

The difficult judgments involve situations that fall between these extremes. And, at the risk of personalizing this issue, I see here a hierarchy of legal talent. The lawyer for whom I have the least respect doesn't even realize a problem exists requiring agency approval. One rung up the ladder is the lawyer who sees the problem, but in all instances automatically pooh-poohs the trip to the agency—"Why do we need them to tell us what we can or cannot do?"—and proceeds to implement the transaction. Somewhat more elevated is the attorney who always takes the conservative viewpoint. He's just not willing to go out on a limb himself and feels it incumbent to run every question that arises by the agency. To be sure, his client is safe this way—if safety is measured solely in terms of not incurring the agency's wrath; but one cannot say his client will never be sorry, since it's entirely possible that certain of the transactions the agency has discouraged *when asked*, might have been accomplished without problems if they hadn't been taken to the agency in the first instance. The best lawyer is the one who realizes that there are times when you should go to the regulator, and times when you should not go; and in order to reach the right decision in a given instance, it takes a thorough analysis of numerous considerations—risks, opportunities, timing, an understanding of the agency's likely position, the probabilities of the issue ultimately coming before them, and so on.

Let's say that you represent a company which is subject to the jurisdiction of a state agency—roughly analogous in function and approach to the SEC—regulating the content of the proxy statement that the company sends to its shareholders prior to meetings. The rules of the agency provide that if any nominee for a seat on the board of directors has been convicted of a crime in the past ten years, that fact should be disclosed in the proxy statement. The provision is ambiguous, however, as to whether the ten-year period is measured from the date of the proxy statement or from the close of the immediately preceding fiscal year (to which most of the information in the proxy statement relates); and other evidence as to what was intended by the agency in this regard is inconclusive.

The company has decided to elevate a certain long-term key employee to its board of directors for the first time this year. In response to your routine questionnaire, the employee discloses the fact of a criminal conviction for possession of two grams of marijuana (an offense now decriminalized in the state). The conviction falls within the ten-year period if measured from the close of the prior fiscal year, but not if measured from the date of the proxy statement. The employee is cha-

grined at the prospects of this conviction appearing in the proxy statement for all his friends and fellow employees to see. He would rather not
stand for election as a director—although it's an honor he greatly
cherishes—if disclosure were required. The president of the company
and other board members would very much like this employee to
become a director.

Well, on balance this strikes me as the kind of case where I would
not approach the agency in advance, but would simply omit any mention of the conviction. If you go to the agency, it's at least an even bet
that they'll come out the wrong way—the presumption being that the
agency will generally interpret its rules to require more, rather than
less, disclosure. Ask them the question and I guarantee you they'll
adopt the view that the ten-year period runs from the end of the last
fiscal year (even though the issue never occurred to them before that
moment). Your argument that the agency should bend its rules
because of the inconsequentiality of the conviction is likely to fall on
deaf bureaucratic ears; and injuries to feelings and reputations rarely
constitute good legal tender in this marketplace. Once you get the
wrong answer, then if the employee stands for election, you must disclose the conviction in the proxy statement or risk serious regulatory
consequences.

But consider the alternative. You certainly have a basis for arguing
that the conviction need not be disclosed because it falls outside the
ten-year limit. The nature of the conviction—particularly in view of
subsequent decriminalization and the employee's long and valued
service to the company—is not such as to raise serious doubts about
his qualifications to serve on the board. And then there are the practical considerations, which can't be ignored: the feelings of the
individual; the desire of management to avoid this disclosure for hu-
manitarian—not venal—reasons; the rather slim chance that such an
omission would ever come to anybody's attention, or that if it did,
such person would be sufficiently concerned to do anything about it;
and finally, even if the agency or a stockholder were to discover the
fact and make a fuss, the unlikelihood of a judge deciding that stockholders hadn't received all *material* information about the
nominees—would this have changed any significant number of votes?
Putting all of these factors together, it's not difficult to decide against
going to the agency and merely omitting mention of the conviction.

If, however, two of the ingredients in the problem were changed,
then I think I'd come to a different conclusion. If, for example, the
conviction clearly fell within the ten-year limit, no matter which way
it were measured; and if the crime consisted of aiding and abetting a
fraud on creditors—then my judgment would be to approach the
agency in advance. You lack any argument here that disclosure isn't

technically required; and the crime involved can be said to bear on the employee's capacity to oversee the affairs of a company—a stockholder might well want to know this before voting. Your pitch to the agency would be that it happened eons ago, that there were extenuating circumstances, that it would injure the man with his peers, and so on—with the hope that the agency was capable of exercising some discretion. If not, and disclosure is required, I would abide by the decision, regardless of the contrary wishes of management and the individual.

Now, I suspect you would like to ask me: what if the crime were a fraud on creditors which arguably fell outside the ten-year period (or for marijuana which was clearly within)? My answer is that *I'm* the one who's supposed to be asking the questions! More to the point, when questions get too close, they don't form the basis for appropriate generalizations. Obviously, I like the idea of having *both* arguments: that disclosure is not required, and that even if it were, the news isn't all that important. It's always a good idea to have two strings to your bow when you go it alone.

7.5.3. Take Me to Your Leader.

Let's assume now that you're in contact with the applicable regulatory body concerning a problem raised either by you or the agency. The next question is: who at the agency—which level of regulator—should you be dealing with? At the most simplistic level, the issue is akin to forum-shopping or angling to bring a case before a particular judge—which regulator has the most soft-hearted reputation? Who is most likely to give you the relief you desire? Beyond confirming the obvious—that all other things being equal, you should seek out a sympathetic ear—there's not much here to generalize about. My point, however, is slightly different; assuming all regulators to be on a single wavelength of liberality, at what *level* in the agency hierarchy is your approach likely to accomplish the most good? It's an important question to ask yourself whenever the occasion arises.

For example, it can be extremely dangerous to go over the head of the individual who's been handling your case to his superior, without even notifying the junior of your intentions. That kind of move is bound to burn up the junior regulator—it might even annoy the senior—and let's face it, you're going to have further dealings with that junior down the road. On the other hand, you have to guard against being shunted to such a low level in the agency that the person who's processing your matter has no authority to make any decisions at all; you simply waste your fire without being in a position to generate the kind of authoritative response your problem deserves. Using the SEC as an example, are you facing the sort of issue where it's sufficient to talk to the examiner in the branch having jurisdiction; or should you direct your efforts to the branch chief; or is it of sufficient seriousness to invoke an assistant director, or associate director, or even the director of the division himself?

Generalizations are difficult here, but I will give you one rule of thumb that can be useful, and it's this: on important matters, always try to present your views personally (or at least in writing) to the agency official who is going to make the ultimate decision.[125] Don't settle for discussing a key issue with a subaltern, when you know it will be decided higher up. The reason is simple: *you* are going to be persuasive; the subaltern is not. In fact, the junior regulator who passes along the problem to his superior might be worse than merely non-persuasive; he might add his own negative, pejorative views, which influence the decision-maker in the wrong direction.[126]

A related matter—which can also help solve the who-in-the-hierarchy problem—is whether to go to the agency in person or handle the issue over the phone.[127] As you might expect, the more significant the question and the more complex the factors that bear on its resolution, the more you should be inclined to appear at the agency. Phone calls are adequate for one-dimensional matters of lesser import. With significant issues, my suggestion is to call the junior and tell him you want to meet with *him* (so you're not going behind his back) *and* with his superior. If you feel the need, you can explain your desire to see the senior in terms of the matter involving "questions of policy," on which you realize his superior's views are important. A recognition that elements of the problem go beyond mere mechanical regulation is an effective means of gaining the superior's attention.

Let's say you've been working on a prospectus for a public offering that's very close to taking place. When you initially filed the registration statement with the SEC in early June, it contained (in addition to audited financial statements for prior years ending December 31) unaudited figures for the first quarter (ended March 31) of the current

---

[125] If you don't know who this will be, but you know someone else well at the agency (even though he isn't directly involved in your situation), by all means talk to him, outline the problem, and ask his advice as to how you should go about handling it—including identifying which individual's attention you should seek.

[126] This is similar to the problem we've adverted to earlier—see, e.g., Section 3.3.1—regarding the danger of being quoted inaccurately, and the consequent necessity to have your own views, in your own words, presented to the person whose judgment counts.

[127] On a similar question with respect to clients, see Section 3.3.5.

year. In late July, the SEC's comments were received; and yesterday's responsive filing included numbers for the company's second fiscal quarter ended June 30. The profit reported was slightly below that of the prior year's second quarter. Assuming the SEC processes the revised material expeditiously, you would hope to become effective and see the offering sold by the end of this week—a tight schedule, which for various reasons the company and its underwriters consider important to meet.

Today, you receive a phone call from the junior examiner at the SEC with whom you've been dealing. The staff, he says, considers the second quarter numbers to be sufficiently adverse that the company ought to recirculate the preliminary prospectus before the registration becomes effective. This is a real blow—not just for the expense involved in printing thousands of copies of the amended preliminary prospectus for circulation, but because this will negate any chance of selling the securities this week.

You assess the situation. Clearly, this decision was made at a higher level than the examiner who—though he might have recommended it—wouldn't have taken the burden solely on his own shoulders. You can assemble a passel of good arguments as to why recirculation is unnecessary: e.g., the second quarter results don't presage any adverse long-term trend in the company's earnings—in fact, preliminary indications from the third quarter show the company to be right back on track; there was specific negative language in the preliminary prospectus indicating reduced expectations for the second quarter; and so on. But the examiner is *not* the staff person who can reverse the preliminary agency position on recirculation. Any ammunition fired at him is wasted. Nor is this the kind of subject you can adequately handle over the phone.

What you should do is to get on a plane immediately[128]—with accountants and businessmen and investment bankers and whoever else can help—for a meeting with the branch chief supervising your client's registration.[129] Make your arguments directly to the man who is in a position to reverse the recirculation edict. Don't rely on your points being conveyed to the branch chief by the examiner who, in this instance at least, is your adversary. *You* can be persuasive; he is unlikely to be and may well come out the other way. There's no time here for a writing; and a telephone call lacks the urgency you want to get across to the regulator.

I think a word may be in order here on the *tone* of your dealings

---

[128] *After* notifying the client of the predicament; see Section 6.5.
[129] As suggested earlier, the appointment can be made through the examiner, whom you should definitely invite to be present—since he'll be there anyway at his senior's beckoning.

with regulators. There is a thin line you have to walk when dealing in non-hostile situations with people who serve the public interest. On the one hand, the regulator does deserve a measure of respect and (at least initially) deference that goes beyond what is called for vis-à-vis a private adversary. Let's face it: you're usually cast in the role of a supplicant, and an abrasive supplicant is not only a contradiction in terms but a likely loser. Make a special effort to avoid creating the impression that you look down on the regulator, that you consider him an inferior species of lawyer. You may be able to get away with arrogance or a supercilious nature in your private dealings (though such traits are definitely not recommended); but put on a different cloak at the agency. Many governmental employees are sincerely dedicated to their work, convinced that they're performing the most useful of functions. It behooves you to avoid actions or statements that suggest you don't share this point of view or that impugn the regulator's competence. The individual at the agency might not comprehend all the intricacies of some complex problem you're trying to work out, but in the last analysis he has to make a decision; and you would be wise not to adversely influence his presumed neutrality in approaching judgment.

On the other hand, avoid being overly deferential to government personnel. They are, after all, merely humans; and they're supposed to be serving the interests of your client, as well as the rest of the country. If they fall down on the job, if they fail to render impartial, intelligent judgments or are inefficient in administering the laws, never feel that you lack recourse. If things aren't getting done, give a push; if you think the agency is taking an idiotic position, scream bloody murder.

7.5.4. Framing and Attaining Objectives.

I want to conclude this discussion with a few thoughts on gaining your objective from the agency. Aiming at limited goals, timing your approach, putting the question in a certain fashion, anticipating objections—all these can help attain the relief you seek.

For example, I've always believed that the *way* in which you pose the question to the agency can make a difference in whether you succeed or not. Compare these alternative approaches by a lawyer to an SEC staffer:

> "We are about to put out a press release relating to the proposed acquisition of a small public company in exchange for shares of our stock. There are no Rule 10b-5 or 10b-6 problems, and I just wanted to run the text of the

release by you—to make sure you haven't recently expanded your views on "gun-jumping" to the point where
anything in here would be troublesome."

> "I have a press release here that I'm not sure you
> fellows will approve of, since it raises possible
> gun-jumping questions. I'd like to read it to you, and of
> course we can take out whatever offends you. . . ."

Now that's a little overdrawn for emphasis, but the point is valid:
too many lawyers adopt the apologetic tone of the second example in
their agency dealings. I'm convinced that their own sense of guilt (or
at best, indecision) suggests to the administrator that *he's* probably
overlooking something heinous if he fails to find fault with what's
proposed. By contrast, the first approach is much brisker and more
routine—just a good careful lawyer, dotting his "i's" and crossing his
"t's", with much less inclination on the regulator's part to get excited
about the issue.

Take another example. Let's say you have a situation that is very
close to the fact pattern of a favorable published agency position.
However, two quite obvious facts in your case—one relatively minor,
one possibly critical—differ from those in the prior ruling. I would *not*
recommend handling this by simply laying out *all* the facts of your
case *en masse* and then asking the agency for a reaction. You run too
great a risk that the regulator, faced with this undigested totality (including the two distinctions), will revert to a negative response. I
would tiptoe toward the issue along these lines.

> Mr. Regulator, you of course recall your published
> ruling *(describe briefly)*. I assume this still represents the
> position of the agency. *(Wait for affirmative response.)* I
> happen to have a very similar case *(and here you go into a
> litany of the parallel facts)*. One small respect in which my
> case differs is as follows *(describe)*, which I assume would
> not change the result; is that correct? *(Note: the small
> point has been raised and a response solicited prior to any
> mention of the more serious point, which could poison the
> atmosphere. Assuming a favorable response is attained,
> you proceed.)* Now, there is one possibly significant dif-
> ference from the published ruling *(describe)*, but for the
> following good reasons, I don't think that this should make
> any difference in the result *(and here you launch into your
> argument)*.

Sure, the hurdle is still there to overcome, and it may well prove fatal—but at least you've positioned the matter intelligently to arrive at a favorable response.[130]

Whenever you contact an agency to ask for a particular clearance or blessing, the question arises as to how thorough you ought to be in presenting the facts applicable to the situation. On the one hand, you must ensure that the decision-maker has in his possession all the material facts necessary to make the decision—not only on an ethical basis but on the highly practical footing that any comfort you achieve is expressly grounded on the facts presented.[131] On the other hand, to simply heap mounds of undifferentiated facts on the decision-maker doesn't adequately discharge your responsibilities to either your client or the agency. The regulator may well get lost in the morass, heading off on unhelpful tangents. So make the original materiality judgment on your own; eliminate from your presentation facts that you deem extraneous—taking care, however, not to delete anything which a regulator could reasonably deem of significance.

The people at an agency such as the SEC can't help being influenced by the legal *conclusion* your firm has reached in the matter under consideration. Ex-staff members have remarked that they were less likely to grant "no action" letter requests when company counsel was unwilling to state his own views on the underlying question—on the theory that if *he* won't go that far, why should *we*? Now, there are times when a lawyer simply *can't* opine on a matter—in fact, what he's seeking is the staff's commitment to non-intervention even though the proposed action may technically violate a statute or rule. But in other instances, when the proposal falls into a more ambiguous area, your client's chances of attaining clearance will be improved if your firm is willing to take a favorable position on legality.

Be sensitive to the question of how hard you should push with a regulator on a certain day. At times, you can force a reluctant bureaucrat to act by emphasizing your time constraints and pressing for an immediate decision. But if no decision is required on that particular day, you might be better off with an uncertain regulator *not* to force the issue and risk a petulant adverse verdict. Defer the matter by telling him that you'll send along some additional factual information, together with a memo containing authorities buttressing your case. This takes the

---

[130] For a discussion of putting facts in their best light in a *written* agency submission, see Section 3.2.7.

[131] In this regard, see Securities Act Release No. 5512 (July 8, 1974). A typical SEC no-action letter contains the following language: "Because this position is based upon representations made to the Division in your letter, it should be noted that any different facts or circumstances might require a different conclusion."

regulator off the hook temporarily; he's not forced to make, on the phone, what for him may be a difficult decision. He'll have an opportunity to consult with others, *after* reviewing your material. Moreover, it removes the suspicious taint which accompanies a lawyer's attempt to pressure a regulator into doing something hastily.[132]

If you are dealing with the agency on a *written* basis, you should anticipate possible objections that may occur to the regulators and attempt to rebut them *in advance*. Otherwise, you might not have an opportunity to get this input before the decision-maker; and his unrebutted objection could lead him to a negative decision. You can't afford to be merely conclusory, since you may not get a second chance.

For example, let's say you're writing a letter to the SEC, requesting permission to omit from a filing certain financial statements which, although technically required by the rules, are unavailable and essentially irrelevant. Now, if you were engaged in a *verbal* dialogue on this subject, and a staff member remarked that these financial statements may be important as providing the reader with information on thus-and-so, you could readily reply that the reader already *has* that particular information from other specific material contained in the filing—and the staffer's point would be put to rest. But if he reacts in that manner to your *letter,* you might not have a chance to reply to the point—and the staff member could use it as one basis for denying your request. So think ahead; *anticipate* this possible objection; and state in your initial letter that it's not necessary to include these financial statements just to furnish the reader with information on thus-and-so, since this is provided by the other specified material.

Finally, give a little thought to exactly what you're seeking from the agency. In some cases, this is relatively clear-cut; a specific statutory approval may be required, a registration statement has to be ordered effective, etc. But more subtle areas also exist, where it might pay not to set your sights too high when something less will do.

The basic distinction I have in mind here is the difference between approval and absence of disapproval—between asking an agency to bless what you're doing and obtaining the agency's indication, by whatever low-key means are available, that it has no real objection to your proposed action. That's really the essence of the SEC no-action process; the staff won't say that what you're doing is right or lawful or that it approves your proposal—rather, you're advised that if you take such action, the staff won't recommend enforcement action to the Commission. And this is solace aplenty, on which businessmen and lawyers routinely rely.

At a less formal level, it's often the case (particularly in securities practice) that before you take some action, you would just like to know

---

[132] For more on regulators' suspicions, see Section 5.3.2.

that the roof isn't about to fall in on you, because a member of the SEC staff will decide that what you're doing violates some regulation. Asking for approval of your action might pose problems for the staff, involving policy considerations, precedents and the like. You don't really need that; and if you ask for it, at best you'll slow things down and at worst you'll be denied. The better course is to bounce the proposal off someone at the staff, and assuming that he doesn't react negatively —and that *you're* persuaded it's all right—then go ahead according to plan.

CHAPTER 8

THE EXERCISE OF GOOD JUDGMENT

8.1. A SHORT ESSAY ON JUDGMENT

You're in the big leagues now. Intellect is fine but insufficient alone. Diligence, a worthy trait, doesn't command big fees. Communicating, people-handling, negotiating skills—all qualities to nurture, yet still not enough. But JUDGMENT—ah, now you're talking. This is where the wheat and the chaff part company.

The early years of practice constitute a cram course in the basics of lawyering, leaving little time for loftier vistas. But as you progress, you'll find yourself increasingly situated in judgmental areas. In evaluating associates, we tend to be somewhat forgiving of questionable judgment during the early years,[1] focusing on the more tangible (and thus more malleable) qualities; the unspoken premise is that judgment will take care of itself as the attorney matures. But as the associate draws closer to partner status and is being viewed in terms of assuming responsibility for decisions that bind the firm—the essence of partnership—we need to feel comfortable that the associate possesses sound judgment. In fact, in considering an associate for partnership, the quality of judgment is probably the single most important professional criterion. Associates who advance to the final rounds of the selection process generally possess the other requisite qualifications; but a lawyer who lacks judgment (or is *perceived* as lacking it, which is almost as bad) will probably not be asked to join the firm.

Some young lawyers appear to possess good judgment right from the outset; others don't. Some from this latter group develop judgment as they progress; the remainder, no matter how skilled they become in other professional areas, never really latch on to this quality. I firmly believe that judgmental skills can be acquired.

---

[1] Which may have been fortunate for me; for a personal experience involving lack of good judgment in a negotiating context, see Section 7.3.1.

What's unfortunate, however, is that we rarely attempt to subject this elusive quality to the kind of analysis that might be helpful to a young lawyer. And so, that's what this chapter is all about: an attempt to analyze lawyerly judgment, to derive some useful general principles.

But first let's agree on what we mean when discussing judgment. Sure, we all know it when we see it—like gymnastic grace or good taste in clothes—but what's it composed of? The dictionary definition is as follows:

> "The ability to judge, make a decision, or form an opin-
> ion objectively, authoritatively and wisely, esp. in matters
> affecting action; good sense; discretion: *a man of sound
> judgment.*"[2]

A thesaurus garnishes the contours of judgment with terms such as "prudence", "circumspection", "levelheadedness", and "rationality".[3]

At the risk of oversimplifying a complex concept, I believe that much of what we consider judgment in a lawyering context comes down to decision-making. Over the course of a day, a mature laywer is called upon to make a great number of decisions—a few large ones, mostly small ones, some conscious, others unconscious. Should we adopt a certain plan of action or not? If we're committed to action, which alternative should we take? Must I tell my adversary about Smith's problem now, or can I wait until after the contract is signed? Should I inject myself into this interminable dialogue between client and accountant?

Judgment doesn't lie in finding a solution to a relatively narrow legal question—that involves legal knowledge, analysis, perhaps some diligent application. But judgment consists of the *next* critical step, to wit: once you have the answer to the legal question, what should you do with it? How can you utilize this knowledge in solving the particular problem at hand? Judgment is often the *practical* step that follows and subsumes and builds upon all the factual, legal and analytical inputs you've been able to muster up to that point.

Perhaps we can get a better handle on this by fiddling with several analogies. One that comes to mind involves piloting a ship out of a harbor filled with other vessels and fixed obstacles. The pilot is engaged in a constant decision-making process. What course should our ship be steering? What's our speed? Should the course or speed be adjusted in order to avoid that ferry over there? Given the ferry's apparent course and speed, where will he be when we reach the bend in the channel? What is the applicable Rule of the Road?

---

[2] *The Random House Dictionary of the English Language.*
[3] *Roget's International Thesaurus.*

Assuming the ferry is the "burdened" vessel, will he observe that status? Are we close enough to give a whistle signal? The first time you do this—I can report from memorable experience—your judgments are necessarily inexpert, because so much of this particular judgmental ability depends on nautical competence. After a while, as you become more familiar with your own ship, with aspects of relative motion, with the reactions of ferry captains—as situations tend to recur and a fund of experience builds up—you develop a certain feel for these ingredients. You can spot a certain ship, watch it for a minute, and realize that it won't come close enough to give you trouble—which enables you to divert the attention that would otherwise attend this non-threat to that *other* vessel on the port bow that appears to be on a collision course. And gradually you become skilled at thinking out the problems in advance, anticipating them, taking early evasive action, and thus accomplishing smooth sailing—as opposed to hurtling from crisis to extremis.

Well, this is all equally true in the practice of law. It's difficult for a young lawyer to be in a position to exercise sound practical judgment on substantial questions at an early stage in his career. He really needs a backlog of experience—a grasp of the underlying principles, a feel for recurring situations, a sense of how people act and what motivates them. That's something worth keeping in mind, especially when you start feeling like a real hotshot—that out beyond knowledge and intellect, there's an extra dimension to lawyering, whose surface you've barely scratched.

The other analogy I like is to the game of chess. At a relatively early point in the game, a player has a great variety of alternative moves to choose among. Many of these can be automatically excluded, because not only don't they help, but they'll clearly make things worse. In theory, you *could* move your king into danger, or place a piece in a position where, without any apparent benefit to you, it can be taken by your opponent—but such moves make no sense, and the good player spends little time considering them. Similarly, a lawyer should give these possibilities short shrift, in order to concentrate his energies on the plausible alternatives.[4]

There will undoubtedly be some chess moves that look good on the surface—a blocking move against an opponent's aggressive attack, your own counterattack on a marauding piece—but which, when analyzed, reveal disadvantages that undercut their apparent validity. Need I say that, in the law, today's seeming solution can prove to be

---

[4] Yet, so often I observe lawyers trotting out a laundry list of absurdities—"in the interests of being comprehensive"—which only serves to generate negative reactions in their more practical listeners.

tomorrow's disaster? Always take a closer look—especially when things seem their rosiest. Then there are the chess moves that are relatively safe, that don't presage any difficulties for you, but offer little in the way of progress. Since one of the objects of chess is to keep pressure on your opponent, you ought to avoid idle moves. This is equally true with respect to lawyering, where you should try to make each action advance toward a defined objective, avoiding time-consuming, ineffectual diversions.

At last, having cleared out the dross, there will generally be several good chess moves which don't present undue risks and which do constitute progress. The question then becomes one of deciding which is best. And it's in this process—choosing between viable options—that judgment enters into both chess and the practice of law. Good judgment *doesn't* consist of merely refraining from a half-cocked plunge into a harmful situation; that's too negative for my taste. Rather, it involves making intelligent, effectual decisions. And occasionally—in chess and in lawyering—perhaps a brilliancy (although most situations, in games as well as life, don't lend themselves to the scintillating stroke).

It's fully as vital in lawyering as in chess to figure out where a particular decision is going to take you. A good chess player thinks several moves ahead; in effect, he says to himself: "If I make move X, my opponent's likely response will be move Y. Assuming it is, which move will I then want to make? There is also the possibility that he will make move Z; how would I react to that? On the other hand, if I make move A instead of X, what is he then likely to do?" As a lawyer, particularly in matters involving an adversary (whether hostile or friendly), you must plug into your decision-making apparatus some speculation on what the response is likely to be. But don't stop there, as so many lawyers seem to do; ask yourself what, given the assumed response, *you* will do next. You're not operating in a vacuum; you have to expect reaction and be prepared for it.

In trying to isolate the quality of good judgment in those lawyers of my acquaintance who possess it in spades, I keep coming back to one characteristic they all have in common: the appreciation of significance, the ability to sort out what is truly material from what is minor or essentially irrelevant. I'm convinced that most faulty decisions occur because the decision-maker allowed himself to be unduly influenced by a factor which didn't deserve nearly so much weight—or alternatively, that the true importance of some other factor (a proper regard for which would have tilted the decision in the right direction) escaped his glance entirely. This motif has been reiterated *ad nauseam* through these pages, but it's worth one more reminder here. You don't make sound decisions by running down a checklist of relevant factors and striking an arithmetic balance of the pros and cons. Rather, in order to arrive at practical solutions to difficult problems, you have to attribute varying *weights* to those factors in terms of their relative significance.

When you come right down to it, what we're dealing with here is the lawyer's real stock in trade: the exercise of judgment on behalf of his client. This is what justifies the fee. The advice you give represents a distillation of a number of other factors, culminating in a judgment call only you can make.

Most of the aspects of judgment that don't quite fit under the rubric of decision-making tend to fall into the areas of discretion and common sense. The advice here is simple: don't park your sagacity outside the door when practicing law. Diplomas and certificates of admission exalt your status but shouldn't create a new person. Proceed with caution; be discreet; worry about people's feelings; use some natural horse sense. Enough said.

Although this chapter is devoted to isolating the quality of judgment, much of the preceding discussion is equally applicable—for instance, such topics as reflecting good judgment in writing and speech,[5] when to consult with the partner,[6] how to stay out of the gears between two partners,[7] and a practical approach to negotiating an impasse.[8] In particular, the question of whether you should advise the client or defer to the partner, which involves very subtle judgmental questions, has been covered in detail elsewhere[9] and will not be repeated here; the assumption in this chapter, unless the contrary is stated, is that you're very much on your own.

8.2. ANTICIPATING JUDGMENT DAY

As with most of the topics we've discussed, some advance planning can be helpful in exercising judgment—both in terms of simplifying the decisions and reducing the necessity to make difficult calls. Putting the proposition the other way 'round, decisions are often rendered more difficult because the decision-maker has neglected to anticipate and prepare for what was clearly on the horizon.

I never cease to marvel at the fact that, in this imperfect world, so many decisions involving lawyers have to be made under time pressure, at a point when the decision-maker's knowledge of the rele-

---

[5] See Chapter 3 generally.
[6] See Section 5.1.2.
[7] See Section 4.4.
[8] See Section 7.3.7.
[9] See Section 6.3.

vant facts, law or other factors is incomplete.[10] Can you picture a
modern dentist blindly drilling into a tooth, without having taken a
prior X-ray? Would an architect commence his drawings before
visiting the site? Well, we do the equivalent in legal practice quite
often—not because we want to, but as a result of pressures imposed
on us by clients, associated parties, adversaries, regulators and
the courts, as well as by the exigencies of the moment.

This won't change. But what you can do is to anticipate what's
coming up and prepare the ground. Get in the habit of stopping at intervals and asking yourself this series of questions: "What significant
decisions will I have to make in the near future? What inputs will I
then want to have? Is it likely that I'll have these inputs at the time I'm
called upon to make the decision? If not, what actions can I take now to
be better prepared?"

For example, you might need to know the answer to a certain legal
question at the point you'll be called upon to make a particular decision—but when the moment comes, there won't be time to stop, do
your research, and come up with the answer. Let's say you represent
a corporate client that is contemplating the purchase of a controlling
interest in another company. Although discussions are still in the
preliminary stage, you have a hunch the minds will meet. And the
president of your client is the sort of man who, once he makes up his
mind to do a deal, likes to move very fast—who objects strenuously
to being held back by what he terms "legal stuff".

So, even though the client has given you no assignment during this
tire-kicking period, your mind ranges ahead. What are the key items
you'll want a handle on at the time the decision to proceed is made?
Well, one basic consideration is whether the acquisition would violate
the anti-trust laws. Now, this is *not* the kind of question that lends itself to snap judgments. It requires a thorough analysis of substantial
factual data, viewed against a complex legal background. If the stakes
are large enough and the client has evinced a definite interest in the
deal, then it makes sense to perform that anti-trust analysis in advance—at least insofar as you're able to do so on the basis of
published data and other less-than-perfect materials that can be pulled
together. Of course, you have to consult first with the client, since
you'll be running up legal time on a project that will prove useless if
the deal falls through. Simply tell him that if, at the point he wants to
do the deal, he would like your opinion on the anti-trust issue, then
you have to work on it in advance; otherwise, you'll be forced to hold

---

[10]   In fact, one definition of "decision" is "the action an executive must take
when he has information so incomplete that the answer does not suggest itself."
Arthur William Radford, *Time*, Feb. 25, 1957, at 19. For an example of this
happening in the acquisition area, see Section 4.3.3 of *Anatomy*.

up the works at the crucial moment when he's ready to move ahead. If he's serious about the deal and his momentum, the president will usually want this done in advance. But *he* can't be depended on to anticipate the problem; the initiative has to come from your side.

That's large-scale advance planning. But situations calling for problem anticipation come up in microcosm all the time. A close friend is coming to your office this afternoon to discuss his will. Although you don't practice trusts and estates law, you believe in staying involved with your clients' personal affairs, and knowing enough about estate planning and will preparation to ask the right questions and transmit the required information to your estates colleague for further analysis and drafting.[11] Now, it so happens that this client has, in addition to several natural children, an adopted child. This issue has never arisen in your experience before, and you simply can't recall whether under applicable state law the presence of the adopted child creates any different presumptions or requires any special provisions to be made.

In my view, it would be just plain wrong on your part, when this issue comes up at your meeting (and it will), to say: "I'm not really sure how to handle this or what's required under the law. I'll have to check with our experts." Contemplating a will can be an emotional experience; don't exacerbate it by creating unnecessary tensions in the testator. And by the way, why not appear well-informed, at least on such a relatively straightforward subject as this? So go to your colleague *in advance* of the meeting, get the answer (which may simply be that he should make his intention clear to treat the adopted child as a natural one), and then be in a position to reassure your friend that there's absolutely no problem.

One important aspect of judgment is determining whom you ought to consult prior to making a particular decision. We have covered previously your deferral to the partner,[12] the need to consult the client,[13] and touching base with counsel in joint and parallel representation status.[14] There are times when you'll be looking for substantive guidance from some or all of these persons; on other occasions, where they're unlikely to have anything to offer, the consultation is more a matter of courtesy and cosmetics. Any doubts should be resolved in favor of inclusion.

---

[11] An admirable position, in my view. The client is your friend; he's coming to you for advice. You know his likes, dislikes, family situation, etc. Don't shunt him off to some stranger; stay involved. By all means, let him know that other "experts" will draft the documents, but that you will relate to them what's needed and review the results on his behalf.

[12] See Section 6.3.

[13] See Section 6.6.

[14] See Section 7.2.

Now, one of the most mundane but critical aspects of advance planning for decision-making is to be sure of the continued availability of each of the important contributors to the ultimate decision.[15] If you sense a decision approaching tomorrow, and the partner is going to be out of the office, alert him to what's happening and find out how you can reach him by phone. But how about the case where a key individual is going to be completely unavailable at the time the decision has to be made—off on an African safari, not a phone in the veldt, completely out of touch—with no way of deferring judgment until his return. Here, the wise course may be to meet with him while he's still around—even though, for other reasons, a decision now would be premature—and on the basis of certain assumptions, make alternative decisions (or at least rebuttable presumptions, recognizing that the final judgment will depend on what actually happens) to help guide your hand when the time finally comes.

For instance, let's say you represent the controlling corporate stockholder of a public company. You have engineered a so-called "going private" transaction, which has managed to stir up some resentment among the minority stockholders of the public company who are being cashed out; as a matter of fact, a class action lawsuit has been brought challenging the merger. Although the court hasn't entered a stay, your client has undertaken not to consummate the transaction until judgment is rendered. The decision is expected to be handed down next week, at which time one of the key men in the client's organization will be completely unavailable for ten days.

In planning ahead, you realize that upon receiving the court's decision, an immediate tactical choice may be required. For instance, if the court delivers a strong, well-reasoned opinion in your favor (which is likely to be sustained upon appeal), you may well opt to move ahead with the transaction promptly (in the absence of any court order to the contrary). On the other hand, a favorable decision on the wrong grounds, with a weak opinion that misses the whole thrust of the plaintiff's argument, could be extremely shaky on appeal; and you might feel this is an excellent point at which to reach an accommodation with the attorney for the minority stockholders, on the basis of an extra half-dollar or so per share for the stockholders and an appropriate legal fee for the plaintiff's attorney. There are also a number of other possibilities. Wouldn't it be prudent to run through these various permutations and combinations *now* with the departing key man, formulating various reactions (although recognizing that final judgment must be deferred until the court decision is in your hands)?

---

[15]   For an example of this principle in action, see the hypothetical "Stud or High Stakes" in Section 9.1.

At least this way, you'll have the benefit of this individual's thinking in your later deliberations—to be extrapolated and applied to results falling somewhere between the cracks.

If you anticipate properly, you'll sometimes spot a situation developing where, unless current evasive action is taken, you're likely to be faced with one of those Scylla/Charybdis decisions—caught between a rock and a hard place, facing two or more undesirable options. In this event, good sense suggests taking prompt action to avoid the morass, even where the action is somewhat unpalatable. This might be termed the cut-your-losses theory of legal practice—equivalent to dropping out of a questionable poker hand early, to avoid the agonizing moment when, holding a weak hand and subjected to repeated raises from the well-heeled bluffer across the table, you're forced to make the ultimate decision.

Let me offer an example. You are acting as outside counsel to a corporation which has a highly vocal, dissident stockholder. In the past, both at annual meetings and in correspondence, this stockholder has been extremely critical of various employee benefit plans adopted by the company, particularly those that benefit top management. The disparity of treatment received by senior executives galls him no end, and he delights in comparing the company's plans unfavorably with those of other prominent corporations which have retained a leading consulting firm to pass on the merits of their plans. This stockholder has let it be known, in unmistakable terms, that he's prepared to institute a lawsuit to enjoin the next "giveaway program" (as he terms it); and from his track record as a litigious gadfly, you realize he's fully capable of carrying out this threat.

Well, it just so happens that the company is about to propose a new benefit plan, which in some quarters could be considered discriminatory in favor of top management. In your view, it would be highly undesirable for the company to be subjected to a lawsuit on this score. Were that to happen, the company would be faced with the difficult choice of (i) sticking with the plan and attempting to steer it through the stockholders and the courts in the face of determined opposition—a course of action which, even if ultimately successful, would be expensive and detrimental to the company's public relations—or (ii) backing down and giving bully boy the satisfaction of knowing he can call the shots at the company. That's the kind of decision you'd prefer *not* having to make.

Why not, then, sit down with the company president and convince him that proceeding with the original plan will likely lead to this difficult juncture. How much better, you suggest, to restructure the plan to be non-discriminatory on its face; and, to really button up matters, how about hiring the very consulting firm which the dissident has previously praised, to place its imprimatur on the plan (including a specific finding of non-discrimination). Sure, management might have to give up a few goodies—although all goodies are relative, and even on a non-discriminatory basis there will undoubtedly be enough for all; and sure, using the consultant might cost the company a few dollars; and sure, doing this might violate management's concept of who's running their show;[16] but at least when the plan is exposed to stockholders in the proxy statement (along with the consultant's blessing), you've undercut this gadfly's potential opposition, and the company won't be faced with a truly unpleasant decision.

The final question I want to address in regard to anticipating judgments is whether it's possible to ease the decisional burden by developing a fixed point of view—a set of presumptions which spring into action whenever a certain type of decision is called for, to help guide the decision-maker's hand. Don't laugh; in some quarters, it's *de rigueur*. I'll never forget my first experience sitting as a member of a special court martial in the Navy—how disconcerting it was, while listening to the evidence, to observe the officers to the right and left of me doodling hangman's nooses on their yellow pads! We've all run across attorneys who exhibit a relentless consistency—for instance, the lawyer who's always on the conservative-negative side with respect to any affirmative action suggested. Or the lawyer who says: "We want to make every effort to accommodate our clients within the boundaries of the law and good taste"—and who goes to quite uncomfortable professional extremes in pursuit of this viewpoint.

Well, perhaps those are unfair examples. I can remember situations where I've given an associate the kind of instructions that bordered on a rebuttable presumption. Representing a potential issuer of securities whose financial standing was rather shaky, my last words to the associate before he went into the final prospectus-drafting session (that I had to miss) were approximately: "I want you to go along with whatever reasonable disclosures the underwriter's counsel wants to make. The important thing is to make sure the issue is sold; and if they feel more comfortable with a parade of horribles and risk factors, so be it." This made the associate's job a lot easier, and I was correspondingly less concerned about my unavoidable absence.

But in the long run, such guidelines don't take you very far. Most of the time you have to roll with the punches—bring your best intelligence and judgment to bear on each question which comes up, without presuppositions or shibboleths, keeping in mind the big picture and assessing how this decision fits into your overall plan.

---

[16]   You might make the observation, if you dare, that management is not exactly in the most objective position to pass on its own compensation.

8.3. THE FINE ART OF DEFERRING A DECISION

So much for anticipating judgments. Now I want to talk about the other side of the coin—the art of ducking a decision that's premature and better postponed.

Let's set the stage. A certain date has arrived on which it would be logical to make a particular major decision[17]—perhaps because a meeting of the applicable decision-makers happens to be taking place, either regularly scheduled (as a quarterly board meeting) or called specifically for the purpose of considering the matter. Although it's *logical* to decide at this time, it's not *necessary* to do so (in the sense that no action is required the next day), so the luxury of deferring the decision exists. We'll assume the decision is a difficult one, where the road to take is not clearly marked, and some risks exist in almost every direction. Finally, you're not in possession of all the information and other inputs you would like to have (and ultimately will receive); either further steps need be taken to round out the picture, or events are likely to occur in the immediate future that may well have an important bearing on the final decision.

Well, in situations with these characteristics (which arise with some frequency), the path of prudence might dictate deferring the decision, rather than forcing the issue through to a conclusion on the spot. I'm so often impressed with the fluidity of business-legal situations—new factors call for new directions, and one's own thinking on a subject has a tendency to change (or at least crystallize) over time as other events occur. As a result, decisions made today, while seemingly suitable under existing circumstances, may appear completely off base several weeks later. And if you've taken actions on the basis of that premature decision, it may be too late to pull back. Putting off the decision—and the action—may well be the better part of valor.[17a]

Here's an example. On the board of directors of a client sits Huckleby, a rather prominent individual whom the powers-that-be at the company would like to see relegated to the status of ex-director. Evidently, he introduces a dissident element to the proceedings, not altogether to their liking. They wish to accomplish Huckleby's removal from the board in the smoothest manner possible, with the

---

[17] Minor decisions, once considered by an assembled group, should probably be made on the spot—on the theory that it wastes valuable time to reassemble the group for subsequent consideration.

[17a] Listen to your maxims. It's true that "One of these days is none of these days" (English proverb), but on the other hand, "Delay is preferable to error" (Thomas Jefferson letter to George Washington, May 16, 1792); in fact "He who hesitates is sometimes saved" (James Thurber, "The Glass in the Field," in *The Thurber Carnival* (1945)).

least ruffling of his feathers—the man has powerful friends. Throwing him off the board is distasteful, and they would rather not have to request his resignation. The best course would be for Huckleby simply not to stand for reelection at the next annual meeting of stockholders. And lo and behold, as the date of the annual meeting approaches, it looks as if they might get their wish. A strong rumor has surfaced, which Huckleby is doing nothing to squelch, that he is about to be appointed to a minor ambassadorship—in which case, being physically out of the country, he would be forced to sever all corporate ties.

The problem, though, is that the last meeting of the board of directors prior to the annual meeting of stockholders is being held this week. Traditionally, this is the meeting at which the board selects the management nominees for director for the coming year, to be submitted to the stockholders for their vote. The announcement of Huckleby's ambassadorship, unfortunately, isn't expected for another two weeks. The chairman of the board asks you how he should handle this situation at the board meeting.

Well, not everyone would come out the same way on this, but here's how I would advise the client. Defer any discussion of the slate of nominees; don't even have the matter on the agenda. To be sure, it's typically done at this meeting, but it doesn't have to be; nominations could be handled by a written consent circulated to the directors in lieu of a meeting.[18] Tell certain key directors why this is being done, so they aren't tempted to raise the subject. And if someone else happens to ask about the annual meeting resolutions, simply state that these will be handled by a written consent to be circulated at a later time.

To me, this is the lesser of the evils. There's no good way to handle the subject at the meeting. If you deny Huckleby renomination without knowing for certain about the ambassadorship, you may incur his righteous wrath. If you explicitly recognize the possibility of his appointment and nominate him conditionally, you run the risk that he won't get the ambassadorship—and then you're stuck with him on the board for another year. By deferring this matter, you have an easy way out if he gets his ambassadorship; and if he doesn't, then that's time enough to face the unpleasant task of telling him he's not up for renomination. (By the way, that's a chore better handled *outside* the boardroom in any event.)

Here's another example at a more mundane level. Your secretary

---

[18] Assuming state law permits this, as most do. A written consent is particularly apt if the slate is to remain the same, or if Huckleby is off but no replacement is being named. If a new nominee were being added, the other directors might want the opportunity to discuss his qualifications at a meeting.

buzzes you this morning to announce that Mr. Dogged (a friendly adversary) is calling on the telephone. You know very well why Mr.
Dogged is calling; he wants to know what you've decided about a
specific issue he put to you last week, on which you promised an
answer yesterday. You haven't quite reached a decision yet; you
need one more item of information, which you expect to receive this
afternoon.

Now, there may be exceptions, but in general my advice would be
not to take the call. I like to answer the telephone as well as the next
man, but the alternatives here are not happy ones: on the one hand,
answering with a premature judgment which can prove wrong later in
the day; on the other hand, conceding that you've reached no decision even though the promised date has come and gone. Much better
to get your final item, make the decision, and call back that afternoon
with an answer. In fact, you should have your secretary say that,
although you're tied up just now, you expect to be free later that
afternoon and will call Mr. Dogged back at that time.[19]

Note this well: the concomitant of deferring a decision is *not*
necessarily inaction. In fact, failure to take action as a result of the
deferral can defeat your whole purpose. What may be called for
instead is the taking of action in a carefully controlled manner, leaving you with sufficient freedom of action to move one way or the
other, based on the outcome of the intervening event and your
resulting decision.

Take this example, which might seem a bit bizarre but is based on
an actual situation. Your client corporation (Bidder) is interested in
acquiring another company (Target). A block of stock representing
55% of Target's outstanding shares is available for purchase from Mr.
Blockholder. Bidder plans to negotiate for and acquire the block, and
then cause a tender offer to be made at the same cash price (representing a substantial premium over current market) to all other target
stockholders; Bidder's commitment to make the tender would be contained in the stock purchase agreement with Blockholder. Following
the tender, the plan would be to merge out the remaining minority
stockholders of Target, presumably at the same cash price—and this,
of course, would be disclosed in Bidder's SEC filings and in the
tender offer document. If the block purchase and tender yield over
90% of Target's shares, then Bidder can effect a so-called
"short-form" merger, which doesn't require proxy solicitation of the
remaining Target stockholders; otherwise, a regular merger will be

---

[19]   I should add that I do *not* recommend this solution when you won't have the
final input for several days. In such a case, you should take the call, explain the
problem, give Dogged your probable answer, and explain that you'll become
definitive later in the week.

utilized, which Bidder will have more than enough votes to approve. Both Bidder and you feel that, as contrasted with the traditional direct merger route, this multi-step approach is the most desirable way to proceed with the transaction—both in terms of preserving the premium and reducing the possibilities of third party opposition.[20]

Just as negotiations over the block are nearing completion, the local counsel you have retained in Target's state of incorporation advises you that by virtue of a recently-enacted law[21] applicable in cases where one company owns a majority of another company's stock, the parent is prohibited from causing the subsidiary to be merged into it for any consideration other than stock of the parent. The only exception permitting the use of cash is where the parent owns over 90% of the subsidiary and can effect a short-form merger. This presents a real problem for you. After Bidder buys the block, it has 55%. If the tender nets at least another 35%, it owns 90% of Target's stock and can effect a short-form merger for cash; but if Bidder receives *less* than 35% on the tender, then the mop-up merger would have to be for Bidder's stock, which is not the consideration Bidder wants to use. And, although you believe chances are good, there's no way to be assured that the 35% will tender.

Your correspondent lawyer goes on to advise you that the state legislature, belatedly recognizing the problems created by this law, has recently passed additional legislation which provides, in effect, that you can effectuate a long-form parent-subsidiary merger for cash if the state commissioner of corporations passes on the fairness of the terms. However, the Governor has yet to sign this bill into law, and there is at least some question whether he will do so. If he does, you would be willing to proceed with your block purchase and tender offer plans. The odds of garnering the 90% are good, and even if you don't make the 90% level, you still have a good shot (given the

---

[20]   The alternative would be to enter into and announce an agreement in principle with Target for a direct merger, which could have the effect of whetting the interest of other potential acquirors of Target at a time when Target is not contractually bound. Mergers can take three or four months to consummate from start to finish; given the competitive climate for acquisitions existing today, and the willingness of deep-pocket suitors to enter situations where they're not wanted, this could result in Bidder either losing the deal, or paying a higher price. By contrast, the chosen approach locks up the controlling stock contractually right from the start, so no other bidding can develop. In addition, there's less risk of a leak leading to rumors which boost Target's market value and reduce the premium inherent in Bidder's price. See Freund, "The Multi-Step Approach to Negotiated Corporate Acquisitions," in PLI *Tenth Annual Institute on Securities Regulation* 501-586 (1978).

[21]   With respect to the situation in this hypothetical, *cf.* Cal. Gen. Corp. Law §§ 1101, 1101.1 and 1110(b).

healthy premium) at a cash merger through the commissioner. If the Governor doesn't sign the bill, you fear the risk of topping out at, say, the 80% level, with an unmergable minority; it might be better to shift gears to a less buttoned-up, more time-consuming direct merger right from the outset.

All right. You have a fluid situation, where all your instincts tell you to defer making the final decision on how to proceed until you find out which way the Governor is going to jump. Now some lawyers in this position might advise the client to refrain from entering into the agreement to buy Blockholder's stock until the Governor's decision is announced. Wrong! Absolutely wrong—just as mistaken as forcing a premature decision right then to proceed definitely with the block and the tender, or to forego the block and move to the less desirable one-step merger. Look, if you've got a seller who is ready, willing and able to sell, this isn't the time to defer action; don't let the man out of the room! The trick is to take action, while at the same time deferring the necessity for ultimate decision on the most desirable route.

And there happens to be a way to do just that. Bidder should enter into a present agreement with Blockholder to buy his stock in 20 days and thereafter to make the tender. But the agreement would include an additional provision to the effect that, at Bidder's option to be exercised within the 20 days (during which time you will learn the Governor's final position), the transaction can be changed from block purchase/tender to a direct merger, with Blockholder's shares transferred in the merger along with all others—and with Blockholder agreeing to vote his shares in favor of the transaction.

Nice work; you have your cake and eat it too. You've properly deferred your ultimate decision on format pending the Governor's action; you've preserved your options; the controlling stockholder is tied up, so third party opposition will be minimal; and the price announcement occurs with no leaks, so Bidder gets credit for the full premium.[22] Moreover, you've carved out the time necessary to scrutinize Target's stockholder list—because even if the Governor doesn't come through, you might decide to take the tender risk should it appear there's a good chance of attaining the 90%.

Let me close with a final word of caution. Don't treat this advice about postponing or deferring decisions as the equivalent of not making decisions. You *are* going to make the decision—but at a more propitious moment. Be very careful here. Businessmen clients, who often tend to be decisive (even to the extreme of rendering premature

---

[22]   In addition, if you have to move to a direct merger, you will be in a position to sign a definitive merger agreement with binding force, rather than merely a non-binding agreement in principle.

judgment), can be extremely sensitive to lawyers they consider indecisive. You'll observe these executives chafing at the lawyer's analytical bent, frustrated by the complexity of the factors introduced into the decision-making process. If the client feels you're passing the buck by putting off the decision, then you haven't handled matters well. Always make an effort to explain to the client exactly what you're up to. Let him see that the delay isn't caused by an inability to make up your mind, but rather by the realization that a better judgment can be made later on, when all the evidence is in.

8.4. THE GO/NO-GO DECISION

For analytical purposes, I've chosen to distinguish between two basic types of decision-making, possessing common attributes but with enough differences to warrant separate treatment. In this section, we'll be discussing the go/no-go decision—whether or not to proceed with a possible course of action, as to which the client is under no duress. This is a voluntary act, the seizing of an opportunity; e.g., whether or not (i) to make a proposed acquisition of another company, or (ii) to initiate a certain lawsuit. In the next section, we'll take up the way-to-go decision involved when the client must take a certain action (or has resolved to do so) and the question before the house is how best to go about it; for example, (i) if a client corporation were under an FTC order to divest itself of a certain subsidiary by the end of next year, and the question was whether to sell it to a single buyer, or offer its shares publicly, or spin it off to the stockholders; or (ii), once it has been decided to institute a lawsuit, whom to include as defendants.

In contrast with the way-to-go decision (where you're comparing possible courses of action), the go/no-go decision measures action against inaction. With a negative decision (refraining from taking the action), you may have passed up a favorable opportunity. But in most cases—unlike the situation where you reject your broker's recommendation to buy 500 shares of Amalgamated and watch in chagrin as the stock climbs 20 points—it's not always so clear how things would have worked out had you taken the action. So, one fact of life to bear in mind is that a decision not to proceed is less likely to produce second-guessing than an affirmative decision, made on the basis of your advice, which turns out badly and leaves you as a tempting target for abuse.[23] I have the feeling, however, that some lawyers have elevated

---

[23] The obvious riposte here (that you can be a hero if a deal you sponsored turns out well) is subject to JFK's favorite dictum, to the effect that victory has many fathers while defeat is an orphan. Don't worry: there will be plenty of eager applicants to share any triumph. And by the way, advising *against* an act that nevertheless gets done and turns out to be disastrous can garner you even more plaudits than advice in favor of an ultimately successful transaction.

this simple observation to the status of a life style—the consistent negativism of their advice betraying an obsessive concern with the security of their own tail. That's obviously *not* what I have in mind.

But it does suggest one significant trait of the go/no-go decision—again in contrast with the way-to-go decision (where affirmative action must be taken even if none of the choices are appealing). Should the scales tip only slightly in favor of proceeding in a go/no-go situation, you might well decide not to take the step. In terms of an acquisition, for example, should a purchaser take on a particular target where the chances of things working out are only, say, 55-45? There are plenty of deals around; why not wait for one with better odds? You might even generalize the point: that there's almost a presumption against taking a voluntary action which appears to be only slightly more desirable than inaction—at least in cases involving substantial risks and where other options are or will become available.

This is precisely the sort of homily that you can proffer to a client when the trees start to obscure the forest. A group of you—including the client and his other advisors—are in the process of exhaustively analyzing a transaction. It's about a half-dozen of one, maybe seven of the other. At this point, you take a few reflective puffs on your pipe and remark profoundly, "Well, George, a lot of people feel that when you end up with a close call like this one, you're probably better off passing it up." And client George sits up and responds: "You know, Sam, you're absolutely right. I'm just not enthusiastic enough about this deal; it's not hitting me in the right way. Let's forget it and move on to something else."

All of which brings me back once more[24] to the role of the lawyer in his client's decision-making. There's more on this subject in the next section, but at this point it's important to note that in a go/no-go situation, a good general rule for the lawyer is to avoid making the ultimate decision himself. In fact, as contrasted with the way-to-go judgment (where I believe the attorney should generally take a position), it might be wise to avoid a strong stand on the go/no-go determination. So often these matters come down to essentially business judgments, which the client ought to make. The principal role of the lawyer should be to clarify, summarize and analyze the various considerations which enter into the determination, in order to assist the client's decisional process.

For example, let's say your client is proposing to make an acquisition in which a critical consideration is whether anti-trust problems will arise. Now, there are at least three elements to this question.

---

[24] See, e.g., Section 6.3. and other portions of Chapter 6.

First, what are the chances that the transaction will come to the attention of the Department of Justice or Federal Trade Commission?[24a] Second, assuming it does, what is the likelihood that one of those agencies will challenge the deal on an anti-trust basis? Third, if they do decide to attack, are the courts likely to agree with the government's position? It's not sufficient merely to advise the client that the anti-trust risk in the transaction is acceptable; in order for his ultimate decision to be meaningful, you have to explain the basis for your analysis.

Suppose your conclusion is based on the assumption that the Justice Department will discover the deal and challenge it, but that your client will ultimately prevail. Now, the client president might be concerned about being subjected to severe criticism by his board if he undertook a voluntary transaction which caused the company to become involved in a fracas with the Justice Department—*whatever* the outcome—and for that reason, notwithstanding your favorable advice, he would spurn the deal. Or, if your view is premised on the practical consideration that the FTC isn't likely to become aware of the transaction—although if it did surface, an attack might ensue and could prevail—a client with a highly tuned ethical sense might pass the transaction, shunning acts of borderline illegality even when unlikely to be noticed; whereas, if your advice were based on the hypothesis that the FTC, fully aware of the transaction, would decide not to prosecute, then the same client may well be inclined to proceed.

You will frequently hear businessmen discussing a "downside" analysis—what's the *worst* that can happen if the affirmative action is taken and everything turns sour. Now, if there's one exercise the typical attorney relishes—even though he might not give it that label—it's the downside analysis. By training and temperament, lawyers are past masters of the art. Here comes the parade of horribles, the "what if's": What if a $1 million lawsuit against the target company were to suddenly emerge from the woodwork? What if the Justice Department were to charge the company executives with criminal conspiracy to fix prices? What if Liechtenstein declared war on us, and all trading was suspended on the Big Board? And so on and on. The natural proclivity of a lawyer's mind is to speculate about what could go wrong.

There's no question that downsiding can be a useful exercise, and I would be the last person to discourage its utility. Just as you ought to view matters in the best light—assuming that everything goes perfectly—in order to assess the maximum advantages inherent in the situa-

---

[24a] Assume, for purposes of this example, that the transaction doesn't invoke the pre-merger notification provisions of the Hart-Scott-Rodino Act.

tion, so you ought to look at the worst that can happen—the disaster analysis, so to speak. Your client is entitled to know what blunt object might whack him on the side of his head, and you can be very helpful in this regard.

Still, while lawyers are inclined to speculate in possibilities, most businessmen are trained to deal in probabilities. And so, I consider it poor lawyering for an attorney to leave the disaster analysis as his last word on a subject. Consider how difficult it is for the businessman to evaluate the lawyer's Cassandra-like musings in terms of the likelihood of their occurrence. Are such matters strictly hypothetical or do they constitute a prediction? Should the client file this scare story away in the recesses of his mind as nothing more than a lawyer covering his tracks—or is it a prospect that ought to give the client pause? He has to respect the lawyer's judgment in legal matters, and unqualified downside speculation can act as an impediment to desirable action.

The proper role for the lawyer, I believe, is to examine both the best and the worst, and then to give his assessment of what may be considered *likely* to happen. It stands to reason that the more you attempt to adjust your thinking to the decisional framework within which the businessman operates, the more helpful you can be to him. Try to speak his language. Parade your horribles, to be sure; but don't let the downside become anything more than a disaster analysis.

So, for instance, when you counsel a client on whether he should become a general partner in a certain partnership, it's entirely proper—even requisite, one might say—to advise him that his personal assets can be reached for a partnership debt. That's the downside. But you can't stop there, leaving him in a total quandary as to whether to take the risk. You have to take him through the rest of the analysis, all of which tends to minimize the risk: how the partnership can insure against tort and product liability claims; how the creditor must first satisfy his claim out of partnership assets—so that if there are substantial properties under partnership control, your client can assess the relative unlikelihood of their exhaustion before a creditor turns on him; how the local law provides for contribution among partners, entitling him to claims over if the worst were to happen; and so on.

Or take this common situation in the corporate context. When businessmen contemplate a course of action with their counsel, you will often hear the lawyer say: "If you do that, you leave yourself open to a minority stockholder suit." Now, that's fair comment for the lawyer to make, but he can't leave it at that; he really should—but many don't—go much further in advising the client on this score. No one likes to be sued, or even to run a risk of being sued; but in the world of business, all things are relative—and the businessman is entitled to a more thoroughgoing analysis.

First of all, how will the transaction come to the attention of minority stockholders or the plaintiffs' bar? When will it be disclosed and in what documents? Second, are there enough dollars involved in the transaction to interest anyone in mounting an attack? For obvious reasons, most shareholders and their attorneys don't go around bringing lawsuits over financially trivial matters. Third, assuming some minority stockholders are enraged about this action, are they likely to vocalize their objections before taking action, thereby giving you a chance to modify your posture before any lawsuit ensues? Fourth, if a lawsuit were instituted, what would be your defenses? Are they valid? Is the plaintiff likely to be able to obtain a stay or a preliminary injunction or some other temporary relief that will provide him with leverage in connection with such an action? Is there insurance coverage or likely claims over against others? And finally, if (as so often happens in these matters) the case will ultimately be settled, can you predict a clear basis for settlement right from the start—so that, for instance, your client can anticipate a maximum exposure of, say, an extra dollar per share. Now, *that's* a helpful analysis to a client assessing a course of action—while simply to say that the proposal might evoke minority stockholder litigation doesn't really advance the ball very much.

Businessmen love to hear legal risks quantified. If you feel comfortable with this sort of thing—"I think it's 80-20 that we'll win in the lower court"—then by all means do so (after the appropriate caveats as to unpredictable judges and your inability to guarantee the result[25].) Personally, I think that's more appropriate for bookies and weathermen than for attorneys. There are other ways to summarize or characterize the situation that can be helpful to the ultimate decision-maker. For instance: "If you're otherwise inclined to proceed with this acquisition, then our conclusion is that the anti-trust risk alone should not deter you." Or conversely: "We feel that the anti-trust risk here is so serious—the likelihood of the Government taking a meritorious adverse position is so clear—that unless you're prepared to get into a long drawn-out struggle with a strong possibility of losing, and unless the rewards here are significantly greater than you can hope to achieve elsewhere, you probably ought to pass this deal by." It's still his decision, but at least he knows clearly where you stand.

That last example leads into my final thought on this sub-

---

[25]   On the subject of caveats generally, see Sections 3.2.8. and 6.5. If forced to quantify, you're clearly best off (from an invulnerability-to-second-guessing viewpoint) shrugging your shoulders and calling it 50-50.

ject—which is that, on occasion, with particular clients to whom you
have close ties and who rely on your judgment, you can and perhaps should go further on a go/no-go decision than simply sorting out
the possibilities. Here are two rules of thumb for this deviation: one,
make sure it's a matter in which the legal inputs are at least as strong
as the business factors; and two, take an exposed position only when
the decision is negative, not affirmative. I don't think a lawyer should
tell his client to *do* something; but the attorney can assert that he
doesn't think a given action is wise.

For instance, take the case of a client who is contemplating the ac-
quistion of a company teetering on the threshold of bankruptcy.
You've seen enough in your limited investigation to know that it will
be extremely difficult to keep the various groups of creditors in line
while the flow of red ink is being stanched. In fact, you have the distinct feeling that your client will be spending the next few years
straightening out the acquired company's past indebtedness rather than
running its business. The problems loom so large that, even though
there are possible rewards, your voice of experience tells you "no".
Well, by all means speak up and take a stand: "My advice would be
to pass this deal."

Make sure, however, that you never give this kind of ultimate advice without spelling out the rationale behind your conclusion and
labeling any non-legal advice as such; and finish on the note that
you're no seer, that life can take funny twists. This leaves the door
open for the client, if he disagrees with your reasoning—if he feels,
for instance, that you've made some unwarranted assumptions about
the acquired company's creditors and that things are likely to work out
much better than you expect—to overrule your advice and proceed.
When a lawyer takes a strong position without providing the underlying
reasoning, it tends to overpower the client who is leery about disagree-
ing with his counsellor—whereas the realization that there's nothing
jurisprudential about your judgment (which is based on certain assumptions that the client, in an equal position to judge, doesn't share) frees
him to go counter to your advice.

Oh, yes. There's one other type of judgment on which you should
have no hesitation about expressing your views. That's where an
ethical issue is involved.[26] It's to be expected that you'll be more
sensitive to this than your clients—after all, you live with questions of
propriety on a daily basis—and your voice ought to be heard loud and
clear. Cut through that heated discussion about the merits of a course
of action with: "Look, we can discuss this *ad nauseam,* but in my
view, it's unethical; and whatever its rewards, I have to recommend

[26] For a discussion of partner-associate differences over the ethical implications of proposed action, see Sections 5.1.3. and 10.5.2.

strongly against doing it." I'm assuming here that the ethical issue is clearly drawn; more ambiguous matters of choice have to be dealt with in a lower key, such as: "All other things being equal, I would prefer course A to B, because of the possibility that some of your directors might feel that B has unethical overtones." Remember, even if the final decision isn't yours, you're going to be affiliated with it; and the judgment had better be one that you can hold up your head and support.

The concomitant of this ethical vigilance, however, is to avoid moralizing on basically non-moral issues—or you'll have minimal credibility left to make impropriety a key consideration when it counts. And in this regard, I find that it's usually an easier pill for the client to swallow if you can couple your ethical nay-saying with a potent practical argument pointing in the same direction. You know: "Not only is it wrong, but you'll probably arouse the Commissioner's otherwise latent wrath. . . ."

8.5. THE WAY TO GO

We turn now to the situation where your client is about to take some action, either because he has to or wants to, and the sole question before the house is which of a variety of ways to go about doing it. As you might expect, this is often less of a business question than the go/no-go situation. Once the decision to move ahead has been made, optimizing the means to accomplish the goal often involves legal and quasi-legal considerations, as to which you're supposed to possess some special expertise. The client is going to be looking to you for advice, which may well transcend the purely legal issues; he is saying, in effect: "Look, we've already made the decision to proceed, so you don't have to worry about *that*. Now, just please tell me the best way to go about it."

These are the kinds of decisions which businessmen are fond of discussing in terms of such concepts as the "risk/reward ratio". That's less arcane than it may sound; actually, it's not a bad way for a lawyer to approach this kind of question, and you probably do it already on a subconscious level. In comparing two courses of action—A and B—if each offers the same potential benefits but there's a lesser probability of problems arising with A, then (all other things being equal) you would obviously choose course A. In another situation, where the risks appear about the same but the rewards from course B are superior, you naturally opt for B.[27] And, of course, in those

---

[27]   Those of you who play backgammon will recognize this principle: in evaluating two moves with roughly equal risks, good players prefer the move which, if the danger *doesn't* come to pass (i.e., if the other player doesn't hit your blot), puts the mover in the position of maximum potential advantage.

seemingly infrequent cases where both greater reward and lesser risk lie along a certain path, your choice is easy. The difficult questions arise when course A holds the greater reward but also entails the greater risk, while B couples the lesser reward with the lesser risk; you have to decide whether A's incremental reward justifies the added risk.

Let's take a pass at this sort of analysis in terms of a specific problem. Upandcoming, Inc., a client company whose 1,000,000 shares of common stock are registered under the Secruities Exchange Act of 1934 and traded over-the-counter, is contemplating the acquisition of a private company in exchange for roughly 300,000 shares of Upandcoming's common stock. In terms of Upandcoming's modest size, this is a large acquisition; and Upandcoming does not at present have sufficient authorized but unissued shares of common stock to pull it off. So, even though there's no requirement under the corporate laws of Upandcoming's state of incorporation for its stockholders to vote on this transaction[28] (board approval being sufficient), the company will have to call a special meeting of stockholders to approve an amendment to the certificate of incorporation, authorizing the necessary additional shares for the acquisition (as well as excess shares for future uses). In accordance with SEC rules, since a portion of the additional shares being authorized will be utilized for a specific transaction, information regarding the acquisition and the acquired company must appear in the proxy statement being sent to stockholders.

Upandcoming's inside counsel then raises the following question: since Upandcoming has to go back to its stockholders anyway for the additional shares, should the stockholders also be asked in the same proxy solicitation to specifically approve the acquisition (even though such approval is not required as a matter of corporate law)? And there's a collateral question: if it's decided to place approval of the acquisition before the stockholders, should they vote on this as a separate issue from the authorization of the additional shares, or should the two be joined as a single issue? The client is looking to you for a judgment call on these issues, even though the company will have to make the ultimate decision.

All right. Since you don't need stockholder approval of the acquisition under corporate law, the initial point of analysis has to be whether anything is to be gained (the potential rewards) by putting the issue to this group. If no advantage is apparent, then there's no point

---

[28]   If Upandcoming were listed on either the New York or American Stock Exchanges, approval of Upandcoming's stockholders would be required by Exchange rules for a transaction which results in a 20% increase (sometimes construed as 18½%) in Upandcoming's outstanding shares.

in doing it. And even if there are potential rewards, these have to be measured against any particular disabilities (the risks) which the action involves.

Well, there does happen to be one factor which suggests that perhaps the acquisition should specifically be approved by stockholders. In setting the stage for this problem, I left out one key fact. It seems that, in addition to the large number of Upandcoming shares being issued in the deal, the proposed transaction is also significant for the fact that one of Upandcoming's directors is a major stockholder of the company being acquired.[29] So there's both materiality and a trace of possible self-interest—factors which may cause the Upandcoming board to welcome being taken off the hook by the Upandcoming stockholders. To be sure, stockholder approval doesn't totally insulate the directors from challenge, but it's helpful to point to if and when the attack comes.[30] On the other hand, the reward is only relative, since even if you don't ask stockholders to vote specifically on the acquisition, they are being told all about it in the proxy statement; and, at least in theory, they could vote against authorizing the necessary additional shares if they didn't like the deal.

Now, what are the risks of putting the acquisition on the ballot? The most obvious risk is that it might not be approved by stockholders; and if that were to happen, Upandcoming (although possessing the necessary corporate power) would be rather foolhardy to proceed with the transaction. This risk would arise only if the two items were separate on the proxy card, and the stockholders authorized the additional stock but didn't approve the deal.[31] Well, what's the likelihood of anyone who's inclined to vote in favor of the

---

[29] This would be another ground for requiring stockholder approval if Upandcoming were listed on one of the Exchanges.
[30] At the very least, it may be deemed to shift the burden of proof to the plaintiff on the "interested" transaction. Of course, if stockholder approval is only a formality because insiders (particularly those related to the director with the conflict of interest) hold a majority of the shares, you can't take much comfort from the vote, unless the controlling shares are "sterilized".
[31] If the two were combined as a single issue and voted down, or if the issues were separate but the stock increase failed to carry, then Upandcoming wouldn't be able to make the acquisition in any event because it lacked sufficient shares. If the issues were separate, it's possible that (even with everyone voting the same way on both) the acquisition could be approved but not the share authorization—since the latter requires a majority vote (in some states, two-thirds) of all outstanding shares, while a majority of a quorum would be sufficient for the former. Note that, if the two matters were voted on as separate issues, the proxy statement would have to make clear that authorization of the additional shares doesn't depend on the acquisition vote; but that even if the acquisition received the necessary approval, it couldn't be consummated unless there were an affirmative vote on the share authorization.

additional stock not voting in favor of the acquisition? This would mean the stockholder approves other uses of the stock, including future acquisitions, but doesn't like this particular deal. Sounds unlikely, although it's at least possible due to the quantity of shares being issued here and the taint of self-interest. On the other hand, if the deal is a really good one, might it garner extra votes for the share authorization? Not very likely.

Another risk of putting the acquisition to stockholders is to focus any opposition that may develop to the deal—i.e., to spur a potential critic into action by specifically asking him to approve the deal (as opposed to merely telling him it will happen). This seems only a marginal risk, however. A further argument is that you furnish the possible opponent of the deal with more ammunition to attack it, since he will be able to claim that there were material misstatements or omissions in the proxy statement pursuant to which the vote was solicited. Where a vote on the deal isn't directly solicited, the effect of any such misstatement or omission is more indirect—since this particular acquisition is only part of what the additional shares will be used for—but not by much.

A final risk is that by going to stockholders for a transaction where approval isn't strictly required, you create a precedent that might present future problems; e.g., if stockholders are bypassed on subsequent major transactions where their vote isn't requisite. However, the size of this transaction and the self-interest feature do help to distinguish it from run-of-the-mill transactions, thus reducing the precedent impact.

Well, that's the analysis; and I leave it up to you whether on balance, the slight added reward of stockholder endorsement outweighs the slight additional risks. I should add that, in close cases like this, a factor that can tilt the balance is whether the additional step entails considerably more work, expense or time. If, for example, a host of extra financial and other information concerning the acquired company were required in the proxy statement for stockholders to vote directly on the acquisition, this might be a substantial negative factor.[32]

Let's say that in a given situation you've gone through your risk/reward analysis, and the ultimate decision isn't obvious. Should you present your own views on the subject or wait to be asked? There's no all-purpose answer here; much depends on the particular client. Be very sensitive to any hints a client may provide that he either wants you to lead him by the hand in making the decision or, conversely, would prefer you to keep your big mouth shut. Don't

---

[32] In the case under discussion, voting on the acquisition involves a relatively simple adjustment, with no major additional cost, time or effort—so this factor is essentially neutral.

become mesmerized by the sound of your own voice; listen very carefully. You might have a client who's silently crying for help, as he faces a decision that's beyond him. If so, and assuming you have a point of view, help him—make the recommendation. Or, you might be getting signals that you're becoming a shade too uppity—lawyers ought to know their place and let businessmen handle these kinds of matters—in which case, button up but good.

Another factor here is how adept your client is at making sound decisions. If the client has notoriously poor judgment (which you've observed in action on numerous occasions), you're more likely to come out of the closet and reveal your feelings on the matter. At least then, he's on notice that if he goes the other way, he's doing so against your better judgment. He still has the right to do so—in fact, he probably will!—but it somewhat reduces the inevitability of his making another poor judgment.

In most cases, after laying out the alternatives and factors as carefully as possible, you ought to defer the decision to the client. After all, if path A holds the greater rewards with the greater risks, while path B presents lesser risks with lesser rewards, the client should be the one to say: "I'm a gambler; let's take path A." What the hell, he owns the ball. Of course, in this kind of a situation you can help him with something along these lines: "Well, it seems to me that, given your basically conservative nature, you would probably feel more comfortable taking path B in this instance. True, you won't gain a windfall, but you're unlikely to get badly burned."

We all know there's more than one way to skin a cat. How many times have you been in a situation where you favor one alternative but haven't been asked for your views; you hesitate to express them directly; and the temptation arises to "load" the risk/reward analysis in favor of your position, thereby leading the client irresistibly (but unconsciously—some would say, unconscionably) to the decision you've decided is the right one. There are so many ways to accomplish this in a basically covert manner—your emphasis, the order in which you place things, pejorative or buzz words or phrases—a thousand nuances by which you can suggest the direction to take. But should you do it?

Well, I'm sure we're all guilty of this, consciously or unconsciously, to greater or lesser degrees. It isn't possible to entirely submerge your own feelings when you present a problem for judgment. And you can always rationalize it: your decision is clearly right; if the recommendation had been overt, the client would have gone along; so what's the harm in letting him feel he's made the decision himself? But, bottom line, it's wrong. You do a client no service to influence his decision by subtle coercion. It's far better to portray all aspects of the problem in as objective a manner as possible—and then ask the client if he wants to know your preference. This enables the client to separate the facts from the judgmental quotient, for purposes of his own ultimate decision. When you impose judgments on him in the guise of objective facts, you distort the decision-making process in an unprofessional manner.

Finally, what about the situation where you're closeted with two executives from a client company, each with a different view on how best to proceed, and they turn to you to break the tie. This can be an extremely awkward predicament. Taking sides in favor of one officer and against the other is not calculated to endear you to 50% of your audience. Still, it's very difficult to cop out.[33] Assuming you do favor one approach, and the problem has a substantial legal content, you just have to step up to the plate and present your own point of view. The key here is to emphasize that it's a close call; and you can further assuage the loser's feelings by a line such as "On balance, I prefer the first approach, but perhaps that's just because I'm extremely conservative by nature"—in effect, acknowledging that different people with slightly dissimilar bents can reasonably emerge at variance on close questions.

8.6. PROCESSING AND PACKAGING JUDGMENTS

I want to conclude this chapter with a few additional observations on both the process of reaching judgments and what may be termed the cosmetics.

As you might expect, correct answers and sensible judgments aren't always sitting around in attendance, waiting to be plucked. Complex problems breed opaque solutions; you need all the help you can get. So, peruse each and every vital document yourself—don't accept their contents from someone else's description. Remember that the breadth of variation in perception, memory and outlook among the population is staggering; so hear all sides of a story before rendering judgment. The discussion under legal analysis[34] regarding the methodology of arriving at solutions to problems is equally applicable here. In particular, discussing a decision with others who have something to contribute—or who at least provide a good sounding-board—can be extremely helpful. The process of exposing all facets of a problem to the light of an open forum—much like a diamond dealer rotating a gem slowly in his hand—often leads to inescapable con-

---

[33] One possible sidestep is: "I see the pros and cons of both your positions, and on balance I feel they're roughly equal. More important, I don't think the company will be hurt whichever way you go."
[34] See Section 2.4.

clusions, as less desirable choices eliminate themselves and the proper path becomes more readily apparent.

Although there are few shortcuts to well-reasoned judgments, occasionally the nature of your approach to decision-making can help to minimize the time needed to reach a conclusion. I have in mind complex questions involving several sub-issues, where, although the order in which you deal with the issues has little bearing on the merits of the ultimate judgment, a particular route enables you to dispose of the entire matter by addressing less than all of the topics.

Let me illustrate this point with a simple hypothetical. Let's assume that the question to be decided is how to handle the disclosure to the SEC staff of a certain troublesome matter, in the course of seeking advance clearance for a particular step.[35] Now, analytically there are three separate issues involved here: (i) should you be going to the SEC for advance clearance; (ii) assuming "yes", are you obliged to raise this troublesome matter with the staff; and (iii) assuming "yes" again, how should it be raised? If you begin your analysis by dealing with the difficult questions of whether there's a disclosure obligation and how to handle it, you may have wasted a lot of time should your decision be not to approach the SEC in the first instance; without a trip to Washington, you never reach the other two issues.

This may sound simplistic, but the tripartite nature of the question might not be readily apparent at first glance; and even then, the logic of the order in which to approach the sub-issues may not be clear on its face. Some analysis is required, both to spot the divisibility of the issues and to assess the possibility of shortcircuiting the analysis. It's worth doing, though, because in this business, speed can be very important—especially when you're sitting around a table with impatient individuals who are prone to make expedited decisions.

One caveat here, however. In many cases, you *must* deal with the second and third segments of a question in order to answer the first segment properly. For instance, in the example given, the issues of whether the item is disclosable to the staff and how to accomplish this might bear directly on the question of whether you should go to the SEC for advance approval. Let's say you decide the matter *is* disclosable but can't think of any good way to handle it; as a result, you're likely to be turned down by the staff; this would tend to reinforce the decision not to ask the staff's permission. Conversely, a judgment that there's no disclosure obligation or that the matter can be handled easily with the staff, might support a conclusion to make the journey.

One of the most difficult choices for a young lawyer in the judg-

---

[35]   Relations with administrative agencies, including whether to seek advance clearance and how to present your case, are discussed in Section 7.5.

mental process is whether, when attacking a problem in concert with other individuals (such as clients, inside lawyers and the like), he should toss on the table ideas which have just popped into his head but haven't been tested in the usual crucible. The ability to generate fresh ideas is extremely beneficial to group decision-making. Even if the particular concept uttered doesn't work, it may stimulate discussion, suggest other possibilities, and ultimately lead to sound judgments. But should *you* be the point man for the platoon?

Different lawyers react in various ways here, and I must confess to some ambivalence on the subject. Many an attorney is loath to be a sitting duck for the pot shots of others, with respect to ideas which he hasn't had a chance to evaluate. Others glory in this role, seemingly untroubled as their ideas are decimated, always ready to proffer another untried concept. For myself, I'll often float an untested idea, but I hesitate to advise others to do the same. It can be quite humiliating to have your brainstorm dashed to the ground within seconds, on the basis of some rather obvious consideration that would have occurred to you had the thought been subjected to real scrutiny before its utterance.[36] This sort of jolt is relatively easy to overcome if the previous relationship with your colleagues is solid, or you possess an unshakable reputation for sagacity; but when you're "on trial", being blown out of the water may suggest to others that you lack maturity or are chronically superficial.

On balance, however, I think you're better off floating the occasional untested idea than not. Counterbalancing the superficiality label is the reputation you'll develop if your ideas are interesting (even though not ultimately usable), plus the points you achieve for trying to be constructive (lighting candles rather than cursing the darkness, so to speak)—and then there's always the possibility that you may come up with a real winner, which will stand greatly to your credit. But any such activity should be performed in a judicious fashion, with maximum guarding of flanks.

Let's assume you're sitting in a room full of people, including the partner on the case, clients who don't know you very well, and the client's regular lawyers (whom your firm has been brought in to assist). The discussion is droning on, as the participants grapple to reach a judgment on some point, and suddenly you come up with what you consider a real brainstorm. Your instinct is to place it on the table immediately;[37] if you delay several minutes to evaluate its

---

[36] In Fitzgerald's words: "No grand idea was ever born in a conference, but a lot of foolish ideas have died there." F.S. Fitzgerald, *The Crack-Up* (1945).
[37] For an analogy (with disastrous consequences) in the negotiating area, see Section 7.3.1.

merits, the discussion may well have moved on to another point, and you would then be in no position to change subjects. Even a minute's deferral seems too long, because someone else might come up with the same inspiration and steal your thunder. What do you do?

First of all, make a quick assessment of the partner.[38] Is he the sort of person who likes all ideas to emanate from him? If so, you might want to whisper your thought to him and let him decide what to do with it. If he isn't that way, but is likely to react critically should your idea (however well-intentioned) turn out to be a dud, then discretion may be the better part of valor—unless you're pretty sure the idea has merit. Let's assume, however, that the partner is someone receptive to new ideas and unlikely to be embarrassed by your initiative. You still can expect problems, however, from the other lawyer, who wasn't overjoyed to see your firm brought into the situation in the first place.[39]

If you do decide to introduce your concept, by all means add a preliminary caveat along the lines of "Now, I'm just thinking out loud and really haven't had a chance to evaluate this, but what would you think if we. . . ." At least no one will be under any illusions that the idea has been subjected to your own critical scrutiny (as they might be entitled to infer from an unqualified introduction). Another helpful technique is to say "I don't know how this will fly from a tax point of view, but how about if we. . . ." This shows your sensitivity to tax concerns, even though you don't know (and probably couldn't be expected to know) the tax answer offhand. Then, if the tax expert replies: "No, it won't fly," you haven't really lost too much—while in the absence of any allusion to the possible problem, your audience might write you off as someone indifferent to the central role of the Internal Revenue Code.

If another participant shoots down your idea on plausible grounds, I urge you *not* to follow the path of atavistic impulse and defend your creation to the last ditch. Instead, bow out as gracefully as possible, turning to the gunner and remarking, with refreshing candor: "You're absolutely right, it wouldn't work. Let's move on." Never become mired in defending an unworkable idea, out of some misguided ego or machismo motivation. Cut your losses and move on.

And, when someone else floats an ill-conceived idea, remember what the pangs of public humiliation are like; so, if you're the one to puncture the balloon, try to handle it in the gentlest manner possible ("That's a good idea, but I'm afraid it would destroy the pooling

---

[38]   The subject of adapting to the idiosyncrasies of the partner is discussed in Section 5.1.1.

[39]   Professional jealousy in joint representation is covered in Section 7.2.1.

. . .'')—avoiding any suggestion that the progenitor is an incompetent who should never have raised such an idiotic point in the first place.

I can't urge you strongly enough, as you approach judgmental decisions, to keep in mind the necessity to constantly question your own thinking, to review the assumptions which circumscribe thought, and—just as previously discussed in terms of analytical reflection[40]—to crack the mold on occasion. Don't get so bogged down with the various factors involved in the decision-making process that you lose sight of the hierarchy of relative significance within which your goals operate. Materiality is as much (or even more) a factor here as elsewhere. Decisions only make sense if they advance the ball toward a meaningful objective. Never feel bound by stated alternatives. Make sure you're aimed in the right direction and giving everything its proper weight.

While you quest after good judgment in substantive terms, don't neglect appearances. You might have a capacity for quite sound judgment, but if you appear unsure of yourself (or conversely, too dogmatic), your resources are likely to be overlooked. A hesitant, indecisive lawyer is akin to a palsied periodontist; he may well be able to handle the job, but who wants to stick around to find out?

There's a narrow line to walk in order to come across as sensible and decisive. Just as you can't let the enormity of the decisional burden appear to weigh you down,[41] so you shouldn't appear cocksure in the face of difficult and weighty matters. There's nothing wrong in letting the client know that you're up against a tough one. Still, once you've mastered the issue and have a point of view, it's best to radiate a quiet kind of confidence, thereby reassuring your client and colleagues that you know what you're about. A cool exterior can be a real plus. Apparent nervousness in the face of difficult judgments rarely inspires trust. Let your words provide whatever caveats your conclusions require; but never allow your manner to mirror the depths of your uncertainty.

Just a word on the level of decisiveness with which you pronounce a judgment. In my view, both consistently unqualified judgments and constant hedging of bets represent inadequate approaches. The fact is that there are some judgments you feel more strongly about than others. If there's room for doubt, then say so—or at least use phrases (such as "it appears" or "one could therefore conclude") that imply something less than omniscience. But avoid these qualifiers on the

---

[40] See Section 2.5.
[41] A mistake in judgment isn't fatal, but too much anxiety about judgment is. Pauline Kael, "Zeitgeist and Poltergeist," *I Lost It at the Movies* (1965).

easy calls; they only serve to irritate and detract from the image of decisiveness you would like to project.

I often hear lawyers say in response to a question that is raised: ''I haven't the slightest notion what to do about that,'' or words to that effect. Personally, I don't dig this particular style. In my view, a lawyer ought to have *something* to say about almost everything. He can label it as assumption, or estimate, or prediction; he can put odds on the nose and qualify it any way he sees fit (''Well, that's strictly a business decision on which I have no real expertise, but. . . .''); he can mull it over for a while; but he ought to make a contribution. Always attempt to be constructive. Once you start excluding relevant areas from your consideration, you rapidly lose control of the situation.

A final word on record-keeping. When an important judgment has been made, it's wise to provide an internal record of what happened by way of file memorandum. If you gave advice, for example, but made no recommendation, record that fact; it may help in the event there's second-guessing down the road. If you made a recommendation on the basis of certain stated assumptions, chronicle these; then if the judgment turns sour as a result of a modified assumption beyond your control, you're protected. And it's always a good idea to have a record of who was there and acquiesced in the decision, just in case they try to dissociate themselves from it at some later date.

CHAPTER 9

PUTTING IT ALL TOGETHER:
AN ILLUSTRATIVE SEPTET

Well, now for some fun and games. I want you to sit back, relax, and picture yourself as the central figure in each of the seven hypothetical situations which make up this chapter. My purpose is to illustrate a number of the principles we've been discussing, through case studies intended to approximate actual experiences. In prior chapters, I've consciously tried to restrict the issue involved in each example to the matter then under discussion. In this chapter, however, the problems are lobbed your way much as they confront a practitioner—a bit fuzzy, with mixed issues of law and fact and practice, often opaque perspectives, overlapping and conflicting considerations, and so on. It's labeled hypothetical, but this is *our* real world.

In addition to matters explored at greater length in other sections of the book (to which cross-reference is made), I've included in this chapter a number of other points not previously discussed.[1] Certain of the studies contain specific associate-partner issues; others do not—but if you're an associate, it goes without saying that all significant conclusions and recommendations should be checked with the supervising partner.

Need I mention once more that the opinions and observations expressed here cannot be measured by any objective standard, are of a highly personalized nature, and will undoubtedly be open to question. Able practitioners can and do take different tacks in these judgmental areas. There is nothing inevitable about most of the conclusions reached; and I encourage you to arrive at your own independent judgments. As a matter of fact, that's the whole idea: to get

---

[1] No doubt, certain of the problems will contain still further aspects that pique your curiosity but which (either for pedagogic reasons or in the interests of keeping matters focused) are not discussed. For this, I apologize in advance.

you *thinking* about these matters, rather than merely going through the motions.

9.1. STUD OR HIGH STAKES?

A thoroughbred racehorse named Widow's Mite is owned jointly by four individuals: Abner, who is your client; Barney, who had been a close pal of Abner's, although their friendship has waned in recent months; Claude, a professional in the racing business, who operates a stud farm; and Dirk, about whom you know little except that he seems to travel a great deal.

Widow's Mite has enjoyed a successful racing career, winning purses totalling almost $500,000. The time is now at hand for his owners to decide whether to continue the four-year-old in competition or retire him to stud. On the track, the possibility exists that he could earn another half million dollars; but there is also a substantial risk of serious injury, which might result in the horse's destruction. Preliminary indications are that Widow's Mite could be syndicated for stud right now for about $300,000.

At the time they purchased Widow's Mite, the four owners entered into a partnership agreement (which your firm didn't draft but reviewed on Abner's behalf), containing the following provisions:

1. All "racing decisions" are to be determined by a majority "in interest" of the owners, while all other decisions are to be decided by two-thirds in interest.

2. The four partners share equally (25% each) in the net earnings of Widow's Mite from racing. With respect to amounts realized by way of stud fees or syndication, however, Abner, Barney and Dirk share 20% each, while Claude is entitled to 40% because of his expertise and some additional stud farm services he's obligated to provide.

3. In order for the partners to take affirmative action at a meeting, a quorum of 80% in interest on the particular issue is required.

The partners intend to hold a meeting next week to determine the future of Widow's Mite. Abner has come to you for advice on how to proceed. He is leaning strongly toward continuing to race the horse—perhaps less for financial reasons than for the sheer pleasure he has derived from this activity. In the past, Barney has usually been on the same wavelength as Abner; but the two have spoken only rarely since their recent coolness, and Abner isn't sure what Barney's position will be. Claude has always been friendly towards Abner, but Abner suspects Claude may be opposed to continuing Widow's Mite on the track because of Claude's larger percentage interest in the horse's stud fees. As far as Dirk is concerned, Abner believes him to be in favor of continued racing; but in view of Dirk's heavy travelling schedule, Abner isn't sure whether Dirk will be able to attend the meeting.

All right. Now, how do you go about analyzing the issues involved here, in order to advise Abner? Well, it's pretty obvious that you have to start out by attacking the problem on an analytical level —sorting out the issues, the relevant facts, the various possibilities, and so on.[2] This is where you usually begin, before making any reasoned judgments or giving intelligent advice. And the key to this problem lies in making an advance assessment of how the vote on racing vs. retirement is likely to come out at the scheduled meeting. This involves both an analysis of "the law" (in this case, represented by the partnership agreement) and dealing with the facts as presented (or as *omitted,* in this rather cryptic précis).

Your initial discovery is that the partnership agreement contains several critical ambiguities:

First, is a decision to stop racing a "racing decision", or not? If it is, a majority in interest will decide the question; if it's not, two-thirds in interest is required.

Second, with respect to such a decision, what does the phrase "in interest" mean? More specifically, does it mean the interests of the partners in racing earnings (which are 25% each) or their interests in the stud income resulting from a decision to retire Widow's Mite (in which case, Claude would have a 40% voice and the other three 20% each)?

Finally, for quorum purposes, are their racing interests or their stud fee interests applicable?—a point which might become relevant if Dirk is unable to attend the meeting.

So, you have a situation—not really so unusual in the practice of law—where ambiguity results because the required decision embodies more than one aspect; i.e., both the *stopping* of racing and the *starting* of stud services. You must spot these ambiguities as a threshold matter. But that's only the beginning. How do you then proceed to analyze the dimensions of the problem and reach some sort of conclusion? Competent issue-spotters aren't necessarily good lawyers; you still need to make sound decisions.

---

[2] Legal analysis is the principal subject of Chapter 2.

It seems to me you ought to approach this problem through an analytical matrix—making certain assumptions, holding certain details constant while varying others.[3] For instance, first assume that all four owners will be present at the meeting. Assume further that this is considered a racing decision, as to which a majority in interest will prevail. Apply the racing percentages as their respective "interests". Viewed in this light, in order for Abner to prevail, he needs any two other owners to join with him. Another way to state this proposition is that, under these assumptions, no single owner can block the decision to keep Widow's Mite racing.

Now, still assuming that everyone is present and it's viewed as a racing decision, what if the stud percentages were to apply in determining interest? In this case, Abner needs the concurrence either of (i) both Barney and Dirk, or (ii) Claude alone, in order to obtain the requisite majority. Again, however, no single individual can block the decision to continue racing.

If everyone's present but the decision is deemed to be other than a racing one (so that two-thirds in interest is then required), what happens? If the racing percentages applied, Abner would need any two other owners to prevail, and no single person could block the decision to keep racing. But if the stud percentages were applicable, Abner would need Claude and one other owner, which means that Claude alone could block the decision.

Now assume that Dirk does not show up. If you used the racing percentages to measure interest, the necessary 80% quorum wouldn't exist; with the stud interest percentages, however, it would.

You have to analyze the realistic effects of these ambiguities along such lines, in order to appreciate the dimensions of the problem and the potential differences in result depending on the assumptions made. But you also have to go on from there—to attempt to *resolve* the legal questions, and then to deal with the practical aspects of the problem. As a first step, you should flesh out your data base. What other provisions of the partnership agreement, or background facts surrounding its negotiation, might bear on the questions of whether this is a racing decision and which "interests" are applicable?

It might be, for example, that other contractual provisions or contemporaneous statements suggest the intention to limit "racing" decisions to the issue of selecting the races in which the horses should be entered—that the lesser vote for such decisions reflects the need to reach judgments quickly, without being able to consult all the owners. In the absence of evidence supporting this interpretation,

---

[3] Various analytical approaches are discussed in Section 2.4. I find that the kind of matrix discussed here is best done on paper, in order to properly assess all the different permutations and combinations.

however, one would hesitate to conclude that the decision to stop racing—arguably, the biggest racing decision of all—can be excluded
from this category. And once you determine this to be a racing decision, then as a matter of internal consistency, you would tend to
utilize the racing percentages in determining interest.[4] This is to Abner's advantage; the only way Abner could profit from the stud
percentages applying to a racing decision is if Claude were to support
continued racing (the two of them constituting a majority)—an unlikely possibility, given Claude's financial incentive to retire Widow's
Mite to stud.

The worst of all worlds for Abner would occur if this were considered a non-racing decision to which the stud percentages were applied. In that case, Claude by himself could (and presumably *would*)
block the decision to keep racing. Therefore, from Abner's point of
view, it makes sense to view this as a racing decision with the racing
percentages applied—with one important exception: that if Dirk isn't
present at the meeting, there won't be a quorum (using the racing interests), and consequently Abner will not have an opportunity to
prevail on the issue.[4a]

All right. That's enough analysis for the moment. Let's turn to
practical considerations. Your goal should be for Abner to know in
advance that, if he attends the meeting, he'll be in a position to
prevail.[5] Start with the presumption that Claude will vote against continued racing. Abner then needs both Barney and Dirk to side with
him in order to keep the horse on the track. And thus it becomes important for Abner to know how his former friend (Barney) stands on
this issue, and whether or not Dirk will be present at the meeting.

There are a number of ways to approach this, but one that appeals
to me is for Abner to contact Dirk prior to the meeting, confirm Dirk's
interest in continuing the horse's racing career, and urge him to be

---

[4]   Interestingly enough, if the racing percentages apply, it really doesn't matter
to Abner whether it's a racing decision or "other" decision, since in either
case he needs the votes of any two other owners (and no single owner can block
the decision).

[4a]   Actually, however, the law of inertia works in Abner's favor here. The
fact is that Widow's Mite is now racing, pursuant to an earlier decision to do
so. One can argue that an affirmative decision would now be required to
overturn this state of facts and stop the horse from racing—so that, in the
event of a stalemate or lack of quorum, the existing situation would be
deemed to continue. Note also, that in referring to the issue, I have used
various formulations: "the decision to keep Widow's Mite racing"; "a decision to stop racing"; "a decision to retire Widow's Mite"; "if Claude were
to support continued racing"; etc. Sometimes, the way a question is
phrased can bear on this matter of decisional inertia. *Cf.* Section 3.2.1.

[5]   This is akin to the discussion in Section 8.2, concerning the anticipation of
judgment.

present at the meeting. If Dirk can't make it, then Abner should ask Dirk to request that the meeting be rescheduled for a day when he can attend.[6] And, in view of the falling out between Abner and Barney, Abner could suggest that Dirk contact Barney and solicit his support for continued racing—on the theory that Barney would be more amenable if such views don't appear to originate with Abner.

If, contrary to expectations, Dirk replies that both he and Barney are in favor of retiring Widow's Mite to stud—and they plan to be present at the meeting to vote that way—then Abner's best strategy might be to avoid showing up at the meeting himself. The effect of his absence, assuming the racing percentages are used to measure interest, would prevent a quorum from being convened, which effectively obviates any decision to halt the horse's racing career. In such a situation, make sure the others are aware of your client's view that the racing percentages apply to this decision for quorum purposes.

To illustrate a different point we've discussed previously, let's assume that Abner agrees with your strategy but asks *you* to make the call to Dirk. This you do, reporting back to Abner as follows: "I told Dirk that we hoped he was in favor of continued racing; that if he was, he should try to make the meeting; and that we would appreciate it if he would please call Barney and solicit his support. Dirk was non-committal, saying in effect that he would take the matter under advisement." Do you consider this a good job of reporting? Or, if it accurately and fully reflects your actual conversation with Dirk, did you handle *that* phone call well?

I don't think so, on either score. In the conversation with Dirk, you should have made a real effort to ascertain Dirk's likely position. And in reporting on that conversation to Abner, you ought to speculate on Dirk's leanings, as extrapolated from any clues he might have dropped.[7]

For example, if Dirk had discussed the merits of the matter with you in some detail without a hint that he might *not* be able to attend the meeting, I think a fair inference to draw is that he expects to be in town. If he were going to be away, that fact would likely have been mentioned. So, here's a case of an omission having possible significance.

Did Dirk ask a number of questions about the falling out between Abner and Barney? Was he interested in Abner's speculations as to Barney's probable position? If so, this would suggest that Dirk is

---

[6]   My experience is that it's better for such a request to emanate directly from the person adversely affected by the scheduling, rather than from another person—like Abner—whose motives may be suspect.

[7]   The subject of making an effective oral report is discussed in Section 3.3.1.

seriously considering making the call to Barney; and since the main reason for him to do that (at your suggestion) is to solicit Barney's support, this could indicate that Dirk is leaning toward Abner's view. On the other hand, if Dirk happened to mention that he had a recent call from Claude, this sounds like Claude might be doing some politicking for the stud result—which is not particularly good news.

So probe—and listen—and draw inferences—and pass along your hunches to the client. Just be sure to label fact as fact, statement as statement, and inference as just that, so no one is misled.

There are any number of collateral issues that might be raised in this problem, but we'll stop at this point. I can't resist leaving you with one thought, though. What about the fact that your firm had originally reviewed (although not drafted) the partnership agreement? Might this give rise to some sensitivity in regard to these various ambiguities slipping by someone—was it you?—and does this affect either the substance or style of your handling of the problem?

9.2. THE UNCOMFORTABLE COMFORT LETTER

Your firm is outside counsel to Byer Corp., a public company, which is in the process of acquiring another publicly-owned corporation, Cellar Inc. The respective Boards of Directors have approved the deal; an agreement of merger was signed; Cellar and Byer solicited proxies from their stockholders by means of a bulky joint proxy statement processed through the SEC; and the necessary votes to authorize the transaction were received at the respective stockholders' meetings. At the point we join the festivities—call it April of 1979—the parties are about to close the deal.

The merger agreement, which details the rights and duties of Cellar and Byer, contains a number of conditions to each party's obligation to close the transaction. For our purposes, the two relevant conditions to Byer's obligation are: (i) that no material adverse change in Cellar's results of operations or financial condition shall have occurred from the situation reflected in its audited year-end (December 31, 1978) financial statements, which had been delivered to Byer prior to signing of the agreement and were included in the proxy statement; and (ii) that Cellar's independent public accountants will deliver a so-called "comfort" letter[8] to Byer just prior to the closing, stating that in the course of their recent review of Cellar's books and records, nothing came to their attention which gives them reason to believe that any of a variety of potentially negative events occurred during the period subsequent to December 31, 1978—including any decrease in the net income for the period as contrasted

---

[8]   Accountants' comfort letters are discussed in Section 8.3.3 of *Anatomy*.

with the comparable period of the prior year. The agreement also contains a standard provision to the effect that any condition to the obligation of a party may be waived by that party.

During its processing of the proxy statement, the SEC staff—with the well-known *National Student Marketing*[9] situation obviously in mind—asked for inclusion in the proxy statement of an undertaking that should a "material condition" to a party's obligation be waived after stockholders had voted on the merger, the stockholders would be notified of this development and their proxies resolicited. The apparent theory was that stockholders are entitled to rely on material conditions being satisifed; when one is waived, they should be consulted as to whether the waiver makes any difference to them. (In this connection, keep in mind the Supreme Court's formulation in the *Northway* case,[10] holding that a proxy statement omission is material if there is a substantial likelihood that a reasonable investor *would* consider it important in deciding how to vote—reversing a lower court which considered material all facts that a reasonable shareholder *might* consider important. The companies, anxious to glide through the SEC as promptly as possible and considering the point a purely hypothetical one, acceded to this comment.

Well, there you are, exchanging final forms of documents at a pre-closing occurring the day before the scheduled closing date, and someone hands you a draft of Cellar's accountants' comfort letter. You scan the pages with a practiced eye and . . . whoops!—it's not clean! Preliminary indications are that income for the 1979 first quarter is below that of the 1978 first quarter. The estimated dollar amount of the difference is neither clearly material (a judgment that, sadly, accountants will no longer make for you[11]) nor plainly insignificant.

You immediately spring into the next room to bring the comfort letter to the attention of Byer's president and chief financial officer. "I'm not at all surprised," says the financial man; "This pretty much accords with what I expected Cellar's results to be for the first quarter." Byer's president nods in concurrence. "So then," you ask (already knowing the answer), "the letter doesn't change your desire to go ahead and close the transaction?" "Absolutely not!" thunders the president—and then he adds, as an afterthought: "Why, does it create any problems for you?" At which point, you mumble something non-committal and slink off to the privacy of your room.

---

[9]   See *Securities and Exchange Commission v. National Student Marketing Corp.*, 457 F. Supp. 682 (1978).
[10] *TSC Industries, Inc. v. Northway, Inc.*, 426 U.S. 438 (1976).
[11] See Section 8.3.3 of *Anatomy*.

After several moments spent gazing blankly at the pictures of your kids on the desk, you face up to the situation, to assess where you stand. Has something happened requiring you to advise your client that the closing should be deferred, stockholders must be resolicited, and—aagghh! The sheer agony of such a course, the furor you can expect from your client, the uncertainties that will attend a month's delay, literally prevent you from completing the thought. You pace the room; but the problem won't go away—you have to deal with it. A sequence of grotesque images passes before you (as in a Fellini movie)—gloating, green-shaded accountants; stern-eyed SEC staffers, ready to pounce; beetle-browed, Cro-Magnon-like stockholders, incapable of reading beyond the cover page of the proxy statement; the twenty people scurrying about in the next room, anxious to get on with the closing. . . .

Okay. Calm down. Get control. You're about to make an important judgment and need your wits about you.[12] You would do well to have another lawyer from the firm in the room—even one who hasn't worked on the deal—to bounce thoughts off.[13] And the very first thing to do is frame the precise question confronting you. This is critical. If your initial analysis of the issue is wrong or superficial, it can distort everything that follows.[14]

What you're faced with is a relatively narrow issue, namely: assuming Byer waives receipt of the clean comfort letter called for by the agreement, and closes the deal on the basis of the actual letter detailing the first quarter downturn, has Byer waived a *material* condition to its obligation? If the answer is yes, then stockholders should be resolicited, because that's what the proxy statement said would happen; failing to do so would constitute a serious breach of faith—not to mention opening Byer up to suits and administrative sanctions. If Byer hasn't waived a material condition, then the closing can proceed and no harm has been done. Note: this is *not* a contract issue; under the merger agreement, the condition regarding delivery of a clean comfort letter (which contained no reference to materiality) has not been satisfied, and Byer has the absolute right to decline to close. And in the first instance, it's *not* really a proxy statement/disclosure issue either (although, as we shall see, this enters the analysis at a later point); the statement concerning waiver and resolicitation is clear and unambiguous. Rather, this is a question of construction; is the condition which your client is about to waive a material one?

Now that you've framed the question properly, how do you go

---

12 The subject of judgment is treated at length in Chapter 8.
13 See Section 2.4.
14 The dangers of superficial analysis are discussed in Section 2.1.

about solving it? Well, let's begin by examining some of your options. And the first possibility that comes to mind, deriving from the play-it-safe school of lawyering, sounds like this: look, we're clearly waiving a condition; I don't want to be in the position of judging whether it's a material condition or not; so let's put off the closing and go back to the stockholders. Some lawyers approach every tough question in this fashion; why take any chances?

To each his own, but that wouldn't be my style. You're being paid to accomplish this deal expeditiously; there are bound to be road-blocks along the way; you owe it to your client to make every effort to overcome them. Now, this is not to suggest that should an in-depth analysis reveal the question to be a close one, it might not be prudent to elect the conservative course; that's perfectly acceptable practice. What I'm criticizing here is the tendency to arrive at that conclusion *without* having undertaken the hard-nosed judgmental analysis that's required. This does your client a real disservice. A deal that is delayed for an unnecessary resolicitation of stockholders could be lost—at the very least, unwarranted additional expenses will be incurred and troublesome uncertainties engendered. So don't duck the judgment and head for the hills; this does scant honor to the profession.

A second possibility, which would be popular with a number of lawyers, is to fly down to the SEC and attempt to get the staff's blessing to close the transaction.[15] If the staff took the position that resolicitation of stockholders wasn't necessary, you would pretty much be home free. Sure, some discontented stockholders could conceivably kick up a fuss, but at least the SEC wouldn't be chasing down everyone in sight (as they did in the *National Student Marketing* case).

If you do decide to go to the SEC, how would you present the question to them? Some lawyers I know would lay out the problem in completely neutral tones—in effect, asking the staff for advice as to what to do. To me, that's the wrong way to handle matters (unless you're covertly seeking a ''resolicit'' response). Assuming you believe that resolicitation isn't required, the better method is to present a persuasive argument why Byer is *not* waiving a material condition.[16] Make the staff overrule your views—force them to sub-stitute their judgment for yours—if they want to come out the other way. Remember, you're an advocate, not a judge.

But the reality of this situation is that no matter what you say to the staff, a substantial risk exists that you'll receive a resolicitation

---

[15] The subject of which questions to take to an agency (and which not to) is discussed in Section 7.5.2.

[16] See Section 7.5.4 on presenting your case persuasively to an agency.

answer. It's so natural for an administrative agency to take the line that promotes their function—in the SEC's case, the function of ensuring full disclosure. And the adverse practicalities to the company inherent in resolicitation will carry little weight. "Go back to the stockholders," I can hear the staff say; "avoid any taint of the *National Student Marketing* situation." But, you argue, our case is different. Have you ever tried to distinguish a case to an agency—especially a case the agency took very seriously? It's a tough uphill fight, I can assure you. And, of course, once the staff tells you to resolicit, you act at your peril in not doing so.

So, seeking the SEC's views on the subject isn't a completely palatable alternative either. Incidentally, as between that and throwing in the sponge by way of resolicitation, which choice do you prefer? Well, under most circumstances (and assuming the question is not open-and-shut), I would opt for going to the SEC. At least this way you have a *chance* of getting the answer you seek. It's also preferable on the second-guessing front. If you resolicit without asking the staff and problems occur, your client will always wonder whether the resolicitation was necessary—maybe the SEC would have said the waived condition wasn't material. Whereas if you go to the SEC and get an adverse response, you're in a position to say to the client: "Look, I'm really glad we asked them, because this proves how unhappy they would have been if we had proceeded to close the transaction—and they had then found out about it on their own."[17]

As a matter of fact, the sole reason I can think of to go back to stockholders without having at least tried the SEC—other than the possibility of a private action lawsuit, which I don't consider terribly significant—is that you might then be better able to set the terms for the resolicitation. For example, since the meeting has already been held, you may consider it sufficient compliance with the *spirit* of the undertaking to write a letter to stockholders, telling about the unclear comfort letter and advising them (if the news changes their decision) to return the enclosed card to signify non-assent to the deal. Only if cards aggregating a certain percentage of the outstanding shares are received (which you're sure will never happen), will Byer initiate a new vote. But once you raise the whole issue with the SEC and generate a negative response, the staff may be inclined to dictate a more formal approach to the resolicitation of stockholders.[18]

---

[17] See Section 7.5.2 on the advantages of approaching an agency voluntarily, rather than having the regulators unearth the facts themselves.

[18] Of course, that low-key letter alluded to in the prior sentence would have to be cleared by the staff; but the atmosphere would less resemble a *cause célèbre* than had you tried to avoid resolicitation with the staff's blessing.

And so, here we are, back at the point of the dilemma once again—trying to see your way clear to proceed with the deal, if you can. And that's just where you should be, because (as with so many judgmental problems a lawyer must face) the *first* step toward an intelligent decision is to resolve the question of what's right in your *own* mind—not in some other lawyer's mind, or the client's mind, or the SEC's mind, but in your own mind. You have to do more than define the issue; you have to find the solution for yourself. That might not be the end of the matter; for instance, you might come out in favor of proceeding to close the deal, but feel the question is close enough and the dangers sufficiently meaningful that it ought to be run by the SEC. But you can't get started on a decision without first knowing where *you* stand. If, upon analysis, closing the deal doesn't seem right to you—if you believe that the stockholders deserve further consultation—then no amount of practicalities or client urging (or the assurances of the client's inside counsel that the problem is manageable[19]) should push you to a conclusion you can't support.

As you begin to face up to this question under time and client pressures, I imagine you'll be troubled by a nagging feeling of guilt—should you have done something differently earlier to prevent ending up in this soup? Was there poor communication between the businessmen (who apparently expected the reduced earnings) and the lawyers and accountants (who made no provision for it in the contractual references to the comfort letter)? Should *you* have taken the unusual step of offering to include a caveat in your own client's comfort letter condition (even though it wasn't sought), providing in effect that Byer wouldn't be able to avoid its obligation under the agreement unless the gap between the anticipated and delivered comfort letters was itself material?[20] Maybe the proxy statement should have stated that the parties were likely to waive certain conditions, including this one—thereby putting stockholders on notice. Or perhaps you should have resisted the staff's inclusion of the resolicitation language—not have been so cocky that material waivers were unlikely to surface. It's hard to keep such thoughts from intruding, and they may even be useful in a *post-mortem* to derive lessons for next time around; but don't let yourself get tied up in knots while you're in the midst of tackling this decision. The fact is that it happened; you weren't prepared; and now you have to deal with the situation.

---

[19] The potential pressures on inside counsel in this kind of situation are explored in Section 7.2.3.
[20] See the discussion in Section 8.3.3 of *Anatomy* as to how sellers' lawyers often forfeit the hard-fought materiality criteria otherwise achieved by failing to insist on just such a caveat in the comfort letter provision of the agreement.

You should begin by determining whether or not the information revealed in the unclean comfort letter—the decrease in earnings for the period—constitutes a material adverse change in Cellar's business. If it does and you were to close anyway, then pretty clearly you would be waiving a material condition (quite apart from the comfort letter)—namely, the no-material-adverse-change section of the agreement. And even if it doesn't clearly rise to the level of a *material* adverse change, the more significant the earnings decrease is, the more the waiver of the comfort letter would tend to be deemed material.

Now, in actuality, this is a business question that you aren't equipped to handle by yourself, but you can and should mobilize the necessary people to come to grips with it. So this is the first order of business—rounding up the financial types, the businessmen, accountants, investment bankers and such—to assess whether or not you've got a material adverse change on your hands.

Let's assume that your interrogation of the financial people reveals the following information: that the earnings decline had been anticipated by Cellar; that it was attributable to certain factors (such as a deteriorating backlog) that were well known (except to the lawyers!) prior to the signing of the merger agreement; that the potential of a disappointing first quarter had been communicated to, and taken into account by, Byer's management and board of directors when they authorized the deal and determined the purchase price; that in reaching its opinion on the reasonableness of the terms, Byer's investment banker had focused, at least peripherally, on this factor; that, according to Byer's accountants, the adverse numbers do not rise to the level of what is considered material under certain tests that auditors and the SEC use; and that for various reasons, the first quarter doesn't presage any negative long-term trend—things seem to be working themselves out, and the last month of the quarter was actually better than the first two months. So the clear consensus is that the development was neither materially adverse nor one that caught anyone (other than you) by surprise.[21] So far, so good.

This then throws you back to the issue of whether, assuming no material adverse change in operations has occurred, there has nevertheless been a waiver of a material condition by virtue of the fact that Byer is closing without the clean comfort letter it was entitled to receive. Put another way, the question is whether a comfort letter, standing by itself, has material independent significance. Some

[21] It's a good idea to document these conclusions of others in contemporaneous signed statements (or at least memos to the file), to avoid any convenient loss of memory if the transaction closes and then comes under attack, with everyone scattering for the hills.

documents, one could argue, do possess just such significance. For instance, the absence of a clean accountant's opinion on audited financial statements—no matter what the "subject to" qualification is—could be deemed material, because of the importance that businessmen, lawyers, and especially the SEC and stock exchanges, place on unqualified auditors' certificates. But where does that leave a comfort letter? Obviously, it has *some* significance. And it was an unclean comfort letter that was at the core of the whole *National Student Marketing* brouhaha—but there, of course, the negative facts revealed in the letter were clearly material.

Well, here's the way I would reason on this issue. When you come right down to it, the comfort letter is analogous to legal opinions, officers' certificates, and other similar documents which the agreement provides to be delivered at the closing. Such documents represent a means of ensuring that the information being conveyed is more reliable than if the subject matter were simply phrased in terms of an anonymous company function—more reliable also, in the case of legal opinions and comfort letters, because an independent professional is putting his firm's name on the line. The comfort letter represents a device for asking a company's independent auditors to focus on and review its most recent operations. Since accountants have retreated from passing on materiality, it's clear that not every failure to give a clean comfort letter necessarily rises to a level of materiality—yet that's the standard by which the need to resolicit the stockholders must be judged. It helps to reduce the concept to an absurdity[22]—an earnings decrease of a single dollar—which could theoretically raise the same question, but with a simple answer. And thus you conclude that waiver of the clean comfort letter is *not* a waiver of a material condition if the unclean matter isn't itself material.

How about that ghost of the *National Student Marketing* case, which has been hovering there in the background?[23] How close are the two situations? Unless you can distinguish the adverse precedent, you're not all the way home—and the District Court decision heightens the risk for lawyers making wrong decisions in this area.[23a] Well,

---

[22] The two-party use of absurd examples as a bargaining device is referred to in Section 7.3.5.

[23] The significance of that case in terms of the waiver of a condition is discussed in Section 12.4.3 of *Anatomy*.

[23a] The nub of the District Court's decision is contained in this quote: "Although it is arguable whether the better business decision under the circumstances was to proceed with the merger, the antifraud provisions prohibit such a course of action when a material misrepresentation or omission has occurred, regardless of the business justification for closing the merger." 457 F. Supp. 682 at 709. For a discussion of the case's implications for securities lawyers, see the commentary by Kenneth J. Bialkin under "Securities Law" in *The National Law Journal*, Oct. 30, 1978, at 22, col. 1.

fortunately there are some very real distinctions. I don't wish to go into the facts of NSM, but in addition to the clear materiality there and some unanswered questions about possible deception, one major difference exists. As contrasted with the question of *Cellar's unreported* recent earnings, in NSM it was the *purchaser's reported* earnings appearing in the proxy statement that were materially overstated. NSM stock was being distributed to the seller's stockholders (and thereafter into the marketplace) on the basis of incorrect financials; that's what much of the fuss was really about. Materially misstated numbers aren't the same as omitted numbers—not materially adverse—which weren't required to appear in the proxy statement in the first place.

It really comes down to what a stockholder of Byer might reasonably have anticipated with regard to Cellar's subsequent earnings, on the basis of what appeared in the proxy statement. If what actually occurred was generally consistent with reasonable expectations, then Byer stockholders can't be said to have been misled. And so, the final part of the puzzle is to take a close look at the proxy statement itself. Lo and behold, you discover language in various places suggesting that Cellar might be facing some short-term hard times in precisely the areas (such as backlog deterioration) that caused the earnings decline. You are also pleased to note that, in the section describing the merger agreement, no specific mention of a comfort letter appears. To be sure, the agreement was attached to the proxy statement as an exhibit, so that a stockholder could have found out that a comfort letter was being delivered; nevertheless, the fact that no big deal was made about it in the proxy statement text is helpful. And so, viewing the proxy statement under the *Northway* test, it doesn't seem there's a substantial likelihood that a reasonable Byer stockholder *would* (not *might*) consider the first quarter news by itself an important element in his decision.

Well, from this point on it's all downhill. You brief the client on the situation; present your analysis; outline the various possible courses of action; explain the risks attendant on each; indicate that, in your view, resolicitation isn't legally required; and let him make the ultimate decision.[24] I think you can guess what it will be. You're no hero—the client doesn't even understand what all the fuss was about. But you've done your job, and done it properly.

9.3. THE CASE OF THE WELSHING ART COLLECTOR

Your wealthy client, Mr. Pristine, is in the throes of a temporary

---

[24] For material on the interaction between lawyer and client in terms of making decisions, see Sections 6.3, 8.4 and 8.5.

cash flow bind. As a result, he has decided to sell a valuable oil painting from his impressive collection. He enters into an agreement with Mr. Slowpay, a well-known (but not always well-heeled) collector, who will purchase the painting for $250,000, payable in six weeks—thereby affording Slowpay a reasonable period to raise the necessary funds. The contract (which you drafted and Slowpay's lawyer reviewed) provides that if Slowpay refuses to hand over the $250,000 at the closing for whatever reason (including his inability to finance the purchase), your client Pristine will be entitled to receive $50,000 as liquidated damages. Sure enough, Slowpay taps out on the financing and defaults at the closing.

The idea behind this rather simple hypothetical is to examine some basic lawyer-to-lawyer adversarial dealings. Although you and Slowpay's attorney could be classified as hostile adversaries[25], the situation you find yourself in holds the potential for fruitful negotiations—which brings into play many of the considerations discussed in the section on friendly adversaries.[26] To get a feel for both sides of the fence, from time to time we'll also view matters from the vantage point of Slowpay's attorney. For reasons which will become obvious, the discussion is divided into three parts, each based on a different basic assumption:

> Situation A, where Slowpay actually advanced $50,000 in cash to Pristine upon signing the agreement, as a down payment on the ultimate purchase price;

> Situation B, where no money changed hands upon the signing; and

> Situation C, where upon signing, Slowpay delivered $50,000 into escrow, to be held by a disinterested third party.

Let's begin with situation A. Here, you and your client Pristine are sitting pretty, holding the $50,000 down payment which is equal to the $50,000 liquidated damages. There's really nothing for you to initiate; Slowpay has to come to you. If he wants part of that $50,000 back—on the grounds that it's too high a price to pay for failure to fulfill his contractual obligation—but you're unwilling to part with it, then Slowpay is going to have to sue. And at least conceptually, this is a difficult kind of lawsuit, because Slowpay is asking the court to rule that a contractual provision he was willing to live with at the time of signing—so willing, in fact, that he put up equivalent funds as a down payment—is not a binding liquidated damages clause but rather an invalid penalty.

---

[25]   See Section 7.4.2. The various categories of relations between lawyers are discussed in Section 7.1.
[26]   See Section 7.3.

Of course, all things being equal, you and Pristine would prefer that Slowpay doesn't sue. Lawsuits are costly, time-consuming and generate ulcers; in addition, there is always the possibility you could lose. As a result, if Slowpay begins to make a nuisance of himself, there might be some inclination on Pristine's part to achieve quiet enjoyment by refunding a small portion of the $50,000 which he holds.

However—and I can't overestimate the point—in this kind of situation it's essential that you exhibit a posture of great strength toward your adversary. Any sign of softness in your legal position or of disposition to settle would be a real mistake. So, when Slowpay's lawyer first begins nosing around to explore the possibilities of some sort of settlement, your initial reaction should be:

"Why are you talking about settling? It's all settled! Look, our clients made a deal; you and I approved it. Your client failed to come through with the price. My client keeps the $50,000. It's a matter of principle for my client, and it ought to be for yours also. Listen, Jack, if the painting had *increased* in value to $300,000 between the time of signing and the closing—as would have been the case if a third party had come in the door waving a check for three big ones—my client would still have felt obligated to sell it to Slowpay for the $250,000 price. We've foregone other potential deals, which are unlikely to be around any more. We firmly believe we're entitled to the liquidated damages provided in the contract."

And so on, *ad nauseam*. But be careful not to get carried away with your own rhetoric and thus blinded to the reality of the situation—which is that the $50,000 is a pretty neat windfall, allowing your client (assuming his cash flow position isn't precarious) the luxury of initiating a search for another buyer at an attractively reduced price.

Now, let's examine this from the viewpoint of Slowpay's lawyer. Poor fellow; his position isn't enviable—as a matter of fact, it's the poorest of the six lawyers' roles involved in these three variants of the problem, because he (i) represents a wrongdoer (ii) who has already put up the money, and (iii) has to initiate a tough court case to overturn the provision.

This may be naive, but if I were to find myself in that kind of posture, I would consider it very important—not as a legal matter, but in appealing to Pristine's sense of fairness—to have a reasonable explanation for why Slowpay defaulted on the deal. This is another way of saying that the strategy of Slowpay's lawyer should be two-pronged: to give Pristine cause for concern that Slowpay might sue and could prevail, and to prevent Pristine from becoming too self-righteous and rigid in his position. If Pristine feels that Slowpay simply changed his mind and decided to renege on the contract, Pristine is unlikely to give Slowpay's proposals for relief much of a reception. On the other hand, if Slowpay had arranged for the necessary funds and then his financing source let him down—or if a sudden family emergency developed in which Slowpay had to use the money for a worthy cause—then at least Slowpay's lawyer can paint his client's case in sympathetic hues. I'm *not* suggesting that Slowpay's lawyer should make up a tale out of whole cloth, but simply that if a reasonable explanation for Slowpay's default does exist, his lawyer ought to make sure that Pristine—not just Pristine's lawyer—is aware of it, and not operating under the erroneous impression that Slowpay's breach of contract was totally arbitrary.

The unspoken premise behind such advice is that when lawyers negotiate, there is considerable verbal jockeying for position—a marshalling of the evidence, both legal and factual, to support the respective cases.[27] There's no question in my mind that, through such dialogue, an able lawyer can meaningfully promote his client's cause. But remember, there's another side to this particular coin; if you carelessly blurt out the *wrong* thought, you can actually hurt your client's case. And perhaps a brief discussion of the need for constant vigilance—for thinking through the possible negative side effects of your words *before* they utter from your big mouth—is in order here.

It's no secret that in this complex world we inhabit, operative facts are multi-faceted and often ambiguous. Propositions that, upon first glance, seem to cut in your favor have an annoying propensity to turn against you. Double edges abound; the argument that's beneficial for one aspect may work to your detriment on another. If the benefit outweighs the detriment, you utilize the argument and seek to minimize the negative impact; but if the opposite is true—and assuming disclosure is within your control—you're better off not introducing the matter at all. This may strike you as an obvious point, and yet we often become careless, focusing only on the positive impact and oblivious to the negative possibilities.

To illustrate, let's assume that you (as Pristine's lawyer) and your adversary are debating the basic question of whether the $50,000 constitutes a valid liquidated damages provision or an unenforceable penalty. Now, without delving too deeply into the applicable law, I seem to recall that a principal issue here is whether the provision was indeed an honest attempt to liquidate the damages; and that two key criteria for this determination are (i) whether the damage actually suf-

---

[27]   This is a subject discussed in Section 7.3.8.

ferable by the aggrieved party upon breach of contract is likely to be difficult to calculate (the greater the degree of prospective difficulty, the more it resembles an enforceable liquidated damages clause), and (ii) whether the provision could be applicable to a wide range of breaches, some serious and some not (which cuts toward penalty status). Your adversary has just made the second argument—that the clause could apply to a whole host of possible breaches and therefore would be viewed as a penalty by the court—and you are casting about for ammunition to rebut that charge.

Suddenly, you remember your client telling you that, prior to contracting with Slowpay, Pristine had attempted to sell the painting to another well known art world figure, Mr. Curator. Aha, you think, this is good rebuttal material. After all, Slowpay's lawyer is arguing, in effect, that it's not determinable whether, in the event of a breach by Slowpay, Pristine would have sold the painting, or kept it, or donated it to a museum, or whatever; and that each of these presents a quite different damage situation. So you say: "Now, wait a second, Jack. Pristine actually tried to sell the painting to Mr. Curator before Slowpay came along. This is a strong indication of Pristine's intentions—good evidence that the clause was really only applicable to a single type of damage situation."

Fine. That's just great; you really made some points with Slowpay's lawyer on that one. But now, let's say that you end up in litigation, and Slowpay's lawyer deposes Mr. Curator (whose existence, but for your remark, might have passed unnoticed). And lo and behold, Mr. Curator's testimony (which you now recall to your chagrin) is that he, Curator, was willing to pay $230,000 for the painting; and that after hearing of the Slowpay contract, Curator told Pristine that if the deal fell through, Pristine should come back to see Curator. This, of course, is devastating testimony on the *other* issue—the relative difficulty of fixing the damages in advance. The knowledge that a third party exists who is willing to take the painting off Pristine's hands at a specified price means that the potential extent of Pristine's damage (the $20,000 differential between Slowpay's price and Curator's offer, plus incidental expenses) was readily cognizable. Your failure to anticipate the detriment flowing from this seemingly beneficial fact could end up costing your client his liquidated damages.

Now, getting back to situation A where Pristine is holding the $50,000, I would consider it totally inappropriate for you (as Pristine's lawyer) to make a first offer of settlement—even if your client is willing to compromise the matter. Let the first offer come from Slowpay's lawyer. Moreover, if Slowpay's proposal is one you would never consider accepting (as where he asks for $35,000 back out of the $50,000 deposit), the optimal strategy would be to pooh-pooh the whole idea and refrain from making an immediate counter offer. What you can do at that point, however, is to indicate[28] that if Slowpay's lawyer were to suggest something reasonable, your client might consider affording him modest relief.

For example—and I realize this is oversimplified, but I want to make the point—suppose your client is willing to refund up to $10,000 to Slowpay. The least you can offer with a straight face is $5,000. To do so before your adversary has opened his mouth is to practically invite a $40,000-to-$45,000 counter, which gets you nowhere. Even to do so *after* Slowpay has proposed a refund of $30,000 suggests a settlement in the $15,000–$20,000 range. Your strategy should be to get Slowpay's lawyer down into *your* ballpark, before *you* start negotiating. If you can induce talk of $15,000 or $20,000 from your adversary, and then make your $5,000 offer, you have the kind of bid-and-asked that should land your final settlement in the area of $10,000.

Well, of course, if you're Slowpay's lawyer, you have to be aware that Pristine's attorney is likely to adopt such tactics. All you can do is put up a brave front, try to get across both your client's strong intention of suing to vindicate his rights and the sympathetic nature of the breach, and attempt to elicit a figure from Pristine's lawyer as early as possible in the bargaining. But I don't envy your task.

Now, let's move to situation B, in which Slowpay has made no down payment, and Pristine's remedies are strictly contractual. If Slowpay won't hand over the $50,000 to which your client is entitled, you'll just have to sue him for it. And since Slowpay realizes that the maximum Pristine can receive throught the lawsuit is the $50,000 claimed as liquidated damages, there is little financial incentive for Slowpay to pay over the full amount. Slowpay and his lawyer will assume that your client is aware of the legal fees he'll incur in going to court, as well as the uncertainty of outcome on the penalty issue; as a result, Slowpay is likely to believe he can settle the matter for less than $50,000. And he's undoubtedly right.

If you look at the situation from Pristine's perspective, no matter how you slice it, Pristine's not going to end up with $50,000 in his pocket—unless Slowpay forks over the cash voluntarily. If Pristine has to go to court, his attorney fees will substantially reduce the amount

---

[28] "Indicate" is a much abused word in lawyers' prose. So often it is used flabbily, where a much more positive assertion (such as "he stated") is warranted. Yet occasionally "indicate" can be useful, where (as in the textual sentence) the writer desires to describe the act of getting across a position without expounding on it in detail.

he realizes, even as a winner. And so, if you can negotiate a good settlement for him—especially one that approximates his liquidated damages less a full trial legal fee—Pristine is probably well advised to snap it up, so as to avoid the risk of losing in court, as well as the inconvenience and delay of judicial proceedings. Even a somewhat lesser settlement might be desirable, simply to resolve the matter and enable Pristine to move on to other things.

Thus, you can readily see how critical to negotiations is the identity of the fund-holder—the old saw about possession amounting to nine-tenths of the law being perhaps the truest of all aphorisms. This is a consideration that lies at the root of practicality and ought to be factored into your analysis of all legal problems involving money or property—not only after the fact (as here) but *in advance,* as you go about negotiating the terms of a business deal.

One of the major questions you face in this situation B is whether to begin negotiating for your damages *prior to* having instituted a lawsuit. It's difficult to generalize on this point—and other practitioners may not share this view—but in my opinion, it's generally preferable to attempt to negotiate before suing. Even the initiation of a suit can be expensive for your client, and it's just possible that Slowpay will come through with a satisfactory settlement. Perhaps even more important, a lawsuit can often serve to exacerbate the already strained relations between the parties, rendering productive negotiations impossible.

Nevertheless, in order to get anywhere in this kind of situation, you have to convince Slowpay's lawyer that (i) you're fully prepared to institute suit, if necessary, and (ii) the odds are you'll prevail. Only when both of these perceptions exist does Slowpay have real incentive to settle at a decent price. He has to be concerned about finding himself in a time-consuming lawsuit which is likely to result in his losing the $50,000, plus paying his own expensive legal costs—an obviously unattractive proposition for Slowpay.[29] Perhaps the only way to get this across to Slowpay is· to serve him with a summons and complaint; if you seem to be going nowhere in the negotiations, it may be advisable to take that step before proceeding with further efforts at compromise.

As to your ability to win, it would be sheer foolishness to admit to any weakness in your position. Quite the contrary, you ought to buttress your case by providing the other side with citations—perhaps even a short memorandum—favorable to your position. And if you could show that your actual damages might be *greater* than the

---

[29] And perhaps equally unattractive for Slowpay's lawyer, who (given Slowpay's penchant for defaulting) has to worry about payment of his own fee!

$50,000 liquidated provision, Slowpay would have less incentive to go to court—since a victory on the penalty point might leave him in even worse shape.

Give some thought to other means of bringing pressure on Slowpay. For example, assuming that Slowpay enjoys a good reputation in the art world (or in some other line of endeavor), the fear that his breach may be publicized could render him more amenable to an attractive settlement. Don't underestimate your position here. You may not be holding the money, but you're a little like the motorist who, while stopped at a red light, is struck in the rear by another car; there's no question about the party at fault, and it's merely a matter of agreeing upon a satisfactory price.

Try to induce Slowpay's lawyer to make the first offer here. If it's a foolish offer (such as total damages of $5,000), you're best advised to simply ignore it. But if the proposal is bona fide—say, something in the $20,000–$30,000 range—then the negotiations can get underway, with you naming a figure close to the liquidated provision. If no offer is forthcoming from Slowpay, then it's permissible in this situation B (as contrasted with your stronger, cash-rich position in situation A) to show your disposition to negotiate by stating you'll accept $45,000. Without giving up very much, at least you've laid the concept of negotiations on the table; you can never tell where that's going to lead.

Now, let's turn to situation C, where the $50,000 is held in escrow by a third party stakeholder. The probable scenario here is that you will claim the funds on behalf of Pristine; the escrow agent will notify Slowpay's lawyer of your claim; and Slowpay's lawyer will dispute the claim. If the escrow agreement is worded the way most of them are, it will authorize the escrow agent to hold the funds pending resolution of the dispute, either through a court judgment or settlement.[30]

Accordingly, in order to get the money out of escrow, you will either have to bring a suit or reach an accommodation with Slowpay. In this respect, your position is not unlike that in situation B—and nowhere near as comfortable for you as situation A. However, as contrasted with situation B, here Slowpay doesn't have the use of the money either. It's sitting there with the third party stakeholder, completely out of play. If interest is accruing, the escrow agreement probably provides that it will pass in proportion to the ultimate dis-

---

[30] Representing Pristine, you undoubtedly would have tried to insert a provision in the escrow agreement directing the escrow agent to turn the $50,000 over to your client automatically upon Slowpay's default; but since matters of default and blame are hard to pin down prospectively, Slowpay's lawyer—as well as the escrow agent, who doesn't want to get caught in the middle between two contending factions—would presumably have resisted inclusion of such a direction.

tribution of the underlying escrow fund. Since it's more likely that Pristine will eventually emerge victorious, Slowpay can't even look forward to any return on the funds—as he could in situation B, where pending resolution of the dispute he has the unrestricted use of the money.[31] And so, additional incentives exist for Slowpay to settle this matter, in order to secure for his own use whatever portion of the $50,000 he can achieve in the bargaining.

If you wanted to summarize the three situations in terms of probable dollar values of settlements, you would say that Pristine will end up with the most money in a settlement under situation A (perhaps $40,000 or $45,000); that Pristine will receive the least (maybe $25,000) under situation B; and that under situation C, he is likely to end up in the $35,000 range.

In this situation C, you definitely ought to talk before suing. Everyone realizes that in an escrow context, if you cannot reach a negotiated accomodation, litigation will have to follow; as a result, initiating a lawsuit doesn't do too much for you psychologically.

In situations such as C, I like to speak to the other lawyer on a man-to-man, down-to-earth basis.

"Look, Jack, we both know where we stand. Your guy owes mine the $50,000. My guy doesn't have the money, and if you want to hold me up, I'll have to sue you for it. And that'll cost my guy something. But on the other hand, your guy will have to pay legal fees, too. So for everyone's benefit, let's strike a deal."

Having an escrow in place makes it very easy to move into settlement talks, leads to much more candid discussions at earlier stages, and is more likely to result in a negotiated bargain.

9.4. A TALE OF TWO ASSOCIATES

Here's a brief vignette concerning the professional relations between two associates—Stan, the senior, and Joan, the junior—and their mutual interaction with Paul, the partner for whom they work. There are three segments to the story. The scenario for part one, which we'll critique through a series of flashbacks, is as follows.

Paul (the partner), whose specialty is tax law, calls Stan (the senior

---

[31] Of course, in situation B, if Pristine were to initiate and prevail in a lawsuit, he would likely be awarded interest at the statutory rate from the date of breach; however, this would usually be less than Slowpay can earn with the money during the interim. Moreover, if there's ultimately a settlement, the interest factor often disappears from the calculation.

associate) to his office. Paul proceeds to describe a transaction that one of his corporate partners has devised for an important corporate client, involving a recapitalization of the company. The tax issue is whether the transaction will qualify as a tax-free reorganization. Paul asks for a memorandum to be prepared on the subject, reflecting appropriate research and problem analysis. Because some time pressure exists, Paul advises Stan that he can utilize the services of Joan (the junior associate) to assist in this task.

Stan returns to his own office, calls in Joan, outlines the problem to her, and tells Joan to research the subject and prepare a memo. Several days later, Stan receives Joan's memo. Stan, who has done no independent work on the project and is heavily involved in other assignments, reviews the memo rather quickly, suggests one or two minor changes, and passes the memo on to Paul. The "From" line at the beginning of the memo contains the names of both Stan and Joan. Nothing in the memo itself, or in any accompanying note, identifies Joan as the principal author.

A few days pass. Then, at a firm luncheon which all three of the lawyers are attending, Paul approaches Stan and says: "That was a fine memo you prepared on the recapitalization." Stan accepts the plaudits, without mentioning Joan's role. Joan happens to overhear the exchange.

Let's pause at this point, back up, and examine what has occurred. We'll begin with the initial assignment. Paul knew that Joan was going to work on the project; should he have invited Joan to his office along with Stan?[32] Well, that might have been a good idea, particularly if there were some nuances to the problem that Paul wished to convey directly to the lawyers involved,[33] and Joan would have been made to feel more a part of the team. But it's certainly not crucial. And since Stan and Joan are in a clear senior/junior relationship, Paul should not have to involve himself in the division of labor between them. Although he knew Joan would be involved, Paul was obviously looking to Stan to bear the ultimate responsibility on what would emerge.

How about Stan's style in calling Joan in and turning the project over to her?[34] Nothing improper about that—assuming Stan has had enough prior experience with Joan to consider her capable, and provided that Joan knows something about the reorganization area.

---

[32] A subject discussed in Sections 5.2.1 (from the junior associate's viewpoint) and 10.2.1 (from the partner's).

[33] The advantage of not having to rely on a second-hand account is covered in Section 3.3.1.

[34] The general subject of relationships between senior and junior associates is explored in Sections 5.2.1 (from the junior's viewpoint) and 5.2.2 (from the senior's).

If, on the other hand, Stan had reservations about Joan's competence or felt she was unfamiliar with the issues posed, then it would have been prudent for Stan to outline the contours of the assignment in somewhat more detail, advising Joan what to look for, pointing out the principal considerations, and so forth.

We come now to Stan's review of Joan's work. If Stan is highly knowledgeable in this particular area of recapitalization, it may be appropriate for him to review Joan's memo without engaging in any original research or analysis on his own. But assuming Stan had never dealt with a problem quite like this one, then I think he should have probed some of the source material on his own—not to duplicate Joan's work, but to place Stan in a position to evaluate what Joan has turned up. Particularly if there is a key case or ruling at the core of Joan's analysis, there's no substitute for Stan doing his homework and forming his own opinion as to its relevance or distinguishability.

And I have to wonder just how carefully Stan reviewed Joan's work, when the sole changes were a few fly specks. To be sure, Joan may have done a superior job (and Paul's subsequent misdirected praise would indicate that to be the case); and yet, I find it hard to believe that a more experienced and presumably wiser attorney cannot add *something* of substance (or style, or organization, or emphasis) to a written document prepared by a junior. It doesn't seem to me that Stan is doing what Paul asked *him* to do—namely, to lend *his* analytical skills and mature judgment to this problem.

Now for the question of the ''From: Stan and Joan'' byline on the memo. If Stan had performed on the task as he should have—reviewing the memo intensively and suggesting significant changes—then the joint authorship designation would have been entirely proper. But in view of Stan's minor contribution, it seems to me he should have chosen a better way to convey the realities of the situation to Paul. Perhaps a covering handwritten note would have done the trick,[35] along these lines: ''Here is the memo on recapitalization that Joan has prepared. I have reviewed it, and concur in the analysis.'' This serves to advise Paul that the memo is not Stan's original work, but rather Joan's; and if that fact bothers Paul—if he wants more of Stan in that memo—then Paul is in a position to call upon Stan directly. Without such information, Paul has no way of knowing whether the memo is in reality a joint product or (as was the case here) the junior's work with the senior functioning solely in a cursory reviewing role. By the way, had Stan recognized that such a note would be appropriate under the given facts, this might have provided him the

---

[35] The subject of attaching caveats to a written product is discussed in Section 3.2.8.

incentive to review Joan's work more thoroughly—in order to be able to
fairly characterize the product as joint.

Another purpose for such a note is to ensure that Joan will reap any
resulting benefits if the memo is first-rate. Otherwise, Paul doesn't
know who deserves the credit—as evidenced by his congratulatory
remark to Stan. Incidentally, do you feel this showed good judgment
on Paul's part, particularly with Joan sitting there in the room? I don't
think so. Paul should have either praised both Stan and Joan equally,
or inquired privately of Stan as to the division of labor[36] and directed
his plaudits accordingly. It's important for a partner to praise an
associate's work when it's excellent;[37] where the authorship is dual,
the laurels ought to be shared.[38]

It's quite clear, of course, that Stan acted improperly in accepting
Paul's plaudits without indicating that the work was principally
Joan's. This is just a matter of basic human relations. And by the
way, Paul would definitely be impressed (as I always am in like circumstances) were Stan unselfishly to shift the credit to Joan; that kind
of self-effacement, much too rare in the competitive world of legal
practice, shows real character.

How about Joan, overhearing Paul's misguided compliment to Stan
and Stan's presumptuous acceptance—should Joan do anything about
this miscarriage of justice? On balance, I don't think so. If Joan does
good work, this will ultimately emerge, and Paul will know. If Stan is
as distasteful a character as he seems to be, there's not much Joan
can do to gain the partner's plaudits short of identifying herself to
Paul as the memo's real author—an action not calculated to endear
her to anyone. The best Joan can hope for is that when the next periodic evaluations are made, and the firm asks Stan his opinion of
Joan's work,[39] her efforts will bear fruit.

Now, let's proceed to part two of our story. A week has passed.
Stan telephones Joan. "Paul wants to see us," says Stan, "and he
sounds hopping mad." They enter Paul's office with some trepidation. Paul is pacing back and forth behind his chair. "I'm furious!" he

---

[36] One can elicit a more candid response on this kind of question if it's
posed *prior to* any indication of whether the questioner liked or disliked the
memo.

[37] See Section 10.4.1.

[38] If the partner has no opportunity to personally convey his favorable reaction to the junior associate, he can ask the senior associate to pass on his
remarks—but the impact is much more effective if the praise is delivered
directly.

[39] I'm assuming that the firm solicits evaluations of younger associates from
their seniors, who are often in a much better position than the partners to
assess the newcomers' worth. See Sections 10.4.3 and 10.4.4 on the evaluation process.

exclaims. "We sent that recapitalization memo on to our client, who turned it over to his accounting firm; and *their* tax people discovered a revenue ruling—not even *mentioned* in our memo—which directly refutes our conclusion! Here, look at this. . . ."[40] And sure enough, the adverse ruling is devastating; the law firm has simply goofed. Paul turns to Stan and says: "How could this have happened?"

I'm sure this will seem painful to readers who have been sympathizing with poor Joan, but I think that she ought to speak up here and accept full blame for the omission. It's a difficult admission, but the right step to take under the circumstances. And if Paul is any kind of person, Joan's adoption of sole responsibility will enhance her in Paul's eyes. Anyone can make a mistake; we've all erred on occasion. The mistake may ultimately be forgotten but the integrity displayed will linger.

But what if Joan doesn't speak up at this point? How should Stan handle the situation? Remember, this is the same Stan who accepted initial credit for the memo without blinking an eye or sharing any portion with Joan. It's a tricky situation and I've wrestled with my recommendation—but where I come out is that Stan should probably say, in effect: "I know I accepted credit for the memo when it was praised, but that was wrong of me to do; the research was Joan's and I performed only a cursory review." Now, I don't suggest this because I feel it's somehow better to lack integrity than to be incompetent; as a matter of fact, this is a more damaging admission for Stan to make than to accept responsibility for the research error—although his forthrightness, however tardy, might earn some points. Rather, it's because at this point, Paul is entitled to know the full facts—i.e., that both Joan and Stan committed errors, but that hers was one of research while his was one of judgment.

The alternative is for Stan to swallow hard and accept his share of the blame. Once Stan has placed his name on the memo with no further elucidation, that's the price of such association. Which illustrates, of course, why Stan would have been better off putting Paul on notice from the outset that the memo was basically Joan's. Had he done so, and assuming Paul (with full knowledge of Stan's minor role) hadn't asked him to do more, it would now be harder for Paul to blame Stan for the omission. After all, if Paul had wanted Stan to perform the actual research—perhaps because of his concern that Joan might miss just such a key ruling—then Paul could have asked Stan to undertake the task. But without any indication of Stan's *actual* role, Paul was entitled to assume that Stan was involved in the research as well as the analysis.

---

[40] Feedback—good or bad—on associates' performance is discussed in Section 10.4.

Now, let's turn to part three of the problem. The corporate partner on the account, the client, and Paul all put their heads together and come up with an alternative means of accomplishing the recapitalization that doesn't run afoul of the particular adverse revenue ruling. Paul directs Stan to analyze the new program in terms of whether it qualifies as a tax-free reorganization. This time, as you might expect, Stan gets much more involved along with Joan in the research and analysis. But now a different kind of problem arises.

It seems that no regulations or published rulings bear directly on the specific question raised by the revised transaction. In order to arrive at a conclusion, it becomes necessary to reason, analogize, distinguish and the like. Joan concludes that the transaction will qualify as a tax-free reorganization and, moreover, that if a ruling were applied for, the Internal Revenue Service would grant it. Stan, viewing the same facts and precedents, emerges with a different view—that the IRS would not grant a favorable ruling, would contest this treatment on audit, and would prevail in court. Stan and Joan discuss the question at some length, but neither becomes reconciled to the other's views. How should they handle this vis-à-vis Paul?[41]

Well, I think they would be doing Paul a serious disservice if they didn't advise him there are two possible views on this subject, identifying each view and viewholder. The alternative—to paper over their controversy and present a united front with which neither is entirely comfortable—is simply not the best way to proceed. Legal questions are difficult and complex; reasonable people often disagree on conclusions, on inferences, on possible courses of action. Paul is in the best position to decide which of the two views will constitute the firm's position.

If, however, instead of this solution, Stan were to ask Joan to re-work the memo in accordance with Stan's views[42] (which Joan doesn't share), then Joan ought to label those views as Stan's and advise Paul—perhaps in a footnote[43]—that she dissents from Stan's conclusions. Otherwise, Paul is entitled to assume that Joan is in full agreement.

Stan, for his part, ought to have sufficient self-confidence to realize that disagreements over such matters can exist, and should not try to

---

[41] The issue of associates' disputes is discussed in Section 5.2.1.

[42] Actually, it might be unwise for the written memo to contain Stan's negative view, as the document may come back to haunt the taxpayer at a later date. See Section 3.2.9 on the decision whether or not to memorialize lawyers' musings. In part, also, the question of whether to communicate with Paul in writing or orally might turn on the associates' reading of Paul's idiosyncracies; see Sections 5.1.1 (from the associate's viewpoint) and 10.3 (from the partner's).

[43] See Section 3.2.8.

overcome the dispute by virtue of his seniority but rather through the substantive rationale he can bring to bear on the point. If that doesn't work, then he shouldn't fear confronting the split openly with Paul. Presumably, Paul will give Stan's more experienced views somewhat more weight than Joan's.

Now, assume the conflict is brought to Paul's attention and, after due consideration, Paul concludes that the transaction should be tax-free and that a ruling would probably be granted. In other words, Paul agrees with Joan's position. What should Stan do at that point? Well, if Stan remains unconvinced by the cumulative weight of Paul's and Joan's views that the transaction qualifies, then Stan ought not to relinquish his views.[44] Paul should fully understand that he hasn't been able to convince Stan of Paul's views on the transaction. This will have the effect of making Paul more cautious in what he's doing. He might call in another partner for an additional opinion. Or he might tinker further with the form or substance of the recapitalization, in order to overcome Stan's problem. Or the additional uncertainty might tilt the balance in favor of going to the IRS for an advance ruling, rather than proceeding on the basis of the firm's opinion alone.

On the issue of whether to apply for an advance ruling or not, however, this is more a matter of feel than of legal substance. Once Stan has staked out his position on this issue, I don't think he should continue to press the point, since this much more judgmental issue is really the partner's call.

9.5. A MATTER OF OPINION

Your firm has been retained as special counsel by Gamy Inc. in connection with a private placement of its equity securities—in this case, an issue of convertible debentures—to a group of insurance companies assembled by Gamy's investment banker. Your firm has represented Gamy from time to time in the past, so you're generally familiar with its affairs and know the top executives. The partner in charge of this assignment, who's quite busy on other matters, is relying on you (a relatively senior associate in the firm) to manage things pretty much on your own; and the principal negotiations thus far have taken place between you and counsel for the lead insurance company.

As in most private placements, the lawyer for the insurance com-

---

[44] See Section 5.1.3. This does *not* mean that Stan should spell out his objections in front of the client. It's really up to Paul as to how the matter should be handled at that level. Usually, the firm presents a single viewpoint—although if the area is particularly murky, Paul might say to the client that *he* believes the deal will be tax-free "although others in my office do not."

panies has prepared a draft purchase agreement. The schedule calls
for signing the agreement within the next week, with the closing to
occur a month later. The draft agreement provides for your firm to
render an extensive legal opinion on various matters, including an
opinion (which mirrors a representation by Gamy to the same general
effect) that the company's operations aren't violative of applicable
laws.[45]

Although you've never performed any investigation into the matter
(and haven't been asked to do so by the client), you're generally
aware that one aspect of Gamy's business could be deemed to violate
the price discrimination provisions of the Robinson-Patman Act. As
with most issues under that statute, this presents a complex question,
and one or more defenses might be available depending on the underlying factual circumstances. You can see, however, that this may
become an issue in connection with the financing; and your training
and instincts tell you *not* to duck the problem now, hoping that things
will somehow work themselves out. Issues such as these rarely
evaporate, and to defer their resolution to a time when you must act
under the pressure of events merely exacerbates the difficulty. Anticipate the problem, and try to resolve it at an early date.[46]

Not unnaturally, your first thought may be whether someone else is
in a position to give the necessary opinion.[47] And sure enough, in
reviewing other recent Gamy transactions (including a bank loan in
which your firm didn't participate), you discover that similar
no-violation-of-law opinions have indeed been rendered by the company's inside general counsel. You know him as an able practitioner;
presumably, he must have satisfied himself as to the potential
Robinson-Patman problem before giving the opinion. If he's willing to
provide the same opinion here, and counsel for the insurance companies is prepared to accept it from him in lieu of your firm, then
you're out of the soup.

But you also have another concern. Assuming inside counsel is of
the view that there's no violation, your conduct shouldn't suggest to
your adversary that a problem exists. If you simply told the
purchasers' lawyer that the inside counsel would provide the

---

[45] I might say this is the kind of opinion that, because of its breadth, many
lawyers—including myself—would balk at giving. "How can I be expected to
know each aspect of my client's business," whines the attorney, "and which
minor laws might be transgressed daily?" At the very least, he would insist
on various materiality qualifiers and knowledge caveats. For purposes of this
hypothetical, however, let's assume that the language is sufficiently hedged
to form the basis for a valid request by the purchaser's counsel.
[46] Anticipating the need for making difficult decisions is the subject of Section
8.2.
[47] Among other things, if a favorable opinion *is* forthcoming, this would tend
to support the company's position in making the correlative representation.

no-violation opinion, your adversary may become suspicious. And if, as is likely, he then starts asking specific questions, you might have both ethical and practical problems in not being altogether forthright—problems which are within bounds at this point, given the fact that you really don't know whether a violation exists.

So, you decide to proceed in the following fashion. In addition to the no-violation opinion, your firm is being asked to opine on a number of other matters which relate to Gamy's day-to-day operations; e.g., that the company isn't in default under any of its agreements, that it's qualified in all states where it does substantial business, and so on. You envision telling the purchaser's counsel that in order to give all of these essentially factual opinions, it would take considerable effort on your part to familiarize yourself with Gamy's operations; that this would not only be very time-consuming but also quite expensive for the company; and that you therefore suggest such opinions be given by the company's inside counsel, who's entirely competent and knowledgeable in these areas—with your firm still opining on the purely legal matters, such as due incorporation, capitalization, authorization, etc. Such an approach would be unlikely to draw attention to the Robinson-Patman Act.[48]

Of course, you have to consult with Gamy's inside counsel before implementing this plan.[49] And it would be foolish not to level with *him*—revealing your concern over the no-violation opinion in view of the possible Robinson-Patman problem. Be careful to do this in a way that doesn't suggest *he* might be more willing to give the opinion than you—without regard to the merits—because of his position as inside counsel. The natural tack for you to take is: "Look, Joe, in effect you've already given that Robinson-Patman Act opinion to the banks. I'd prefer not to get involved in such a complex question, and for me to do so would cost Gamy some unnecessary fees. So it makes sense for you to give the opinion here also. But I don't want to single out this one area, since that might make the purchaser's counsel nervous."[49a]

Let's assume that inside counsel goes along with your plan—after all, anything that saves the company outside legal fees can't be all bad! So you approach counsel for the insurance companies to request

---

[48]   The subject of "creative motivation" such as this is discussed in Section 7.3.5 *N.B.* I would *not* be recommending this approach if you knew or were pretty sure that the violation of law existed—in which case ethical restraints and potential problems under Rule 10b-5 would enter the picture.

[49]   Relations between outside and inside counsel are explored in Sections 7.2.3 (from the outside viewpoint) and 5.3.1 (from the inside).

[49a]   I'm assuming here that the inside counsel knows more than you do about the Robinson-Patman problem. If the degree of knowledge were reversed, then this conversation would involve unacceptable deception.

that this entire segment be carved out of your opinion and handled by company counsel. Shift gears now, and put yourself in the place of the attorney for the insurance companies: viewed from his vantage point, how should he deal with this request?[50]

Well, as the number of companies hiring experienced inside counsel has proliferated, it's not uncommon for certain opinions to emanate from them. The real key here for purchaser's counsel is his perception as to the competence and independence of inside counsel. If suspicion exists that the inside counsel would elevate his sense of company loyalty above his professional responsibilities, purchaser's counsel is unlikely to accept the inside counsel's opinion. In practice, a distinction is often made between matters that are particularly within inside counsel's knowledge or are fairly routine—where use of outside counsel could be deemed to represent an unnecessary expenditure of company funds—and areas which trouble purchaser's counsel enough to seek an extra degree of comfort.

And so, a typical reaction of the attorney for the insurance companies to your request might be: "Well, I don't mind if inside counsel gives the opinion on due qualification in various states, but I want *you* to give the opinion that the company isn't violating any laws." Not that the purchaser's counsel suspects a particular violation of law exists, but merely that the potential harm from a material violation warrants having your firm address the issue. Let's assume that this *is* his response here. What do you do?

You're in a difficult position. Pressing the issue further can suggest to your opposite number that a problem exists. Sure, you can stress the potential expenses to the company from your investigation; you can proffer some absurd examples[51] of laws whose petty violation you wouldn't uncover in a month of digging (minor OSHA violations are always useful in this regard); but if he stands firm on the point, acquiescence is probably the better part of valor.

At this point, it's time to call a meeting with the inside general counsel and the Gamy executive who's in charge of the financing—in this relatively small company, probably the president. You relate the problem, indicating your concern about being able to give the no-violation opinion at the closing; if it turns out you can't, the purchasers will have an out—since your favorable opinion is a condition of their obligation to close. After digesting the matter, the president speaks to you as follows:

"Look, Don, it's no secret to you that I'm extremely anxious for this agreement to be signed. I want those in-

---

[50] See Section 8.4 of *Anatomy* on popular sidesteps by lawyers in giving opinions, and how the recipient ought to deal with them.
[51] See Section 7.3.5.

surance companies to cross the bridge—to fix their names to the contract. And I'll be frank; I don't want to introduce any problems at this stage—problems that could, under any circumstances, cause them to change their minds.

"Now, as I understand it, at this juncture—the signing of the agreement—you don't actually have to *give* your opinion; the agreement merely recites what your opinion will have to say at the *closing* in order to keep them obligated. So my suggestion is to say nothing more at the present time and go along with the opinion language recited in the agreement. Once the agreement is signed, you can pursue your investigation into the Robinson-Patman question. If you feel, on the basis of what you find, that you can't give the opinion at the closing, then we'll put you into a position to give the opinion by discontinuing any practices that violate the Act."

Well, now you're on the spot. In fact, it's one of those times you wish a partner were available for consultation![52] You're not very comfortable with your client's stance of less than full disclosure. Yet, you can well understand his nervousness—and his undertaking to change the practice should you find it unlawful sounds pretty reasonable. . . . In situations like this, it's wise not to respond immediately. You really need time to think, in order to arrive at a reasoned conclusion. And so, you pose some questions and deal with certain collateral issues, as follows.

How about the fact, you say to the president, that the ambiguous wording of the opinion language may apply more broadly than just to the state of affairs at the closing. The provision could be construed to cover not only present violations of law but past violations also—at least violations that existed at the date the agreement was signed. "All right," answers the president. "If that's the case and you feel it's necessary, then once we've discontinued the practice, you can disclose to the insurance companies what we did in the past; and I'll take my chances that this won't kill the deal."

You try another tack with him.

"You should understand, Harold, that, in addition to the legal *opinion*, the company is also asked to *represent* that its operations aren't in violation of law. If that representation turns out to have been untrue at the time it was made

---

[52] And, of course, this sort of decision should *always* be kicked upstairs to a partner—although for purposes of this example, we're going to assume you are forced to handle it yourself.

(and it's not clear that *this* problem is solved by curing the misrepresentation before the closing), then not only do the insurance companies have the right to walk away but, at least in theory, they have a lawsuit against you for damages—at the very least, for the expenses they've incurred in the deal. And if they find out there's a problem *after* the closing, since the representations survive, the debentures you're issuing could accelerate and become due.''

Strong stuff. But the president understands; he appreciates your advice; these are risks he's willing to take as a business matter. At bottom, the president is convinced he can talk the institutions out of calling the debentures or taking other action against Gamy. "Listen, Don, they're going to have so much invested in our company that they can't *afford* to call a default!" And so, you're just going to have to confront the ultimate question.

It's a tough call, but on balance, I think you can permit the agreement to be signed without raising the point. Here's your line of reasoning. First, the president's undertaking to square things away prior to the closing removes the real sting from the situation. Second, you're not really *sure* any violation exists—you've never investigated the matter and inside counsel seems relatively comfortable. (If, on the other hand, the violation were certain, the decision to proceed would be more difficult—which suggests the advisability of delaying commencement of your investigation until after the agreement is signed.) Third, the Robinson-Patman issue has never been raised specifically by the insurance companies; the opinion language on violations of law is broadly stated, without specific reference. (Your decision might be altogether different if the insurance companies had focused on this aspect of the company's operations and asked pointed questions about price discrimination.)

Finally—and this is the toughest reason for me to articulate, the pill that many young lawyers find most difficult to swallow—the strong feelings of your client on this issue have to count for something. You don't practice law in a vacuum. In matters such as these, you bear no juridical responsibility as an ''officer of the court''. You're paid to be an advocate, a partisan.[53] And while you should never do anything that's dishonest or unethical or can't be squared with your conscience, once you're over *that* hurdle (here, by virtue of the first three reasons[54]), why not help your client keep his deal warm.

---

[53] See Sections 6.1 and 6.6.

[54] In this regard, it would be wise to write a memo to the file, making clear that you aren't sure at this point whether a Robinson-Patman violation exists, that the subject has never been raised by the insurance companies, that the client has

All right. Let's assume now that the agreement has been signed, several days have passed, and you're meeting with the client's president to discuss the next step. Before you can open your mouth, the president hits you with the following:

"Listen, Don, I've looked into this price discrimination situation more fully, and I have to tell you that, no matter how your investigation turns out, I just can't cut out this particular practice. All of my marketing people tell me we would be operating at a tremendous competitive disadvantage if we were to switch gears.

"Now, I'm sure you can understand, I just don't want to say *anything* about this to the insurance companies, since it could make them nervous. I'm perfectly willing for the company to give the flat representation and run the risk of the debentures accelerating down the road. And for obvious reasons, I would like you to give an unqualified opinion. Forget the investigation; it's such a murky area anyway. The company will indemnify your firm against any harm it could possibly suffer.

"I'm asking you to do this, Don, as a real favor to me. I've been very happy with your work on our account and am looking forward to a long and fruitful relationship between our company and your firm. As you know, a number of other matters are coming up in the near future where we'll want to employ outside counsel. . . ."

Well, this is the first really easy question I've posed in the whole book. Your answer should be a flat, unequivocal "no", delivered without hesitation.[55] You simply cannot render an opinion under these circumstances; and the indemnity would only serve to make your conduct more blatant. You have to advise the client in no uncertain terms that if he doesn't want your firm to resign from the engagement—a development which, it goes without saying, would appear extremely suspicious to the other side—this matter must be resolved to your satisfaction.

The president of your client happens to be a realist; he was testing the water, but he didn't expect you to go for that deal. He doesn't try to push it now, but agrees to cooperate toward resolving the matter in

---

agreed (if necessary) to stop the practice before the closing and disclose its prior existence, and that you've advised him fully as to the possible consequences of signing the agreement without further disclosure. See Section 6.5 on the general topic of covering one's tail.

[55] See Section 8.4 on facing up squarely to ethical-type decisions.

the least damaging way—at which point he turns to you for a suggested course of action.[56]

Assuming you haven't bolted the premises in righteous protest over the president's flagrant attempt to renege on his prior undertaking—perhaps you've learned to take his occasional intemperate utterances with a grain of salt—you might start out by subjecting the attitude of those marketing people to a little more searching inquiry.[57] Their initial reaction—rejecting any suggested change in business methods impairing freedom of action—was entirely predictable; you have to make sure it didn't represent merely knee-jerk self-interest. Be certain the prospective adverse impact of the change is adequately scrutinized. Then too, the president may have posed the question in a negative manner, subtly suggesting the anguished reply—a verbal wink, as it were. Or possibly, the marketing people weren't really so negative; the president may have exaggerated the degree of their reaction to justify his dilemma.

But now, let's say that the marketing people stick to their guns; it really would hurt the company to cut out the practice. What's your next move? You don't possess the power to *make* anyone alter the system; that's strictly an executive decision. So the question becomes how to handle this with the insurance companies—how to introduce the subject in a way that doesn't undermine the financing. And the initial decision you must make is whether or not to conduct your own investigation first.

Let me give you a very practical approach to this decision. If there's a reasonable chance your investigation could result in a clean bill of health, then by all means undertake it immediately. With a favorable determination, you won't have to raise the point, you can give the opinion, and no harm will have been done. If Gamy is actually unsullied, then confronting the purchasers with a non-existent issue is a disservice to your client. However, if you sense this result is unrealistic to expect—you've seen and heard enough at this point to believe there's probably a violation—then it may be better *not* to have, made a personal investigation at the point when the purchasers are advised of the problem. This enables you to be a trifle more removed from the fray in discussing the subject with your opposite number; and when pressed, you can honestly state that you haven't investigated in depth and really don't know for sure whether a violation exists.

The next consideration is one of timing[58]—when should the revela-

---

[56]   The role of the lawyer in the decision-making process is explored generally in Chapter 8 and more particularly in Sections 8.4 and 8.5.
[57]   The subject of not feeling bound by the assumptions the client provides is discussed in Section 2.5.
[58]   A key factor in negotiations, which is discussed in Section 7.3.4.

tion take place? There's no hard and fast rule here; each situation has its own dynamics. But timing can be crucial, and you shouldn't ignore it in your strategic planning. Other things being equal, if there's a serious risk of the insurance companies discovering the problem themselves, then I would waste no time in exposing it to them first; it's crucial to resolving matters for the disclosure to have been voluntary—not something called to your attention by the other side.[59] If discovery isn't likely, then some lawyers would make a good practical case—if not ethically elevating—for waiting until most of the other obstacles to the deal have been removed. There usually comes a point when everyone is gearing up to complete the deal, where a certain momentum has developed that can be useful in setting the tone for this disclosure.[60] Early revelation, at a time when positions haven't changed very much and expectations aren't set in stone, can make unwinding too easy.

The next question is, who should talk to whom? This can also be very significant. Perhaps the worst of all ways to handle the disclosure is the one that might seem the most natural—lawyer-to-lawyer. Information of this sort coming from *you* makes the client look bad; the optics are that you've been playing cop, have caught the client in a misrepresentation, and are now squealing on him against his will. What's more, the purchaser's lawyer can be counted on to view himself as a latter-day Paul Revere—spreading the alarm across the institutional investor countryside. No, it's much better for the news not to emanate from the lawyer, and for the initial recipient to be someone with a practical view of such matters.

And, for these purposes, no one fills the role better than the investment banker who put the financing together in the first place.[60a] After all, he's been operating in that no-man's land between the corporate client and the insurance companies, with good relations on both sides. And he's used to overcoming obstacles on the way to consummating deals.

So, your client's president calls in the investment banker for a breakfast meeting. I don't usually attend such sessions, but I have a hunch that the president, after mentioning that a possible problem ("involving a much ignored statute") has arisen, is likely to declare with some fervor ("as one practical businessman to another") that a change in practice would be harmful to all concerned ("*including* the insurance companies") and that the investment banker's assistance in selling this concept to the purchasers would be much appreciated.

---

[59]   This distinction is explored in a regulatory context in Section 7.5.2.

[60]   See Section 12.4.1 of *Anatomy*.

[60a]   For a discussion of your relations with the client's investment banker, see Section 6.7.

Just remember: as a lawyer, you *don't* have to play hero. What matters is for the disclosure to be made; it does *not* have to issue forth from you to your counterpart.

All right. The insurance companies have been advised of the possible Robinson-Patman violation and have decided they can live with the practice—which means you won't have to render an opinion on the subject. However, they would still like your opinion that the company isn't violating any *other* significant laws. Assume that you're willing to deliver such an opinion. The question is: how do you phrase the exception in your opinion (or alternatively, revise the agreement) to exclude the Robinson-Patman Act, without calling attention to the fact that the company might be violating that particular law? You should presume that the documents will some day become a matter of public record or the subject of a subpoena; and you wouldn't want to encourage customers, or others who may be adversely affected if a violation exists, to lodge any claims.[61]

There's no point in changing the agreement which has already been signed and is the one document most likely to enter the public record. If the inside counsel is still willing to give the Robinson-Patman opinion, then your opinion could allude to that fact, which (particularly if he's rendering other opinions, such as due qualification in foreign jurisdictions) doesn't sound too sinister—just a division of responsibility among lawyers. But what if the inside counsel has now gotten cold feet and won't opine?

Well, one technique I would *not* use is to give a broad "no violation of laws" opinion, together with a side letter which says, in effect: "Oh, by the way, that opinion shouldn't be read to include the Robinson-Patman Act." Documents generally ought to be complete on their face. Side letters can *interpret* them, but not alter their plain meaning. Your opinion could contain a reference to the side letter ("This opinion is limited by the matters set forth in my letter of October 3"), which would solve the ethical problem—but which clearly alerts the reader to the concealment.

Another possibility is to include a paragraph in the opinion stating: "It is understood that the purchasers are making their own investigation into Gamy's compliance with the anti-trust laws. Accordingly, we have made no special investigation of such matters, and the opinions expressed herein are not intended to refer to the anti-trust laws." In other words, the omission isn't based on anything being

---

[61] This kind of question commonly comes up in connection with an item of potential tax liability not yet claimed by the IRS (such as in the accumulated earnings area), which a seller has disclosed to the purchaser, who has agreed to take subject to the possible liability; the question is how to exclude this from the tax representation without alerting the IRS to the problem. See Section 7.4.3 of *Anatomy*.

wrong; it's just an area that the parties have decided to exclude. By broadening the scope of the exception beyond the Robinson-Patman Act to the anti-trust laws generally (assuming the purchasers can live with the larger exclusion), there's less in the way of finger-pointing. It's not perfect, but there's really no ideal solution to this thorny kind of problem.

9.6. THE BALLAD OF FASTTALKER AND DEEPPOCKET

In this rousing saga of the brave men who develop residential real estate, you play the role of a senior associate in the firm representing the well-heeled Daryl Deeppocket. The partner who services Deeppocket's account, Ralph Rainmaker, is generally off on other matters. So you have considerable discretion in handling things—as long as Ralph is kept generally informed of events and consulted on questions of importance.

Deeppocket owns some land that's ripe for development. Lacking the experience to undertake such a project on his own, Deeppocket is negotiating a joint venture with Freddy Fasttalker, an experienced (albeit, somewhat shoestring) developer of real property. The basic deal calls for Deeppocket to contribute the land, which Fasttalker is to develop and sell off in lots. All important joint venture decisions will be made jointly, and the parties will share 50-50 in any net profits. The businessmen have made a preliminary estimate that $1,000,000 of their money will be needed to fund the project initially; they have agreed in principle that Deeppocket will put up $750,000 (in addition to the land), while Fasttalker is responsible for the remaining $250,000.[61a] It is understood that monies contributed to the venture would be paid back to the contributor before any division of profits, but without interest.

Up to this point in the negotiations, the subject of eventual cash requirements beyond the initial $1 million has received only brief attention, but it's an issue that bothers you. Actually, two interrelated questions are involved: (i) should the parties be obligated in advance to put up additional monies in some specified amount (as contrasted with omitting any provision, and thereby leaving it to their mutual agreement at the time the cash is needed); and (ii) if more dollars are required, in what proportion should they be contributed (e.g., the same 75-25 split as the initial $1 million, or 50-50, or some other formula)?

[61a] I realize that it may be more typical in such transactions for the parties to cause the venture to borrow the funds from a financial institution, with the obligation personally guaranteed by each of them jointly. For purposes of this problem, however, let's assume that borrowed funds are not available.

As you might expect, Fasttalker has taken the position that the agreement should obligate the parties to contribute up to an additional $1 million, if and when the venture needs the money, and in the same 75-25 proportion as the initial $1 million. His argument is that he doesn't want to get heavily involved in developing the property, exhaust the $1 million, and then find that Deeppocket has cooled on the venture—refusing to advance further funds, resigned to his $750,000 beating, and opting for the return of his land via the breakup provision of the venture agreement. Although the initial $1 million represents a reasonable estimate of costs, it's not clear this will cover all needs; the pace of development, fluctuation in interest rates, materiel prices and other factors outside the parties' control could produce cost overruns. The obligation to put up additional funds is Fasttalker's security blanket against unforeseen (but not unforeseeable) adverse developments.

However, your client Deeppocket, who doesn't have complete confidence in Fasttalker's ability to complete the project, is extremely leery about agreeing in advance to invest more money. He's certain that—to the extent the additional money may be *his*—such a provision will become a self-fulfilling prophecy, causing laxity in averting cost overruns and reducing the tempo of development. Deeppocket would much prefer that Fasttalker worry a little about whether or not the extra cash will be forthcoming. Moreover, Deeppocket would like to be in a position, if and when additional funds are needed, to negotiate *at that time* the terms on which those dollars enter the venture—with Fasttalker then under pressure to put up half the excess, or at least have the venture pay Deeppocket interest on the differential.

So that's the situation at present. And this, of course, isn't taking place in a vacuum. A number of other issues are under discussion, factual investigations are underway, tax advice has been sought, drafts of documents are making the rounds. This particular question about subsequent contributions occupies a back seat at present; still, it's lurking there, and you realize it may ultimately prove a significant issue between the parties.

Well, this is *just* the time to display a little initiative—to exhibit some of those self-starting qualities partners prize so highly in an associate.[62] Start thinking about the final resolution of this issue, and plotting whatever strategy is required to reach the desired goal. Don't let the ball play you; dominate your subject matter.

The first issue to address is a political one: what should you do about Ralph Rainmaker, the partner? Can you ignore him or should you seek his advice? The answer depends in part on Rainmaker's idio-

---

[62] See Section 4.2.

syncracies, which you've observed over the years.[63] On the basis of the sketchy details provided above, I would think that (i) you would *not* approach Rainmaker solely on this issue right now; (ii) during your next overall briefing of Rainmaker, you should refer to subsequent contributions as a potential problem; and (iii) rather than ask Rainmaker's advice on handling the question, you ought to tell him *your* proposed plan of action.[64]

As you evaluate the additional contribution issue, your gut feeling is that Deeppocket won't win this one entirely. (And maybe he's better off with a partial victory—since an obligation on Fasttalker's part to make an additional investment might help to maintain the developer's interest in the project.) As badly as Fasttalker wants this deal, he probably won't proceed without reasonable assurance that sufficient monies will be available for total development. The figure of $1 million for openers came from Fasttalker and was undoubtedly a somewhat lowball number, designed to stimulate Deeppocket's interest. And as for Deeppocket, well, he *has* the money; he really wants this deal to take place; if he gets the land back, he'll only have to finish the development himself; and so he probably won't let a contingent additional outlay stand in his way.

At this point, you begin thinking about the shape of the ultimate compromise on this issue.[65] Deeppocket will strive to keep the commitment for additional funds as small as possible, perhaps half of the additional $1 million sought by Fasttalker. You probably won't be able to negotiate a 50-50 split on the additional contribution, but perhaps you'll be able to reduce it from 75-25 to 65-35. And the venture ought to pay your client interest on the differential between the two parties' contributions—or at least on Deeppocket's excess over a 50% share.

Most important, you'll seek to protect Deeppocket from having to put up more cash in a disaster situation by conditioning the obligation on the accomplishment of certain specified objectives in developing the property. Typically, this would be handled by setting up a schedule of dates for completion of plans, the receiving of requisite regulatory approvals, putting in roads and sewers, and the like.

Now, this is the kind of compromise that will ultimately work, but it would be imprudent for you to introduce it—or even to hint at the possibilities—at this stage of the proceedings. As soon as you indicate Deeppocket's willingness to commit to additional funds, no matter what protective penumbra you throw up, Fasttalker will make a

---

[63] See Section 5.1.1.
[64] See Section 5.1.2 on reporting to the partner and proposing your own solutions to problems.
[65] The subject of compromise is explored in depth in Section 7.3.

strong case for the full $1,000,000, the 75-25 split, no interest to Deep-pocket—and any schedule of significant progress would be leisurely at best. You're much wiser to start positioning Fasttalker for this ul-timate compromise *before* your client has signified his assent to sub-sequent contributions or Fasttalker's attention has been focused on the introduction of conditions precedent.[66]

So, for example, at a time of your choosing—but unrelated to any discussion of the subsequent contribution issue—you ought to inter-rogate Fasttalker as to the likely progress of development.[67] Since he's still concerned about Deeppocket getting cold feet for the proj-ect—and not on his guard as to the role of his words in a possible compromise—Fasttalker will wax optimistic about the completion dates for various aspects of the project. When you do get around to discussing subsequent contributions, be sure to let Fasttalker babble on about the relative unlikelihood of the additional funds ever being needed—they're just set aside for a rainy day. Perhaps you'll get lucky, too. For instance, Fasttalker might overplay his hand and remark—in the course of bemoaning how he's strapped for funds—that he'd be delighted to borrow his full share from the bank if he weren't leveraged to the hilt—a potentially damaging concession of willingness to pay in-terest.

Now, Fasttalker is set up for the compromise. Since he's minimized the extra amount needed, you'll probably be able to limit the overage to $500,000. If you lose on your pitch for a different proportion than 75-25, you should at least be able to get interest on the difference. And your client's obligation on the extra funds will be tied as closely as possible to the optimistic time schedule that emerged from Fasttalker's own mouth.[68] But you might have blown the whole thing by introducing the compromise prematurely.

A few words here on your relations with Deeppocket, the client. Make sure to clear your overall strategy with him since the decision is ultimately his.[69] Maybe he just won't want to compromise on this issue; that's his call. Assuming he's agreeable, then by all means brief him on how you intend to accomplish this—let him observe your skill in setting Fasttalker up.[70] And if you feel particularly bold, make a prediction as to the ultimate outcome;[71] your seeming clairvoyance could net you considerable respect.

---

[66] For a general discussion of laying the groundwork for compromise, see Section 7.3.8.

[67] Since there's an element of creative motivation here (discussed in Sec-tion 7.3.4), Fasttalker's lawyer ought to be present at this meeting.

[68] See Section 7.3.5 on petard-hoisting.

[69] See Section 6.6.

[70] See Section 6.5.

[71] See Section 6.5.

Now, let's assume that while compromise negotiations are in process, Deeppocket says to you:

> "Look, I need some mixed business-legal advice. Rainmaker never seems to be around when I need him. I don't know whether to agree to the $500,000 additional contribution or not, and I'm not sure whether the development schedule really gives me adequate protection."

How do you handle this? In particular, would you proceed to advise Deeppocket yourself or should you defer to Rainmaker?[72] And if you do give advice, how far should you go in passing judgment?[73]

Well, Deeppocket didn't *say* he wanted the answer to these questions to come directly from Rainmaker—just that he was annoyed at the partner's absence from the scene. It strikes me that this is the time to earn your spurs by offering Deeppocket your own views. If you duck and refer his questions to Rainmaker, you may never fully develop your own relationship with the client. Moreover, you'll only exacerbate Deeppocket's frustration in being dependent on a lawyer who's seldom present. And finally, your proximity to the bargaining puts you in a better position than the absent Rainmaker to offer sound advice.[74]

So, I'd suggest that you take a pass at Deeppocket's questions. But in my view, the two issues are quite different. The second matter regarding the time schedule and its contractual significance is right up your alley; after all, the whole concept was your idea in the first place. You ought to be able to give Deeppocket an excellent fix on just where he'll stand on this—in effect, to provide him with your opinion or judgment on the matter. The dollar issue, however, is mainly a business matter, as to which lawyers should hesitate to pass judgment. What you can do is review with Deeppocket the course of the bargaining, give him your assessment of how firm or flexible Fasttalker is on the point, and suggest what other factors bear on Deeppocket's decision. But then back off and let him make the call.

9.7. THE CORPORATE OPPORTUNIST

For a number of years, you have acted as regular outside counsel to

---

[72]   A subject discussed in Section 6.3.

[73]   See Sections 8.4 and 8.5.

[74]   If, however, you feel that Deeppocket would really like Rainmaker's views, tell the client that you'll bounce your thoughts off the partner. And by all means, at the earliest time and in as diplomatic fashion as possible, advise Rainmaker of Deeppocket's seeming irritation, which a simple phone call can perhaps mitigate. See Section 5.1.2.

a small, unlisted public company ("Publico"). In the process, you've developed a fairly close relationship with Publico's president ("Twomasters"), although you don't handle his personal legal affairs. One of the key components for the products manufactured by Publico is supplied by a single privately-held concern ("Source").

On this particular day, without any warning, Twomasters calls you to his office and advises you, first, that he has just personally purchased a 35% interest in Source from the estate of its co-founder; and second, that he would like Publico to acquire Source for two million dollars cash, which he feels is a fair price. Now, this comes as somewhat startling news. You're surprised—perhaps even a trifle hurt—that Twomasters hadn't sought out your advice *before* buying the Source shares. He must have known this could create some problems . . . which, you realize with a twinge, is just why he *didn't* consult you—he was afraid you'd advise against the purchase.

As thoughts such as these flash through your mind during the moments following Twomasters' revelation, don't lose sight of the fact that you're dealing with a sensitive issue in lawyer-client relations. Twomasters happens to be the president of your client. Unless you want one less client, you can't react to his disclosure as if the man is some kind of criminal, regardless of your personal feelings in the matter. Twomasters himself didn't consider this improper—or at least not sufficiently improper to deter him. Moreover, Twomasters' personal funds are involved, a factor which always makes things extra sticky. On the other hand, you can't simply say "Fine" and proceed to implement his plan. There's a thin line for you to walk here, proceeding with utmost caution.

The fact is that you're dealing in an area—usually known as "corporate opportunity"—which is particularly murky. There are few laws on the books prohibiting specified conduct. Fiduciary responsibilities exist, but are somewhat vague; the dividing line between proper and improper conduct is not well-defined. So, avoid a self-righteous tone as you cope with the predicament you find yourself in. For example, I *wouldn't* begin by asking Twomasters how much he paid for the Source shares. You'll find out soon enough, and until then you can assume it was less than the amount he'd net on Publico's acquisition of Source—but why start out by rubbing his nose in this rather embarrassing comparison.

It's wise to begin here—as in so many mixed legal/practical situations—by distinguishing between what has *already* been done (Twomasters' purchase of the 35% Source interest) and what is *planned* for the future (the proposed acquisition of Source by Publico). There's a world of practical difference in your ability to respond to a *fait accompli* (where your options are severely limited), as contrasted with a contemplated transaction. In this regard, make sure the purchase from the estate has in fact occurred—that it doesn't represent merely an unconsummated meeting of the minds.[75]

Dealing first with the accomplished fact, a bit of client education may be in order to set the stage for what's to follow. Make sure Twomasters understands that his ownership of Source must be disclosed in Publico's next proxy statement. The glare of public scrutiny can sometimes deter executives from taking certain actions. "I know that," Twomasters replies impatiently. Next, explain to him that, though you're sure he intended no wrong, the fact that Source is a major supplier for Publico could cause his purchase to be viewed as the appropriation of an opportunity belonging to Publico—the company to which he owes a duty of undivided loyalty. Without referring specifically to the facts of *his* situation, acquaint him with the broader aspects of the corporate opportunity doctrine.

Now, let's assume that Twomasters is a shrewd operator whose mind is clicking rapidly as you proceed through your exposition. At the finish, he says that *this* wasn't a corporate opportunity because "the estate would never have offered the shares to Publico." Everyone involved—the deceased, the executor, the other Source stockholders—"knew me, trusted me, and wanted *me* to own the shares." Well, now you have your weapon to head off the *second* transaction. Tell Twomasters that he can't have it both ways. If he wants to take the position that the investment opportunity wouldn't have been available to Publico, he can't turn right around and have Publico buy the entire company. Moreover, facts tending to negate Publico's interest in making such a purchase are helpful in justifying Twomaster's purchase of Source stock—a consideration which would be severely undermined by Publico's acquisition of Source.

Having scored once, you quickly warm to your subject. It's one thing for Twomasters to acquire these Source shares. You can deal with that—perhaps by erecting some protective barriers—and any personal gains he might ultimately obtain are purely speculative at this point. But it's quite another matter to provide for Source's acquisition by Publico, for cash, in a transaction in which—and here you'll have to confirm your suspicion—the amount Twomasters will receive exceeds the cost of his recent purchase from the estate. Under scrutiny, this quick profit will look terrible.

---

[75] Clients tend to be somewhat imprecise in describing the legal status of transactions, engaging in a fair amount of inadvertent hyperbole. Note that the fact Publico is an unlisted company has significance, inasmuch as the stock exchanges discourage conflict situations. See, e.g., NYSE Company Manual, §A2, pt. IV, at A-29: "Once they are listed, companies obviously are expected to conduct their affairs in such a manner as to prevent conflicting interests from arising. . . ."

Stated forcefully, the logic of your argument will become apparent to Twomasters. His rational decision should be to shelve the second step for the foreseeable future. Make sure this is indeed the case—that there's no present secret intention to effect the acquisition—since it affects your disclosure obligations. A practical precaution here is to elicit a promise from Twomasters that, should he decide to press the acquisition down the road—making sure he realizes that "down the road" doesn't mean just a matter of months—he'll consult with you prior to taking any irrevocable step.

All right. You've succeeded in separating the two transactions. Now you're in a position to deal with Twomasters' purchase of the Source stock without the spectre of the proposed acquisition. And the next step is to deal with the Publico board of directors. Twomasters may put up some resistance ("*I* bought the stock. What in blazes do *they* have to do with this—especially if Publico's not going to make the acquisition?"); but you shouldn't be deterred. After all, what you're doing here (as with so many lawyers' procedures) is for the client's own good—a doctor-knows-best approach that most clients, after some obligatory kicking and squirming, do seem to accept.

Directors of public companies are growing more independent each year—less cowed by management, thinking for themselves, asking probing questions. As the company lawyer, you should do nothing to discourage such independent judgment, no matter what pressures are imposed on you by management. But most small company boards are still somewhat wary of locking horns in a direct conflict with the president—who is probably responsible for the presence of most directors on the board—over a matter which is neither overwhelming in significance nor a clear-cut violation of law.[76] And so, the first thing to do is get a feel for how the directors react to this matter *in advance* of any formal board meeting.[77]

If, for example, you sense that the directors are indignant over what Twomasters has done—if they believe the purchase was a bargain that should have been made by Publico—then you might suggest to Twomasters that he avoid a confrontation with the board over this issue by offering the Source stock to Publico at his price to the estate. Twomasters may well balk at this, but he may also be sensitive to the

---

[76] I have in mind here the typical board of the smaller public company, where the members are really serving at the sufferance of the chief executive officer—either because they report to him as employees of the company or have been invited into the boardroom from outside at his instance.

[77] Generally speaking, advance consultation with directors is desirable to avoid unnecessary confrontations in the boardroom—or the sullen silence of directors who haven't been informed, who are worried that something improper or unwise is happening, but who don't want to antagonize the chief executive officer by speaking up in open forum.

criticism of his colleagues—and if the negative reaction is universal, he might surprise you and go along. But if, on the other hand, you discover that the board isn't really disturbed by all this—that the directors aren't interested in having Publico acquire an interest in Source and, assuming it's legal, are anxious to validate Twomasters' transaction—then you can't ignore their evident wishes. Let's assume that the Publico directors fall into this latter category.

In the first place, it's important for the Publico board to make a concurrent determination (as contrasted with a judgment made two years later in the face of a pending lawsuit) of its lack of interest in owning a piece of Source and its absence of objection to Twomasters making the purchase. Sure, it would have been preferable to consult the board *first*, before the transaction took place, but you don't have that luxury—and it's idle to fantasize over what might have been.[78] Do the next best thing; get the board on board right now.

Your approach should be keyed to the case law on the corporate opportunity doctrine, attempting to touch as many of the approved conduct bases as possible. For example, the board should indicate (if true) that Publico has no wish to integrate vertically, so that purchase of the Source block would have been of no interest; in fact, had it been offered to Publico, the board would have turned it down.[79] The board should further declare (if true) that it has no problem with Twomasters' ownership of the interest in Source, and that it wouldn't have raised any objection had he solicited board approval in advance of the purchase.

Then, in order to eliminate any trace of impropriety, Twomasters should agree to be a completely passive investor in Source—at least to the extent that he won't become engaged in anything involved with the terms of the Publico supply contract. Nor should he be involved in such matters on the Publico side; this task ought to be delegated to others, who bypass Twomasters and report directly to the board on this issue. If it seems necessary, independent experts can be retained by Publico to pass on the commercial terms of the Source-Publico contract, in order to assure its arm's-length character—to satisfy the

---

[78] If the opportunity presents itself, however, you might point out to Twomasters—for future reference—that this would have been much simpler had he come to you in advance, so that all the bases could have been touched *before* the purchase occurred.

[79] To the extent it may be true, the other side of the coin should be covered also—namely that the investment would not have been made available to Publico even if Publico had wanted it and Twomasters didn't. If you don't wish to approach Source or the estate on this point, and no third parties are available, then you'll have to make do with a representation from Twomasters on the subject.

board that Publico is receiving as good a deal from Source in terms of price and quality as it could find elsewhere.

Sure, it's a difficult situation, but there will be plenty more like this one; and you just have to learn to make the best of it—always taking a constructive approach, extracting the maximum from the materials at hand.

Let's assume you've crossed these hurdles and obtained board ratification. Six months pass. The whole program has receded into the distant passages of your consciousness, when suddenly Twomasters—who hasn't forgotten for a moment—drops the other shoe. "Okay," he says, "*now* I want to merge Source into Publico. I've waited a decent interval, and you said I'd be able to do it down the road. I've already talked with the key directors, and they have no objection." Well, there it is—complete with a misstatement of your position.[80] What you had *said* was that he shouldn't have a secret acquisition plan or else disclosure would be required; that proposing an acquisition of Source in the near future would be circumstantial evidence of such a secret plan; that this didn't mean he was *forever* foreclosed, but as a practical matter—oh, what the hell, it shouldn't come as a surprise that those carefully chosen words (remember, you were still trying to dissuade him from the second step at that point) would come home to roost, bereft of caveats and nuance.[81]

Unlike the stock purchase, however, at least Twomasters has come to you in advance this time, so you have a chance to head off his proposal. Make your arguments practical and down-to-earth, not judgments hurled to earth from some lofty moral firmament. The deal will *look* bad—stockholders could object[82]—Publico's stated position is that they *don't* want to integrate vertically—wait a little longer. . . . You give it the old college try, but just can't change Twomasters's mind. So, once again, you have to be constructive and deal with the situation you've been handed.

First, a valid reason should exist for the board to change its mind and decide to acquire its supplier. I'm not suggesting that the lawyer should invent rationale or manufacture facts, but you can be helpful in identifying useful criteria. Perhaps there has been an intervening development since the time of Twomasters' purchase—a change in circumstances, as it were, such as an industry-wide spectre of poten-

---

[80] The proclivity of clients to misquote their lawyers is referred to in Sections 6.5 and 3.3.1.

[81] It's also possible that your words were themselves slightly ambiguous—a subject covered in Section 3.3.4. By the way, unlike other possible situations, memorializing your views in written correspondence would probably *not* have been appropriate under these circumstances. See Section 3.2.9.

[82] But see Section 8.4 on overdoing this.

tial shortages, making vertical integration a desirable business strategy. You have to counter any inference that the acquisition was planned all along or that the board didn't mean what it said in hypothetically "turning down" the offer of the Source stock.[83]

Second, you ought to suggest that the deal be done on a basis where Twomasters makes no personal profit. Assuming that the purchase price would yield him, on a pro rata basis, more than he originally paid for his 35% interest, an arrangement could be worked out to net him only an amount equal to his purchase price—while the other Source stockholders receive their regular profit, but Publico ends up paying a lower overall price. Believe me, suggesting to your client that he forgo profit isn't a pleasant business, but it would clearly improve the appearance of the deal. In the last analysis, however, this has to be Twomasters' decision, and he might not be willing to go this far; after all, he'll argue, I put up the funds and took the downside risk on the investment—Publico wouldn't have bailed me out if the investment proved improvident—so why shouldn't I reap the benefits?[84]

Third, you should insist that an independent investment banker bless the purchase price as fair and reasonable from the standpoint of Publico. This helps to remove part of the taint from Twomasters' ownership of Source stock, and mitigates the implicit influence he could be expected to exert on the Publico board.

Fourth, it's clear that Twomasters should be as far away as possible from the acquisition negotiations. The Publico board should appoint its most independent members to act as a negotiating committee. And if *you* have any hesitation over vigorously representing Publico's interests—or sense that the board might *perceive* you as tainted by your closeness to Twomasters—then bring in an independent law firm to work with you on this deal.[85]

Finally, it would be desirable to submit the acquisition to Publico stockholders for their approval, regardless of whether stockholder approval is required by the applicable corporate law. To be sure, there are negatives associated with this program—the added exposure of

---

[83] If this development were foreseeable at the time of the Source purchase, then to the extent the board considered various rationale in its rejection, appropriate emphasis should have been given to reasons—such as the board's general disdain for holding minority positions in privately-held companies—that would be inapplicable at the second stage (when 100% of the company is offered).

[84] Because, the lawyer replies quietly, Twomasters is creating the opportunity to reap the benefits by furnishing the receptacle and paying agent. . . .

[85] The phenomenon of joint and parallel representation by counsel is covered in Section 7.2, with particular emphasis in Section 7.2.5 on conflicts of interest.

misstatements or omissions in the proxy soliciting material, the possibility of litigation prior to consummation of the deal, the spectre of being turned down on the vote—but these must be weighed against the added degree of comfort directors derive by not taking the responsibility totally on their own shoulders.[86]

Let's close by examining three issues that arise in the course of the acquisition. As you might have expected, Twomasters refuses to stay out of things; rather, he positions himself right in the middle of the negotiations over the merger agreement, as well as the proxy statement disclosures to be made by Publico (the board having decided to seek stockholder approval).

In the first place, Twomasters isn't exactly a disciple of full disclosure. He's willing for the proxy statement to reveal his 35% stockholding in Source, but he doesn't want any specific mention of his recent purchase of the stock, nor the price that he paid, nor the amount that he'll be receiving. If Publico were subject to SEC rules on proxy solicitation, these facts would have to be disclosed. But even if Publico isn't under the SEC's jurisdiction, you simply have to convince Twomasters that anything less than full and candid disclosure is self-defeating.

Here's the argument I use with clients under similar circumstances. In any transaction such as this, even assuming full disclosure, the risk exists of a lawsuit over the substance of the transaction. But if disclosure is incomplete or misleading, then, in addition to the risk on substance, you add to the plaintiff's arsenal the opportunity to allege inadequate disclosure. I don't like to give a plaintiff that extra weapon—and neither should the client. Even half-hearted disclosure alerts potential troublemakers to the pendency of a delicate transaction; if they're going to sue, they'll probably do so anyway. When it then unfolds that you've been misleading the public, you have a *real* lawsuit on your hands, with a judge who's likely to be less than sympathetic; whereas, when you lay everything out for the world to see, at least nobody can fault your candor—if not your good judgment in devising the deal.

Secondly, Twomasters takes the position that, because Source has been operating without an outside auditing firm, Source shouldn't have to make the standard representation that its financial statements fairly present its results of operations and financial position, in accordance with generally accepted accounting principles consistently

---

[86] The pros and cons of such a risk-reward analysis are discussed in Section 8.5. If Publico were listed on the New York Stock Exchange, the decision might be easier: "Where unusual circumstances make an isolated 'non-arm's length' transaction unavoidable, stockholder approval should be obtained to reduce objections to a minimum." NYSE Company Manual, §A2, pt. IV, at A-29.

applied—although he insists that Publico give just such a representation to Source. Again, you must argue Twomasters out of this. The acquisition not only must be fair in fact, but it should also have the *appearance* of fairness. To omit this common and vital representation—to be asymmetrical in the degree of comfort offered by the two sides here—can be very dangerous; and those inclined to oppose the deal can read a great deal of unintended cupidity into such an omission.[87]

Finally, Twomasters wants Source to have the right to walk away from the deal at the closing, virtually without conditions precedent—in effect, to have almost an option. "Why is this necessary?" you ask; "Does Source plan to utilize this out?" "Oh, no," says Twomasters. "Well then," you reply, "it shouldn't be in the contract." Never insert a questionable provision into an agreement if you don't intend it to have any significance. Why give yourself a right you don't need and which has the added infirmity of being perceived as overreaching? And yet, you'd be surprised how often that kind of misstep occurs in affiliated transactions.

---

[87]   See Chapter 1 note 9 *supra*, and Section 13.3.3 of *Anatomy*.

CHAPTER 10

A WORD TO THE PARTNERS

10.1 NOBODY'S PERFECT

This final segment is aimed at partners in law firms who are willing to indulge in a little soul-searching over their relationships with associates. I would hope these thoughts are equally applicable to those who act in supervisory capacities in corporate counsel offices or governmental agencies.

Let's begin on a sympathetic note. As a partner, the practice of law is damned hard work, calling for virtually all of your attention. The time pressures can be overpowering. All the tough decisions are filtered through to you—the easier ones being resolved at lower levels. Dealing with clients can be frustrating and time-consuming. To take on a capable adversary requires skill and mental alertness, while regulators and judges impose substantial burdens. Many of you also carry part of your firm's administrative burden, which further gobbles up your valuable time. And you may well have other professional responsibilities—bar associations, lecturing, writing, etc. All in all, some handful.

Against this backdrop, it's readily understandable why, when it comes to dealing with associates—to supervising their education, guiding their hands, providing feedback on their performance, recognizing their sensitivities and needs—this aspect of lawyering is often relegated to the back burner. And yet, how unfortunate this is. No longer can we indulge ourselves in the fiction—if we ever could—that an associate will evolve into an effective lawyer by merely observing a partner in action. An associate can't be filed away for three or four years, suddenly to emerge, full-blown and mature, ready to practice. On the contrary, the pace is such that we often plunge tyro associates into difficult, tricky situations, hoping that they'll prove to be responsible and competent. And when it doesn't

337

work out (as happens all too often), we find ourselves reiterating that ancient theme: "*What* are they letting out of law school nowadays?" But the more relevant question might be: "Where have we *partners* let these associates down? Just what have *we* done to prepare them for the cold shock of practice?"

The suggestions contained in this chapter as to desirable partner conduct represent actions I would like to have taken—*not* what I've actually done with any degree of consistency. As I review my own performance against the suggested standards, I'm aware of some woeful shortcomings. I'm often brusque with associates; my temper should be under better control; too seldom do I stop to examine a situation from the associate's viewpoint; and so on. For those of you who know me, this is clearly a "Do as I say, not as I do" kind of chapter.

I don't intend to rehash everything we've talked about previously, with the emphasis shifted to the partner's role ("*Tell* the associate to write concisely. . . ."), nor have I attempted to be comprehensive in selecting materials from prior chapters. Rather, the focus is on those matters which should particularly concern a partner in the course of his professional dealings with associates.

For purposes of analysis, I've divided the subject matter into four major sections. First, there's the educational function—the means by which you impart to associates practical knowledge. Second, we'll examine the division of labor between the two of you, as well as certain other aspects of the relationship. Third is the area of feedback on performance—specific and general critiques to provide the associate with an idea of where he or she stands. Finally, there's a section on sensitivity to the associate's particular needs.

I admit to approaching this chapter with some trepidation. Not only is it presumptuous to be counseling my peers, but I expect to find it difficult living up to my own advice! Still, I want to take dead aim on the self-deception that deludes us into believing this key function can be achieved through osmosis—when what's really required is specific performance. Somehow, each of us must carve out the time from that mélange of other pressures to come face-to-face with the associates working at our sides.

10.2. THE EDUCATIONAL FUNCTION

There are any number of obvious ways in which partners can and should stimulate the education of associates—ways I don't intend to detail here—such as: exposing associates to issues of professional responsibility and the ethical precepts by which we practice; encouraging associates to participate in continuing legal education programs; giving young lawyers opportunities to express themselves outside the court or conference room (for instance, by speaking on topics of current interest at a firm or departmental luncheon). I want to concentrate, however, on certain less cut-and-dried educational aspects.

10.2.1. Observation and Comprehension.

The most natural and simplest of all learning opportunities for an associate is to watch the partner in action—observing how you handle a potentially explosive client situation, noting your negotiating tactics directed at the lawyer across the table, having a bird's-eye view of a knotty administrative agency problem being resolved, listening to your argument before the court. When an associate hears you make a certain point, it gives him the confidence to make a similar point in a subsequent matter. Tactics receiving your implicit imprimatur are filed away for future use. I *know* how this works—if only because I never fail to play a better game of tennis after just having watched Bjorn Borg perform on television.

But in order for the associate to view you in action, he has to *be there*. Thus the first axiom in the educational process: make an effort to have the associate with you when all the activity is taking place.[1] And this does involve some minimum effort on your part. There you are, about to place a phone call to the SEC staff. You know all the necessary facts; you've outlined in your mind what you're about to say. There's some time pressure. It's awfully easy to make that call right now, and tell the associate what transpired later on—but that's not nearly so beneficial to *him* as being present when the call is made, to listen to your pitch. Or how about when the client comes to the office for a short, unexpected meeting; do you pause a moment to invite the associate on the case to join you?

On the other hand, the continuing education of a young lawyer is only a number of considerations that you have to balance in drawing up the guest list for events of the day, and the balance sometimes tips in the other direction. For instance, there might be a high-level meeting that the parties have decided to keep within as small a group as possible, and the associate's presence is otherwise unnecessary. At other times, you might be concerned about bringing in passive junior associates lest the client feel the meter is ticking excessively.[2] Oc-

---

[1]   This subject is discussed from the associate's point of view in Section 5.1.1.

[2]   As one top executive put it recently, lawyers "travel like nuns, in pairs or three at a time, and the clock is running and it's very annoying for a client to observe it hopelessly." Jay Pritzker, Chairman of the Board of Cerro-Marmon, quoted in the *N.Y. Times* (*Magazine*), Nov. 20, 1977. Of course, you can always advise the client that a junior associate is there for education, and that the client will not be billed for the associate's time at the meeting.

casionally, where a single lawyer is representing the other party, you may feel it works to your psychological disadvantage to position additional talent on your side of the table.

In terms of using the telephone, if the associate is in your office when the call is made, it's preferable educationally for him to hear the other party to the conversation as well as yourself. This can be accomplished by putting the associate on another extension or making the call on a speaker telephone—with the associate's presence always identified to the other party.[3] In certain conversations, however, you may feel more progress can be made if the other party believes he's talking to you alone. Perhaps he'll speak with a greater degree of candor when there are "no witnesses". In such cases, don't hesitate to tell the associate why you consider it advantageous to take the call alone—he'll understand perfectly. Excluding him without a stated reason, however, is subject to misinterpretation.

In any event, if valid reasons for exclusion *don't* exist, then let the associate take advantage of the educational opportunities inherent in being present and involved. Sure, if you had *thought* about inviting him in, you probably would have done so. The question is: how often do you think about it? Self-discipline is required to put the associate in the right position—not the library or *his* room—to see what's going on.[4]

But the opportunity for observation is not sufficient by itself. You can't assume that the associate appreciates the full significance of what he's observed. If the associate is present at a negotiating session when you engineer a subtle gambit successfully, make sure later that he understands what took place and how you set it up—even at the risk of appearing to blow your own horn. When you're struggling with a new adverse development, and you pause in the midst of your travail to call the client and convey the bad news, a word to the associate on your motivation is appropriate;[5] otherwise, he may be unlikely to attach any special significance to the call. And, by the way, don't limit your focus to instances where you've played a hero's role; if you've committed a real blunder that illustrates an important point, have the self-confidence to direct the associate's attention to your gaffe—it will probably make more of an impression than all your successes combined.

In order to accomplish this, try to set aside time for a brief postmortem after the event. Following a meeting at which the associate

---

[3] I consider it improper to have someone listen in on a conversation without advising the other party. Similarly, taping a call without telling the caller you're doing so is just not cricket—and may violate the laws of certain states.

[4] In this regard, the senior associate can be helpful in further involving the junior associate—a subject discussed in Section 5.2.2.

[5] See Section 6.5.

was present, take two minutes to point out some significant developments that he might not have noticed or appreciated: "Did you see how Jones began to hem and haw when I asked him that question about . . . ?"; "Were you aware how we allowed a consensus to form on the one issue before moving ahead to the other?"; "Remember when I cut Smith off because he was rambling on interminably . . . ?"[6] If you have enough time, it might be worthwhile to conduct this drill through questions—asking the associate what matters of significance he observed at the meeting (or, more pointedly, what did he notice about Jones' demeanor, etc.).

It's even more effective if, during the actual meeting, you can whisper to the associate what you're planning to do next—so that he can watch the action taking place, not merely view it later in retrospect. Best of all is when you have a hunch *prior to* the meeting that you'll be doing something cagey, and you give the associate a preview of what to be alert for.

The educational content of this sort of exercise is immeasurably increased if you're able to generalize from the specific point under discussion, so that the associate can appreciate the broader applicability.[7] Lawyers tend to deal in specifics and, for some, generalizations don't come easily. Still, while we should beware of glib overstatements, it's important that you attempt to expand the point; the exact pattern is unlikely to recur, but the associate should be able to recognize analogous situations and react accordingly. Let me give you an example of something that occurred recently.

An associate reported to me that he'd been having a difficult time persuading another lawyer that a certain procedure we had suggested would work. We outlined our strategy—developing some good, although not conclusive, answers to the questions previously raised—and then placed a call to the other lawyer on a speaker telephone. The minute the other lawyer started to talk, I could tell that he had already picked a path through the problem and had come out our way—although he didn't *say* this at first, choosing instead to plow once more through the gory details. In the course of his monologue, he made one point to which we had concocted a plausible reply. The associate started to interrupt, to jump in with our argument. I almost literally clapped my hand over the associate's mouth, wordlessly silencing his well-intended rationale. We continued to listen without comment as the other lawyer rambled through his presentation, finally concluding that our suggested procedure would be all right. "Great," I said; "We'll be seeing you."—and hung up.

---

[6]   The general subject of conducting a meeting is discussed in Section 3.3.3.
[7]   The related point about generalizing your specific comments on the associate's performance is covered in Section 10.4.4.

"Sorry about the muzzle," I said to the associate. "But when you can sense the other guy's coming around, keep quiet. Don't interrupt. Let *him* work it out. This way, he can't say later on that we talked him into it. Besides, an interruption could serve to distract him, and he might never get back on the right train of thought." Then I further generalized the point. "*Listening* can be so important. Hear what the other person is saying. Read between the lines. We all talk too much and don't listen enough."

And then I reminded the associate of an incident that had occurred in the course of another joint phone call several days earlier. I had been holding forth at length on a certain subject, when the other party interrupted and began to say something that, in retrospect, might have been very important—but I was so intent on the point *I* was making that he didn't get a word in edgewise. Later, when I'd finished my dissertation, there seemed no obvious route to reopen what the other party had started to interject; so we never did hear what he had on his mind. "If I'd only stopped when he interrupted," I bemoaned. "But I was talking and not listening, and that's the price you have to pay." I have a feeling that this incident, the discussion, and the generalization made a strong impression on the associate—particularly because it related to something he was in the midst of experiencing for himself.

10.2.2. Learning By Doing.

So much for observation and comprehension. From an educational standpoint, it's extremely desirable to take the next logical step—to let the associate, in your presence, actually run a meeting or mollify a client or handle a negotiation. This enables you to see how well he performs, not only for evaluation purposes,[8] but also to rectify his mistakes and offer a constructive critique. Unfortunately, however, associate participation may be easier to propose than to accomplish.

Let's face it; when you're there in the room, the natural tendency is for you to be running things. If the client is there, he expects it. Questions and comments are usually directed your way. You become the actor, while the associate retreats to an observatory role. When a matter has significance, it's hard for you to sit silently, letting the associate call the shots. His responses, lacking your accustomed polish, make you wince. In a negotiation, he may cede points he shouldn't or stick where compromise is in order, to your evident chagrin. It's a lot less frustrating to manage things yourself.

But then, you fall into a vicious cycle. The less the associate does on his own, the less experience he develops, the less competent he is to handle things, the less freedom you allow him. Similarly, the more

---

[8] See Section 10.4.

you dominate, the less chance he has to perform, the more difficult for you to critique or evaluate his performance. What's to be done about this?

One possibility, obviously not too satisfactory, is the hypothetical approach. Before the meeting starts, ask the associate how *he* would handle certain matters which you expect to arise. After the meeting, compare notes with him on what actually happened, to see if his reaction would have been different from yours. Still, this isn't actually *doing* it, which is what's really important.

A better choice is to single out in advance a particular issue expected to arise at the meeting or during the negotiation, and designate this as the associate's responsibility. It could, for instance, be a briefing on a point of law he's researched, or the recapitulation of a fact investigation he's conducted, or an argument against certain provisions in the other counsel's draft that the associate considers outrageous. If you have the time, review with the associate what he intends to say prior to the event, so there won't be any unpleasant surprises; but don't attempt to dictate his entire presentation, which undercuts the whole purpose of the exercise.

When the applicable point in the meeting arrives, you should simply say, "I am going to let my associate Andrea handle this issue." Just a short, straightforward introduction; no further elaboration is needed, and apologies are definitely *not* in order; everyone will accept this routinely. The more difficult task lies in resisting the temptation to jump in with your two cents while Andrea's doing her thing. Try to remain an observer, even though the words aren't precisely what you'd hoped to hear. Of course, if the associate makes a real error, then rectify it—as diplomatically as possible, so as not to destroy the associate's confidence.

If you can work this out, it provides an excellent opportunity for the young associate to get a feel of what you face daily, and what he or she will be doing solo in a few years. I have a hunch, though, that you—like me—don't arrange for this often enough. And yet, without taking this step, your adverse view of the associate's lack of élan in joint sessions with you may be somewhat unfair. I confess to having doubted the ability of certain associates to negotiate a deal, partially premised on the muteness of their prior participation—not realizing that, while the partner's in the room, the associate might feel intimidated from entering the negotiations without a specific invitation. I'd never tell an associate, "Now, just jump in whenever you feel the urge"; in a negotiation, for example, you may wish to preserve certain natural rhythms which the associate's abrupt intervention can sidetrack. The specific issue approach, however, accomplishes the purpose of providing the associate with an active role, without relinquishing your control of the proceedings.

As time goes by and the associate performs these cameo roles with distinction, you should vary and expand his active participation to provide more experience. There's a broader principle involved here, also. When an associate handles a particular assignment well—let's say, a certain kind of acquisition—the tendency is, when the next similar acquisition arrives in the office, to let the same associate handle it. After all, he now has some experience with the subject matter, and can be expected to perform more efficiently than another associate approaching the task *de novo*. But if such logic were carried to its extreme, associates would never achieve the well-rounded background that's so desirable. So, combat this tendency whereever possible, and try to provide the associate with a broad variety of situations.

We've previously discussed this next point from the viewpoint of the associate,[9] but I want to emphasize it again for the benefit of the partners. At least in situations when no clients or outside lawyers are around, always give the associate an opportunity to answer the question he raises before interjecting your own response. If you don't encourage the associate to take this initiative, he may feel it's inappropriate for him to presume a reply; what he should be told is that it's not only appropriate but *expected*. When an associate comes to you with a question but without a suggested response, your reaction should be: "And what do you think the answer is?" This gives you a chance to evaluate the associate's thinking process; it also helps your own analysis of the problem, since it's easier to review a solution than create one yourself. Unless you provide the associate with an opportunity to offer his own reactions, you'll never know how he might respond if you weren't around.

There's a related point of some importance here, a mixture of substance and optics. It's so easy for associates to develop a bad habit of reacting to actual problems in an indecisive manner. In a sense, this is nurtured in the law schools, where the stress on opening up young minds to multiple possibilities elevates the "it can be argued" exam approach above adherence to "right" answers. But in legal practice, after examining all the options, you do have to take a position, to make a decision.[10] If the ultimate determination is always left to the partner, the associate may begin to feel that his sole role is to lay out the choices. But that's not the case; he should start honing his own judgmental skills at an early stage; he ought to appreciate the importance of appearing decisive in dealing with clients and other lawyers. You should encourage this, by giving the associate both opportunities to exercise judgment and reminders of the key role decisiveness plays in his professional maturation.

---

9   See Section 5.1.2.
10 See Chapter 8 on decision-making generally.

10.2.3. Sprucing Up Written Work.

Let's assume you ask an associate to draft a certain letter to the client. Unfortunately, his draft turns out to be deficient in a number of respects—some substantive, others stylistic, still others in terms of organization. Now, there are two basic ways for the partner to handle this situation, with quite differing educational content.

The first alternative is to revise the letter yourself and send it out. If you remember (and have the time), you'll explain to the associate after the fact why you made the changes you did—although in my experience these after-the-fact critiques seldom take place. Even if you don't get around to this explanation, the associate will observe your modification from his prior draft, and should appreciate the superiority of your product—but he might not understand what went through your mind in making certain changes. The subtle reorganization you introduced into the revision may escape him entirely; he won't necessarily realize what aspects of his writing style require improvement. When you do take the time for a critique, there may be an undesirable confrontational edge to the session—the attempt to justify your revision against his draft can result in dutiful, dour nods or possibly even hostile reactions.

If you have the luxury of time, however, the preferable course is to call in the associate and go over his draft *orally*—presenting your thoughts, indicating the portions you'd like to see modified, and asking him to produce a revised second draft. This is far better educationally than simply doing it for him. Direct the associate to the deficiencies, but let *him* perform the actual surgery—rearrange concepts, shift emphases, organize more forcefully, reduce prolixity, and so on.[11] This way, he's more likely to grasp the principles of persuasive writing[12] and experience the crucial role of rewriting in legal prose.[13]

Now, should the associate's second draft still not measure up, you could send him back to the drawing board for a third draft; but at that point, you normally take over the job and finish it yourself. The associate can see the final document, and observe the further revisions (along the lines you had previously suggested) to improve the product.

Never let slipshod work leave the office because you're embarrassed to revise what an associate has drafted. If something is unsatisfactory, then it ought to be modified notwithstanding the associate's reaction. If the associate can't accept the fact that you're capable of a

---

[11]   See Section 3.2 generally.
[12]   See Section 3.2.7.
[13]   See Section 3.2.1.

better piece of work, he's not going to last long around the firm. This is not to say, however, that you must mold each writing to the precise form you would have used had you drafted it in the first instance. To do so—especially when the revisions are primarily stylistic rather than substantive—can be particularly dispiriting to the associate. Still, most of us can't resist stamping our imprimatur on important documents; and if you write well—so that your imprimatur represents a definite improvement in the overall presentation—then it should constitute an educational experience for the associate.

10.2.4. Don't Ignore The Nuances.

To be really meaningful, your educational efforts with the associate should extend well beyond the basics (such as writing) to some of the subtleties discussed in prior chapters that might not otherwise be readily apparent to a young lawyer.

For example, the issue of how to deal with other lawyers in the joint and parallel representation area[14] isn't something that a new associate is fully prepared to handle. The technique of making the sponsoring lawyer look good;[15] an awareness that the seemingly cordial lawyer who *didn't* bring you in is capable of backbiting or second-guessing;[16] the realization that you needn't suspend judgment on what an acknowledged trademark specialist is telling you[17]—these bits and pieces should find their way into the education of an associate.

Conflict of interest is another issue that must be discussed with young lawyers.[18] On the one hand, some associates dream up conflicts where none exist; others, however, overlook clear cases of dual responsibility. At what point does a seemingly satisfactory situation become untenable, and what's to be done when that happens? Another pedagogic opportunity exists in dealings with administrative agencies[19]—whom to seek out, the line to be drawn between deference and obsequiousness, the distinction between approval and absence of disapproval. Teach the associate to give you the *sense* of a conversation after finishing a more specific report; elicit his more subjective observations—while making sure he labels nuance as nuance and fact as fact.[20]

---

[14]   See Section 7.2.
[15]   See Section 7.2.1.
[16]   See Sections 7.2.1 and 7.2.4.
[17]   See Section 7.2.2.
[18]   See Section 7.2.5.
[19]   See Section 7.5.
[20]   See Section 3.3.1.

As the associate progresses in the firm, the most important subject for you to stress—yet often the most difficult to articulate—is the elusive element of good judgment. The associate should be made to understand that this quality extends beyond the merely mechanical aspects of the practice of law. Although generalizations may not come easy, you can point to specific situations and characterize the judgment used favorably or unfavorably, in hopes that something will stick to nourish future good habits. And when you're in the midst of exercising judgment—assuming you recognize the symptoms yourself!—let the associate see what's going on in your mind.

So, for instance, if you ask an associate to check on whether the client's financial vice president will be available next Tuesday, tell him *why* you're doing this—that by anticipating a forthcoming decision where the executive's input will be critical, you'll be in a better position to make a reasoned judgment.[21] The idea is to get the *associate* thinking about the necessity for advance planning, so that he'll take similar steps himself the next time. But if you just ask the associate to check on the executive's availability, with nothing more, the associate may have no idea what's behind your request. Similarly, if you've decided to defer a particular judgment but are taking certain interim actions to maintain all of your options,[22] point our your game plan to the associate. Make sure he appreciates the superiority of this course over the alternative of rushing through to premature judgment.

When difficult questions arise, rather than just deciding them, you should attempt to lead the associate through your reasoning process—if not at that moment with other people around, then later when you're alone.[23] Perhaps the issue involves a risk/reward type of analysis;[24] let the associate see your mind at work in this sometimes subtle area.

10.3. THE GROUND RULES OF THE ENGAGEMENT

Answer truthfully now: how often do you actually *communicate* with associates about the basic ground rules under which the two of you will be operating? I'd bet your reply is "infrequently". And yet, proper communication here could avert a number of problems that potentially affect the relationship.

We assign an associate to a certain task; we outline the substance

---

[21]   See Section 8.2.
[22]   See Section 8.2.
[23]   Remember, in the presence of clients, don't flaunt your reasoning prowess unnecessarily (see Section 3.3.1), although it's sometimes important to let the client understand your analysis (see Section 8.4).
[24]   See Section 8.5.

of the problem—probably all too cryptically, as we shall discuss in a moment; but how much further do we go in informing him what we're really after? For example, do you ever tell an associate which aspects of a matter you'll want him to deal with and which ones are to be reserved for your attention? Have you ever thought to acquaint an associate with your particular policies and quirks[25]—matters assimilated by associates who have worked for you, but which the novitiate can't be expected to divine at the outset. I believe this to be among the most neglected aspects of the partner/associate relationship.

For example, let's say you're one of those lawyers who insists on personally reviewing every piece of paper leaving the office on your projects *prior to* transmission. Well, you're entitled to your whim, and the associate ought to adhere to it—*if* he knows about it. This is a rather simple policy to lay before the associate; and yet, if you don't, he may be entitled to assume that his *modus operandi* with other clients—handling relatively routine correspondence on his own, without prior partner approval—is perfectly satisfactory. Or, perhaps you're the contrary type, who has no desire to be bothered unless the sky is actually falling; you've got enough problems of your own, associates have to sink or swim—you know the attitude. Then, by all means, *inform* the associate accordingly; otherwise he might feel obligated to run everything of any substance by you—especially when the two of you are working together for the first time. If you don't articulate this attitude, then your irritation over his frequent visits is on unsure footing. Do you prefer written memoranda or would you rather receive oral reports? Have you definite feelings about which of you ought to be speaking to the client, and the particular individual at the company to be contacted? Communicate these morsels to the associate. Don't expect the associate to glean your preferences; take the mystery out of the relationship.

One of the sins from which many of us suffer is the all too cryptic description of the specific project to the associate. We're rushed; it's boring to plod through the details; we figure the associate will discover all he needs to know from reading the papers or talking to the personalities involved. But the soul of wit is not the stuff of associate efficiency. Brevity without guidance leads to wasted motion—lost hours and mounting legal fees while the associate attempts to get his bearings.

But what if there just isn't time for elaboration when the assignment is handed out? One possible technique is to have the associate start on a relatively narrow portion of the task—something he can fo-

---

[25] The importance of this information to an associate is discussed in Section 5.1.1.

cus on without necessarily comprehending the full picture. Later, at a less frenzied moment, you can get back to him with more details. Another alternative, assuming there's someone else in the firm with a grasp of the details and issues, is to point the associate towards that person. Whenever you're aware that others in the firm have useful knowledge on a particular subject, let the associate know this at the time you hand out the assignment; otherwise, he might be reluctant to check around.

Spell out the ground rules for the project at hand. For instance, if the assignment involves preparing a memorandum, you ought to advise the associate whether this memo is for your eyes only, or whether it's intended to be sent to the client (and if so, whether the reader will be a businessman or a lawyer), or to an adversary or other person whose interests aren't identical to your client's. You can even go one step further and suggest the purpose which you wish the memorandum to serve—to inform, to persuade, perhaps to defuse a potential irritant.[26]

An associate is entitled to assume that you want his best and most complete effort on every project assigned to him, unless you advise him otherwise. If the task at hand happens to be one of those infrequent matters where, because of the need for speed or client-imposed limits on your authorization to proceed fullspeed, shortcuts are in order, this has to be spelled out for the associate. When you don't say anything, and he gives it the full-blown treatment—research, memos, the whole bit—that's not *his* error. What you then do with the bill is your business; the associate shouldn't be involved or made to feel guilty. You're entitled to complain only if you explained to him in advance that your goals were limited and he chose to ignore the message.

Always provide the associate with a deadline, assuming you have one in mind. When you tell an associate to have a certain memo on your desk by next Thursday and it's not there, your gripe is warranted. He had a week to budget his time; and barring unforeseen circumstances, he should have produced it on time. But if you never mentioned Thursday to him—although this was the logical interval you had in mind—and the memo doesn't arrive by then, your complaint is on less secure grounds (unless the project is such that its non-completion in this interval constitutes *prima facie* evidence of neglect). If instead of mentioning Thursday specifically, you had asked that the memo be done with all due haste, then you can probably take him to task when Thursday (but not the memo) ar-

---

[26] Discerning the purpose and intended readership of a memorandum is a topic covered in Section 3.2.1.

rives—although in fairness, your idea of haste and the associate's might not mesh precisely.

Even if you don't suggest a deadline, at least you ought to indicate whether the project is of high, low or medium priority, so that the associate has some idea of the intensity with which to approach it. And where you give an associate several projects to work on at one time, always spell out the relative priorities; otherwise, you may have to live with *his* judgment on which should be attended to first.[27]

10.4. FEEDBACK ON ASSOCIATES' PERFORMANCE

In the panoply of partner/associate relations, nothing exceeds the need for partners to convey to associates how well they're doing. Associates want and deserve feedback; how else can they effectively gauge their performance? While one would expect an underachieving associate to recognize his malady from other indicia—e.g., the cries of anguish escaping the partner's lips as he assaults the associate's draft—the power of self-delusion is remarkable indeed. It's not infrequent for an associate, upon being advised he's in trouble, to respond: "I never knew." And while part of that ignorance may stem from wishful thinking, some portion is undoubtedly attributable to an absence of negative feedback. At the same time, positive feedback, while perhaps less vital, forms a necessary ingredient in the associate's self-esteem and morale.

Feedback to associates involves several overlapping dimensions. Most basic is the critique of a specific task the associate is performing contemporaneously.[28] ("Hey, Joe, on this draft memo, I think the material under paragraph 3 ought to be moved up to the start of paragraph 2 for the following reason. . . .") The specific instance can also be utilized to dramatize a more universal point of lawyering technique. ("Joe, remember yesterday when you asked the client which state his company was incorporated in? That's *not* the kind of question you really ought to pose to a longtime client, since presumably we have the information in our files. . . .") Second, as aspects of an associate's performance tend to recur, these can be used as the basis for more general comment about his strengths and weaknesses.[29] ("You

---

[27]   This is *not* to say that an associate's foolish judgment on priorities won't subject him to criticism. Recently, I assigned an associate (i) a draft letter which the client had to mail before an approaching deadline, and (ii) a low pressure memo for the file on the same subject. Out of an excess of caution, I mentioned the obvious fact that the letter ought to be done first. Had I not spoken up, however, I would certainly have expected the associate to do just that—and if he reversed the order, I undoubtedly would have had some choice words to deliver.

[28]   See Section 10.4.1.

[29]   See Section 10.4.2.

know, Joe, watching you at that meeting today, I can see great improvement in your handling of clients. . . .'') Third, there's feedback of a more far-reaching sort, occurring at periodic intervals, representing an attempt to reach a consensus view of various partners.[30] ("The feeling around here, Joe, is that you're just not careful enough with your written work. Too many typos, mistaken cross-references, that type of thing. . . .'') And finally, there is the foray into providing the associate with some idea of where he stands in the firm.[31] ("Joe, you're on track, but we have to assign you to a few more securities projects so you can show some other partners what you're capable of. . . .'')

A truly effective feedback system should employ each of these variants. Specific performance critiques without generalization fail to provide an adequate framework for improved performance. Generalized principles in the absence of specific examples are much less meaningful or memorable. Periodic evaluations are a necessity to let the associate assess whether he's up against some basic problem, but constructive criticism ought to be more consistently rendered. And indications of standing are an associate's main means of ascertaining how he stacks up to his peers.

I find that partners vary widely in their feedback capabilities. Some excel at specific critiques but find it hard to generalize the point or give an overall appraisal of an individual's performance. Others, who blossom with insight during periodic evaluations, fail to speak up on the spot; "You need some work in drafting" may not be as helpful at year-end as in the wake of a badly blundered memorandum. And particularly when the message is negative, we could all stand some improvement in the difficult task of conveying an overall firm appraisal and a notion of relative standing on which to base that most vital of all associate decisions—whether to stick around or move on to greener pastures.

10.4.1. On-The-Spot Specifics; The Dramatic Gesture.

I suppose it's theoretically possible to take notes on an associate's performance during the course of a substantial project and then, when it's over, sit down with him to critique the past four months. But although the concept of a summing up has attractive features, it lacks the immediacy of constructive criticism offered on the spot. As you might have guessed, I firmly believe in the principle that a partner ought to *react* to an associate's output—the documents he produces, the meetings he conducts, the negotiations he handles.

---

[30] See Section 10.4.3.
[31] See Section 10.4.4.

Now, in the majority of cases, the document or action will fall into that broad middle area of competence, without great distinction or glaring defects. Obviously, that sort of work is less likely to provoke specific reactions from you, other than to point out particular technical aspects. But if a product is sub-par, you ought to let the associate know it—right there and then. Similarly, if the associate achieves excellence, tell him so; there's no substitute for partner praise. Many associates have good days and bad days; if you only criticize and never praise, your unbalanced reaction fosters an erroneous impression. A partner who abjures the neutral posture should be careful to mete out *both* criticism and plaudits (where warranted).

When giving feedback on a specific matter—let's say, a letter of advice to a client—it's not sufficient to single out the sentences or aspects you dislike without also making a comment on the work as a whole. If your only comment is directed at one offensive phrase in an otherwise well-done letter, the associate has no way of knowing—other than through negative inference, which doesn't count for much—what you thought of the rest. A much more helpful synopsis would be: "I liked this letter; it accomplishes its purpose. My only adverse comment relates to that phrase in the second paragraph. . . ." Or, in the taxi returning from a pretrial hearing: "I thought you handled the argument on the liability issue with intelligence and force. It would have been even better, though, if right after the factual synopsis, you had alluded to. . . ."

Why is it that so many partners find it relatively easy to point to the specific—especially where an adverse comment is involved—but resist providing an overall characterization to the work? Since you're more likely to specify negatives than positives, associates end up with mostly negative feedback—which not only may distort your generally favorable feelings, but needlessly bruises sensitive egos. I believe that an associate, having been told his product is fine with one exception, is more likely to listen to—and learn from—the specific item of criticism.

Babe Ruth hit 714 home runs in his major league career, but the one everyone remembers is when the Babe called his shot—pointing to the centerfield bleachers and then proceeding to knock the ball out of the park. I have a feeling—admittedly undocumented—that the more dramatic the educational gesture to an associate, the more likely the lesson is to penetrate and stick. And so, at times it's worthwhile to try something just a little different—perhaps even a mite melodramatic—to make your point forcefully.

Opportunities for a dramatic gesture often present themselves in terms of inadequate written work produced by the associate. Assume you receive a draft memorandum that rambles endlessly. You want to emphasize that the style is too long-winded—that conciseness itself can be a virtue, especially when it involves an appreciation of materiality.[32] You call the associate into your office, hand him back his draft, and say: "There are some good things in here, and you've got the general idea, but it's much too long and flabby. You don't need twenty pages to discuss this subject. I want you to give me a ten-page memo on the subject tomorrow, containing everything material that's in your first draft."

Now, this will appear to be a completely arbitrary demand on your part, since there's nothing magic about the number of pages in a memo. Yet, the associate is forced to attempt compliance; and wonder of wonders, he'll find the task isn't as difficult as he thought. The discipline of performing the compression, of witnessing its accomplishment, and finally of realizing the superiority of the shorter draft—together with an appropriate lecture by you on the importance of brevity in a world where clients are unwilling to read lengthy documents—should imprint a lasting message upon his consciousness.

Earlier, we discussed the importance of rewriting[33] and its role in the educational process.[34] When an associate hands you a document possessing all the earmarks of a first draft, and you want him to realize that he hasn't produced his best work, try this forceful approach: "I think this looks like a first draft. It's sloppy; it's not internally consistent; you didn't choose the best words or phrases to express your thoughts; and so on. I'm not even going to give you any specifics; I just want you to go back to your room, rewrite this thing, and come up with a better, more refined draft." If the revised draft emerges in a more polished state—as it should—you ought to compliment the associate and then ask whether *he* sees the difference between the two. He will; and you just might have a lifetime convert to making that extra effort.

Similarly, when you receive a memorandum that lacks organization,[35] point out the shortcoming with a flair: "I'm unhappy with this memo; it lacks form and structure; I was never sure which point was under discussion or the intended flow of the argument. I want you to go back to the drawing board and do an *outline* of this memorandum before proceeding further." Now, an outline is obviously something he should have done *before* writing the memo, but probably didn't; your proposal to create one *after* the piece is finished illustrates to the

---

[32] See Section 3.2.5.
[33] See Section 3.2.3.
[34] See Section 10.2.3.
[35] The importance of good organization in written materials is discussed in Section 3.2.2.

associate how important you deem its preparation. Moreover, the discipline of constructing the outline after the fact should reveal how disorganized his original memo was. Assuming the associate delivers a satisfactory outline, he can then rewrite the piece accordingly.[36]

The striking gesture is equally usable outside the contours of the written word. For example, say an associate comes to you with a new problem. You ask him for his proposed solution. He obviously hasn't thought the matter through, and his reply is analytically off base. It's simple enough to tell him where he's gone wrong, but much more dynamic to say: "There's a basic flaw in your reasoning. Do you know what it is?"—and let *him* try to figure out the missing link. If he does, discovering it himself leaves a more lasting imprint than being told what it is. If not, you've lost only a few moments.[37] You can use a modified Socratic method here, not unlike the professorial role in law school. The associate will be used to this, and there's no reason it can't possess post-graduate merit.

Another instance of this occurs when an associate begins an oral report to you in long-winded fashion with a good deal of background. It's very forceful to cut him off with: "Okay, what's your bottom line?" That's obviously *not* the way he wants to give the report; he prefers to built up a superstructure from the basement, show you the brilliance of his reasoning, etc. But forcing him to state his conclusion early, and then stressing why that's so important—particularly in contacts with the client—makes the point in more graphic fashion.[38]

10.4.2. Generalizing The Criticism.

Let's turn now to the more generalized critique of an associate's performance, occurring either in the course of an assignment (as when a particularly negative trait exhibits itself several times and generalization seems appropriate) or periodically (as when the firm evaluates its associates and provides them with an overall picture).

You should be extremely careful about generalizing on the basis of a single experience. Keep in mind this important distinction: on the basis of one experience, you can generalize with respect to the *shortcoming* itself (*i.e.*, as it applies to lawyers generally), but not as regards the associate's performance. So, for example, when an

---

[36] If he produces a bad outline, however, you'll realize that his disorganized work wasn't accidental or the result of undue haste, but that his thinking on the subject is muddled. This will give you the further opportunity to discern whether this shortcoming relates to just this project—which is correctible—or whether his analytical skills are just not up to the standards of the firm.

[37] Again, his inability to spot the problem might indicate some basic analytical flaw, which it's better for the firm to learn about early on.

[38] See Section 3.3.1. In effect, you're telling the associate: "*I* am your client."

associate writes an unclear sentence, you can pontificate on the desirability of lawyers producing prose of great clarity;[39] but you cannot say, based on that one sentence, that this associate's draftsmanship tends to the ambiguous. The generalization regarding his or her performance should only take place when you have sufficient personal experience to recognize lack of clarity as a relatively common occurrence. Similarly, if an associate fails to meet one deadline, that might call for a mild reprimand and perhaps a brief lecture on the importance of productivity;[40] it's only when the second and third deadlines are ignored that the criticism should be directed to solving *his* evident shortcoming.

When you do generalize about a lawyer's performance, be careful not to overstate any tentative conclusion you may have reached. At least when raising the matter for the first time, it's enough to point out that a deficiency exists; it's not necessary to portray the deficiency as sufficiently glaring to affect the associate's entire career. And where appropriate, always indicate to the associate that you consider the deficiency a correctible one.[41] For openers, a low key approach along the following lines is best: "There's something I would like you to work harder on . . ." or "Your ideas would really come across better if you were to. . . ." Remember, almost *any* generalized criticism emanating from a partner can prove devastating to an associate's self-image, so you needn't exacerbate the damage by an overly negative tone. A specific suggestion for coping with the shortcoming is also helpful ("I think your problem may be that you're not sufficiently knowledgeable about the securities laws. I understand NYU has excellent evening classes that might be just the ticket. . . .").

If possible, the generalized critique should be uttered in proximity to a particular instance of the genre. Using the specific occasion to venture into generalization allows the criticism to flow more naturally than an out-of-nowhere approach—which implies you've been dwelling on the deficiency, thereby rendering it more devastating to the associate.

If you have previously generalized a criticism to the associate, and he later performs in a manner indicating a constructive response to the problem—for example, his disorganization in former deals has been replaced by a real sense of structure in this one—make sure to direct a specific compliment the associate's way, showing your awareness of his efforts. Praise is essential to reinforce his per-

---

[39] See Section 3.2.4.
[40] See Section 4.4.
[41] Assuming, of course, that you do believe this to be the case. Otherwise, it's wrong to encourage self-deception in the associate.

formance—while having his efforts ignored by the critical partner implies to the associate that the upgrading isn't worth the effort.

Although it's far more usual to generalize criticism, opportunities for generalizing praise shouldn't be overlooked. If a certain associate has turned out a number of well prepared documents, there's nothing wrong with saying: "I really like the way you write". We don't seem to do that sort of thing too much, but we undoubtedly should.

10.4.3. The Periodic Evaluation.

Equal in importance to on-the-spot feedback is the periodic evaluation. An associate is entitled to know how he's doing on the broader canvas—how these various specifics mesh in evaluating his progress as a lawyer. From the firm's point of view, to reflect on these matters at periodic intervals assists in identifying associates who excel (or should be shown the door), in fixing salary levels or bonuses, and in singling out individual characteristics that need improvement.

Each firm has its own procedures for compiling the periodic evaluation data and presenting the results to associates. Obviously, the sheer size of the firm is central to how formalized the process tends to become. Whatever the method, however, the necessity for precision in results can't be underestimated. It's awfully easy to oversimplify, to distort—and a young person's career might well hang in the balance. Minor faults can be elevated into fatal defects; serious deficiencies may go overlooked and consequently stand uncorrected.

Let's first examine the situation where you are only one of several partners for whom a particular associate has worked, and someone other than you will be transmitting the evaluation to the associate. Your sole responsibility here is to convey to the firm your personal evaluation of the associate. This may be done orally; or, in some larger offices, forms have been developed for partners to fill out—forms which, in addition to seeking overall evaluations, attempt to single out specific lawyerly skills that the associate appears to lack. Such forms can be helpful in obtaining widespread participation in the evaluation process, and in developing some uniformity of approach. However, I firmly believe that no amount of box-checking can substitute for an evaluation spelled out in words, in order to get across the nuances of an associate's performance and problems.

"Spencer exhibits a great deal of seeming competence
and efficiency in his work, but I have the nagging suspicion
that a really complex problem would be beyond him intellectually. The job he did for me was relatively routine. I
think we should make an effort to get him into something
more demanding and see how he functions."

That's a thoughtfully qualified affirmative with a suggestion for further action—an analysis that would be difficult to convey other than in words. On the basis of your experience, to say of Spencer that he either "has it" or doesn't pass muster, would be unfair. While his past performance can't be knocked, it likewise shouldn't be overly exalted. You have to evaluate not only the associate but your own experience with the associate. How demanding was the work? How much opportunity did the associate have to strut his stuff? Which lawyer-like qualities were measurable and which weren't?

In pointing out certain deficiencies in a generally capable associate, be sure that these are recognized for what they are: selected negatives in an overall good performance. Curb that unfortunate tendency to unduly emphasize the negatives (which are, unfortunately, more interesting to discuss than competent craftsmanship).

If possible, you should always try to distinguish between a deficiency that suggests an absence of legal ability in the associate, and one that simply indicates a lack of experience. In this regard, if you have worked with the associate before, be sure to mention how his work has improved or deteriorated since the prior occasion. To merely note certain deficiencies in an associate's performance, without stating that he's come a long way since your last experience with him, doesn't do justice to the associate's progress. Conversely, an associate whose achievements remain merely satisfactory with the passing years may lack the capacity for growth which is the hallmark of the first-rate lawyer.

The interchange of information regarding an associate's performance can be of real benefit to the partners as well as the associate. For instance, let's assume that a certain associate has fared rather badly with clients on several occasions. Other partners—who might otherwise be inclined to give the associate his head—should be warned that, at least at this stage of his development, he's not quite ready to deal with clients on a completely one-on-one basis. This is not to say that he shouldn't be encouraged to develop these skills, or that the next partner utilizing his services should quarantine him from clients entirely; such an approach would inhibit progress in this vital area. What it does signify is the existence of a question in the client contact area requiring further work; and that, pending improvement, the partner on the case should be careful to supervise the associate's client activities. If the knock on an associate is that his writing tends to be disjointed and rambling, the next partner to oversee his labors will be on the lookout for this trait. If it re-emerges, the partner will realize it's not a one-time deficiency, thereby enabling him to generalize the need to write concise prose, in hopes this will aid the associate in overcoming his problem.

Let's deal now with the situation where, because you are the partner who has worked closest with a particular associate (or for whatever other reason), you're selected to deliver the firm's consensus view on his progress. This is a delicate task, one which I'm afraid too few of us take the trouble to perform as well as we should. There are two principal components here: collecting and analyzing the input from the other partners,[42] and then conveying the results to the associate.

You should first try to synthesize the several comments so as to minimize the variations traceable to the other evaluators—their personalities and relative degrees of perceptiveness, the differing levels of excellence they typically demand. Weigh the depth of experience each partner has had with the associate. When another partner's view is particularly negative, don't accept it secondhand or from a piece of paper; to insure the accuracy of your report to the associate, interrogate that partner directly—to assess, for instance, whether the associate is showing at least marginal improvement. If there's an apparent split of opinion about an associate, make a real effort to determine whether the associate himself blows hot and cold, or evaluators react to him differently. In other words, *whom* are you charging with inconsistency—the associate or your own partners?[42a]

After you've collated the necessary information, stop for a moment before speaking to the associate, and outline the major points you want to stress. What is your basic thrust—positive or negative? If the overall evaluation is affirmative with just a few minor problems, then start with the good news rather than the deficiencies. If the associate is in trouble, be sure to let him know that's the case, no matter what positive aspects you elect to include.

Two questions frequently arise in connection with periodic evaluations: should your criticism be specific—related to a particular job the associate botched up—or merely general; and should you identify individual partners as the source of certain comments?

On the latter issue, it's probably best *not* to associate partners with

---

[42] Don't neglect the comments of senior associates for whom a junior associate has worked. Often they will be in the best position to evaluate the junior's abilities, although you may have to discount their report by some indeterminate factor.

[42a] It may unfortunately be true that some partners tend to evaluate associates on the basis of whether the latter mirror the strengths of the former; e.g., an evaluating partner whose outstanding attributes are creativity and imagination may criticize an associate whose principal abilities lie in the area of attention to detail. More secure and mature partners will recognize and appreciate disparate qualities possessed by an associate which complement the partner's own shortcomings. See Rosenberg, "Are Your Associates Insecure?", 51 *New York State Bar Journal* 103 (1979).

comments. You're trying to communicate the view of the firm; relating each remark to an individual unduly diminishes the collective force. The associate knows which partners he's worked for and should be able to sense their respective reactions—particularly if he's been receiving the specific feedback referred to earlier.[43]

However, when the associate has worked primarily for me, and my views are negative, I'll indicate this fact to him—so as to emphasize that the opinion isn't broadly held (and therefore, theoretically more correctible). I must say that, although many partners seem distressed at the prospect of an associate putting two and two together and discovering the source of a specific criticism, this has never really bothered me. I think that a partner who criticizes an associate to other partners should be willing to repeat that criticism to the associate face-to-face. I don't like the idea of hiding behind the collective skirts of "the firm".

As for reference to specifics, your critical remarks should always be specific enough to provide a basis for improvement. To tell an associate that the firm is dissatisfied with his performance, but without revealing why, is inadequate. If the partners can't articulate what's wrong with the associate's performance, how can he be expected to improve? So, in terms of skills or characteristics, some specificity is in order. But I would try to stay away from citing specific instances of shortcomings that emanate from other partners, since this only leads to further questioning, rebuttal or rationalization—all of which dilutes the message you're trying to get across. If the associate demands chapter and verse, then refer him to the partners who rendered the adverse reviews; don't attempt to recapture the moment through hearsay.

A little analysis on your part—psychological or otherwise—can be helpful here. Try to figure out *why* the associate was found lacking in a certain area. For instance, let's assume you're dealing with an associate who hasn't been turning out assignments on time, yet doesn't seem like a slow worker. What's the reason? Could it possibly be that he's taken on too many other jobs for different partners and isn't adept at juggling projects?[44] If you suspect this might be the case, interrogate the associate to confirm your thesis; and if you're right on target, give him some tips on solving this problem.

Unless the associate is a total dud, there will usually be some bright spots in an otherwise mundane performance. If your evaluation is generally negative, don't neglect to mention the positives also. I wouldn't worry that he'll get the wrong idea, or think he's doing fine. The very mention of serious negatives has presumably shaken the

---

[43]   See Section 10.4.1.
[44]   See Sections 4.4 and 10.5.2.

associate's self-image; you don't have to destroy his confidence entirely.

10.4.4. "Here's Where You Stand".

A perceptive associate ought to have a pretty good idea of where he stands as he moves through the firm. The type of work assignments he's receiving, his salary raises (and bonuses, if applicable), the reactions to his performance from partners and clients, information conveyed through periodic evaluations—all these offer the young lawyer clues to how he's doing. But as he becomes more senior, it becomes increasingly important for the firm to advise the associate directly of his status in the partnership chase.

Firms differ widely in their procedures with respect to making partners, and generalizations on this subject are risky. Nevertheless, there are a few observations I wish to make.

At the outset, let's distinguish between (i) firms in which the opportunities are such that, if the associate performs with distinction, he will become a partner, and (ii) firms where, for policy or financial reasons, only a limited number of places are available, and the resulting competitive situation denies partnership to some high-performance lawyers.

In the first kind of firm, more often than not, the associate who displays real talent from the outset will become a partner; and the associate who falters badly in the early years, will ultimately fail in the quest. To be sure, there are associates who seem to be doing fine work in the early years and yet don't qualify for partnership; the usual reason is that some of the important qualities—such as good judgment—entering into the ultimate partnership evaluation aren't really tested by the limited responsibilities given a junior associate. Conversely, from time to time the associate whose early spotty performance appeared to doom his future, becomes more comfortable in his work, executes an about-face, and through maximum effort achieves partner status. But in most cases, the concept exists of being "on track" (or not) as the years go by, and the associate is entitled to know the firm's appraisal of him in this regard.

And so, at least after a few years have passed, it's important to add to the associate evaluation a comment indicating that he or she is on track toward the partnership goal or has some catching up to do. Telling an outstanding associate that he's headed in the right direction has the decided advantage (in addition to ego gratification) of reducing the risk that he'll suddenly decide to seek greener pastures elsewhere. Informing an associate that he's not performing up to par may stimulate him into getting his act together, if it's capable of improvement; if not, the information serves to lay the predicate for an ultimate negative judgment.

And this latter point is so important. There's no excuse for the inadequately anticipated decision to aim an associate out the door—so painful to the individual who's been living in a dream world because no one told him he was in real trouble. Sure, this kind of message can be signaled through miserly raises in salary (or disappointing bonuses), backwater work assignments, and the like. But don't let these peripheral clues speak entirely for themselves, because they're subject to rationalization and may even convey misleading messages. For example, you may award a handsome bonus to an associate who possesses serious analytical and judgmental shortcomings, as a way of rewarding diligence and long hours over a sustained period—but the associate may read the gesture as an indication that he's pointed in the right direction.

Coupling a status report with your critique of the associate's performance can make the criticism much more meaningful to him. For example, you might tell an associate that in all respects but one he appears qualified to become a partner, but that single factor—let's say, a seeming inability to gain the confidence of clients—is quite significant and could hold him back. The associate would then have to be really opaque not to concentrate his energies on remedying this problem—which is exactly what you're trying to achieve.

Assuming the chronology is somewhat fluid within the firm, the more senior associates should be given an idea of how long they have to go before being seriously considered for partnership. Practice differs on this subject, but my view is that the amount of time since law school graduation constitutes only one of several criteria evidencing an individual's ripeness to become a partner. A more crucial determination is whether or not the partners and clients of the firm have full confidence in the associate's abilities and judgment. And for some associates, this point arrives more quickly than for others. If an associate is heading in the right direction, but isn't quite there yet—even though some of his peers are—I believe he should neither be made a partner nor passed over for partnership.

What *should* take place is a candid conversation with the associate, in which he's told that he hasn't yet made it all the way home; that although in many ways he's doing fine, the firm has certain reservations about his performance (which you specify); that you believe these reservations can be eliminated through the application of concerted effort over a period of time; and that you suggest he get started immediately. If his reaction over the next few months is a positive one, that's a strong indication you did the right thing. To have elected him to partnership prematurely might have resulted in the deficiencies never being corrected; to have passed him over would have meant missing out on a good potential partner who merely needed more experience under his belt.

In the situation where it has become clear that the associate is unlikely to become a partner, the discouraging word should be relayed to him promptly, so that he can begin to decide about his future. Don't wait, for instance, until he comes up for consideration with his chronological group and is passed over; if the handwriting is on the wall, let him know at an earlier date. If the associate is competent and useful to the firm, this negative message may be coupled with a statement that he's free to remain in place. And if he's comfortable there, handling interesting matters and receiving good training, he might choose to stay on for a while. But at least he's under no illusions—he realizes his future is limited—and sooner or later, he'll have to seek his fortune elsewhere.

In firms which play a "numbers game" for limited partnership openings, I would think this policy should be made clear to all associates from the outset. They ought to know they're not merely competing against abstract criteria of what makes a good lawyer, but also against their fellow associates—that economic or policy factors constitute significant impediments bearing on their admission to the firm. Once an associate is thus on notice, he can proceed at his own risk.

In order to convey a proper evaluation to an associate in this type of firm, some notion of how he's doing relative to his peers would seem essential. It's not enough to say: "Your work is good" if the bulk of his class is performing at a higher level of excellence. As the years pass, those without a real shot at the prize ought to be so advised; no one should remain ignorant of a stacked deck.

10.5. ON THE SENSITIVITY FRONT

Finally, let's take a brief look at associate sensibilities, as well as some possible pitfalls in the partner/associate relationship.

10.5.1. Dealing With Heightened Sensibilities.

It's quite remarkable, in view of our former associate status, that we partners can so often be insensitive to the needs and apprehensions of associates. It's almost as if we were determined to erase from mind that most difficult period in our own lives—a period of insecurity and uncertainty, of not knowing exactly where things stood, of feeling that one's life was not his own, of reading symbolic meanings into innocent gestures, and the like. In order to deal effectively with associates, we should attempt to put ourselves back into that frame of mind. Just as a good lawyer is conscious of how he appears to clients and adversaries, we ought to become aware of how the younger lawyers in the office react to us.

Don't limit yourself, however, to just the obvious aspects, such as whether a particular associate is being worked too hard and ought to go on vacation. There are so many subtle areas where associates can go astray. For example, each year we hold a firm dinner party, the seating arrangements for which are designed to bring together individuals who have little opportunity to deal with each other on a professional basis—very senior partners with very junior associates, corporate partners with litigation associates, and so on. But it never fails that some associates read into particular seating arrangements matters of great—but completely unintended—significance.[45]

The associates' search for meaning proceeds apace in many ways that just don't occur to our preoccupied minds. You walk down the hall, concentrating on a knotty new problem that has just arisen. An associate who's working for you on another matter passes; you ignore him. The associate reads a bad omen into your omitted greeting. "Did I do a poor job on yesterday's memorandum?" he asks himself. A phone call has to be made to the client. Impulsively, you decide to make it yourself, advising the associate of your action after the fact. The associate wonders: "Doesn't he trust me with the client?"

So, you have to be alert to the unintended negative inference. But your associate sensitivity quotient needs to reach beyond that—to the establishment of positive values in your relationships. And most of this boils down to making the associate feel that he's an important member of the team, with the freedom to voice what's on his mind.

Remember, a law firm is a special kind of mechanism. The lawyers are all professionals. Each one, down to the newest associate who's just been admitted to practice, can go out into the world, hang up his shingle, and compete with the rest of you. In banding together to

---

[45]   Here's my favorite example of associate paranoia. One year, a firm held a party for lawyers at the summer home of a senior partner. Because a number of new associates and summer law students were present, it was decided to use name tags to avoid embarrassment. The tags were prepared in advance and placed on a table near the entrance to the house, to be picked up as the lawyers arrived. The following year, in the course of planning a similar party, it came to the attention of the partner in charge that several associates had objected to this procedure—*not* to the name tags themselves (which they recognized as a useful device under the circumstances), but to the fact that they had been prepared *in advance*. Why so, asked the partner? Because, came the reply, the name tags remaining on the table at the party's end constituted a list of those associates who chose not to attend the senior partner's party! And so, at the next party, a secretary was assigned to write out each name tag as the individual *arrived*. . . .

practice law, you (the partners) are—at least temporarily—in a category above the others (present associates). But it's a delicate hierarchy at best. The partner is in no way equivalent to the army officer who orders the enlisted men "over the top" and expects blind obedience.

Partners should be sensitive to this difference. Assignments should be phrased in terms of requests rather than orders. "Since the meeting is coming up Thursday, I would like you to try to complete this memo for me by Wednesday" is far better than "Have it on my desk tomorrow." As a much too frequent offender, I firmly believe that civility can pay large dividends.

And what if the answer to your request is: "I'm sorry, but I have a dinner date with my parents tonight, so I won't be able to finish the memo by tomorrow." Well, first you ought to determine whether it's really necessary for you to have the memo tomorrow; if not, let the associate deliver it on the following day. If promptness is requisite, then your tack ought to be:

> "Look, Bill, it's very important for me to have this memo tomorrow for the following reasons . . . [explain]. . . . You're the one associate who is most familiar with the subject matter, and it would be difficult at this late date to find a substitute. Is there any way you can put off the dinner with your parents until tomorrow night? Or, if you'd like, you can take the next day off once the memo is finished."

If the associate still persists after this explanation, I think you have to realize that the parent situation is a serious one to him; you'll just have to find someone else to complete the memo.

Still and all, you do have to function efficiently; and it would be equally wrong to abdicate completely your leadership role. Associates shouldn't be coddled. The practice of law is demanding, and some personal sacrifice will be in order. Your proper course lies somewhere between martinet and egalitarian.

10.5.2. The Disputative, Overextended, Unhappy Associate.

Now for the problems. Let's start with the situation where an associate disagrees with you on a matter of law or strategy or even ethics.[46] Take a case where you are knowledgeable on the general law concerning a certain subject; you ask the associate to prepare a

---

[46] These matters are discussed from the associate's point of view in Section 5.1.3.

memo on that topic for the client; and to your surprise, the conclusion of his memo is opposite to the result which you expected.

The first step is to test your own premises, as well as the reasoning of the associate. After all, here's a disagreement between two professionals; and although you may have experience and more mature judgment on your side, you haven't gone down to the library recently and hit the books on this topic. Assuming you then conclude that your view is the correct one—that the associate is taking an unnecessarily restrictive view of what the rules permit (perhaps substituting some law professor's opinion as to what *should* be the law for what it actually *is*)—you ought to send the associate back for another round of research, this time taking your comments into account. Make it clear to him, however, that he's not expected to change his views simply because *you* have demurred—intimidation is out of place in this context.

If a reasonably competent associate still persists in the disagreement after his second foray into the books, then I think it's wise on your part to involve a third lawyer; let him take a fresh look at the problem, unencumbered by any hang-ups—psychological or substantive—that you and the associate may have on the subject. It takes real courage for an associate to stand up to you at this point. To simply overrule him leaves a sour personal taste that's worth trying to avoid. If, however, the disagreement comes down to the reading of a single case or regulation—where he reads the text as saying one thing and you as another—then, although a third party's opinion can be comforting, you're in as good a position as the associate to make the judgment; and you might as well bite the bullet.

If the associate takes issue with a tactic or stratagem you plan to use, or a proposed method of dealing with a client or another lawyer, you should certainly listen to his views without disparagement, and to the extent they have merit, take them into account; but I don't think you need be quite so concerned here with persuading the associate that the path you've chosen is correct. In the last analysis, this has to be *your* decision, and the associate should realize that fact. Make it clear to him that this is a matter of judgment, as to which you can't prove objectively that your proposal is preferable—but that you're calling it the way you see it.

When an associate calls into question the ethics or propriety of a proposed course of action, that has to be a serious matter. Few associates would venture in this territory—where angels fear to tread—unless they felt very strongly about the matter. I don't know that any of us has such confidence in his own sure sense of legal ethics that he wouldn't want to obtain a second opinion from another partner in this kind of case.

So much for disagreements. How about the associate who is so enthusiastic, so anxious to please, that he's incapable of turning down any partner's request to take on an assignment; and as a result, he's in a terrible bind—hopelessly overextended, with the quality and timeliness of his work suffering accordingly. If you sense this kind of situation developing, don't just let it continue; step in and do something about it. The associate may feel trapped and unable or unwilling to extricate himself. He'll try to cover up the fact that he's not spending enough time on your task. You have to be perceptive here; if you sense that the associate is the sort of person who ordinarily turns out timely work of high quality, you can bet that the problem emanates from another source.

Once you've diagnosed the ill, you have to be somewhat gentle in prescribing the remedy; after all, the associate is knocking himself out trying to please, and that sort of enthusiasm ought to be encouraged.[47] You should explain to him that overextension doesn't do him or the firm any good; that partners are getting the wrong impression of his abilities; that you're pleased with his enthusiasm, but he has to learn to say "no" at times—to strike a happy balance. Most important of all, be sure to emphasize that when he inadvertently gets into this kind of bind, he should not try to paper it over, but rather should make you aware of what's happening; perhaps you can rectify the situation.

That's the associate who's *too* enthusiastic. But how about the one who's not enthusiastic enough? He's just going through the motions; you can tell he's not really involved. Did you ever stop to think that *you* may be partially responsible for this? Is it possible that you've failed to convey to him your own sense of enthusiasm for what you do? Perhaps if a little more zest radiated from you, it might be reflected in his work. An associate tends to work harder for a partner who is himself putting out. Are you? And if so, is the associate aware of it? And have you shown him proper appreciation for the hard work he's doing?[48]

One of the most difficult problems for a partner occurs when he has an unhappy associate working for him.[49] Why is he unhappy? Because he doesn't enjoy what he's doing, due to either a personality conflict with you or a distaste for your kind of work. In some cases the associate is obvious about his attitude; in others, it might be dif-

---

[47] The virtues of enthusiasm are discussed in Section 4.2.

[48] There are also other ways you can encourage him. For instance, if there is an opportunity for the associate to start to develop a specialty or subspecialty within the firm, by all means encourage him to do this, as it will stand him in very good stead later on; see Section 2.7. Without that push from you, he might not make the extra effort required to forge such a skill.

[49] For the associate's point of view on this subject, see Section 5.1.3.

ficult for the partner to ascertain. And let's face it, we all possess something of a blind spot here; no one enjoys thinking he's difficult to work for or that his assignments aren't interesting.

If you spot this happening, the best course is to bring it out in the open with the associate; don't let it fester. Perhaps talking about the subject will partially solve matters. The problem may have arisen because you took little notice of the associate—failed to take him along to meetings, never let him handle the negotiating or oral argument. A frank and candid conversation could alert you to the sensitive areas. On the other hand, if the problem seems irremediable, then it's probably in your mutual best interests for the associate to transfer to another partner or a different area of the law.

POSTSCRIPT

An unhappy associate—that's a poor note on which to end this book. I'd rather conclude on an upbeat, with a bit of verse—designed to be sung at late hours, over a few beers, to the tune of "Hello, Young Lovers" (from Rodgers and Hammerstein's *The King and I*).

Hello, young lawyers, wherever you are
(Which is probably *not* in your home).
Your future's all planned,
Your assignment's just grand:
"Take two depositions in Nome!"

Be brave, young lawyers, associates still,
When partners are giving you grief:
"Finish that draft
By Saturday aft'—
And then start right in on the brief!"

I know how it sounds when you're making the rounds
Of the firms and they promise the moon;
But then in mid-winter, 4:00 a.m. at the printer,
They're singing a quite different tune.

Hello, young lawyers, with talent galore,
But doubts just beginning to gnaw.
It's hard to decide
If your witness has lied. . . .
Or just which conclusion to draw.
Still you're in awe of the law, *like me;*
You're just in awe of the law.

*   *   *

Be strong, young lawyers, at frustration's door,
Chafing at edicts and rules;
It's not Blackstone's era—
But OSHA and FIRA—
And a stiff lip while suffering fools.

You strive, young lawyers, to rationally judge
(Please pardon that last split infinitive),
Each day growing wearier
Of opaque criteria
And the need to be calm and definitive.

I know how it feels to negotiate deals
While the client gets tanned by the sea.
You argue with verve, and bargain with nerve,
And get stiffed for the bulk of your fee!

Hello, associate, grasping the grail—
Anxiety, displaced by peace—
As you finally hear
Those words dear to your ear:
"Congrats, *partner;* please sign the lease!"
Now you're in love with the law, *like me;*
You're just in love with the law.